BACK to BYZANTIUM

Travels through a Balkan Conspiracy

Antonin Grook

2017

ISBN: 1548862401
ISBN-13: 978-1548862404

for Lucie and Pierre

*who share my love for
Central and Eastern Europe*

Acknowledgments

Special thanks to Edmonde Grutchfield and Jane Salvage for their patience, encouragement and invaluable advice. Thanks to Natalia Murashova for help with Russian and to Lili Sotkovsky for teaching me Hungarian.

All verse quotations in the book are taken from Byron's *Childe Harold's Pilgrimage*

> For dear Janey,
> without whose heroism in reading the draft and suggestions for improvement this book would not have existed in print.
> Much love
> Antony Grook

Transliteration from Cyrillic

The author has adopted the American Library Association and Library of Congress (ALA-LC) Romanization tables for Slavic alphabets (updated in 1997), used in North American libraries and in the British Library since 1975.

Back to Byzantium

Contents

Map 1: Europe	ix
Map 2: Balkan Peninsula	x
Map 3: Central Europe	xi
Map 4: Russia: Transsib	xii
Avant-propos	1
Prologue - Jean Jaurès	2
Chapter 1 - Simplon	3
Chapter 2 - Skopje	16
Chapter 3 - Plovdiv	33
Chapter 4 - Crusade	49
Chapter 5 - Sack	64
Chapter 6 - Klinika	73
Chapter 7 - Convalescence	85
Chapter 8 - Sarajevo	99
Chapter 9 - Mamaia	111
Chapter 10 - Malbork	120
Chapter 11 - Transsib	136
Chapter 12 - Siberia	148
Chapter 13 - Algiers	161

Back to Byzantium

Chapter 14 - Tirana	175
Chapter 15 - Transylvania	193
Chapter 16 - Leningrad	208
Chapter 17 - Istanbul	219
Chapter 18 - Budapest	231
Chapter 19 - Moscow	252
Chapter 20 - Coup	275
Chapter 21 - Games	287
Epilogue: A. Malakoff	300
Epilogue: B. Ramstein	312
Postscript	320
Appendix 1: Timetable Trans-Siberian 1977	325
Appendix 2: Chronology of author's travels	326
Appendix 3: Chronology of current events	328
Appendix 4: Chronology of historical events	331
Glossary of proper names	335
Glossary of place names	361
Bibliography	378
Index	384

Back to Byzantium

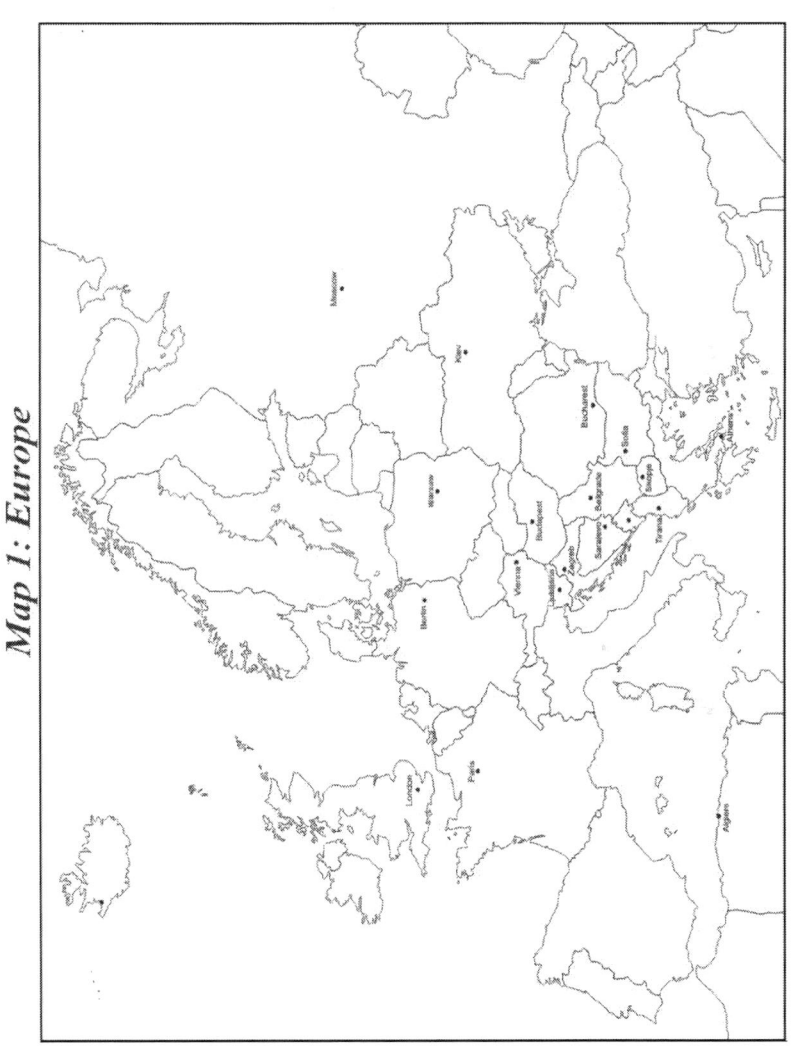

Map 1: Europe

Back to Byzantium

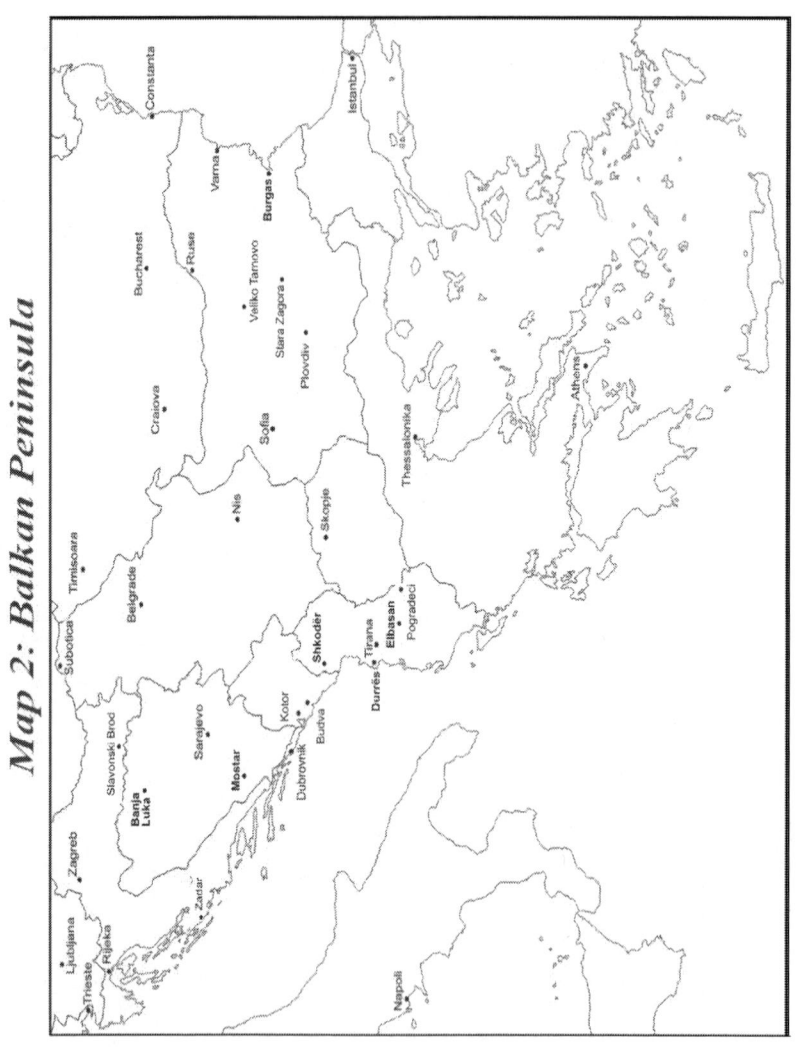

Back to Byzantium

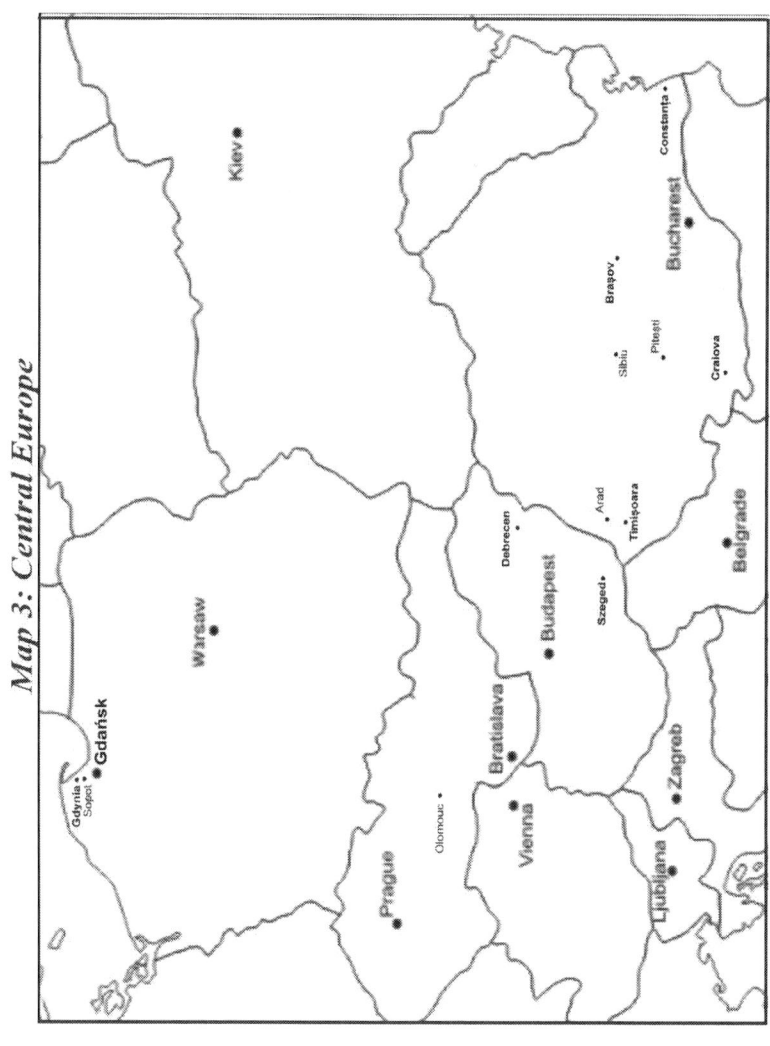

Back to Byzantium

Map 4: Russia Transsib

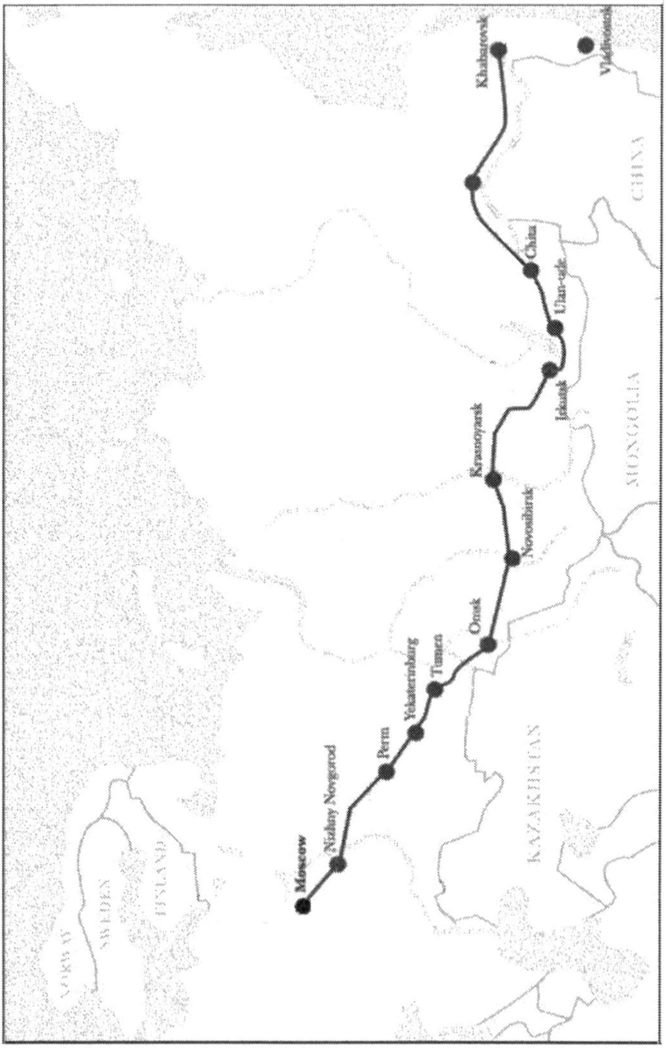

Associations

PARIS

Tsé-Gué-èNe

réunion d'information

mardi 13 avril 2004
20 heures

association France-Byzance

13 rue de Constantinople
MALAKOFF

EK 6713

800 ans

Souvenez-vous !

Prologue
Jean Jaurès

Late-afternoon commuters crowded the platform of *Jean Jaurès* metro station in Toulouse. A young Hungarian woman stood waiting for the train. What told me that she came from Hungary? Those who have been there may know what I mean, the robust hour-glass legs, the same that you see on Hungarian bronzes of the *Secessionist* period, sprung rooted from the soil beyond the Danube in the Great Hungarian Plain.

We got onto the same metro carriage and I forgot about her. I took out a copy of the women's magazine, *Nők Lapja,* which a Hungarian friend had left me. I had nothing else to read. After learning the language for some time I could just about decipher the interviews. A hand tapped me gently on the shoulder: '*Magyarul beszél,* Do you speak Hungarian?' She later told everyone of her surprise at discovering an Englishman *d'un certain âge* reading a Hungarian women's periodical in a metro carriage in South-West France. Just too embarrassing, I was lost for Hungarian words.

I first visited Budapest in the early seventies on my way back from Bulgaria, where I had spent a couple of months in Plovdiv, first in hospital and then in convalescence. Budapest in those days was a sad place and I didn't have the maturity or imagination to look past the decrepit walls to the beauty beyond. My thrill at then was Sofia.

The previous year I had set off by train from Paris for Piraeus.

1
Simplon

Forty-three years after its introduction in Britain and twenty-four since its adoption in newly-independent Pakistan, Switzerland's male population had just voted to grant suffrage for women. One hundred and seventy-seven years after France, the United Kingdom had switched to decimal currency. In the coming autumn, fourteen years after its six founding members had signed the Rome Treaty creating the European Economic Community, the House of Commons would vote by a slender majority in favour of British membership, a decision that would be reversed by the British electorate forty-five years later.

In Yugoslavia, Marshal Tito was beset by disturbances with Croatian nationalists and Serbian pro-Soviet sympathisers. In the coming winter Leonid Brezhnev was to travel to Belgrade to meet Tito and reaffirm Yugoslavia's political independence. I was on my way via Yugoslavia to Greece.

A Macedonian colleague met me at 10:30 PM on a warm June evening at the *Gare du Nord* in Paris. The Direct Orient Express already stood waiting at the platform. I was travelling via Piraeus to the island of Poros just off the Peloponnese, where my brother ran a holiday villa. On my return journey I planned to visit my colleague's sister and her husband in Skopje in Macedonia. 'Watch out for the Serbs, Grook', he said.

Yugoslav guest workers returning home for the holidays had already filled several compartments. We found one occupied by a Greek family, a young student

Back to Byzantium

reading naval architecture in the UK and his parents. 'These look all right, Grook', said my colleague. The journey to Piraeus would take three nights and two and a half days, with four of us in the compartment, sharing our food and our snores.

It was my first real train journey. On subsequent occasions I felt the exhilaration each time as I boarded the same train at 10:55 PM at the *Gare du Nord*.

Replacing the prestigious Simplon Orient Express in the early 1960s, the so-called Direct Orient had become a train for domestic travellers, impecunious intrepid tourists and migrant workers. It was now just a *bummel* train, stopping in each major city in Italy and every town through Yugoslavia.

Destination plates on each side marked *Istambul* or *Athinae* identified the coach.

Dijon, Vallorbe, Lausanne, the Simplon tunnel, Domodossola, Milan, Verona, Venice, Trieste, Villa Opicina, Sežana, Ljubljana, Zagreb, Belgrade, Niš, where the train divided, then on to Piraeus through Skopje, Gevgelija, Thessaloniki, and Athens. The names sounded magical!

The foreign coaches had a dated, exotic appearance. The old-fashioned Bulgarian coaches were upholstered with *moquette*-covered seats. In the opulent Italian coaches you could pull the seats all the way out to transform the compartment into an integral bed for two or for three, designed for an encounter with the *Madonna of the sleeping cars*. The cheap and nasty French coaches had rigid *couchette* seats covered with mouse-grey imitation-leather. And there was that steep metal staircase to let you climb and off the train at stations, none of which had platforms.

You think train journeys are a bore. So they are if they last less than three hours. But set off for three days and it's an adventure. Sharing your picnic with new compartment companions, cruising the corridors for an encounter, standing by the window for a smoke and a chat in a foreign language, having lunch in a real dining car when they hooked one onto the train beyond Trieste. But especially getting that feeling of being in suspension, outside time and space.

At each border the train halted to change locomotives. Men with large metal stamping devices, that left an ink smudge on the facing page of your passport, passed through the coach for border control, followed by plain-clothed customs officers. In Yugoslavia each one bore a screwdriver, the tool of his trade for removing plastic laminate panels from the ceiling of the corridor and toilet, traditional hiding places for contraband. At night stops, only the wheel-tappers broke the silence, checking the integrity of the wheels with their long hammers. Cracked wheels, like cracked bells, do not sound the same as those that are sound. Ladies in headscarves cleaned out the compartments each morning. I got used to shaving in the minuscule basin in the toilet to the sway of the coach and the rhythm of the wheels, and on a subsequent journey even washed my hair in it.

The early morning halt at Frasne on the Jurassian plateau: gently drawing back a corner of the blind from my *couchette* to peep out through the silence over the moonlit black-velvet fields; ambling at first light along the Northern shore of Lake Geneva through Lausanne and Montreux; exiting the Simplon tunnel, currently the world's longest, to arrive in the early morning in Domodossola, where hawkers tried to sell you repulsive dolls in wedding attire; discovering the Borromeo Islands in Lake Maggiore through intermittent flashes between the clumps of trees; arriving at 10 AM at *Milano Centrale* station, Mussolini's massive marble masterpiece, for a pizza (a new phenomenon) for breakfast. Up to then I hadn't been further east.

The overnight smell of our compartment had become foetid. Elegant Lombards queening through our coach turned up their noses ostensibly. The train spent the afternoon and evening cruising across the plains of Lombardy, past the lakes, through Venice to Trieste, my favourite Italian city, the gateway to the Balkans. This was a city that Stendhal, as French consul, had despised, as did Lawrence Durrell, who could smell in Trieste the Great Hungarian Plain.

We entered Yugoslavia late at night and slept until Belgrade with stops in Ljubljana and Zagreb. Leaving Belgrade, the train took on a leisurely pace along the wooded Morava river, then through short low valleys of maze and poplars. We watched ox-carts dawdling over unmade roads, past naked rough-laid brick houses. The Yugoslav government provided aid for the building materials, but not for the rendering. We stopped at each handsome country station, where peasants joined the train with live poultry, baskets with holes cut out to reveal a live goose craning its neck through one on each side. The Serbs, less squeamish than the Milanese, joined us in the compartment for political discussions in rudimentary German.

Like many of my generation I had always had a certain admiration for Tito, though I knew little about Yugoslavia, just that it had become a soft Communist country and that I no longer needed a transit visa to get through into Greece.

> According to my travel guide, modern Yugoslavia followed the principle that Communism in each country could be reached only by taking local specific conditions into account, quite distinct from Stalin's *Socialism in*

One Country.

After first opposing, then encouraging Tito's attempted *rapprochement* with Georgi Dimitrov of Bulgaria to found a Balkan Federation, Stalin had finally scuttled it, accusing him of being a covert agent of Western imperialism. Tito's refusal of Soviet domination had led to the rift with the Soviet Union in 1949. He was now promoting cooperation between nations outside the bipolar cold-war blocs in his non-aligned movement.

The Soviets also denounced as social democracy his policy of *camoupravlenie*, or self-management, and profit sharing. After the death of Stalin, Khrushchëv normalized relations with Yugoslavia, and now, six months after my trip, Brezhnev would once again pay a visit to Tito and give him a fraternal hug, if not yet a kiss on the lips.

I learnt that though Tito was half Croat, half Slovene, in fact Serbs dominated the federal administration.

A nondescript Greek in his forties in a blue tweed jacket with an open-neck shirt under a golfing pullover stood smoking in the corridor. He was a banker, though he didn't look like what I thought a banker should and I didn't imagine that bankers travelled by train on second class. We got talking.

Just after Kumanovo, on the plain about an hour before Skopje, we slowed down almost to a halt through a bucolic village with low-slung, red-roofed houses. Except that, from the tiled roof of a house identical to all the others a minaret shot up like a *doigt d'honneur*.

Back to Byzantium

Muslims in Europe! Imagine the almost physical shock that it felt to realize that I had entered a different world. I was travelling for the first time beyond Munich, Florence or the Costa Brava and I hadn't done my homework. I had seen Muslims every day in Paris, but they were always from North Africa.

We stood smoking in the corridor when the train slowed down almost to a halt. The temperature had risen sharply and we had pulled the window down. From nowhere appeared a swarm of dark-brown urchins in tatters. They signalled to us that they wanted cigarettes and we tossed a few through the window.

'Who on earth are these', I asked the banker. 'They look like Pakistanis. And what's that minaret doing there?'

'Oh, it's just a Muslim village, like lots of others in the region', he said. 'Muslims have been here, you know, just like in every Balkan country, for seven hundred years or so.'

'Really? Where did they come from?'

'There are two categories', he said, 'some of them are Turks, who descend from the Ottoman occupants, and the others are mainly native Slavs who converted to Islam. They now make up the majority of the population of Bosnia and Albania and a fifth of that of Macedonia.

'The Ottoman Empire, under the so-called *millet* system had divided the populations into *true* believers on the one hand, meaning the Muslims, and *infidels* on the other hand, meaning the Orthodox Christian population, making no distinction of either language or ethnicity.

'When Constantinople had become the Eastern capital of the Roman Empire, though the Greek language later replaced Latin, the Orthodox populations, whatever their own language, continued to call themselves Romans, *Rum* in Turkish, *Romai* in Greek. So the Orthodox Balkans under the Ottomans came to be known as *Rumelia*', he added.

'A *millet*?' I asked.

'Soon after their conquest of Constantinople in 1453, the Turks reorganised the state according to principles of the *sharia*, distinguishing other religious communities *of the Book*, which they considered to be inferior to Muslims. They regrouped the Orthodox Christians throughout the Balkans into the Greek dominated *Rum Millet*.

'Under the *millet* system Christians were governed by their own Orthodox Patriarch, who was nominated by the Sultan. With their own legal system, Christians did have a certain degree of autonomy, though in cases of litigation with Muslims, of course their testimonies were not considered to be valid. The Ottomans prohibited all sorts of activities for Christians. They forbade them from serving in the army, bearing arms and even riding a horse - which meant that peoples of the different regions could no longer travel or communicate with each other. They didn't even allow them to build churches more than a certain height, and reserved green clothes for Muslims only.

Back to Byzantium

'And Christians had to pay a capitation tax, levied for a fixed amount per head irrespective of wealth. Above all, they were subject to the *devşirme*.'

I didn't know the word.

'The *devşirme* was the most abominable feature of the Turkish occupation. Every five years or so, one pre-adolescent son was snatched from each Christian family (it applied neither to Jews nor to Gypsies), sent to Constantinople, circumcised and raised as a Muslim. At adolescence, they enrolled him into the army or civil service. The majority became *janissaries*, or foot soldiers, but the cleverest went to the palace, where they could reach the very highest positions, even become Grand Vizier. Though technically slaves owing absolute loyalty to the Sultan, many became wealthy and powerful.

'The result was that the Ottoman ruling class, originating totally from the *devşirme*, became in fact genetically European, as you'll see if you go to Istanbul. Among its famous members were Sinan the architect, Skanderbeg the Albanian national hero, and Vlad Țepeș the Impaler (better known as Dracula).'

'But what you say is absolutely horrifying', I said. 'Didn't the parents try to resist it or hide their children?'

'Parents' attitudes of to *devşirme* were varied. Some of them did resist at all costs, even resorting to mutilating their male children. Others, though, had aspirations for their sons and volunteered them, hoping to obtain advantages in the Ottoman bureaucracy.

'At first, the Ottomans seized boys indiscriminately from Christians of all regions, but they later showed a preference for those from Albania and Bosnia. As I told you, in those two regions, although the Ottomans never required non-Muslims to convert, Christians did convert to Islam very soon after the beginning of Ottoman occupation. Even so, many of the conversions were not genuine and a lot of people continued to practise their Orthodox faith at home. And, despite mass conversions to Islam, Turkish rarely replaced the local language, even for leaders like Ali Pasha, the Albanian, who spoke no Turkish.'

'From what you say, the majority of Muslims in Yugoslavia are in fact converted Slavs. But these urchins don't look like Slavs to me', I said.

'No, they're not', replied the banker. 'As you can see, these are gypsies'.

'How did they get here? I always thought gypsies were nomadic. These look pretty sedentary to me.'

'Many Gypsies have been in the Balkans even longer than the Muslims, others arrived with the conquering Turkish army', he said. 'You were not far wrong when you asked if they were Pakistanis. They in fact originated in India and still speak to some extent a language that resembles Hindi, though it's usually very polluted by the local language.

'The Turks, considering them to be a separate, inferior ethnic group, encouraged them to settle in their own villages and work as agricultural workers. Gypsies became an integral part of the cultural environment and were influenced by local peoples.

'They call themselves *Roma*, *Rom* being the word for *man* in their language, *Roman*i. You shouldn't confuse them with Romanians, in whose country many Roma live, nor with Romaic peoples from the Eastern Roman Empire.

'As for their religion, as you can see, in this area they are Muslims. Until the 16th century most Gypsies were Christian, but this was reversed in the 17th century, when Muslims became the majority.'

An hour later at five o'clock the train arrived in the shell that remained of the station in Skopje.

Eight years previously, on 26th July 1963, Skopje, formerly the Ottoman city of Üsküb, had been eighty percent destroyed by an earthquake of a magnitude of 6.9 on the Richter scale. More than 1,000 people had died and 100,000 had been left homeless. The city was rebuilt after the earthquake with the help of 78 countries.

The clock at the modern railway station, part of which remained standing, still showed the time of 5:17, when the tremor stopped it.

An elderly American couple, burdened with luggage, climbed down from the train and disappeared into the remains of the station building. No other foreigners alighted. Thirty minutes later the train doors closed ready for departure. The couple reappeared, very flustered. They clambered up the metal staircase, complaining so that everyone could hear: 'Nobody here even speaks English'.

We had bought foreign newspapers, *L'Unità* in Italian and *l'Humanité* in French, the only ones that we could find, both Communist. As soon as the train reached the border at Gevgelia my Greek companions pushed them hurriedly out of the window onto the tracks. We had left the relative freedom of speech of Yugoslavia, where you could criticize almost anything and anyone except Tito, for the recently totalitarian state of Greece.

Throughout Yugoslavia I had been talking politics with my Greek travel companions, but as soon as we arrived in Thessaloniki conversation stopped. I recognised the characteristic *squirrel* glance, right then left, before speaking, that I had already witnessed in Franquist Spain and would later see in each of the Soviet satellite countries. During our ride through Serbia and Macedonia my naval-architect companion had already explained the situation in Greece and how it had come about.

'As I am sure you know, Greece has been under military rule for the last four years. The *coup d'état* took place after thirty years of conflict between Right and Left since the Civil War.'

'Of course', I said, 'but what triggered it?'

'After years of conservative government, the new King Constantine II, in a clash with George Papandreou, his new Socialist Prime Minister, called elections. Afraid that, if Papandreou won, he could govern only in coalition with former Communists, Brigadier General Pattakos and Colonel Papadopoulos led a *putsch,* arresting more than 10,000 people, including the caretaker Prime Minister. They suspended the constitution and declared martial law.

'When King Constantine refused to oppose the *coup* and swore in the insurgents as the new legitimate government of Greece, Papadopoulos abolished the constitution and ruled by decree.'

'But didn't the West and specially the USA object?' I asked.

'The *CIA* has always maintained a close relationship with the Greek intelligence services and the army, considering Greece to be vital to NATO during the Cold War. Even so the *coup* took them by surprise. The leaders of the putsch are strongly anti-Communist, pro-Western and pro-NATO, so in the Cold-War context the US has maintained its support to some degree.'

Back to Byzantium

'Yes', I said, 'I remember reading that, when the ambassador had described the *coup* as *a rape of democracy*, a local *CIA* chief in Greece answered, "How can you rape a whore?".'

'With US encouragement', continued my companion, 'King Constantine eventually attempted a counter-*coup*, which failed. His loyalist generals got arrested, but he succeeded in fleeing the country with his Prime Minister. The *Revolutionary Council* then nominated Papadopoulos as new Prime Minister and soon after as Regent with full powers.

'By today Papadopoulos has suspended civil liberties, freedom of speech and of the press, established martial law, dissolved political parties and repealed legislation. Our country has become a police state with 3,500 people in torture centres. Others are in exile. An index has been compiled of prohibited books and songs.'

'All the exiles seem to be currently living in Paris', I said. 'Konstantinos Karamanlis, Mikis Theodorakis, Melina Mercouri, Costa-Gavras, whose film *Z* we all saw.'

'Yes', he answered, 'but, on the other hand, Papadopoulos has been actively encouraging tourism for people like yourself, and there has been strong economic growth with low unemployment.'

'You make me feel guilty, and you are quite right to do so, for having come to Greece at this time', I said. 'You know what surprises me? It's the mediocrity of the image of this revolution, with its surgical metaphors describing the *junta*'s action on the Greek *patient*, Greece reborn like Christ resurrected. Even its nationalist emblem, usually the only strong selling point of a fascist *regime*, looks cheap. A soldier with fixed bayonet before the backdrop of the phoenix arising from the flames (the emblem of the Greek war of independence) looks tacky like Greek fascism itself.'

'I quite agree', said the naval architect. 'Don't forget that the Greeks are a demotic people. This revolution is typically demotic.'

We arrived in Thessaloniki at 10:30 PM. Pedlars sold *souvláki* on wooden sticks with chunky Greek yogurt, handing them up from the platform through the train windows. I ate with relish after our extended two-day picnic.

The sun over the corn fields of Northern Attica woke us up the following morning. In the early afternoon, we arrived in Piraeus. I said goodbye to my Greek companion of three days.

'Remember', he said, after glancing left and then right, 'that, though you Europeans see the Greeks as Hellenes and Greece as the land of Pericles, the birthplace of democracy, for us Greeks our country is Byzantium and we are Romaic, with an enduring, active nostalgia for our long-lost Constantinople.'

I was flabbergasted. Nobody called it by that name any more. It had been Turkish for over five centuries and called Istanbul for as long as anyone could remember. Had I been travelling with a crank, or did many other Greeks really believe that they still had a claim to it? Was this what the Greek *regime* of the colonels was about, reconquering the lands lost to Turkey to recreate the Byzantine Empire?

2
Skopje

I bought my ticket from an efficient young man at the shipping company and located the boat for Poros, already at quay. There was an hour and a half to wait. I found Piraeus an agreeable place. Due to the seventy-five percent destruction of the city during the Second World War and ensuing Civil War, it had little artistic interest apart from the old Turkish harbour. Today Europe's largest passenger port, it is the perfect place for lounging in an open-air café drinking *café frappé,* waiting and watching. Piraeus is also a place to eat fish and drink *retsina*, resinated white wine. 'Yuck', I said after my first glass. 'Drink a litre of it and you will never touch anything else', said my brother, and he was right.

By the time I came back the boat had become crowded, in fact more than full, floating a good metre over the Plimsoll line. But, no matter! The crossing lasted a couple of hours over calm enough water under a perpetually cloudless sky. A small boy beside me, who didn't agree, threw up over the shoe and sock of an elderly gentleman. The gentleman watched it with philosophy and didn't move until the mother had wiped his leg and foot clean if not dry. A smart woman in her late forties queened across the deck in all directions, revelling in the apparently admiring smiles that both men and women gave her. She wore an immaculate white jump suit, except that... I imagined her retrospective embarrassment that evening.

I disembarked in Poros, sat down outside a café and ordered a coffee. No one knew of my arrival, not even my brother, and we don't even look much alike. 'How much?', I asked 'No charge, Jim's brother.' No-one ever charged me for a drink anywhere during my stay on the island. Greece had remained the land of the family, with its *dynasteia*, political dynasties covering three or more generations.

My brother ran a holiday villa. In those days Greek banks had no clearing system. He went each month to his bank, filled a small suitcase with banknotes and took it to his landlord, who then carried it to his own bank. The drachma being highly inflated, the rent filled the small suitcase. Greece was one of the last countries in Europe to have a bankers' clearing house or even a television service, which first started transmitting just a year before the *coup d'état*. As Lenin did for the fledgling cinema, the *junta* lost no time in understanding its propaganda uses.

The season was beginning and nurses from London were my brother's only clients. What do you do with thirteen English ladies when the sales pitch of the holiday is the balanced ratio of men to women? His friend, an officer at the Greek naval academy and trainer of the Greek Olympic rowing team, had the answer. They rented a couple of boats, requisitioned thirteen Greek naval cadets and set off with the English nurses in the evening darkness for a barbeque on a minute uninhabited island. Around the camp fire, though the girls, replete with *retsina*, were willing, the cadets were too well-bred and didn't really know the routine. Each of the nurses subsequently found her own solution with one of the less aristocratic working men in the town.

Early every morning I went running through the luminous Aleppo pine forests with my brother's friend, the Olympic trainer, finishing with a sprint and a dip in the warm sea. I have never felt so fit before or since.

While waiting for a boat for a day trip to Hydra I watched the one of the two *junta* leaders disembark. He was General Pattakos, a clone of Mussolini.

Back to Byzantium

'And history, with all her volumes vast,
  Hath but one page…'

Bathing in the sea one morning I got into conversation with a young Greek girl in her late twenties, who was staying in our hotel. She had got bored with spending her holiday with her family and wanted to go into town one evening. Could I invite her out with the members of our English group? They would provide a chaperone to reassure her father. She was so insistent that I agreed for her introduce me to her parents at the end of dinner and for me to ask them if she could join us. The patriarch courteously offered me coffee and when I invited his daughter to join our group he replied in French *'Ma fille est très fatiguée ce soir'*, his daughter was too tired to go out.

I got in a verbal battle with a slovenly Englishman about personal hygiene. He claimed that the Greeks were a dirty people, which I found offensive and gratuitous, specially coming from him. I tried to explain that the inhabitants of Mediterranean countries washed more frequently than those of Northern Europe, if only because the heat made it a necessity. I quoted the Marquis de Custine's remark that the general filth of peoples of the North, always pent up due to the climate, seemed more repulsive than that of the peoples who live in the sun. I didn't convince him. As a last resort I told him that, though the English abroad may be very demanding about bathing facilities, I didn't think that they actually used them much. He reminded me of the gentleman in the advertisement, who had used Pears soap two years previously and since then had used no other. Was that the case for him?

The time had come to leave and I set off back home. I spent the last day in Piraeus in a small hotel overlooking the delightful former Turkish harbour, now known as *Mikrolimano*, the little harbour. At the end of the afternoon *siesta* I left my room for a minute to find the corridor full of men enveloped in white sheets moving peripatetically backwards and forwards in serious conversation. Plato would not have felt disorientated here.

Two years later the regime of the Colonels was to collapse.

Papadopoulos abolished the monarchy and had himself designated by plebiscite as President of the new Republic. He concentrated more and more power in his hands, sometimes occupying several key cabinet posts. In the absence of democratic control there was nepotism and corruption.

Not only students and the intelligentsia opposed the colonels, but also the business people, the middle classes and even the traditional Right. Due to attempts by Papadopoulos at liberalisation, opposed by hard liners, a political rift appeared within the *junta*. Dimitrios Ioannidis, the head of the Military Police, would soon overthrow Papadopoulos, accusing him of abandoning the ideals of the *Revolution*.

In July 1974 Ioannidis was to trigger a *coup d'état* in Cyprus to overthrow Archbishop Makarios as President, replacing him by the former terrorist, Nikos Sampson. Turkey retaliated by invading the island. Fearing a war between two NATO allies, Greek army officers withdrew their support for Ioannidis, created a government of national unity and invited exiled Konstantinos Karamanlis to return.

The *junta* leaders would be condemned to death, their sentence commuted to life imprisonment, at a mass trial reminiscent of Nuremburg. Papadopoulos and Ioannidis died in confinement after refusing amnesty.

The fracture in the Balkans between Orthodox

Back to Byzantium

Christians and Ottoman Muslims had begun to fascinate me. Cyprus seemed to be its modern incarnation, but no-one in the Greece of the colonels was willing or able to tell me about it. It was only when I got home to the UK that my curiosity was satisfied when I ran into the son of the local *lord of the manor* of the London suburban village where I lived as a boy.

He was a young army officer, who had served for more than a year under permanent fire in Cyprus, in those days a British crown colony. On leave to stay with his elderly parents, he went out one evening and came home late. At 11 PM his mother rang the police to report a missing person... He explained Cyprus to me.

'Cyprus has remained the last active line of fracture between Greeks and Turks, the inheritance of the Ottoman Empire', he said. 'The goals of the two communities have always been incompatible. For the Greek Cypriots it was *enosis*, while that of the Turkish Cypriots was *taksim*.'

'*Enosis* and *taksim*?' I queried.

'*Enosis*, meaning union, was the Greek Cypriot movement to annex Cyprus to mainland Greece. *Taksim*, meaning *division*, was the Turkish Cypriot concept of partition of the island.

'Britain had gained control of the island in 1878 at the Congress of Berlin to prevent the Russians from replacing the Ottomans. After the Second World War Britain tried in vain to create a constitution for Cyprus.

'When the Turkish islanders set up a paramilitary group, Georgios Grivas, a Greek Cypriot right-wing extremist, set up the *EOKA terrorist organisation*, with the objective of *enosis* by armed combat. *EOKA* caused hundreds of British deaths. When Makarios became

Archbishop of Cyprus, as *Ethnarch* or leader of the Greek Cypriot community, he also aimed for *enosis*, but only by political means. That was the difficult time when I was part of the British peace-keeping force.'

'When did Cyprus get its independence?' I asked. 'Were you still there at the time?'

'No, I left several years before. The Republic of Cyprus was created in 1960, with Makarios as President, based on power-sharing at all levels with a dual right of veto for Greeks and Turks. Due to the veto, power-sharing inevitably collapsed and insurmountable violence arose between the communities. All successive attempts by Britain, Greece, Turkey, and later by a UN peacekeeping force failed in the face of intransigence on both sides.'

The *coup d'état* on the island triggered by Ioannidis three years later, after the death of Grivas, would pass without intervention by Britain or the US. Turkey sent troops to invade the island. Thousands were killed, hundreds of thousands in both communities became refugees. The Turkish Cypriot community, representing less than one fifth of the population, gained a third of the territory. The international community then recognised *de facto* the partition of Cyprus.

Back to Byzantium

Back to my train journey home from Athens. We arrived late the following morning in Skopje (still no-one spoke English). I had been talking with a couple of German engineers on an assignment in the city. '*Skopje ist ein großes Dorf*', a big village, one of them said. They took me to the only hotel in town, a boarding-house on the first floor of a building. I booked in and then set off to find my Macedonian colleague's sister's house.

Macedonia, true to its name, was one of the most ethnically diverse regions in Europe, comprising amongst others nearly sixty-five per cent Slavs, twenty per cent Albanians and five per cent Roma.

> 'The Turk, the Greek, the Albanian, and the Moor,
> Here mingled in their many-hued array...'

You could easily recognise the Albanians by their Muslim *qeleshes*, white felt skull caps in the shape of an egg that has been cut in half. In the early afternoon I could see only Roma in the streets.

The city, which had been rebuilt in haste along the axis of a single interminable avenue, the *ulica Maršala Tita*, was said to be one of the longest in Europe. I had the address, but no map of what was a vast reconstructed council-housing estate. A young man offered to help me. We took a couple of buses, got lost and asked a militiaman for help. He got onto his police headquarters on his walkie-talkie and found out the way. You didn't find police with high-tech equipment like that in Western Europe. The young man accompanied me almost to the door. We stopped in front of a house that he recognised by its appearance as not being a Slav dwelling. 'But this is a Muslim house. Your friends are not Muslim, are they?' he asked with some concern. No, they weren't. We'd got the wrong house.

In the prefabricated single-storied construction next door a young couple welcomed me: 'You must be Antonin.' They gave me a Macedonian late lunch, which I ate alone, and the husband then drove me into the centre, picked up my bag and paid my hotel bill. They gave me presents for my family. Eastern hospitality!

The couple, both architects, were employed in rebuilding the city.

In the afternoon of the next day my host drove us up the road into what was then called the *Serbian Autonomous Province of Kosovo and Metohija*. On the way we witnessed the beginning of a battle between two Albanian peasants in white *qeleshes*, each holding a wooden stave, ready for combat. Over what, I asked. About boundaries, my host thought. Together we visited a minute Orthodox monastery housing less than ten nuns. The Mother Superior, a tiny woman bent double from scoliosis, compensated for her physique by her energy and charisma. Along the whole length of the monastery, in fact a large farm house, ran a broad timbered outer corridor known as a *chardak*. I had fallen in love with the Balkans!

Kosovo Polje was not far away, the site of the historic Battle of Kosovo, but we didn't have time to visit it. My Macedonian architect host told me about the myth that was the essence of Serbia.

> 'Kosovo Polje is the symbol of the Serb nation. This is where, on 28 June 1389, the Turks definitively defeated the Serbs, who from then on became Ottoman vassals. The Serbs celebrate the defeat on 28th June under the Gregorian calendar, as a public but working holiday.
>
> 'Try to imagine an event engraved on Serbian collective memory with an impact equivalent for you English to the sum of the Battle of Hastings, the retreat from Dunkirk and Boudicca's defeat against the Roman invaders. Or, even better, to Culloden for the Scots. The defeat marked the end of the golden age of Serbia. Yet through epic

poetry the Battle of Kosovo has become the symbol of heroism in battle, the moment of national glory in Serbian collective consciousness. But it has also turned into the bloody lens through which Serbs see and interpret events of the past, the present and the future.'

'Did it actually take place?' I asked the architect.

'Yes, it did, but… though we know the date and place of the Battle of Kosovo, we are unsure of everything else about it, even whether in fact it turned out to be a defeat for the Serbs or just a stalemate. It took place on what the Serbs call *Vidovdan*, St. Vitus' Day. At the end of the battle flocks of birds are supposed to have swooped down to devour the dead, thereby giving the place the name of Kosovo Polje, the *Field of Blackbirds*. The Turks would eventually rule over the region for over five hundred years, though they actually completed their conquest only a good seventy years after the battle was over. The Serbian leader, Prince Lazar Hrebeljanović, with a coalition of Serbian lords and a diverse collection of warriors from across the Balkans, faced a Muslim army led by Sultan Murad

'The trouble is that factual history has been replaced by mythology, which many people in the Balkans believed and still believe to be the truth.'

And what about the myth? It's said that ethnic interpretations of history form the basis of memory in the Balkans. Myths and symbols are used to make the past contemporary and turn the present into history, thereby justifying ethnic cleansing and worse. Thanks to *the Mountain Wreath*, a play in verse by Petar II Petrović-Njegoš the Montenegrin Prince-Bishop known as

Serbia's Shakespeare, religious mythology has replaced the actual history of the Battle. Oral folklore tradition, epic poetry and literature, and the Serbian Orthodox Church, with the help of generations of illiterate bards, have kept alive the spirit of resistance against the Turks. By providing continuity between the Serbs of the Middle Ages and the contemporary Serbian nation, the myth also justifies their claim to Kosovo.

Kosovo Polje has become the story of Serbian sacrifice, a fight between Serbian good and Muslim evil. The battle is sometimes presented as the Serbian *Golgotha*, an event of great suffering and agony, the crucifixion of the Serb people. With its tale of heroism, martyrdom, sacrifice, betrayal and revenge, the myth became a justification for war. Once they saw themselves as victims, the Serbs could identify their enemy and were no longer bound by considerations of morality.

The Communist leader and partisan hero, Milovan Djilas, claimed that if the Battle had not taken place, the Serbs would have invented it.

The protagonists of the battle were Sultan Murad I, accompanied by his two sons, the future Sultan Bayazid and Yakub, on the Ottoman side. Prince Lazar led the Serbs, seconded by his two sons-in-law, Vuk Branković and Miloš Obilić.

Like most myths, the battle it had its divinity, its hero and its villain.

Prince Lazar, who was decapitated during the battle, is its divinity. He was canonised, becoming the myth's Christ figure.

Miloš Obilić is the hero of the myth, the Serbian national hero. During the battle he is said to have pretended to desert to the Ottomans. When the Turks, not realising that it was a trick, presented him to Murad in his tent, Miloš pulled out a dagger and stabbed the Sultan to death. In his flight he was killed by the Turks. Miloš became the ultimate martyr in Serbian legend. As the Joan-of-Arc figure of the myth, he also was canonised.

Vuk Branković is the traitor in the myth. Jealous of Miloš's courage, Vuk had accused him of conspiring to betray Lazar to the Turks (which Miloš had pretended to do to fool them). After the death of Prince Lazar, Vuk fled the battle to save his troops and was thereafter cast in the role of Judas.

As for Sultan Murad's son Bayazed, after tricking his brother Yakub and having him strangled, he became the new Sultan. Believe it or not, he then married the daughter of Prince Lazar, whom he had previously decapitated in battle. When the Mongols later captured him, he died in captivity, a prisoner of Tamerlane.

The central theme of the myth is God's visit to Prince Lazar on the eve of the battle in the form of a grey falcon, offering him a choice between defeat of the Serbian forces in exchange for the kingdom of heaven for his people, or alternatively victory over the Ottomans and a kingdom on earth. In what is known as the Kosovo Covenant, Lazar chose defeat against the Turks and salvation for the Serbs.

Before the battle, to encourage his countrymen to follow him into battle, Lazar put what is known as the *Kosovo curse* on those who should refuse to join the fight. Any Serb refusing to join him would have neither offspring nor would he reap harvest from what he sowed and he would be accursed for all time.

It seems only logical that the Turkish mythical account of the battle should be symmetrical to that of the Serbs. On the eve of the battle Murad also had a dream, offering himself to God as a sacrifice for the faith and for the victory of his own men and his ascent into heaven. Both myths share the themes of sacrifice, religious martyrdom, and heroic action.

During their *National Awakening*, the Serbs once again used the legend against the Habsburgs. After the assassination of Archduke Franz Ferdinand in Sarajevo on 28 June 1914, the 525th anniversary of the battle, they cast Gavrilo Princip in the role of its assassin-hero Miloš Obilić. As a teenager who knew *the Mountain Wreath* by heart, Princip pulled the trigger in the name of the Serb people, inspired by Njegos's ideology that the assassination of a tyrant could not be considered as murder.

Other events of importance have also taken place on *Vidovdan*. It was on that day in 1921 that the Yugoslav state of the Kingdom of the Serbs, Croats, and Slovenes received its constitution. After the First World War the Serbian memorial day was established on 28 June. It was also the day that Stalin chose to expel Yugoslavia from the Communist Bloc.

'Is the myth still alive?' I asked the architect.

'No, at least not theoretically. Of course, the German occupants banned all Serb culture and traditions. During and since the War, Marshal Tito and the Partisans always ferociously opposed all nationalism. The Communists have deliberately been downplaying the national histories of all the peoples of Yugoslavia, and doing their best to eradicate the Kosovo myth.'

Yet, despite all their efforts, it would survive Communism. After Tito's death everyone would begin to feel insecure in ex-Yugoslavia and start to return to their ethnic roots. Kosovo mythology would survive largely thanks to the Serbian Orthodox Church. A group of scholars from the Serbian Academy of Arts and Sciences were to publish a memorandum, which became the justification for Slobodan Milošević's policy of *Greater Serbia*. It claimed that ethnic Serbs were suffering physical extermination, forced assimilation, religious conversion and cultural genocide. A coalition within Serbia of nationalists and communists manipulated the myth of Kosovo. They defined the nation not as the geographical territory of Serbia, but as an ethnic territory, the holy blood-soaked earth wherever Serbs lived and died. Historical facts became irrelevant.

Serbian clergy blessed Serb militia with references to Lazar and Kosovo Polje as they set off to wipe out entire Muslim populations in Bosnia-Herzegovina. Serbs would once again perceive Kosovo as a land occupied by foreign Muslim oppressors. The Serbs, as victims of Albanians, needed the protection of a strong leader like Slobodan Milošević.

On the 600th anniversary of the battle a million ethnic Serbs from across the globe were to arrive in Kosovo Polje to watch Milošević alight from a helicopter as the new Prince Lazar. In accordance with the Kosovo myth, he would present the Serbs as victims of Muslims, reminding the world that by their sacrifice they had defended Europe from Islam and would continue to do so. Kosovo was Serbian and this fact depended on neither Albanian natality nor Serbian mortality.

He would later stand trial before the International Criminal Court, accused of genocide. Ironically, it was on *Vidovdan*, the anniversary of the Battle, that he would surrender to authorities of The Hague. He was to die before his trial, ten years before the Court posthumously acquitted him.

During the civil war in Bosnia, on the 606th anniversary of the Kosovo Polje, General Ratko Mladić, after taking communion, would proclaim his mission, identifying personally with Prince Lazar, and his Bosnian Serb countrymen with those who fought in the Battle. At Srebrenica, his troops were to murder about seven thousand Muslim men and boys, announcing that the moment of revenge against the Turks had finally arrived.

For this and other crimes in Bosnia, Mladić would be brought before the International Criminal Court, accused of genocide and crimes against humanity.

The Serbian Orthodox clergy would later support Serbian military actions in Kosovo, proclaiming a new battle of Kosovo Polje against its Muslim enemy. In Kosovo, an estimated twelve thousand Albanians were to die during the Serbian campaigns against the civilian population, with countless revenge killings against Serbs (compared with the horrors in Bosnia with 237,500 dead and 2.7 million displaced persons).

When Kosovo would finally be granted its independence, Serb nationalists were to brand Slobodan Milošević as a traitor more treacherous even than the battle's mythical Judas, Vuk Branković, for abandoning his people to the Turks. There was to be no Greater Serbia. Though inseparable from Serbian national identity, Kosovo would finally be lost for ever...

We drove back to Skopje for a traditional *al fresco* dinner on the hill of Vodno, with a distant view over the sparse glitter of the hastily reconstructed city below. With

Back to Byzantium

our *ćevapčići*, tiny spicy kebabs, and *ajvar*, red-pepper purée, I discovered *šljivovica*, damson brandy drunk throughout the dinner, in which I was later to indulge in to excess.

On my last morning, we made a visit the local museum, where my host's father worked as curator. He was also an iconographer, currently in charge of restoring and reassembling the collection after the earthquake. Only the Turkish buildings had resisted destruction because, he told us, mosques, *caravanserais*, *hamams*, had all been constructed on rocky ground.

'Your son tells me that you also paint and restore icons', I said.

'Well', he replied, 'strictly speaking I don't *paint* them. Icons are *written*, not painted. Iconography is a strictly coded language, with its own vocabulary and syntax, designed as a way of communicating with those unable to read and write. Figures of the Christ and the Virgin are drawn with minimal expression, the function of the icon and the fresco being to display dispassion and not passion. You know that an iconographer is not free to change an icon to be original or creative? They have nothing to do with decoration. Iconography is not concerned with aesthetics, but with liturgy. It is part of a whole that includes architecture, vestments, utensils, chants, whose aim is to elevate the soul.'

'But I find these icons most aesthetic', I objected.

'They are of course, but you shouldn't consider the ability to write icons as a gift of artistic talent, but rather as a calling from God. Only those who have faith can do it, because writing an icon is a liturgical act.'

'What about representation in Catholic

churches, especially those of the Counter-Reformation?'

'Western religious art since Giotto has depicted Christ, the Virgin and the Saints as ordinary, contemporary human beings. They were painted in a naturalistic style, sometimes sentimental, other times horrific, while their divinity was neglected. They may be aesthetically pleasing, but they appeal to the senses and the emotions, rather than the spirit. Western ecclesiastical art confuses the profane with the sacred. Catholic portraiture since Giotto has been a perversion of iconography'.

He showed us round the museum and as a parting gift gave me an icon of Saint Nicolas *Thaumaturgos* (the Wonder Worker), that he had copied himself.

To my untrained eye it looked as orthodox as an icon can be. I knew nothing about the symbols or the inscriptions. I was later to discover on closer examination that it was far from being as orthodox or as benevolent as it had seemed at first sight.

I decided to leave the next day for Venice. My hosts had convinced me: 'Why waste your holiday time in Skopje, when you can visit Venice'. I later regretted my decision. Why visit Venice, which I could see any time, and miss the unique opportunity of spending another two days in Skopje with a Macedonian family?

The following morning I took the train for Belgrade. At Niš the train from Istanbul merged with ours. I got talking in the corridor with a young Frenchman returning from Bulgaria. He enthused about his brief stay in a small town there, telling me about how the people made him welcome and particularly about the evening *razkhodka*, the *passeggiata* along the streets of the whole of the town's population. Bulgaria, that's where I had to go next.

I met an Israeli woman and we made use of the Italian compartment with its pull-across seats. We visited Venice together. With New York, Venice must be the only place that forbids ethnocentrism. You just can't say 'It reminds me of ...' Entering by train through miserable Mestre, you walk out of the station directly onto the Grand Canal and are overwhelmed – impossible to avoid the cliché.

I still regretted not spending two more days in Skopje. I wouldn't make a mistake like that again. And yet... I made a similar one ten years later, on the same train to Piraeus, *en route* for Jerusalem, amongst other things to see the Hassidim at Mea She'arim. I met a Turk who invited me to stay with his family in Istanbul, but I was too inflexible to change my plans and accept his offer.

3
Plovdiv

President Richard Nixon had made an official visit to the Soviet Union that spring to complete negotiations for the *SALT 1* agreement, to be signed the following year, signalling the beginning of *détente*. Strategic Arms Limitation Talks restricted the number of anti-ballistic missiles and banned bacteriological weapons. Autumn had begun and, inspired by my conversation on the train in Niš the year before, I was on my way to Bulgaria.

I was sharing a flat in Paris with a German painter. One of his friends, an English programmer of computer graphics, had come to visit with a young Bulgarian girl who had been staying in London. She gave me the address of her elder sister, a medical student in Plovdiv.

A couple of days before my departure I went rambling in the forest of Fontainebleau with a botanist. What better guide for mushrooming than a botanist writing his thesis? He nibbled at a foul-looking fungus regurgitating from the bark of a tree before spitting it out but, when I approached a mushroom that looked both familiar and appetising, I heard him say 'Don't even touch that one!' The nine courses of our dinner that evening were composed just of mushrooms, each one of a different shape and colour. Most of them, just generic toadstools to my eye, I would never have even brushed against had it not been for the expert. Our dinner was memorable in more ways than one, at least for a few days while I continued to look for symptoms of poisoning.

Parasols and horns of plenty, *trompettes de la mort* in French, had not succeeded in killing my stomach, so I went out on a binge with a colleague on the night before my departure. I cannot remember why, but we first limited our libations to green *Chartreuse* and then, when that had run out, to *liqueur de Verveine*. Imagine what I felt and feared the following evening as I boarded the Direct Orient once again at the *Gare du Nord*. Never in a lifetime would I touch the green stuff again.

I chose to share a compartment with three girls. Two were Flemings from Belgium, the other from the Netherlands. I since learnt from experience that, when travelling in Yugoslavia, it was preferable not to be sitting as a lone man in a compartment with more than one woman. When asked: 'Is she your wife?' it was always advisable to answer that yes, of course she was.

I was travelling for the first time behind the *Iron Curtain* and felt a little apprehensive. But that was not where the danger lay. As my Macedonian colleague had warned me the previous year, it lay in the next compartment. A drunken Serb with designs on the women in mine began to pester them. In this case a gentleman knows his duty. Or does he? The women could have better defended themselves without my help.

'Toi *Shadok*', said the Serb, when I tried to mediate. The *Shadoks* were spiky, bird-like cartoon characters who appeared each evening for two minutes on French TV. They were stupid, devious and very nasty, but never a real threat to others. The Serb in his fury yanked the sliding door of the compartment off its rails, leaving it hanging askew, and disappeared. At the Italian-Yugoslav border at Vila Opicina an immigration officer pulled him off the train. Thirty minutes later at Sežana on the Yugoslav side he reappeared. 'Come in here and hide', said some Yugoslavs in another compartment. 'He will kill you.' I lay on the floor until Zagreb, then found another compartment. I didn't see him when we arrived in Belgrade the next morning. He must have got off at Zagreb. Perhaps my Serb was a Croat.

Back to Byzantium

The following afternoon, at the Bulgarian border post at Dimitrovgrad no-one made a fuss. Bulgaria imposed a visa charge for people in transit for Istanbul. I had decided to stay in Bulgaria for a couple of weeks, so it was free of charge. So much for crossing the *Iron Curtain*!

I got talking on the train with a clean-shaven Palestinian student returning to the university in Sofia. He had just shaven off his beard after the dean of the faculty had sent him down for a month. 'Only hooligans wear beards', the dean had told him. 'In that case Lenin was a hooligan', he had replied.

At eight o'clock in the evening I left the train in Sofia. I had no idea which way to go, just the name of the national tourist agency, *Balkanturist*. I got on a bus hoping that it went to the city centre. Night had fallen and I soon understood the American couple in Skopje. No-one here spoke English, French, German or Italian. Everyone I questioned in my state of alarm gave me a look of animosity tinged with envy.

> 'Now Harold felt himself at length alone, …
> Now he adventured on a shore unknown, …
> Peril he sought not, but ne'er shrank to meet
> The scene was savage, but the scene was new;
> This made the ceaseless toil of travel sweet…'

A fat man, reeking of alcohol, offered his services. 'Privat', he repeated. '*Balkanturist*', I replied. I left the bus in the central square, *Ploshtad Lenin*, surrounded by Stalinist buildings. With the help of an elderly gentleman I found the tourist agency. 'Didn't you know?' said the employee. 'Sofia is playing Italy today and the hotels are full of Italian football fans. We only have room in the Grand Hotel Sofia'. So be it, I took the room, though the price was well over what I had budgeted for several days stay.

Sofia was one of the first cities in Europe to ban

traffic from the city centre. Large shiny yellow bricks paved the streets. I took my room at the hotel, which may not have deserved its name, but it seemed pretty grand to me. Where did they hide the microphones, I wondered. This is Communism, the room must be bugged. I decided to leave the next day for Plovdiv to avoid the football fans.

As in every town and village in Bulgaria, propaganda banners dominated the city, proclaiming *Glory to BKP*, the Bulgarian Communist Party, or *Slava na Georgi Dimitrov*, glory to its national hero.

You could hardly overlook Georgi Dimitrov. He had been leader of the Communist party and head of the government of Bulgaria from the end of the war until his death in Moscow in 1949 under mysterious circumstances.

After working for years as a trade unionist and for the fledgling Bulgarian Communist Party before and after the First World War, he was arrested and sentenced to death. He managed to escape to the Soviet Union, from where Stalin sent him to Germany to head the regional *Comintern*.

The newly elected Nazi government had him arrested in Berlin in 1933, falsely accusing him with other Bulgarian Communists of conspiring to burn down the Reichstag. During his trial, he became an international hero with a brilliant, witty defence, cross-examining both Goering and Goebbels, whom the court called as witnesses against him.

I love this part! Called a *Balkan barbarian*, he reminded the court of the time when the Holy Roman Emperor, Charles V, while he spoke Spanish to God, Italian to women and French to his men, spoke German only to his horse. At the time when the German nobility were so ashamed of their mother tongue that they wrote only in Latin, in barbarous Bulgaria Cyril and Methodius had already created a script that enabled Bulgarian culture to survive the five centuries of the Ottoman yoke. Amazingly, the court acquitted him.

Dimitrov became a Soviet citizen, which he remained until his death. As one of the few foreign Communists whom Stalin respected and trusted, at least until after the war, he miraculously survived the Great Purge. Stalin consequently appointed him General Secretary of the *Comintern*, a position where he remained until Stalin dissolved it. At the end of the war he returned to Bulgaria, a country in which he had not set foot for more than twenty years.

His attempt to create a Balkan Federation with Tito made him unpopular with Stalin, who summoned him to Moscow. Within days, according to overwhelming evidence, Beria had him poisoned. It was officially announced that he had died of cirrhosis of the liver. After the fall of Communism, forensic analysis of a lock of his hair and later of part of his brain would reveal abnormal levels of mercury. Nevertheless, opinion was not unanimous. The Bulgarian tabloid, *24 Chasa, 24 Hours*, would later reveal that the Bulgarian Institute of Criminology had no doubt that he had been poisoned.

Dimitrov became the subject of a Bulgarian *calque* of the cult of Lenin, with ubiquitous banners to his glory in every town and village. His mummified corpse lay in an *ersatz* mausoleum. With his physique and moustache, he became the prototype for the post-war Communist boss, Gino Cervi in the role of Peppone to Fernandel's Don Camillo.

Back to Byzantium

The Grand Hotel, a non-descript modern building, was situated behind the Royal Palace, which stood directly opposite Dimitrov's mausoleum. I waited in a queue and then slowly traipsed round the catafalque with the country people paying homage.

His mausoleum had been built within a week out of white marble, a squatter version of Lenin's tomb. At the entrance two soldiers stood guard, dressed in flashy uniforms from the Bulgarian war of independence.

A year after the end of Communism the Bulgarian government would remove Georgi Dimitrov's corpse. The cult of Dimitrov had finally been a failure and very few people came to see him. His embalmed face, which looked just like a waxwork, was too yellow to be believed. In the true Balkan vampire tradition, rumours had begun to circulate about his miraculous state of conservation.

A few months into the new post-communist *regime*, thousands of inhabitants planted a tent village in front of the mausoleum to protest about electoral fraud. They succeeded in forcing the new government to set up a commission to dispose of the corpse. Not daring to bury it to avoid pilgrimages to his tomb, the government had the corpse cremated.

After the corpse had been removed no-one really felt concerned any more with the mausoleum. Inside they had discovered an office, a secret bar for official ceremonies and a urinal... Of course, from then on people equated the mausoleum with a public toilet. Graffiti soon adorned its walls.

The government held a competition to find a new use for it. Among the soberest suggestions were to maintain it as a historical monument or to turn it into a museum of oppression, from the Turkish yoke through Nazism to Communist totalitarianism. A businessman wanted to install a luxury bar or a high-tech supermarket. The most original proposal was to get Khristo, the environmental artist, to *wrap* it.

None of the projects were accepted. Despite the wish of two thirds of the population for it to be maintained, the government had it destroyed. But it wasn't that easy... Like Hitler's *Hochbunker*, the concrete blockhouses that he built in Viennese parks, the mausoleum was almost indestructible. It took four attempts to blow it up and they finally had to finish it off with bulldozers. Learning later the destruction of one of the few monuments in Sofia gave me a slight twinge of sorrow.

Next door to the tourist office I found a book shop. I just had to learn Bulgarian, but the only language manual left in the shop was in Italian. I had been reading the letters that Lady Mary Wortley Montagu had written during her eighteen-month stay in Ottoman Turkey in the early 18th century. She had learnt Turkish using a textbook in Italian. I was in illustrious company, I thought, I'll learn Bulgarian and improve my Italian at the same time. I went to pay. 'Are you Jewish?' asked the cashier in English. 'No. Why?' I asked. 'Because Jews are so clever and gifted for learning languages.'

Sofia, an agreeable city at the foot of the mountains, is one of the few capitals in Europe with neither a river nor a sea front, just a canal. Architecturally it lies at the intersection of the Byzantine and the Ottoman, of early 20th century provincialism and Stalinism, with some French Second Empire added.

I had by then discovered that Bulgarians shake their heads vigorously when they mean *Yes* and nod when they mean *No*. They have this in common with other Balkan peoples, an inheritance from the Turkish yoke. I found it disconcerting that even sign language would be difficult. To avoid misunderstanding with foreigners, Bulgarians usually wag their index finger to say *no*.

The benevolent gushing smile like in the USA, which at first delights but quickly exasperates, is totally absent from Bulgarian as from many Slav cultures. Most of the time people seem completely expressionless and, I felt, even scowling. This doesn't mean that they don't laugh, which they do often and heartily.

> According to the language manual's introduction, Bulgarian was a Slavonic language using the Cyrillic alphabet, whose ancestor became Church Slavonic. Modern Bulgarian differs in some of its language features from other Slavonic languages.
>
> Due to its geographical and ethnographic proximity to other Balkan languages from entirely different language groups, it shares with them certain features not found in other languages of its own group. This is known in linguistics as a *Sprachbund* or language area, which transcends language groups. In the Balkans, it includes, amongst others, Albanian, the Illyrian language, Macedonian, a Slavonic language similar to Bulgarian, Romanian, a Latin language, and even Romani, an Indo-Aryan language spoken by gypsies.
>
> Bulgarian is a phonetic language with few exceptions. Alone among Slavonic languages except Macedonian, and in common with some of its neighbours, Bulgarian has lost its declensions, replaced by prepositions. Like Albanian and Romanian, it has gained a definite article that is appended to the end of the noun.
>
> All this makes it much easier to learn for a Westerner than other Slavonic languages. The main problem is, as in English, to know which syllable bears the stress.

'I would like to buy a second-class ticket for Plovdiv', I said. 'Take first class!' the woman at the ticket office replied. 'Second class is not suitable for you.' 'Why?' 'You will not like it, take first class!' I obediently purchased my first-class ticket, found a compartment with three Bulgarians and started reading my language manual. Learning Bulgarian became an immediate talking point with my compartment companions, a young man doing his military service and a female student.

We arrived in Plovdiv and my companions took me to the *Balkanturist* agency to look for a place to stay. I found a flat that was comfortably filled with furniture from the thirties. My young soldier became ecstatic about the *antiques*.

He accompanied me to Plovdiv's luxury hotel, the Trimontium, called after the three hills on which ancient Phillipopoli had been built. By now only two hills remained. The Nazis are said to have blown up the third. A host of hopeful diners waited for a place under an arcade to eat *al fresco*. As a foreigner, I had second-level priority after nationals of sister nations, but before the Bulgarians, who came third. My soldier friend and I succeeded in enjoying our dinner and each other's company despite the lack of a common language. He gave me his phone number (or was it?), but I never tried to contact him.

The following day I met Biliana, the sister of the girl whom I had met in Paris. We visited the old town together, the wooden masterpiece in the Bulgarian *National Revival* style, that followed independence from the Turks. She introduced me to three students from Sofia, one of whom her sister's boyfriend. They all had long, black beards, like Orthodox *popes*. Did they allow that, I asked, remembering the Palestinian on the train? Each one' took out of his pocket an official paper with the stamp of the municipal authorities permitting him to wear a beard for the duration of a film about mediaeval iconographers that they were shooting for the cinema academy. Each looked like the Christ *Pantocrator*. We spoke together in rudimentary German. I had just had my long hair cut short in preparation for my trip and felt rather uncomfortable. 'I must look like a member of the *Hitlerjugend*', I said. 'More like *Zhivkov Jugend*', said the boyfriend, lowering his voice. Todor Zhivkov had been the Bulgarian leader since he had been so dubbed by Nikita Khrushchëv, and after nineteen years had become somewhat stale. This wouldn't prevent him from surviving a further sixteen. So Communism was not as monolithic as we thought in the West. Here was my first encounter with dissident talk.

'Tell me about your film', I said. 'It's about *iconoclasts*', replied the boyfriend. 'I suppose I need to explain.

'As you may know, *iconoclasm* was a ban on religious images and their deliberate destruction by the Eastern Church. Meanwhile, your Western, Latin Church continued to support images.'

'I'm a Protestant', I remarked. 'Our Church doesn't encourage images either.'

'To some extent it was a sociological split', he continued, 'what Karl Marx and our dear Communist leaders would call a *class struggle*, between *Iconoclasts*, those who wanted them destroyed, and *Iconodules*, who venerated them. *Iconoclasts* were mostly poorer, non-Greek people from the East, who had been directly affected by Muslim raids. *Iconodules* were mainly city people, monks, women and those from the Western part of the Byzantine Empire, the Balkans and Italy.

'But this wasn't Judaism or Islam. What was their problem with images?'

'Icons were based on two principles:

intercession and proximity. The Church had defined a hierarchy for gaining access to the divine: Christ at the top, then the Mother of God, finally the Saints. Physical proximity could magnify the power of intercession, for example, by pilgrimages to places where Christ had been physically present, such as the Holy Sepulchre, or by access to relics, remains - a bone, or something having been in contact - a thorn from the crown, a nail or a splinter from the true cross, ... even a feather from the Archangel Gabriel's wing...

'By the 7th century, it was the images themselves that were beginning to be treated as relics, becoming themselves points of access to the divine to increase the power of prayer. Believe it or not, it reached a point where icons were made godfathers to children. They were also used as a *palladium* for protection in battle, like *Our Lady of Kazan*. It had begun to get out of control.

'In answer to your question, Judaism and Islam were both relevant. First Judaism: the second of the Ten Commandments, of course, forbade making and worshiping graven idols and images. Then the rise of Islam with its prohibition of images also had an influence, due to the prestige of its military successes.

'The *Iconoclasts* believed that the only true religious images must be of the same substance as the original, meaning the Body and Blood of Christ in the Eucharist. They objected that Icons could not represent the dual nature of Christ, both God and man in two natures. They considered images to be a return to paganism, with Christ *Pantocrator* replacing Zeus.'

He paused for a gulp of beer, wiping his jet-black beard with the back of his hand.

'How about the *iconodules*? What were their

arguments?' I asked.

'Just as God had been visibly incarnated in Jesus, so icons represent God in the world. As you no doubt know, icons are written not painted. There was also the crazy theory that Christ and the Mother of God both sat for portraits during their lifetime. They used it as an argument to prove that Christ supported icons.

'Who won in the end?' I asked.

'Iconoclasm came and went over two cycles, one century apart, first in the 8th century, then in the 9th. External events had been considered as divine punishment for images, for example, a submarine volcanic eruption that had caused a tidal wave in the Aegean and a military defeat by the Muslims.

'Constantine V instigated the first removal of an image of Christ and decreed iconoclasm at a phoney ecumenical council. After his death and that of his son, his daughter-in-law, acting as regent for the under-age heir, called a real ecumenical council, which abolished iconoclasm.

'Then in a *déjà vu* occurrence, after the reigns of three more Emperors, the process began again with images being banned after another humiliating defeat. Once again after two generations of iconoclasm, another widow acting as regent definitively restored the veneration of icons in what is known as the *Triumph of Orthodoxy*.

'But I am much more interested in detective stories', he said. 'My own hierarchy has Dürrenmatt at the top, then Simenon, followed by Conan Doyle, with Agatha Christie at the bottom. How about you?'

His girlfriend had been living in London for too long

for his liking and she thought that he had terminated their relationship. Afraid of being bugged when ringing her himself in Bulgarian, he asked me for help. I rang my brother in English, who communicated the message to her that all was forgiven and that he was waiting for her to come back home. I felt that I had entered a spy novel and I had just discovered totalitarianism. She returned to Plovdiv the following week.

I stayed in Plovdiv for several days, broken up by a trip into the Rhodope Mountains. My new friend Biliana tried to teach me Bulgarian, which with my twenty-nine-year-old connected neurones I found remarkably easy. My hotel filled up with a group of Russian tourists, women with platinum-blond beehives in black mini-dresses, those who had remained slim, that is. Bulgaria for them was the West and they were letting off steam vigorously, to the discomfort of those in the adjacent rooms. I left Plovdiv for Burgas on the Black Sea.

The train was full, but I found a seat in a compartment with a red-headed young man and six elderly Bulgarians. When the young man revealed that he originated from the Soviet Union, three of the gentlemen in our compartment opened their wallets and each pulled out a photo of Stalin the size of a cigarette card. The young Soviet, showing acute embarrassment, eighteen years after Khrushchëv's secret speech before the 20th Congress had debunked Stalin, joined me in the corridor where we chatted until he left the train at Stara Zagora. We managed to communicate in Bulgarian, in which we had the same primitive level. He told me he came from Georgia, but I didn't believe him. I really think he was ashamed to say he was Russian, not colourful enough for him, though exotic for me.

This was in fact only my second encounter with a Soviet citizen. You didn't see them much in Western Europe back then. I had got talking with one ten years before on a café terrace in Paris. I just couldn't believe that this affable man in his fifties was actually from

Russia. Had he been from the planet Mars I would hardly have been more surprised.

I continued my journey, studying my language manual with the help of a doctor, who gave me lunch in the courtyard of the station restaurant in Burgas. I spent one night there in a hotel full of Italian engineers, then to be seen all over Bulgaria, before continuing down the coast to spend a few days in a bungalow on a campsite behind the dunes of a Black Sea beach.

I had read that the Black Sea resorts were full of spies. I don't know about that, but it was full of Germans of both varieties. This was the no man's land where *Ossies* and *Wessies* could meet, though not always in perfect harmony. When you met an East German climbing out of his *Trabant*, the first thing he said while clasping your hand was: 'You know, we are not Communists.' Out of a *Mercedes Benz* stepped a bombastic young man from Frankfurt, declaring: 'Lenin was the greatest man of the century.' This was perhaps the authentic, if mirror image of the Cold War. I found the nationals of the *Deutsche Demokratische Republik* invariably both modest and charming. I shared a dinner table with two couples of psychiatrists from East Germany. In my basic German, we discussed psychoanalysis, formerly considered as anti-socialist. *'Die Deutschen sind ein ganz sprachfauler Volk'*, one of them said. A lazy people for languages? I always thought of Germans as polyglots, but not these from the east.

I never liked campsites. Two days of shaving in a communal wash-house with Czech campers leaning across my lathered face to dampen their tooth brushes were enough. I moved down the road to another more luxurious site. Biliana came to stay with me for a few days. This was a no man's land in more ways than one, where the authorities turned a blind eye on fraternisation. My friend left, I tired of the camp site and the end-of-season water had got cold. I decided to leave for Veliko Trnovo, the former capital at the time of the second

Back to Byzantium

Bulgarian Empire.

I arrived in the dark. The station was far from the town centre, so I took a bus. I had great difficulty asking where to find the hotel with my smattering of Bulgarian. When I arrived, there was no room at the inn. A man whom I had met on the bus offered me a bed on the couch of the room that his company had booked for him. We had dinner together and with every glass of *slivova* my Bulgarian improved. Always chase it with a soft drink, even so, *slivova* leaves a nasty hangover. My room-mate from Sofia installed neon signs for a living. We had fun laughing at the group of elderly small-town English tourists, who were the cause of the hotel being full. I had a chat with one of them. How did he like Bulgaria? 'The buses are dirty', he replied.

The next day I explored this remarkable town. In need of shoe laces, I found a cobbler but no laces. 'Sell me your razor blades', he said. I had to return to my hotel to bring my own razor to demonstrate that his own worked better. Razors and blades seemed to be a national obsession that polarised Bulgarians' perception of Western quality.

Veliko Trnovo straddles a hill over a deep wooded gorge encasing the river Yantra. The squat houses with their corbelled over-jutting first floor date from Ottoman times and from the Bulgarian *National Revival*. Just outside the town stood the wreck of the Tsarevits citadel. Little of it remained, but they were rebuilding it. I found it strange that they seemed not to be rebuilding it entirely, but leaving it as a reconstructed ruin. The most famous part was Baldwin's tower.

> After their Sack of Constantinople during the Fourth Crusade, the Crusaders had set up a new Latin Empire. They crowned Baldwyn of Flanders in the basilica of *Hagia Sofia* Emperor Baldwyn I of Constantinople.
>
> Soon after, the Greeks revolted in Thrace with

the help of King Ivan II Kaloïan of Bulgaria, known as the Roman slayer. When Baldwyn laid siege to Adrianople the Bulgarians wiped out his army and captured him.

Kaloïan first treated Baldwyn well as a hostage. He kept him in captivity in the tower now known as Baldwyn's tower, on the hill of Tsarevets in Kaloïan's new capital, today's Veliko Trnovo. It is said that he later had Baldwyn's arms and legs cut off at the elbows and knees, and finally had him flung from the rock of execution. Some said that Baldwyn had tried to seduce Kaloïan's wife.

Baldwyn's tower may have been restored, but it needed a clean. Across the rough stones of the wall someone had stencilled a large, very elaborate piece of graffiti, though today you would probably call it a tag. And yet it was too neat to be just a regular squiggle sprayed on by a narcissistic punk trying to affirm his identity.

ᑫ%ᑭ

I was unable to determine to which alphabet the three strange letters belonged. It certainly wasn't Cyrillic, but what could it be? Who had spent time defacing a historical monument so neatly with such an elegant script? And why put it here of all places? More interested in Baldwyn and his Crusade, I forgot about the graffiti until after returning to Plovdiv a couple of weeks later.

I was eager to find out about the infamous Fourth Crusade.

4
Crusade

It was now nearly 770 years since the Sack of Constantinople in 1204.

I decided to leave Veliko Trnovo by the evening train for Ruse, a border town separated by the Danube from the Romanian town of Giurgiu. The train was full. Burly police officers patrolled the corridors, at night flashing their torches into the faces of the slumbering passengers. My beige corduroy jeans fascinated the young man sitting opposite me. 'Sell them to me', he said, glancing into the corridor for the police patrol. 'It's forbidden to sell them', I replied. 'Anyway, I need them'. He insisted. 'Give them to me then!' He was of very short stature, almost miniature. I stand one metre ninety-three in my stockinged feet. 'They are not even your size'. He gestured that his mother would cut all along the seams, demolish the trousers and then reconstruct them. I gave in, changed trousers in the toilet and, after a precautionary glance into the corridor, made him a present of them.

We arrived late in Ruse. I joined a collective taxi to the hotel, which again was full. They could only offer me a room shared with a Swedish salesman from a large telecom company. We had dinner together. He told me how he had tried to go by car from Giurgiu in Romania to Ruse, but the taxi had refused to enter Bulgaria. He had had to cross the more than two-kilometre-long *Friendship Bridge* over the Danube on foot with his luggage. So much for friendship between Socialist sister states!

Who do you work for?' he asked. 'Your French competitor', I answered. I worked as a small-time contract worker, part of a group providing tools for testing their new mid-range computer. I had dinner with a paranoid Swede. 'Why are you in Bulgaria?' 'I'm on holiday.'

Back to Byzantium

'People don't come on holiday to Bulgaria, they go to the Costa Brava.' 'It depends who you are', I replied, leaving him terrified that his competitor would steal his customer.

I have always had *itchy feet*. The following morning at breakfast an East German couple offered to drive me to Varna on the coast in their big black Mercedes. They were apparently trafficking in something, but it wasn't my business and I didn't ask.

I found Varna exactly as I had imagined a Black Sea town, agreeably flower-bedded, but nothing spectacular. I watched a debonair Nicolae Ceaușescu, in Bulgaria on an official visit to Todor Zhivkov, his enduring Bulgarian counterpart, salute a skimpy crowd on the way to the war memorial. Child sentries bearing rifles guarded it in fifteen-minute shifts.

I had dinner at my hotel, sharing a table with an odd couple. One of them, a lean crew-cut Bulgarian army officer, sat ram-rod straight in his chair opposite a hairy, bearded, slovenly-dressed artist. Apparently, they had been school friends. We drank *slivova* together and within a couple of hours had solved all the problems of post-Yalta Europe at the level of my Bulgarian learnt so far. We had reached an agreement that went far beyond simple peaceful coexistence, when the officer suddenly asked me: 'What about Northern Ireland?'

I left Varna the following day to go back to Sofia. The night train was standing room only, full of delegates on their way to a *Kongreso de Esperanto* in Sofia. An elderly academic chatted with me in pompous French. I had a bottle of *slivova* and offered him a sip, but he was teetotal. 'Je ne bois jamais d'*alkokhol*', he said.

    'How long have you been in the Balkans?' he asked.

    'Just a couple of weeks', I said. 'I always thought that the *B-word* was pejorative'.

'It depends for whom', said the Esperantist. 'For Bulgarians, it has never been so. For us the Balkan mountain range has always been a positive symbol. You must have noticed that the name here is ubiquitous, with *Balkan*, the national airline, *Balkanturist*, *Balkanton* records, etc. It was you people from the West who turned it into a disparaging word.'

'When did people start talking about *Balkanisation*?' I asked.

'It probably all started with the Balkan wars at the beginning of this century. The first Balkan war was popular in the West, because people saw it, despite its barbarity, as a war of independence of the weak from the strong, the Orthodox nations against the Turks. It was the second Balkan war, with each nation fighting against the others, that you rejected. *Balkanisation* came to mean a reversion to barbarianism.

'The term was coined at the end of the First World War, during the collapse of the Ottoman Empire. As you know, it came to mean fragmentation into small nationalist non-viable states. And yet this was totally unjustified. Every one of the so-called Balkan nations, including Albania, had already existed for years. Yugoslavia was the very reverse of *Balkanisation*, with the creation of the Kingdom of the Serbs, Croats and Slovenes. In fact, it was in the Habsburg and Romanov empires that there had been real fragmentation, with the creation of Poland, Czechoslovakia and the Baltic states.

'You have to admit that it is also unjust to talk about barbarity. In spite of prejudice, the level of slaughter in the Balkan peninsula has in fact never been on the scale of that of Europe, of Nazi Germany, the Soviet Union, Turkey, or even of modern-day conflicts.'

'Why is it called the Balkans anyway?' I asked.

'Before the 19th century the mountain range that today we Bulgarians call *Stara Planina*, the Old Mountain, had been known by its classical name *Haemus*. The name Balkan was Turkish. Despite geography the name of the mountain range became extended to the whole peninsula. Today we prefer to speak of South-Eastern Europe. This is the area between the Carpathians in the North, the Aegean in the South, the Black Sea in the East and the Adriatic in the West.'

'So how did the name of a mountain range in Bulgaria become a derogatory adjective?'

'The image of the Balkans was a pure creation that had no foundation in reality. The West created a model, with itself as the standard by which it defined all *others*, with the Balkans as its negative *alter-ego*. The inhabitants of the Balkans, being white and mainly Christian, became the repository of negative characteristics. In this way, Western European nations could keep a clear conscience while avoiding being accused of racism.

'You know, the Balkans have always been considered as a bridge between East and West, also a bridge in time between different stages of development. Have you read *A Bridge on the Drina* by Ivo Andrić, the Serbian Nobel prize-winner?'

I had discovered the book in the small library in the Hotel *Kastela* in Piraeus during my previous trip. How could I forget the chapter-long graphic description of an impaling? The bridge at Višegrad marked the border between Islam in Bosnia and Orthodoxy in Serbia.

'South-Eastern Europe was always perceived as a non-European civilisation', continued the Esperantist, after drinking a sip of tea from his flask. 'In the Middle Ages it first constituted the frontier between Catholicism and Orthodoxy for 1,000 years with Byzantium, then between Christianity and Islam for 500 years with the Ottoman Empire.

'The division of Europe between East and West really dates from the 18th century philosophers, who identified the East with superstition and irrationality, uninfluenced by the Enlightenment. Then, during the Romantic period, travellers, perhaps like yourself, turned the Balkans into a kind of folk museum of Europe for those in search of a romantic adventure, an escape back to the Middle Ages. This did not last long though. Travellers soon began to neglect the Balkans in favour of the real Orient. They considered the inhabitants of the Balkans as mongrels.

'In Greece, after the period of *philhellenism* came disillusionment, the perception of a lack of continuity between the Ancient Greeks and their modern heirs. The English preferred the Turks to the Greeks, whose land, language, antiquities they loved, but not its people. The Germans during the Second World War treated the Greeks as *Untermenschen*, thus justifying their massacre with a clear conscience.

'As for the Americans, with a few exceptions, they still view the Balkans as being in the lesser evolutionary stage of tribalism. They later rediscovered the image of the Greek as the *noble savage*, as in Jules Dassin's film *Never on Sunday.*'

'So Greece is in the Balkans", I remarked.

'What are the other countries?'

'Ah. That's the problem. Each nation except Bulgaria considers that the Balkans is elsewhere. For Croatians, the Balkans begins at the border with Serbia and Bosnia, for Serbians it is *down there* in Bosnia or Macedonia, for Romanians it is across the Danube. For Arnold Toynbee, it began at Bruck an der Leitha (at the Austrian border with Hungary) and for Metternich in the *Rennweg* (in an outer district of Vienna)!'

(Emir Kusturica, the Bosnian Serb film director, would later define the Balkans as wherever he was to be found at a given moment!)

'And for some people in Britain the Balkans begin in Calais', I added.

Eighteen years later, when the last Russian soldier had left Hungary, I would meet this phenomenon in Budapest. Outraged at receiving from the US what we used to call a *care package*, containing tinned food such as corned beef, a young woman asked: 'What do they think we are, the Balkans?' Newly affluent Hungarians had begun travelling to the Mediterranean for their holidays. How was Greece, we asked a young man. 'Oh, you know, just the Balkans', he replied.

'Believe it or not, only the Turks take pride in the Ottoman Empire's Byzantine heritage', the Esperantist continued, 'as saviours and protectors of the Orthodox Church. They perceived the loss of their Balkan territories as a disaster. Some Turks still talk of *Bizim Rumeli*, Our Rumelia.

'If nobody feels Balkan except the Bulgarians, then how do its inhabitants consider themselves?'

'The negative outside perception of the Balkans has been internalised. The inhabitants of the Balkans, when travelling west, talk of *going to Europe*, just as the English, travelling east, of *going on the Continent*. Isn't that proof that, like the English, they don't really feel part of Europe? The essence of Balkanism is to be *in-between*, European, but not quite.

'Do you know the Bulgarian comic anti-hero, *Baj Ganjo*, by the writer Aleko Konstantinov, who personifies this image?'

'I'm afraid I don't.'

'Baj Ganjo is an uneducated ignoramus, a self-made buffoon, both unscrupulous and chauvinistic. He is the prototype for Bulgaria's new lower middle class. At the turn of the 20th century, personifying Bulgarian crudeness abroad, he was an embarrassment to his Europeanised compatriots, who at the same time both despised and delighted in his ethnocentric behaviour. Baj Ganjo superficially mimicked *civilised* Western behaviour without adopting its values, what is known world-wide as *vulgarity*.'

My train eventually reached Plovdiv on a sunny autumn morning. Biliana met me at the station. A Roma woman had brewed Turkish coffee over a make-shift fire outside across the forecourt. It tasted exquisite.

Biliana had an appointment with her friend, who lived on the other side of town, beyond the Maritsa River. We decided to go there on foot. The time had come to ask her about the Fourth Crusade.

'It's a very long story', she said, 'but it is important to hear it if you want to understand the centuries-old antagonism between East and West and the persistent suspicion between the Orthodox and the Roman Catholics. I'll tell you about it if you have the patience to listen.'

'My attention span is limited', I said, 'but, of

course if you think it is relevant and can help me understand the story of Baldwyn's tower in Veliko Trnovo, which fascinates me…'

'The Sack of Constantinople by the Franks during the Fourth Crusade, culminating on the 13th April 1204', she said, 'was probably the worst atrocity in the history of Christianity. The battle took place not between Christians and Muslims, but between the Latin Catholics and the Orthodox Greeks. A Christian army sent to defend Christendom in the East against the Muslims perpetrated atrocities on fellow Christians. Meanwhile, during the whole of the Fourth Crusade not a drop of Muslim blood was shed.

'The leaders of the Crusade handed over the greatest city in the world to its soldiers to do as they pleased for three days. The Franks sacked the city in an orgy of rape, butchering its citizens, robbing its churches of their greatest treasures. Constantinople never really recovered from this and became prey to the Turks in 1453. The Fourth Crusade contributed to opening up Eastern and Central Europe to centuries of Muslim domination.'

We strolled down the *ulitsa Vasil Kolarov*, Plovdiv's main shopping street, recently repainted in pastel shades, leaving behind us the massive Socialist Hotel Trimontsium and the smart glass and steel building of the *BKP*, the Bulgarian Communist Party. Western towns had developed under the protective shadow of the castle and the church until, just after the Fourth Crusade, the merchants had taken over, pushing them both out into the periphery, building *bastides* geometrically around the market square. Socialist towns, I liked to think, on the other hand, had replaced the church with the Party building, and the castle with the hotel.

We passed shops selling machine-made *handicraft*

and squalid soup kitchens, where sad-eyed unshaven workers stood nibbling on greasy *kebabches*. On our right stood the brick and stone *Dzhumaya* mosque, with its sleek striped and checkered minaret and leaded cupolas, and the church of *Sveta* Marina.

'I know about Christian-Muslim antagonism, but how did this conflict between Catholics and Orthodox come about?' I asked. 'Was it something new?'

'No, it wasn't. Events had been leading up to this conflict for hundreds of years. Mutual excommunication had finalised the Great Schism by 1054. The Turks had defeated Byzantium at the Battle of Manzikert in Eastern Asia Minor less than twenty years later. The Normans had been gradually advancing in Italy, gobbling up Byzantine territories. The Byzantine army relied more and more on Western mercenaries against the Turks, including Normans.

'The Emperor of Byzantium, Alexios I Komnenos, had requested help from Urban II to raise a mercenary army against the Turks. The Pope saw the opportunity for channelling the aggression of the Christian warlords and at the same time reaching some kind of reconciliation with Byzantium. He launched the First Crusade.'

'What could have been the motivation for Western Crusaders to travel so far from home at such risk?' I asked.

'A good question! You realise that a crusade not only meant undergoing great personal danger and hardship, it also required enormous financial sacrifices. Crusaders naturally expected a decent spiritual and material return on their investment.

'Their motivation was complex, at the same time both disinterested and mercenary. They certainly had deeply spiritual motives, accompanied by a quest for glory. Don't forget that the so-called *Age of Chivalry* was just beginning. Their aim was Jerusalem, the Holy City. They also had both religious and material motives that were much less glorious. They wanted Papal *indulgences*, meaning that, when they died, all their sins would be instantaneously forgiven. But above all, they were looking for land and plunder.'

'It sounds a bit like the martyrdom of a Muslim *mujahid*', I remarked, 'with the promise of seven virgins as a reward - or is it seventy? But were the cultural differences really that big between Latin and Greek Christians?'

'Oh yes, very much so! It was what you'd call a classic conflict of cultures, which has lasted at least to some degree until today.

'Since the Great Schism the Franks had always considered the Byzantine church and the Greeks as semi-heretics. Apart from the political issue of the primacy of the Pope and the doctrinal and liturgical questions, there was the ethnic aspect. In Byzantium they read the Apostles in the original Greek, not in the Latin translation. Its language and culture were Greek, but its political and legal systems were Roman.

'Byzantium, though it was multi-ethnic, was fairly unified. This wasn't so for the Franks, where there was rivalry between French and Germans, Venetians and Genovese, the Pope and the Holy Roman Emperor, the Templars and the Hospitaliers. The Byzantine Empire was autocratic, whereas the West was feudal, with local lords. Crusader leaders were equal, without a sovereign, each one wishing to accumulate more wealth than his peers.

'And Byzantine political culture used diplomacy as its main weapon. The Greeks didn't glorify battle in its own right. They used it only a last resort, whereas the West had always thrived on military combat. The Greeks believed in negotiation and peaceful coexistence, whereas the Franks had a perception of the world in black and white. Does that sound familiar?'

'But that's not really enough to explain the Franks' antipathy for Byzantium?' I said. 'What were the concrete reasons?'

'The Eastern and Western halves of the Christian world were in different cycles: Byzantium in decline, the West in the ascendant. As the economic superiority of the West increased, relations between Byzantium and the West deteriorated.

'Yet Byzantium before the Fourth Crusade was still far richer and more developed than Western Europe. There was a lot of jealousy on the part of the Franks, who, as you know, were also looking for personal enrichment through the Crusades. The city of Constantinople and its palaces, which exceeded by far what you could see in the West, quite overwhelmed them. This meant that the Byzantines behaved in a condescending manner to the Franks, whom they made to feel inferior.

'The Greeks too had their share of jealousy. Though commerce in Byzantium was a state monopoly, it had gradually been devoured by unscrupulous Western merchants from Genoa and Venice and by the crusaders. Byzantium wasn't really equipped for commercial competition.

'In a word, Byzantine civilization was opposed to Norman-Viking barbarity. The West considered the Greeks to be a devious people, and in the Byzantine Empire they were suspicious of the West. Between the Franks and Byzantines it was *them and us*.

'Give me some examples.'

'During the First Crusade, Western Crusader lords were *in transit*, so to speak, through Byzantine territory on their way to the Holy Land. To let them pass, the *Basileus,* Byzantine Emperor Alexios I Komnenos, required them first to take an oath of allegiance to him. Secondly, he demanded that they made a commitment to hand back to Byzantium any of the land previously lost to Islam that they should re-conquer. Some of the Franks took the oath, others refused outright. Alexios then put pressure on the Crusaders by cutting off supplies to their army.

'Over generations came a succession of what each side considered to be treachery on the part of the other. The Byzantines secretly negotiated with the Turks and later with the Arabs behind the back of the Franks, thereby denying them of an opportunity for looting. They granted refuge to a Turkish force that the Franks had defeated. The Franks refused to abide by the oath of allegiance that the Emperor had more or less forced upon them, unwilling to hand over their conquests to him.

Back to Byzantium

'The last straw was when, during the Third Crusade, Jerusalem had fallen to the Muslims. The Byzantine Emperor Isaac sent their new leader, Saladin, a message of congratulations and even made a secret alliance with him. The Greek Christians in Jerusalem, who had suffered at the hands of the Latin Christians, in fact welcomed the return to Islamic rule, known for its relative tolerance. Saladin improved their situation significantly. The Greeks preferred political submission to the infidel to a spiritual capitulation to Latin Catholics.

'All this contributed to a complete lack of trust by the Crusader Franks in the Byzantine Greeks.'

'And by the Greeks in the Franks?' I asked.

'Emperor Manuel I Komnenos had already begun to adopt Western customs at the time of the Second Crusade. This alienated the Greeks, embittered by Italian merchants swallowing up Byzantine markets. They also remembered how the Normans had burned down the Greek city of Thessalonica.'

'How did Venice fit into all of this?' I asked.

'There was also rivalry between different Italian city states. Byzantium had begun to favour Genoa and Pisa, and Venice had lost some of its importance. John II Komnenos, son and successor to Alexios, refused to grant them the trading privileges which penalised the Greek traders. The Venetians became openly hostile to Byzantium.

'After the Venetians attacked the Genovese trading quarter in Galata, the Emperor captured ten thousand of them and confiscated their goods. The Latins became the general Byzantine scapegoat, with the inhabitants of Constantinople turning on them and massacring each one they could find. The slaughter was comparable to that of the Sack of Constantinople by the Crusaders twenty years later.

'The conclusion is that both the Franks and the Venetians had serious material reasons for their antagonism to Byzantium.'

We were now on our way to Biliana's friend's house across the Maritsa. This was the river that the Bulgaro-Armenian pop idol, Sylvie Vartan, who originated in Plovdiv, had made famous in France with her nostalgic hit *La Maritsa*.

We branched off to the left through a modest residential area of single-storey houses. Passing one of their dusty yards we were startled by loud squawks. A headless chicken scampered around while its owner cleaned the blood off his long folding blade. I had heard about this phenomenon, but never witnessed it before. Years later I would experience a similar one in Korea with raw octopus tentacles. Long after being severed they continue to convulse on the plate and even wriggle onto the table. When you pick them up, first they cling to the plate with their suckers, then to your chopsticks and finally to the roof of your mouth, almost asphyxiating you unless you bite into them fast enough.

Three doors further down the hill, the blast from a radio had nearly drowned the frantic squawks. It was a Bulgarian western-style pop song with a repetitious refrain that sounded like a very garbled 'Say it again' in English. It reminded me of French pop music during the sixties, with its own version of 'yeah, yeah, yeah' taken from the Beatles, causing it to be called *Yéyé* in France over a whole generation.

Four decades later, the panel of judges of a Bulgarian talent show would almost laugh candidate Valentina Hasan off the stage of *Music Idol*. She had just sung *Ken Lee*, replacing 'I can't live, if living is without you', made popular by Mariah Carey, by her very own phonetic rendering. 'Ken Lee, Tulibu dibu douchoo...' was to become a world-wide hit, with 35 million web-surfers viewing Valentina's version.

But was the singer on the radio really singing his own rendition of 'say it again'? It sounded more like ***Say Gay Hen***. Biliana said that it was a pumped-up version of a nostalgic patriotic song.

5
Sack

'What about the Fourth Crusade itself', I said at last.

'Let me try and keep it simple. At the end of the 12th century, Alexios Angelos had deposed his own brother, Emperor Isaac II Angelos, and in the pure Byzantine tradition put out his eyes, thrown him into prison and taken his place as *Basileus*. The German Emperor, who had previously captured Isaac's daughter, gave her as a bride to Philip, Duke of Swabia.

'The newly elected Pope, Innocent III, launched the Fourth Crusade to heal the rift between East and West, reunite the Latin and Greek churches and, above all, reaffirm his supremacy over the whole of Christendom. The Crusade appointed Boniface of Montserrat as its leader. Now Boniface happened to be Philip of Swabia's vassal. Among other leaders was Baldwin, Count of Flanders, who, as you know, was imprisoned and murdered in Veliko Trnovo, in the tower that today bears his name.

'Philip of Swabia's wife's blinded father, Isaac, managed to send messages from his prison in Constantinople to his daughter at the court of Swabia, begging for help. Meanwhile, Isaac's son, also called Alexios, had succeeded in escaping from Constantinople. Boniface devised a plot with his liege lord, Philip of Swabia, to hijack the Crusade and replace the usurper, Alexios III Angelos, by his nephew, young Alexios, who was also Philip's brother-in-law. It's rather confusing with distinct protagonists named Alexios. Are you managing to follow?' she asked.

'I think so, but it's pretty complicated so far', I replied.

'Finance was the main issue of the Fourth Crusade. How to pay for transportation by sea to the Holy Land and avoid the dangers of the land route of the previous Crusades. The sea route was expensive and required a major logistical organisation. They needed to equip a large fleet, which they were unable to do on their own. Only Venice was able to provide it.

'So the Frankish Crusaders negotiated with the Venetians, who were led by the Doge, Enrico Dandolo. Already an old man in his eighties, he was blind, but he was a shrewd man. Dandolo agreed to provide transport, but at a heavy price. Venice would provide the ships, which had to be built from scratch, also food and provisions for six months for the Crusaders.

'The Franks calculated that they would need transport for four thousand horses and some thirty thousand fighting men. But they made a fundamental error, which would compromise the whole Crusade, by basing their calculations on wildly optimistic assumptions. They assumed that the projected numbers of men would all arrive in in Venice on the same appointed date.

'Each individual Crusader lord was responsible for paying for his own transport and that of his men. Sufficient new recruits did not arrive, while some groups had travelled separately at reduced cost, embarking from other Mediterranean ports in France and Italy. As a result, the number of Crusaders who actually reached Venice on the appointed day were significantly less than what had been *costed*, as they say nowadays.'

'So there wasn't enough money to pay the Venetians what they owed?'

'No, not by a long way. The Doge Dandolo understandably demanded payment for the enormous investment that Venice had made to build a fleet of fifty warships. Commercial activity in Venice had virtually stopped during construction. The Crusaders managed to raise less than half of the amount. As you can imagine, the Venetians were furious and the Crusaders embarrassed.'

'How did they pay the Venetians what they owed them, or did they?' I asked.

'Dandolo came up with various solutions. He had an idea whereby he would make do for the moment with what had already been paid by the Crusaders and let them pay the remainder from future gains during the Crusade. That meant, of course, with loot and spoils of war.

'First he asked the Crusaders to help him retake Zara, on the Dalmatian coast, today the Croatian city of Zadar. When this former Venetian territory had freed itself from Venice, the King of Hungary had granted it his protection. Zara was a Christian city and the King of Hungary a Catholic monarch.'

'So this was the first battle against fellow Christians instead of Muslims.'

'Not only against fellow Christians, but against fellow Latin Catholics.

'Dandolo decided to join the Crusade himself. Pope Innocent half-heartedly condemned the attack on Zara by excommunicating the Crusaders. The city surrendered without a fight after five days. The Crusaders looted it and split the spoils after violent wrangling between the Venetians and the Franks.

'Philip of Swabia - you remember him? - proposed that the Crusaders join forces with his brother-in-law, young Alexios, son of the deposed Isaac, to restore him to the throne of Byzantium in place of the usurper, Alexios III. You remember that it was he who had deposed and blinded his own brother. They hoped that in this way the young pretender would reunite Byzantium with the Church of Rome.

'Young Alexios made a commitment that, once he had been placed on the throne, he would compensate the Crusaders with a huge sum of money, provide them with provisions for the onward journey to the Holy Land and five hundred Byzantine troops. This was of course completely unrealistic. To provide the promised amount, the treasury of Byzantium would be totally insufficient. He would have to increase massively the taxes paid by the people, and thereby add even more to the resentment they felt for the Latins.

'But they signed contracts, as this seemed to be the only way of refunding the huge sum that the Franks owed to the Venetians.'

'So, in fact the Fourth Crusade was doubly hijacked', I remarked, 'first by the Doge, Dandolo, to retake Zara, and then by Philip of Swabia and his vassal, Boniface, to take Constantinople in order to put young Alexios on the throne and reimburse the Venetians. Dandolo seems to be the most devious in the story.'

'Probably, but don't forget that he had the most to lose.

'The decision to make a diversion to Zara had been kept secret, so most of the Crusaders didn't really know where they were headed. When they found out, they were outraged. They had made a vow to complete a pilgrimage to the Holy Sepulchre in Jerusalem. Many of them deserted with their troops and made their own way to the Holy Land. Simon de Montfort returned to Europe to persecute the Cathars.

'The leaders of the Crusade then enrolled the bishops, who took up their traditional role of providing moral justification for prior political decisions. The bishops proclaimed that not only would it not be a sin to proceed to Constantinople, but that the Catholic Church would grant full *indulgences* to those who did.'

After tea with Biliana's friend at her flat, we crossed back over the Maritsa and proceeded up the hill to the old town, stopping for a glass of the exquisite peach nectar found only in Bulgaria, in a café inside an ochre wooden house dating from the *National Revival*. Its corbelled first floor overlapped the street, almost touching that of the house opposite.

Back to Byzantium

A Roma family was barbequing in a field down below what was known as Lamartine's house, the finest on the hill. A swarthy young man beckoned to us. These were nice gypsies, said Biliana, why didn't we go down and say hello. At the bottom of the slope they gave us some of the lamb that they were roasting on a spit. Biliana seized the huge knife that the Rom used to cut the meat and put it to my throat while the whole family laughed. We walked back down to the city centre.

'So the Crusaders took the decision to proceed to Constantinople?' I continued.

'Yes, they finally arrived before the walls of the city, setting up camp on the opposite bank of the Bosphorus, at Scutari. The *Basileus* pleaded that an attack by the Franks on fellow Christians would be against the very principles of the Crusade. He promised them food and provisions for their onward journey provided they left Byzantine territory as soon as possible.

'Don't forget that the Crusaders had sailed to Constantinople with the main purpose of raising enough money to pay off the Venetians.

'After the first major attack by the Crusader coalition, the usurper Alexios fled with all the money he could take. The Byzantines restored blind Isaac to the throne as co-Emperor with his son, young Alexios.'

'That sounds like a typical Byzantine compromise', I remarked.

'The Crusaders ordered Young Alexios to respect his commitments, so he began emptying the treasury and tried to impose Latin Catholic rites and generally westernise the Greeks. The people soon deposed him, replacing him by another Alexios, Alexios Muzurfulos, who threw young Alexios into prison. When the Crusaders failed in their next attack, the Byzantines stood on the battlements and displayed their naked bottoms in defiance.'

'It sounds like what General Cambronne was said to have done during his last stand at Waterloo', I remarked, 'when he returned the British offer of a surrender by scribbling the word *merde* on it. I suppose that the outcome was similar.'

'Yes, it was. The Venetians finally managed to breech the city wall and a fire broke out which spread rapidly.

'The Crusaders entered Constantinople and threw the city open to its army for three days to do whatever they pleased. This was probably the worst massacre of Christian by Christian in history. Drunken soldiers pillaged, raped, even the nuns, murdered women and children. They ransacked the churches, stole the jewels from Emperor Justinian's embalmed body, tore the gold from *Hagia Sofia* and are said to have placed a prostitute on the Patriarch's throne.

'The Venetians, being more cultured, stole what they could, including the four bronze horses that now adorn Saint Mark's. The Franks, being less educated, just destroyed whatever they encountered.'

'I can imagine', I said, 'it sounds a bit like xenophobic British football fans on the *Continent*, except that in Constantinople it was with swords, armour and official condonement for the Franks' behaviour. Things haven't changed that much over the centuries, have they? What happened at the end of the three days?'

'The Crusaders designated Baldwyn as Emperor of Constantinople. Dandolo in person crowned him Baldwyn I in *Hagia Sofia*. King Kaloïan of Bulgaria captured Baldwyn the following year, and you already know the rest.

'Sixty years later, the Byzantines retook Constantinople, but they had become terminally weakened. The Balkans lost their protection against the Turks. Pope Innocent III concentrated his efforts on another Crusade against Christians, this time against the Cathars in South West France. The only real winners were the devious Dandolo and the Venetians, who strengthened their presence in the Aegean.

'The word Crusade became derogatory and provided the basis for East-West antagonism for nearly eight centuries.'

We had dinner in the hotel restaurant in Plovdiv. The dining room filled with young couples. Every few minutes a couple got up from their table and left the dining room. I did the same and went down the corridor to the *Gentlemen's* lavatory. There standing outside the door to the *Ladies* stood the young lady's knight errant, mounting guard like the *Chetniks* outside the Dimitrov mausoleum, waiting for his damsel to come out. I saw this parade of chivalry every time outside the hotel toilets of Bulgaria.

Inside the Gentlemen's toilets, in addition to the usual lewd drawings, phone numbers and racist insults, someone had covered one wall with tags, in fact scrawled the same one several times. They looked familiar. I had seen them not long ago, but where? With the usual irritation caused by an elusive recollection, I spent the afternoon trying to recall what they reminded me of.

I returned to my room and had a shower before going to bed. A diminutive window looked out over a bleak wall on the other side of what was a more of a shaft than a yard, ascending to the top of the building.

Glancing out from under the shower head across the yard at the dirty smudges on the wall, it came to me.

Of course, the incongruity of it had left an imprint. It was the same tag that I had seen stencilled so neatly on Baldwin's tower.

V9°p

Here it looked more like a punk's personal signature, but that didn't fit in with the elegant figures printed on the tower in Veliko Trnovo. Scrawled on the wall of a toilet or an air shaft, could it have the same meaning, whatever it was? It looked like a code of some kind. Could it be the logo of an anti-establishment rock 'n roll group?

I spent the last two days of my holiday in Sofia. We went to the city's classiest restaurant, the *Russki Club*. A couple whispered loudly about the *provincials* at the next table. In Plovdiv I had heard its counterpart, the disparaging remarks about Sofia people. Parisians, believing that the *Midi* began at the *Porte d'Italie*, Paris's southern gate, had got me used to the expression *en province*. I hadn't heard it elsewhere since the age of eighteen, when alighting at Birmingham New Street station from the London train to my friend's cry of 'Welcome to the provinces!' Polarity and snobbery to my surprise were universal, even under Communism.

I returned to Paris by train to resume my job, having promised Biliana that I would return within six months to go skiing with her in the Rhodope Mountains.

6
Klinika

Great Britain, Ireland and Denmark had officially joined the *EEC* that year on 1st January. President Nixon was about to devalue the US dollar by ten per cent.

In late spring the Greek military *junta* would abolish the monarchy and proclaim a republic, with Colonel Papadopoulos as President, whom they would depose five months later.

At the end of January, about to set off again for Bulgaria, this time to go skiing, I had a seafood dinner in a Paris *brasserie*. With oysters and clams I particularly enjoy raw mussels. A couple of weeks later, with a fever, I rang a friend who was a doctor. He didn't think the symptoms that I described justified postponing my trip.

This time I was taking the Orient Express from the *Gare de l'Est* overnight to Munich, then down to Belgrade and on to Plovdiv. When I arrived in Munich I was already in a cold sweat.

The city had changed since my first visit. After seven years in a boarding school in Derbyshire, I had spent my first week of real freedom here at the age of sixteen. They had just finished restoring the *Frauenkirche* cathedral. Munich was for me the ultimate city, the first big town that I saw without either my parents or my school. With horses in the streets it was a very traditional city, and yet at the same time modern with its high-tech industry.

Since then it had hosted the Olympic Games, turning its centre into a pedestrian area. Is there a more effective way to turn a dynamic city into a village than to ban motor vehicles? In lieu of entrance doors to the department stores vertical jets of warm air shot from floor to ceiling. This was the famous consumer society that I had read about, but not yet encountered. Probably intensified by my febrile state, I was suffering from culture shock.

I joined my *couchette* at 10 o'clock that evening for Belgrade and slept through Bavaria, Salzburg and Carinthia.

At 3 o'clock in the morning at Jesenice in Slovenia on the Yugoslav border they pulled me off the train. Not the customs men with their screwdrivers, but lean men with slim trilby hats and even slimmer moustaches, *java* dancers from the Paris *fin-de-siècle* riverside *guinguettes*. They took me to a pokey office. 'Your visa not good', one of them said in bad German. 'You must to go to the consulate in Vienna.' 'I don't need a visa for Yugoslavia', I said. They were unwilling to negotiate, so I boarded the first train up to Vienna, arriving the following morning.

I found a hotel opposite the *Südbahnhof* and easily diagnosed my disorder. I drank cola and eliminated the same with no visible difference in colour or density. 'Pissing mahogany' was the expression. I had hepatitis.

It had snowed in Vienna, but it had all turned to slush. My friend Biliana expected me the following day in Plovdiv, so I went to the telephone office adjacent to the station. Above the desk I saw a xenophobic hand-written sign on a piece of cardboard. It was an officious order for people not to wait around the desk for their calls. They had got someone to write it in Croato-Serbian, meaning in Latin script. They hadn't even taken the trouble to write it German. Who said that the Vienna of that time had been neither de-Nazified nor de-Stalinised? I don't mean the monument to the in *Schwarzenbergplatz*, briefly *Stalinplatz*, with Stalin's embossed signature, whose perpetual maintenance had been one of the pre-conditions for the departure of Soviet troops in 1955. I mean those cheap officious signs everywhere and the general atmosphere of depression and suspicion of foreigners.

The consulate of course was closed until Monday. If the Yugoslavs wouldn't let me in I would have to go via Romania. On Sunday I returned to the telephone office. The same woman who had been on duty the previous day informed me that today the international switchboard was not available. Her offensive sign may have been in Croato-Serbian but apparently she spoke no language other than German. I would have to make the call myself. French was fortunately still the language for international communications. I had to navigate through the international switchboard in French until I reached the local exchange in Bulgaria. There I dictated the phone number to the operator with infinite slowness in Bulgarian, digit by digit. When my friend's grandmother answered I just about managed to communicate that I had a visa problem and wouldn't arrive until Tuesday. I felt worse now, spending most of the day in bed, drinking only cola. My eyes had started to turn yellow.

On Monday morning I went straight to the British consulate. It was located near the Belvedere in a Viennese renaissance building with galleries encircling a central courtyard. I showed my British passport, issued in Paris, to the consular official. 'The Yugoslavs won't let me in', I said. 'They think you're a Uganda Asian', she laughed. I may have been jaundiced, but no-one could have taken me for a Gujarati Indian. 'Where were you born', she asked. 'Amersham', I replied. 'Amersham? You can't get more British than that!' She took out a stamp and printed on my passport the words *Citizen has right of abode in the United Kingdom.*

It reminded me of the standard British passport renewal procedure. A passport photo needed to be countersigned as a good likeness by *a Justice of the Peace* or by *a person of good standing in the community* who had known the applicant for at least two years. 'But I don't know any justice of the peace', I said, when making my application at the British consulate in Paris. 'Don't worry. We'll make an exception', said the civil servant behind the counter. In the waiting room the *huddled masses* sat waiting patiently. Would an exception be made for them?

'Is that all?' I asked. 'That's all', replied the consular official.

'Since Idi Amin expelled them last year from Uganda, thousands of Indians have been roaming all over central Europe, including Communist countries, in search of a place to live. Belgrade must have sent an order to its border posts to refuse any British passport issued outside the UK. The authorities in Jesenice just applied the rule without discernment.

'You must have read about it in the papers', she said. 'In August last year Idi Amin Dada, the dictator of Uganda, who was jealous of the wealth of his Gujarati citizens, had a vision in which God told him to expel them. He gave them ninety days to leave Uganda. You may remember that Amin is a semi-literate former assistant cook who succeeded in becoming a chief warrant officer in the British army.

'Though many of the Asians from Uganda have British passports, Edward Heath's Conservative government has refused them residence in Britain. It makes you wonder whether this decision couldn't have been based on colour. Heath tried unsuccessfully to find a remote location to house them, like the Falkland or Solomon Islands.

'You no doubt remember Enoch Powell's *rivers of blood* speech four years ago. That caused Harold Wilson's Labour government to pass the Commonwealth Immigrants Act, designed to give second-class status to non-whites and deprive them of basic rights, such as right of abode. Giving *British Overseas Citizen* status to 35,000 people means that, as non-whites, their passports are worthless. These people have become effectively stateless.'

The 27,000 Indians from Uganda who would finally succeed in entering Britain became the successfully integrated *Huguenots* of the modern era. Only thirty years later would they at last be granted full British citizenship.

With my improved passport, a little dubious, I moved on to the Yugoslav consulate. 'I need a visa', I said. 'British citizens don't need a visa', replied the official. 'But they won't let me in.' He took my passport grudgingly and left the room. I sat down in a small waiting room full of Yugoslav guest workers waiting for documents. He came back with the visa. '*Jugoslavisch und zürück*', *Yugoslavish* and back, he repeated in atrocious German, while all the guest workers snickered loudly.

I took the *bummel* train to Villach and waited for the night train for Belgrade, where I re-joined the Direct Orient for Plovdiv. I had begun to feel very ill. The train was empty, except for a few Turkish guest workers, who were making a lot of noise in the next compartment. At the border post at Dimitrovgrad the immigration officer was atypically friendly and welcoming. I now knew enough Bulgarian to tell him that I was going skiing at Pamporovo in the Rhodope Mountains. He wished me an enjoyable holiday. I arrived in Plovdiv and, in the absence of platforms, crossed the rails to the station building by clambering from one train through the next. My friend was waiting for me. We went to a large suburban hotel, where she confirmed my diagnosis.

The following morning an ambulance took me off to the *Ivan P.Pavlov Infektsiozna Klinika*. A pleasant, professional doctor who spoke good English examined me. I could distinguish the physicians by the foreign language that they spoke. The older ones all spoke

German, the younger ones English, and the Armenian doctors, of which there were several, spoke fluent French. I saw an old German-speaking professor with a mouth full of gold teeth spit vigorously on the ground outside the hospital. I wondered if visible gold teeth and spitting in public weren't a permanent fixture of most second and third world countries. They gave me a two-bedded room for distinguished guests to myself with a private enamelless bath and barred windows. The other patients were crammed into small wards with just enough room between each bed for a minuscule table, touching on each side.

The doctor explained to me that I needed to stay in the clinic for at least a month. Viral hepatitis was apparently one of the infectious diseases which, by international agreement, prevented the patient from travelling. In the circumstances, I was happy to stay and had complete trust in the clinic and the physicians. All the hospital care I received during my stay at the clinic was entirely free of charge. And, of course, Biliana was a medical student.

They told me of a young American in transit from Istanbul, whom they had hospitalised the previous year with hepatitis. He had objected so much to being *detained against his will* that he went on a hunger strike. It had caused a minor diplomatic incident.

> Travel in Communist countries had become simpler for Westerners. It was the period of *détente* in Europe, *razrïadka* in Russian.
>
> When Richard Nixon had become President four years earlier, tension gradually began to recede between the United States and the Soviet Union. A summit on security and cooperation in Europe led to the Strategic Arms Limitation Treaty, known as *SALT1*. Thirty-five European countries would soon sign the Helsinki Accords, with trade agreements made contingent on the

reduction of human-rights violations.

At the same time in France, the Socialist and Communist parties signed the *Programme Commun*, which would lead ten years later to a joint government. For me it was a sign of hope for peace in Europe, and perhaps even the possibility of a reversal of its division since Yalta.

Détente was to end ten years later under Jimmy Carter, when the Soviet invasion of Afghanistan triggered the Western boycott of the Moscow Olympics. Ronald Reagan finally buried it with his *evil empire* bombast, to return to cold-war confrontation.

I rang the British consulate. They said that they would come and visit me. Nobody came. I was only mildly surprised.

The clinic for infectious diseases had two main hospital buildings, one reserved for hepatitis, the other for dysentery. Due to renovation work in the other building the patients with dysentery had been moved to one end of our main building. Of course, the clinic had taken precautionary measures, and each time we touched even a door handle we had to dip our hands into a basin of disinfectant.

Our un-ironed sky-blue sheets and pyjamas had been daubed with paint the colour of faeces to indicate building number 1 or 2. Why, I asked. This was to discourage the gypsies from stealing them, they told me. And why not? They miss-fitted me out with a pair of pyjamas at least two sizes too big for me, without equipping me with a belt. To amuse the other patients strolling in the hospital corridor I would let my pyjama trousers fall to my ankles beneath my dressing gown.

They had prescribed me diet number five, which seemed to be based exclusively on rice. Every day I drank a couple of litres of cold tea brewed from rose hips, a strong concentration of vitamin C. After a couple of weeks, they promoted me to diet *Pet A, Five A*, a significant improvement. My friend regularly brought me bottles of peach, apricot and tomato juice. I have never since tasted such nectar. And yet I felt constantly hungry. The other patients recognised the glutton that I have always been, calling me *Aç kopek*, hungry dog in Turkish, the only foreign language they had a notion of, as they fed me with shards of cucumber.

The toilets were revolting, if not insalubrious. The patients went there for a smoke, wearing Japanese-style clogs on the permanently soaking-wet floor. I continued to smoke in my room until admonished by the terrifying head of clinic, a young woman whom the patients called *veshtitsa*, the witch. 'Vous voulez *se* plaindre', she asked in execrable French, using a *calque* of the invariable reflexive pronoun in Bulgarian, to ask me if I wanted to complain. Why did she imagine that I had anything to complain about?

I immediately stopped smoking for the first time since starting at age seventeen. Thanks to the other patients I now knew enough Bulgarian to write out a solemn commitment that I had just smoked the last cigarette of my life. It turned out not to be true, but my intentions were honourable at the time. When I wanted a smoke, I would raise a laugh saying '*cheren drob bolen, byal drob gladen*', literally 'black fraction (liver) sick, white fraction (lungs) hungry'

I spent more and more of my time with the other patients. We had a sing-song together. Our favourite song was *Oche Zheulti, Yellow Eyes*, an appropriate variation on the Russian classic, *Ochi Chërnije*.

The Bulgarian pop singer in vogue, Emil Dimitrov, had a major hit with a song called *Grozde ne nabrakh, Mamuma, I didn't pick any grapes, Mama*. He had transformed a folk song into a pop hit while retaining its specifically Bulgarian style. With my limited vocabulary, I sang my own variation, *Nishto ne razbrakh, maïmuna*, meaning *I didn't understand anything, monkey*. I found it funny, but I am not sure about the other patients.

Seeing them all every day in identical sky-blue pyjamas with a faecal-brown *1* daubed on the back made it seem very egalitarian and un-exotic. I was agreeably surprised to see an older man, who had just been discharged, appear outside my barred window to say goodbye. He wore a magnificent grey felt suit with a frogged cape across one shoulder, baggy felt trousers with a low crotch, tied with bands into his felt boots, a wide waist sash and a conical felt hat. They were obviously his best Sunday clothes.

Each young patient had a similar carved wooden shaving box, a kind of fetish which he showed with pride. It seemed to be a symbol of maturity that each boy received when he finished secondary school. Once again, I encountered the national obsession with razor blades. Each in turn tried my own razor to reach a final unanimous decision that theirs were better. That didn't mean that blades were always available in the shops. They weren't and neither were light bulbs, even in the *TSUM, Tsentralni Universalny Magazin,* Sofia's department store.

For a couple of weeks, the nurses all appeared masked. All I heard from them at first each morning was a single-word question, *golïama?,* accompanied with explicit gestures. It was short for *golïama nuzhba*, what English children used to call *big jobs*. They were enquiring about my bowel movements. When I had become less infectious they dropped the mask to reveal pretty faces. One day I had a surprise visit from a young woman, a friend of my favourite nurse, who had seen the film *Lawrence of Arabia* and thought that I looked like Peter O'Toole. Her friend was disappointed.

Due to her association with me, my friend Biliana was summoned to the secret police, the *KDC.* Her interrogation took place amicably over a drink in the police headquarters. She said that thanks to her Stalinist former partisan father she had a degree of protection. Her only risk was to be refused travel documents.

March came and my friend brought me what looked like a tassel from the end of an old-fashioned dressing gown. It seemed that everyone in the hospital, patient, nurse and doctor, wore one on their lapel. This was the *Martenitsa*. My friend explained.

The *Martenitsa* is a pagan tradition that is followed in Bulgaria, Romania, and all over the Balkans. Depending on the country, it is said to be of Thracian or Dacian origin.

Spring starts in Bulgaria on 1st March. The month of March is known as the holiday of *Baba Marta*, Grandmother March.

So on 1st March Bulgarians offer members of their family, friends and colleagues little red and white woollen dolls or, more often, just tassels, known respectively as *Penda* and *Pizho*. They are supposed to wear them on their lapels or their wrists until end of March or until they see the very first stalk, swallow or bud on a tree.

My level of *bilirubin* had now come down close to normal and the doctors said that I could soon leave the clinic. They told me also that I wouldn't be fit to travel for another month. My concern now was how to pay for an extended stay in hotels when I had budgeted only for a month. In addition, the company I worked for in Paris had informed me that they had deducted my month in hospital from my annual leave and that any subsequent absence from work would be without pay. One of the patients I appreciated the most came into my room, jubilant: 'Nixon has just devalued the dollar'. I had changed all my holiday money into US dollar travellers' cheques. I was consequently ten percent poorer.

Every day this friend came into my room with the same obsession. He said that I just had to come to his village for 8th March.

International Women's Day had begun in the first years of the century as a commemoration by the Socialist Party of America of a women's strike in the clothing industry.

In 1917 a lockout in a factory in Petrograd had set off a huge strike, mainly led by women calling for bread and for the end of the war. The Bolsheviks had taken it as International Women's Day on 23rd February under the Julian calendar. When the Soviet Union adopted the Gregorian calendar the following year it became 8th March.

Though it began as a socialist political event, it has been celebrated in diverse ways across the world, becoming a public holiday mainly in Socialist countries. In the Soviet Union, it had been a public holiday since 1965, but here in Bulgaria, though widely observed, it was still a working day.

In Eastern Europe, it had generally ceased to be political, to become a cross between Saint Valentine's Day and Mothering Sunday, when men offered flowers and presents to their mothers, wives, girlfriends, daughters, teachers and female colleagues. In Western countries, where it would only be officially established after a decision by the United Nations in 1977, it concerned above all women's rights.

Finally, on Women's Day I wasn't free, so I would have to wait until my stay in Moscow before celebrating it.

I left the hospital cured, with strict instructions not to smoke or drink a drop of alcohol for at least six months. I had a sheet of paper in Bulgarian listing my diet and especially what I was not allowed to eat. 'No beef, no horse, only young animals.' Veal was recommended. On returning to France, my general practitioner gave me another sheet with the recommended diet, specifying

'Beef, horse, avoid veal.' Medicine has always had an important cultural component!

Needing to speak to the French Social Security office about paperwork, I went to the post office to make an international call. The Bulgarian *Kilroy* had been here again. In the phone booth on the wall I noticed the same hieroglyphs that I had seen on Baldwyn's tower and in the toilets at the Plovdiv hotel, but this time neatly stencilled with, underneath, three letters from the Cyrillic alphabet.

$$\text{ⱱ⁒ꝑ}$$

$$\text{ЦГН}$$

So this time he seemed to have signed with his initials. But I still couldn't identify the three characters above. Or had he just transliterated them into Cyrillic?

7
Convalescence

The Social Security office in France informed me that they needed the *epicrisis*, or case history, from my stay in hospital: 'If you can't obtain it in French, try to get it in Latin.' With Biliana's help we identified a translator. 'She's Greek', said my friend. She looked pretty Bulgarian to me. In fact, she was an ethnic Greek Bulgarian, who had never set foot in Greece. Conditioned by my French and to some extent my British education, I couldn't understand how a Bulgarian could be Greek at the same time. I didn't realise that the concept of the nation-state was far from universal.

Under Byzantium and the Ottoman Empire little relation had existed between nationality and language. People defined themselves by their religion, as Serbs and Croats do today, somewhat like in Northern Ireland. They were Orthodox, whether they spoke Bulgarian, Greek or Serbian. But there were still rivalries within the Orthodox world, hence the creation of autocephalous churches, which the Ottomans later abolished.

Nationality, at least outside France, means belonging to a group with a common language, culture, tradition, history, or religion. *Citizenship* is strictly a legal status, meaning that an individual has been officially registered as a member of that country.

France, which invented the nation state during the French revolution, Britain and the United States apply *jus soli*, the law of the soil, whereby a person born within its territory has the legal right to citizenship. The UK makes a distinction between its four component *nations*, but not between their citizens. France, on the other hand, with its politics of assimilation, recognises no minorities, not even in border regions where the traditional language is not French, such as Alsace. For historical reasons, particularly since the deportation of Jews during the Nazi occupation, it has outlawed publishing ethnic statistics. In accordance with the law on separation between church and state, France has a policy of strict secularity.

'It is difficult, coming from Britain, to understand how you can at the same time be Greek and Bulgarian', I said to the translator.

'I realise that', she replied. 'Your problem is that, making no distinction between the concepts of *nationality* and *citizenship*, the French and, to some extent, you British are not really equipped to understand the complexities of the Balkans. This is not the case for countries of Central Europe or for large multi-ethnic empires like the Soviet Union

'Socialist Yugoslavia, as a federation, for example, makes a clear distinction between its constitutive peoples, *narodi*, those for whom a majority live inside the country itself, like Serbs and Croats, and non-constitutive peoples, *narodnosti*, those for whom the majority live beyond its borders, like Albanians and Hungarians. An inhabitant of Serbia is called *Srbijanac*, Serbian, an inhabitant of Bosnia-Herzegovina *Bosanac*, Bosnian, whatever their respective language or religion. On the other hand, an ethnic Serb is known as a *Srbin*, a Muslim from Bosnia as a *Bosnjak*, whatever republic they live in. The term *Muslim* is also used throughout Yugoslavia as a nationality in a secular sense, for both believers and non-believers.'

'The Soviet Union too has always made a distinction between *natsional'nost'*, nationality, and *grazhdanstvo,* citizenship. They call ethnic Orthodox Russian native speakers *Russkiï*, whatever republic they live in. Citizens of the Russian Socialist Republic from other republics or those whose native language is not Russian or whose religion is not Orthodox are known as *Rossiïane*. Soviet citizens have to specify their nationality in their passport. As you may know, the Soviet Union even recognises *Jewish* as a nationality as distinct from *Russian*. Each nationality is at least theoretically entitled to self-determination, even the Jews. You know that Stalin set up his own *Israel* in the Extreme Orient, called Birobidzhan?

'Yes, but all that applies only to countries of the Eastern Bloc', I objected, 'not to Western Europe.'

'On the contrary', she replied. 'They make the same distinction in other European countries, those that apply *jus sanguine*, the law of blood, that is, whereby you are a citizen because your parents were. You know that an ethnic German from the Volga who hardly speaks German has the right to apply for citizenship of the German Federal Republic, whereas a Turkish child born on German soil has great difficulty in ever becoming a citizen.

'That is the situation in this country. It is why I am a Bulgarian Greek, Greek by my culture, Bulgarian as a citizen of Bulgaria.'

We left for the mountains. While travelling in the Rhodope, we arrived at a small railway station. To get into the town we took a horse and trap, functioning as the town taxi. The first thing we noticed was a cross, daubed in black paint on a front door. As we strolled down the high street we saw that it was far from an isolated case. One door out of three bore a black cross. Could this be cholera, I wondered. No, it was just amoebic dysentery. Hungry and thirsty, we sat down in the restaurant of the local hotel. They had no drinks in cans, so we stayed thirsty, but took the risk of eating some hot food. We finished our lunch and left the town.

I was reminded of giving blood in the street in Naples the previous year. I had just witnessed a neo-fascist rally and had become obsessed with conspiracy. Wondering whether the young man recruiting blood donors was not a neo-fascist himself, that's what I asked him. 'We have to give the blood to whoever needs it, fascist or not', he replied. Feeling foolish, I gave my blood. Within a year two unusual events occurred in Naples, probably not due to my contribution. The first was the exceptional absence of a recurrent miracle. The blood of *San Gennaro*, Saint Januarius, the patron of Naples, for the first time failed to liquefy as it has for centuries three times a year. Secondly, if not consequentially, five months after I left the hospital in Plovdiv an epidemic of cholera broke out in Naples, said to be due to imported mussels, causing several deaths. Mussels again!

We took the bus to Pamporovo, a pine clad ski resort in the Rhodope Mountains. The hospital had forbidden me to smoke or drink, hadn't left me with much that I was allowed to eat and had said, like Churchill, 'No sport!' Pamporovo quickly lost its charm. We returned to Plovdiv after a couple of days, and then I continued alone to Sofia.

Everyone told me I had to see Koprivshtitsa, the cradle of the liberation movement from the Turks, the place where they fired the first shot in the April uprising in 1876.

I made a day trip there from Sofia. It took a couple of hours by train through the snow, then by bus up to the most picturesque of historic villages. The houses, built at the time of the *National Revival*, were painted in pastel colours, particularly the cobalt blue unique to Bulgaria. Armed with my *rezhim* sheet, containing my dietary prohibitions, I went to lunch at the hotel. The manager welcomed me like a returning hero, giving me a guided tour of the kitchen, asking me 'Can you eat this, or this?' I returned that evening by train to Sofia.

Vaguely considering getting married, I am ashamed to admit, partly out of a desire for something out of the ordinary, I went to the British consulate for advice. The consular official opened a drawer and pulled out a duplicated sheet entitled 'British citizens wishing to marry Bulgarian nationals.' He explained the procedure in Bulgaria. It was unlike that in force in some Communist countries in Northern Europe, where obtaining permission to marry, though difficult, gave the spouse the right to emigrate. It's easy to get married here, he told me, but it doesn't help obtain exit permission for the spouse. It no longer seemed such a good idea.

I liked Sofia. It's a medium-sized, compact city, lively and green, with a certain elegance. I loved the trams filling the narrow streets, sometimes leaving little room for pedestrians. With its opera and thirteen theatres, it could compete with most capitals. On the train from Plovdiv I chatted in the corridor over a cigarette with a theatrical producer. His production of Shakespeare's *As You Like It* was playing in Sofia, and he gave me a couple of tickets. I didn't know the play and didn't understand the words, but why let that sort drawback stop me from enjoying it?

    I was looking for some easy reading for beginners in Bulgarian. In an antiquarian bookshop, I discovered with some excitement what I soon recognised as my *Rosetta stone*.

Back to Byzantium

Названия	КИРИЛЛИЦА	ГЛАГОЛИЦА	Названия	КИРИЛЛИЦА	ГЛАГОЛИЦА	Названия	КИРИЛЛИЦА	ГЛАГОЛИЦА
аз	А а	Ⰰ ⰰ	мыслете	М м	Ⰿ ⰿ	ща	Щ щ	Ⱋ ⱋ
буки	Б б	Ⰱ ⰱ	наш	Н н	Ⱀ ⱀ	ер	Ъ ъ	Ⱏ ⱏ
веди	В в	Ⰲ ⰲ	он	О о	Ⱁ ⱁ	еры	Ы ы (ꙑ)	Ⱏ Ⰹ (Ⱏ Ⰺ)
глаголь	Г г	Ⰳ ⰳ	покой	П п	Ⱂ ⱂ	ерь	Ь ь	Ⱐ ⱐ
добро	Д д	Ⰴ ⰴ	рцы	Р р	Ⱃ ⱃ	ѣ	Ѣ ѣ	Ⱑ ⱑ
есть	Є є Іє	Ⰵ ⰵ	слово	С с	Ⱄ ⱄ	ю	Ю ю	Ⱓ ⱓ
живете	Ж ж	Ⰶ ⰶ	твердо	Т т	Ⱅ ⱅ	и-а, я	Ꙗ ꙗ	
зело	Ѕ s ꙃ ꙅ	Ⰷ ⰷ	ук	Оу оу ꙋ	Ⱆ ⱆ	малый юс	Ѧ ѧ Іѧ	Ⱔ ⱔ Ⱗ ⱗ
земля	З з	Ⰸ ⰸ	ферт	Ф ф	Ⱇ ⱇ	большой юс	Ѫ ѫ (Ѫ)	Ⱘ ⱘ
иже	И и	Ⰺ ⰺ	хер	Х х	Ⱈ ⱈ		Ѩ ѩ	Ⱙ ⱙ
и	І і ї	Ⰹ ⰹ	от	Ѡ ѡ	Ⱉ ⱉ	кси	Ѯ ѯ	
	Ї	Ⰻ ⰻ	цы	Ц ц	Ⱌ ⱌ	пси	Ѱ ѱ	
како	К к	Ⰽ ⰽ	червь	Ч ч (ꚇ)	Ⱍ ⱍ	фита	Ѳ ѳ	Ⰾ ⰾ
люди	Л л	Ⰾ ⰾ	ша	Ш ш	Ⱎ ⱎ	ижица	Ѵ ѵ	Ⱛ ⱛ

The book was old and, on a faded page, I identified some characters that looked familiar.

'This looks interesting. What is it?' I asked the bookseller.

'It's a correspondence table between the Glagolitic and Cyrillic alphabets.'

'Which alphabet is that?' I asked.

'The Glagolitic alphabet, created by Cyril and his brother, Methodius.'

'I always thought that it was the Cyrillic alphabet that they created?'

'Not at all. It shouldn't really even be called *Cyrillic*. You remember that the purpose of the two brothers was to translate religious books and the liturgy into the Slavic vernacular. In the mid-9th century Prince Rastislav of Moravia had asked the *Basileus*, that is to say the Byzantine Emperor, to help him to reduce the influence of Frankish Catholic priests. The Emperor sent him the two brothers who had elaborated the Glagolitic alphabet. They implemented it in Moravia, where the government used it for the next twenty years.

Then the Catholic priests succeeded in having the alphabet banned and those who used it thrown into prison. The priests seem to have won the battle in the long term. As I am sure you know, in Czechoslovakia they still use the Latin alphabet!

'Some of their disciples, including Clement of Ohrid, escaped to Bulgaria. The Bulgarian Tsar, Boris, welcomed them with their alphabet. Hoping to replace Greek and reduce the influence, this time, of the Byzantine clergy, he had the liturgy translated into Glagolitic. At the end of the century, Clement devised a new alphabet, which he named *Cyrillic* in honour of his mentor. He compiled his alphabet mainly from Greek, adding a few Hebrew characters at the end.

'Glagolitic turned out to be resistant, surviving well into the Middle Ages, when Cyrillic finally replaced it. The paradox is that it is the churches of the two Slavic nations which for the longest continued to use Glagolitic that today use the Latin alphabet. I mean the Czech and Croatian churches.'

He found me a legible table of correspondence.

Glagolitic	Cyrillic	Latin
ⰀⰁⰂⰃⰄⰅⰆⰇⰈⰉⰊⰋⰌⰍⰎⰏⰐⰑⰒⰓⰔⰕⰖⰗ	А Б В Г Д Е Ж Ц З И Й І Ђ К Л М Н С П Р С Т У Ф	A B V G D E Ž Dz Z I J Dž K L M N O P R S T U F
ⰘⰙⰚⰛⰜⰝⰞⰟⰠⰡⰢⰣⰤⰥⰦⰧⰨⰩⰪⰫⰬⰭⰮ	Х О Щ Ц Ч Ш Ъ Ю Я	H O Šč C Č Š Ju Ja

I could have slapped myself. Here were the three

hieroglyphs that I had seen on Baldwyn's tower and as tags in public places. I checked the tag.

Yes, Ⅴ ℅ Ᵽ in Glagolitic did transliterate as **ЦГН** in Cyrillic. But what could **ЦГН** stand for?

Tse-Ge-eN, it sounded familiar. I remembered the refrain from the nostalgic song blaring from a transistor during my walk across Plovdiv, that I now heard several times a day on the radio, something like *Say Gay Hen*. Or was it the name of a racehorse or of a footballer.

An Asian-looking gentleman at the bookshop was helpful. '*Tsegeen*, or rather *tsagaan*, means *white* in Mongolian. Have you heard of the Great White Lake, Terkhiin Tsagaan Nuur, situated in Mongolia? *Tseegeen* is as common a name there as *White* is in England.'

So *Kilroy* was Mongolian, but why did he sign his name in Glagolitic?

Biliana had joined me in Sofia and we said farewell. I never re-contacted her. On arriving back in Paris I fell unhealthily and unsuccessfully in love with a girl from New York and forgot her. I have never lost a gnawing feeling of guilt that will remain with me until I die.

I was finally returning home, this time through Budapest. I boarded the train for Belgrade, sharing the compartment with a *bourgeois* couple in their late forties. Like many professional men in the Balkans, the gentleman wore a suit jacket with ill-assorted trousers.

We talked about Yugoslavia and Bulgaria. 'You know', he said, as we crossed into Yugoslavia. 'If Tito and Dimitrov had had their way, there would be no border here. Yugoslavia and Bulgaria almost merged into a Balkan Federation in 1949.'

'Really? What went wrong?' I asked.

'The movement started around the end of the 19th century as a socialist initiative to liberate the Balkan peoples from the Turks and federate them across the whole peninsula. Although the Bulgarians had no real Pan-Slav feeling, unlike the Southern Slavs, the people and the intelligentsia in Bulgaria liked the idea.

'Serbia and Bulgaria had already set up a customs union in 1905, which the Austrians forced them to dissolve. Then, after the revolution of the Young Turks, the first Balkan Social Democratic Congress was held in Belgrade in 1910, already with Georgi Dimitrov of Bulgaria. Their project was a federal republic containing all the small Balkan states, even including a free Turkey and an autonomous Macedonia. The Young Turks were contemptuous. Austria had annexed Bosnia-Herzegovina. The Macedonian question and the second Balkan war provisionally killed off the federalist movement.'

'I get mixed up with the Balkan wars', I said.

'In the First Balkan War in 1912, a coalition of Bulgaria, Greece, Montenegro and Serbia defeated the Ottoman Empire, which lost almost all its territory in Europe.

'In the Second Balkan War in 1913, Bulgaria, which had started it by opposing a secret agreement between Greece and Serbia over Macedonia, lost all the territories that it had gained. This was a blow to Russia, the protector of the Slavs, who had encouraged Pan-Slavism and Balkan unification to counter Austria-Hungary and obtain access to the warm seas.

'Between the wars the Soviet Union and the *Comintern*, headed by Dimitrov again, resurrected the idea, this time based on Socialism and Internationalism, with the aim of spreading revolution to the Balkans.'

'I learnt in Sofia that Stalin was against merging Bulgaria with Yugoslavia.'

'He wasn't at first. It was only after the War, when Marshall Tito took an independent stand, that Stalin opposed the Balkan Federation. When Dimitrov returned home from Moscow, he realised that Bulgaria could not survive economically without cooperation. So, in 1947 he signed a treaty with Tito. Their long-term aim was to merge Bulgaria and Yugoslavia into a Balkan Federative Republic, recognising a specific Macedonian people and language.

'Stalin and Molotov fiercely opposed the project. They were more concerned with moving the anti-fascist liberation groups that governed the newly created people's democracies towards Socialist revolution. Stalin was afraid that the West would dominate the Balkans through Tito. He disavowed his former trusted ally, Dimitrov, and his political treaty of alliance with Yugoslavia, and forced him to denounce Tito's expansionist position in Macedonia.'

'Perhaps they thought that Tito's attempt to set up a Balkan federation really a means of dominating Bulgaria, Albania and Greece like his precursor emperor Stefan Dušan?

'That maybe so. Anyhow, in April 1949 Stalin summoned Tito and Dimitrov to Moscow. Beria flew into Sofia to fetch Dimitrov, who went alone without Tito. Officially he died of cirrhosis in a Moscow sanatorium, but there has since been general suspicion that he was poisoned.'

'Are you Bulgarians', I asked. 'No, he replied. We are Yugoslavs from Belgrade. We are returning home after a long weekend in Sofia. And you, are you German?' I told him that I was an Englishman and that I had just spent a couple of months in Plovdiv. They both knew some Macedonian, which is very close to Bulgarian. We had already been talking for a good half hour. Getting the gist of what they said, I realised that I must by now know enough Bulgarian for a very simple conversation, albeit political.

'Tell me about Pan-Slavism', I said. 'Is that what inspired the creation of Yugoslavia?'

'Yes, but it went beyond that. It was again a 19th century movement to unite all Slav peoples, mainly in the Balkans, of course, currently under the Ottoman yoke, but also under the Habsburgs, and, to some extent, the Venetians.

'Pan-Slavism was the ideology of Russian imperialism. Russia used it as a pretext to invade the Balkans against Turkey and try to take control over all the Slav countries, as did the Soviet Union after the Second World War until Tito's split with Stalin.

'The first Pan-Slav congress, mainly composed of Czechs, had different factions. The right wing was for *Austroslavism*, believing that only within the Habsburg Empire could the Slav peoples feel protected and preserve their language and culture. This was the case for Poland, who agreed to Pan-Slavism, provided of course that Russia was excluded. The left, on the other hand, considered itself to be part of the Central European revolutionary movement. The majority were against both the Austrians and the Russians.

'In the Balkans, after the creation of a Serbian principality under the Ottomans, a project appeared for a Greater Serbia, grouping all the Southern Slav peoples of the three different faiths, Catholic, Orthodox and Muslim. With the exception of the Bulgarians, they united a century later in the Kingdom of Serbs, Croats and Slovenes, later to become Yugoslavia.

'It may interest you to know, as a linguist, that Pan-Slavic languages on the lines of Esperanto have been appearing regularly since the 17th century until today.'

On arrival, my new Serbian acquaintance slipped a few Dinar banknotes into the pocket of my coat. 'You seem to be a nice, educated young man. Here is something to help you enjoy Belgrade', he said. The couple separated inside the train and walked as strangers in the same direction along the platform.

I explored Belgrade between trains with a shabbily-dressed Bulgarian girl. She was an IT specialist, travelling to work in East Berlin. In Belgrade we had definitely returned to Western Europe. We browsed together through a smart department store on the hill opposite *Kalemegdan* Park. The young people were well-dressed in stylish Western fashions. I felt for my dowdy Bulgarian companion in her imitation astrakhan coat, visibly uncomfortable under the scornful looks of the young Serbian customers. We continued by the night train to Budapest.

Arriving at five o'clock in the morning. I booked into a hotel for one night and visited the city. If there is one city in the world that I love as one can love a human being, it is Budapest. On this my first visit I found Budapest a sad, grey place with its unfriendly *petit bourgeois* women in their *Robin Hood* hats. Due to my lack of imagination at the time and my obsession with Bulgaria and the Slav world, I was unable to look beyond the leprous walls at the eclectic beauty beneath. The Hungarians built the Budapest between the Austro-Hungarian compromise in 1867 and the First World War. Within the space of forty-five years they had constructed Pest in every style from the history of architecture.

'There's nothing authentic. It's all neo-something', I thought with pathetic short-sightedness.

At 6 o'clock the next morning I walked the boulevards while waiting for my train for Vienna. The Italian fans had followed me here for a football match. I found what looked like a public convenience, with two entrances. But which door? They were marked *Nők* and *Férfiak*. The streets were empty in the early morning and no-one was going in or out. I was tempted by *Nők*, but Hungarian is a Finno-Ugric language, I thought, so the rules of Indo-European languages do not apply. I entered the door marked *Férfiak* and used the urinal.

I returned by train to Paris, where my doctor put me on sick leave for a further six weeks. The French Social Security authorities allowed me to spend my convalescence with my parents in the UK, but I needed official permission. It came after five weeks waiting in Paris and I was able to spend the remaining week of my sick leave at my parents' house South of London. I returned to Paris and took up my job once again. After six weeks back in my company, it was the turn of the British National Health Service to ask me when I was intending to return to work.

While still at my parents' house, I noticed the icon that the museum curator in Skopje had made me a present of two years previously. Regretting somewhat having given it to my parents, I took it down from its hook on a wooden beam to admire it. Something about the cross on Saint Nicolas's right lapel looked unusual. I had by now learned enough about. iconography to know what was typically written there.

A cross on a Byzantine icon has two inscriptions. Vertically it says **ICXC**, an abbreviation in mediaeval Greek of **IHCOYC XPICTOC**, **Jesus Christ**. The horizontal inscription is **NIKA** in Greek, or **НИКА**, in Cyrillic, meaning *conquers*.

But on the vertical branch of the cross it was not **ICXC** that I read. Instead it said **ЦГН**.

Whatever could it stand for in Church Slavonic? As this was an icon of Saint Nicolas, perhaps it meant:

Црькы Господь Никола: *The Church of Lord Nicolas.*

Or did it mean something else? One thing that was sure was that it was no Mongolian *Kilroy*. I would have to ask a specialist. Why would you profane the cross on an icon with the letters that I had seen in Glagolitic on Baldwyn's tower in Veliko Trnovo, in a Gentlemen's toilet and transliterated into Cyrillic in a phone booth in Plovdiv in Bulgaria? I knew that Bulgaria and Macedonia had languages that were very similar and mutually comprehensible. Could it concern the Bulgarian claim to Macedonia?

8
Sarajevo

Following publication of the *Gulag Archipelago* and his expulsion from the Soviet Union, the Swedish Academy had awarded Aleksandr Solzhenitsyn the Nobel Prize for Literature. After nine years as General Secretary of the Romanian Communist Party, Nicolae Ceauşescu had been nominated First President of the Socialist Republic of Romania.

In early summer the Greek Colonels sponsored a *coup d'état* in Cyprus against Archbishop Makarios. The subsequent Turkish invasion of the island brought about the collapse of the colonels' regime. Konstantínos Karamanlís returned to Greece from exile to form a provisional government and re-establish the constitution. After a horrific year at work I needed a quiet Mediterranean holiday.

Leaving from the *Gare de Lyon* in early June on my now usual night train for Zagreb, I continued through Banja Luka, sleeping alone in a seating compartment, to arrive the following afternoon in Sarajevo. It had always been my ambition to visit this cosmopolitan town, the city of nine mosques.

In the buffet car after Banja Luka a dark Serb and a dusty-blond Croat, both in business suits, argued animatedly about the Second World War. It fitted comfortably into my preconceived idea of Yugoslavia. I chatted with an environmental specialist about the level of pollution within the Sarajevo basin.

The *Turist Biro* found me a room in a private house, where an American was staying in the adjacent room. The following morning, looking around mine, I saw various family photos dating from between the wars. All the men in the pictures wore *tarbouches*. A Muslim house at last! I must ask my landlord about the city.

According to my landlord, Sarajevo was a multi-cultural society, practising religious tolerance, as had been a general rule across the Ottoman Empire. The elite of Bosnia had always been mainly Muslim, making up more than a third of the population, in addition to some Sephardic Jewish. Under the Ottomans, Bosnian Serbs had been peasants. He reminded me that *Bosnjaks* were not Turks, but Islamised Slavs, what the peasants called *renegade Serbs*.

'You know that our oral tradition in Bosnia, particularly our folk music, is Islamic, but not Turkish.'

I had already learnt during my trip through Macedonia that there had been mass conversions to Islam. My landlord said that, during the 15th century, it had been mainly the *Bogomils*, the wealthiest class, who had converted to Islam, in an attempt to keep their privileges.

'For us *Boznjaks,* our community has always been distinct from Croats and Serbs', he said. 'By converting to Islam we found a way to maintain our identity. Some of our intellectuals claim that we never were Slavs at all, but Illyrians, like the Albanians, who already lived here before the Slav invasions and just adopted the language of Serbs and Croats.'

I remembered reading about the *Bosnjak* bourgeoisie described by Ivo Andrić in *A Bridge on the Drina*. When later my wife, in prolonged labour for our second child, asked me for something to read, it was another book by Andrić that I lent her, *The Time of Anika*. On the second page a woman dies in labour!

'I read somewhere that the Bogomils had some kind of a link to the *Cathars* in South West France', I said.

'Yes', he said. 'That is what they say, but who knows whether there is really a direct link, as the Inquisition believed, or whether they were just similar manifestations of a refusal of the authority of church and state? The Albigensian heresy was known as the Bulgarian heresy. Names such as *bugger, bougre, bulgari* probably originate from Bogomilism in Bulgaria. The Albigensian Crusade followed closely on the Sack of Constantinople during the Fourth Crusade.'

'So it originated in Bulgaria?' I asked.

'Not quite. Bogomils were said to descend from *Paulicians*, nearly a quarter of a million of which settled in Bulgaria after being expelled from Armenia. It was the priest Bogomil, meaning *dear to God*, who founded the sect during the first Bulgarian Empire in the 10th century in what is currently Macedonia.'

'Were they Christians? What did they believe in?'

'The Bogomils were dualists, believing that God had created Man's soul, but that the World and Man's body, and in fact all matter, had been created by Satan. It followed that they refused governments, taxes, feudalism. It was not just a religion, but also a political movement, which rejected, as did Catharism, church and state hierarchy. You might even say that it had something of modern-day Anarchism.

'They saw the Orthodox Church as a creation of Satan. Bogomils had no churches or clergy.

Each community had its own twelve elected *apostles*, which included women. In some ways it was rather *avant-garde*.'

'How did Bogomilism come to Bosnia and then reach France?'

'It spread to the West first into Serbia, where the Church decreed it a heresy and expelled its disciples to Bosnia and Dalmatia. After the *Ban*, or King, of Bosnia converted to Bogomilism the religion began to thrive here in opposition to the Catholic and Orthodox neighbours, who both persecuted it as a heresy. Despite attempts by the Pope, a Hungarian crusade and the Inquisition to remove Bogomilism, it remained in Bosnia until the Ottoman conquest. Bogomils then became ideal candidates for conversion to Islam.'

Sarajevo at that time was a grey Socialist city, with the exception of the old Muslim quarter and the romantic Muslim cemetery flanking it. Ottomans tombs dotted the slopes, cylindrical funeral *steles* coiffed in stone with the turbans of the deceased.

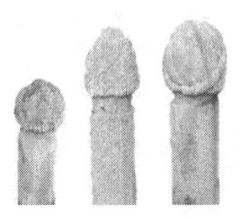

Every man and woman in Europe and North America had heard of Sarajevo, due to the act of one man, Gavrilo Princip. I placed my feet on the marks of his shoes in the asphalt, where he had stood to shoot and kill Archduke Franz Ferdinand, heir presumptive to the throne of Austria-Hungary, and set off the worst massacre in history.

Before returning to Yugoslavia I had read Rebecca

Back to Byzantium

West's *Black Lamb and Grey Falcon*. I never got tired of reading her chapters on Sarajevo. I love her story of the tragicomic visit of the Turkish delegation to Sarajevo in the thirties. She describes the embarrassment of the ultra-secular *Kemalists*, ostentatiously dressed in Western suits and ties, who are acclaimed by the entire Muslim population of Sarajevo, turned out in *tarbouches* and their finest traditional clothes removed from moth balls to welcome their Muslim *elder brother*.

Matija Mažuranić, a young Croatian, had travelled in Ottoman Bosnia for a year and a half at the same time as Lady Mary Wortley Montagu lived in Istanbul. He had described the Bosnjak Muslims aping their Ottoman occupiers without really understanding either their language or culture.

Was it by chance that Franz Ferdinand, despite all advice to the contrary, decided precisely on the date of 28th July 1914 to make his visit to Sarajevo? It was Saint Vitus' day, the 525th anniversary of the historic defeat of the Serbs by the Turks at Kosovo Polje, a date engraved in the Serbian national memory.

His assassin, Gavrilo Princip, identified personally with Miloš Obilić, the Serbian national mythical hero-cum-saint, who had assassinated Sultan Murad I in his tent just after the defeat at Kosovo Polje. I remembered him from my brief excursion into Kosovo.

The young woman in the *Turist Biro* in Sarajevo was surprisingly friendly, calling out into the street to me to come in her office for a chat. 'When you have visited Dubrovnik, go down the coast to Budva, in Montenegro. I am sure that you will like it. You can get a bus from there, she said, holding out a brochure. The tattoo of a flower adorned the inside of her bronzed right upper arm.

Back to Byzantium

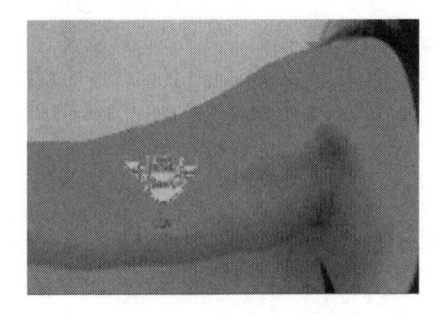

That's pretty', I said, responding to her friendly approach. I took a closer look. 'What sort of flower is it?' I asked.

'My name is Lili, and it is the flower of my country, the yellow lily of Bosnia', she said. Something was tattooed underneath, the letters **CGN**.

'What does it stand for', I asked.

'They are the initials of my boyfriend, of course', she replied. 'His name is **Cvetan Gavrilović Nadarević**.

Despite her answer, which was perfectly plausible, something sounded wrong. I wasn't quite sure that I believed her. When I asked her if we could take a picture together as a souvenir, without hesitation she passed my camera to her colleague and put her arm around my neck, revealing her tattoo.

The wooden bench in my compartment on the train was uncomfortable, but I slept so well that I missed the terminus at Ploče. At half past five in the morning I rubbed my eyes to find that the now-empty train was moving slowly toward the distant sidings. Together with another late sleeper I jumped off the moving coach and walked along the track for twenty minutes back to the station. I had three hours to wait for my train to Dubrovnik.

Back to Byzantium

I had bought myself a language manual in Sarajevo. Serbo-Croatian, also known as Croato-Serbian, depending on the republic, would become known by linguists after the collapse of Yugoslavia as *BCMS*: Bosnian, Croatian, Montenegrin, Serbian. Twenty-or-so million speak Serbo-Croatian worldwide. It was currently the official language of all the republics of Yugoslavia, except Macedonia and Slovenia.

Two separate sets of criteria exist for a spoken idiom to be considered as an independent language rather than a dialect. One is linguistic and the other sociological or political. A number of local dialects of the southern Slavs were considered to have sufficient linguistic structure in common to be called a single language. Bishop Štrosmajer in Croatia in the mid-19th century had been one of the first politicians to elaborate a programme to unite the Southern Slavs; with a language based on the *Shtovakian* dialect, considering the language of the Serbs and that of the Croats to be the same. *Shtovakian*, so-called because *shto, што* in Cyrillic meant *what*, was adopted as a common language. It had two variants, the *Ekavian* pronunciation in Serbia and the *Jekavian* in Croatia. This distinction concerned the pronunciation of the letter *e*, pronounced *e* in Serbia and *ye* in Croatia.

After the creation of Yugoslavia between the wars, Serbia attempted to impose *Ekavian*, but this never succeeded with the Croats, who always tried to set up Croatian as a separate official language. During the Second World War the German satellite Independent State of Croatia of Ante Pavelić attempted to purify Croatian of foreign elements. Later, under Tito, an attempt was made to blur regional differences.

Ploče is situated at the end of the main part of Dalmatia, just before the sliver of land separating it from the remaining shard of the Dalmatian coast. It gives Bosnia-Herzegovina access to the Mediterranean. They were all Yugoslav republics at the time, so it wasn't a problem.

The train idled through an arid rocky landscape with cypresses until we arrived in Dubrovnik, the former Venetian city of Ragusa. It was beautiful indeed, but I moved on the next day by bus down the coast around the Gulf of Kotor to Budva. We drove beside the two islands bearing one an Orthodox and the other a Catholic church face to face, symbols of religious harmony in Yugoslavia.

I spent an uneventful week on the beach in Budva. A lone musician, seated on the hill above the beach played Serbian traditional *narodna musika* on his clarinet with exquisite melancholy.

Six months after giving up smoking after my viral hepatitis, I had reverted to cigarillos. That was all right, I thought. I didn't inhale, even if it gave me toad's breath. Not finding small cigars in Budva, I started smoking again. That first cigarette tasted so good, why had I waited so long?

I bought some postcards. There wasn't much choice. The colour portrait of Petar II Petrović-Njegoš the national hero of Montenegro, was prominent on every stand.

I asked my friend at the *Turist Biro* who he was. He was both bishop and prince of Montenegro, titles that he held from when he inherited them from his father at the age of eighteen until he died of tuberculosis at the age of thirty-seven. Njegoš was a poet, whom Serbs and Montenegrins consider as their Shakespeare, though he wrote only one major work, his masterpiece, *The Mountain Wreath*.

He was also a politician who aimed to awaken

a Montenegrin nation and restructure the old tribal society into a modern nation state. Montenegro, due to its mountainous remoteness, had benefited for centuries from relative independence from Ottoman rule. Feuds had been going on between clans. Njegoš struggled during his short life to ensure the continued existence of Montenegro, seeing conversion to as a creeping disintegration of traditional values.

He certainly looked like a charismatic figure with his black beard, traditional red *jelek*, the sleeveless embroidered jacket, and his black cap.

The Mountain Wreath, an epic drama in verse which he wrote in the mid-19th century, takes place a hundred and forty years previously. A British Serbophile had translated in the 1930s into English verse. I bought the translation and read it almost at one sitting.

The drama tells of Bishop Danilo's attempts to bring together the feuding tribes of Montenegro. In the poem, Danilo has a vision of the spread of Turkish oppression and influence in Europe. The main threat to Serbian unity that Njegoš describes through the voice of Bishop Danilo is not the invasion by the Turks, but the insidious poison represented by Turkified Christians. Danilo calls on leaders to persuade converts to Islam to return to Christianity. Those who agree will be welcomed back, those who refuse must be massacred.

The poem is built around an event that is said to have taken place on Christmas Day in 1707, when the Montenegrins who had converted to Islam were executed *en masse*, although there is no proof that mass slaying of converts to Islam in fact took place. Njegoš is one of the creators of the Southern Slav myths of both Kosovo Polje and of the Christmas-Day massacre. God had punished

Serbians by their defeat at Kosovo Polje. It had been a national fall from grace, which only the sacrifice of the mythical hero Miloš Obilić had redeemed.

The Mountain Wreath, probably the most important work in Serbian literature, is variously perceived today by different peoples of Yugoslavia. Serbian nationalists would later consider it as a justification for creation of a Greater Serbia. Croatians see it as proof of the incurable oriental nature of South-Eastern Slavs. Muslims, of course, consider it to be Islamophobic, a manual for ethnic cleansing. It has recently been called a blueprint for the *Final Solution*.

A week on a beach was more than enough, so I moved up the coast to Dubrovnik, which I gave the attention that it deserved. I had lunch on the *corso* in the old town. The waiter asked me what I wanted to eat. 'I don't speak Serbian', I said in Serbo-Croatian. 'I think that you mean Croatian', he replied in Croato-Serbian.

Digital forests of cypresses in their late spring greenery stood by as we continued up the coast. I stopped off on the way in one of the delightful Croatian villages, a crossroads with a chestnut tree and a café, to lunch again on *ćevapčići* with red pepper purée.

In Split I spent a night in a hotel within the palace walls of Rome's Illyrian emperor, Diocletian. I met a girl from Czechoslovakia, staying in the same hotel as me. The following morning I left her at the quayside, where she boarded the hydrofoil for the airport. She didn't give me her address. The Cold War was on, the *Prague Spring* over and chance encounters had no future. I would briefly meet a Czech woman in Paris a year later. Though she refused to give me her address in Czechoslovakia, three months after I received a mysterious call from an *Air France* pilot. He had a packet for me. She had managed to find a way to send me a photographic guide to Prague, which she had signed without leaving an address.

There had never been a real rail network linking the Yugoslav republics, which belonged to separate worlds, Austria-Hungary and the Ottoman Empire. That was, of course, apart from the main line between Trieste and Belgrade, which ran through Ljubljana and Zagreb. Other inter-republican transport was all by bus. A brand-new direct *Intercity* train linked Split to Zagreb, both in Croatia. Smart Croatian businessmen in elegant suits sat preparing their files on this clean, modern train. Fifteen minutes after departure, someone had defecated on each toilet seat on the train.

I stopped for the night in Trieste, a city that I love for its scent of mystery and *espionage*, where I bought some cheap shoes. The saleswomen spoke to me directly in Serbo-Croatian, or was it Slovene? The Slovenes were all buying their *corfam* shoes. I took the train back to Paris and returned to work.

Thinking about my enigma, my mind turned back to Sarajevo and the girl with the tattoo. With my photos developed in Budva I looked closely at the picture of the girl. **CGN**, I thought. That's **ЦГН** in Cyrillic, ⱅ ⰆⰑ Ⱃ in Glagolitic. And then that *Bosnian lily* didn't really look too much like a flower.

Back to Byzantium

If you looked at it the other way up, however, it appeared to be an oriental temple of some kind, with a large shallow dome surrounded by smaller ones.

9
Mamaia

That summer thirty-five European states, excluding Albania, signed the Helsinki agreement on security and cooperation in Europe and the rights of Man. I was on my way to Romania, to discover a Latin country in the Balkans.

Taking my usual route, I arrived in Belgrade a couple of nights after my departure from the *Gare de Lyon*. A large friendly woman presided in the ticket office. She spoke some English, but forced me to speak Bulgaro-Serbian pidgin. She obviously thought it normal for me to make an effort to speak her language, and she was right. Or did she think I was a Slovene?

Belgrade had that familiar fragrance announcing that I was abroad. One of the characteristics of Communist Europe for me has always been the smell of poorly refined low-octane petrol. In all honesty, it is something like my Proustian *madeleine*. It means that I have arrived in Central Europe.

I changed stations to join the Bucharest train. An ethnic German from Arad joined me in the compartment. He seemed tired of explaining to Westerners why he was German, when it was obvious from his appearance and style that he was from Romania. I learnt from him by imitation the rules for dealing with Romanian officials. The Romanian customs officer boarded the train. 'How nice to see you. Have a cigarette ... Keep the packet' 'What have you to declare, young man?' the officer asked me. 'Oh, he's all right. He's with me', said the ethnic German.

Back to Byzantium

I would remember the rules six years later, only after my wife and I had crossed by road from Hungary into Romania. We spent five hours at the border post, while the customs officer meticulously dismantled her tampons one by one until I remembered the procedure.

Arriving in Bucharest I found a hotel not far from the station. 'How much', I asked the hotel manager. 'Your shirt, your shoes and a carton of *Kent* cigarettes!' I preferred to pay in cash, but bought him the cigarettes. Thirty years previously in Paris a tailor had also required payment with a carton of *Kent* for alterations to my suit. Tax evasion I understand, but what made *Kent* so special?

Smartly-dressed African students filled the hotels with their gaiety and the generous student scholarships that Ceaușescu had granted them to the resentment of the local population. I met several of them, from both French- and English-speaking countries. They all told the same story of the press conferences that the university required them to give on arrival in their respective towns in Romania. 'Do you live in a tree? Do you live with the monkeys? Do you have a father?' featured among the innocent or not so innocent questions. One from Kenya complained that people told him constantly that he must feel at home with the stifling summer weather in Bucharest, ignorant of the fact that Nairobi, situated at 1,800 metres, had an average temperature of 17 degrees Celsius.

I spent a day and a half exploring this charmingly elegant, old-fashioned, dusty central European capital. I was eager to get to the Black Sea, but buying a ticket for Constanța was not so easy. To travel on a train in Romania it was not sufficient to have a ticket. You also needed a seat reservation. The reservation office opened half an hour before the train left and so many people were queuing that you had the choice between missing the train and travelling illegally in the corridor. The train was about to leave so I jumped on without a reservation.

My smoking companion in the train corridor was a

Rom who admired my cheap *Timex* watch. He indicated by signs that he wanted to buy it or exchange it for his Soviet model. I was foolish enough to refuse. The myth of Western razor blades and watches was still alive.

When the train emptied somewhat I found a seat. In the compartment sat a female university professor, like many Romanians, fluent in French.

'You know that the man who liked your watch was a Rom', she said.

'Like you', I said.

'No', she replied, 'I am Romanian. You Western Europeans always get it all mixed up. I know it's confusing for a foreigner.' She gave me a course in vocabulary about the *R*-words.

She told me, as I had already known since my stay in Skopje, that the Orthodox populations in the Balkans had used the word *Roman* to describe themselves, the inhabitants of the Eastern Roman Empire, as opposed to those the Western, whom they called *Latin*.

'*Romaic, Ρωμαϊκός*', she said 'refers to modern Greece, especially to modern Greek language.

'*Rūm* is the name that the Ottomans used for the inhabitants of the Orthodox *millet*, the Balkans being generally known then as *Rumelia*.

'*Romanian* is the name of the Romance language, *Românește*, and of the majority population, *Români*, of the provinces of Moldavia, Wallachia and Transylvania.

'*Rom* is the name used by the Romani gypsies to describe themselves, meaning *man*, plural *Roma*. They live in all parts of South and Central Europe, but mainly in Bulgaria, Hungary, Macedonia, Romania, Serbia and Slovakia.

Romanians are not all Roma, and Roma are not all Romanians, as a lot of the French seem to think.

'*Aromanian* is another word for *Vlach*, a Latin people living throughout the Balkans. Confusing, isn't it?'

'And *Romansch* is a Romance language spoken in the Swiss canton of Grisons', I said, not wanting to lose face, 'not forgetting the Vatican. But what about *Vlachs* and *Wallachs*, are they the same?'

'The origin of the names is *Walhi*', she said, 'what the German peoples called the *Celts*. The name later became extended to all Romance-speaking peoples. For Slavonic speakers *Wallach* meant Romanian. The name is said to be the origin of the names *Welsh* and *Walloon*.

'*Wallachia* is located between the Danube and the Carpathians. With Moldova and Transylvania, *Ardeal* in Romanian, Wallachia is one of the main regions of Romania. The name is not generally used by us Romanians, who call the region *Muntenia*.

'As for the *Vlachs*, their origin is contested, Thracian, Dalmatian or even Illyrian. The Byzantines, who called the Franks *Celts*, called the Latin-speaking inhabitants of Dacia *Vlachs*. They live in most Central and South-Eastern European countries, from Poland to Greece and from Ukraine to Czechoslovakia. In Greece and Albania, they call themselves Aromanians, using their language just for speaking, with Greek for written communication.

'Vlach, or one of its many variants, has become a generic term covering Romance-language peoples of Central and South-Eastern Europe. It is used colloquially for Romanians living outside their country. By occupation,

Vlachs were mainly shepherds, so the name also became synonymous with *shepherd*, whatever their language or ethnic origin. Use of the term *Vlach* or one of its variants has been extended to multiple meanings, depending on the country, usually with a pejorative connotation, for nomads, immigrants and vagrants in general, in fact for any group that one doesn't like. I hope everything is now clear.'

I set out on foot from the station to the centre of Constanţa, the city of Ovid, and then took a bus to the resort of Mamaia. Pale-mauve hibiscus bushes seemed to border every road in Romania. Mamaia, some said a kind of anagram of *Miami*, was one of the longest beaches in Europe. At the tourist office, the queue seemed endless. All the hotels in town were booked out. A middle-aged Italian, who claimed to have been sleeping in his car for three days, came in periodically to shout his mind. I went out to a shop and bought a couple of cans of cold refreshment. 'I'm thirsty', I said to the young man at the desk, when my turn finally came, 'and I think you are too.' 'You are first on my list', he thanked me. 'I have a room for you. In addition to the price of the hotel, it will cost you half a carton of *Kent* for the concierge at the hotel and the other half for me.' I bought the cigarettes and paid for a week.

I booked into the hotel. Looking over the top of the desk I saw the list of rooms with their occupation status. The letter ***L*** filled almost the whole column. *Liber!* That meant that a room was free. Why bother to rent them out when it only meant more work?

I wanted a Romanian lunch, but where to find it in a resort centred on foreign tourism. In all the restaurants, they offered me only the notorious *international cuisine*, *Wiener Schnitzel* and chips on all the menus. 'Have you anything Romanian?' 'You will not like it, it is not suitable for you.' It sounded familiar.

Back to Byzantium

After lunch, I went back to my room. In Mamaia they had built the hotels more-or-less simultaneously along the interminable beach in groups of three at right angles to each other. Some of them stood several stories high. I went into my hotel, took my key at reception and walked down the corridor. Peter Falk was playing *Columbo* on the TV in the *foyer*. I entered my room, undressed and lay down on my bed. They had repainted the ceiling since I had gone out for lunch. Instead of being duck-egg blue it had turned pale green. I got dressed, exited the room and left the key at reception. In retrospect, it was the story of a more recent Soviet film, *The Irony of Fate or Enjoy the Steam*, in which the Muscovite hero is so drunk that he gets on a plane to Leningrad by mistake and enters the same room, in the same flat, in the same block, in the same street, that bears the same name as the one where he lives in Moscow. After walking a couple of hundred metres down the promenade I found the second configuration of hotels and took my key from the identical reception desk and went to my room. *Columbo* was still on TV in the same corner of the *foyer*.

When the original *Columbo* series ended a year later, Romanians thought that their government had refused to import the show. Protest was so intense that the Romanian government asked Peter Falk to read a declaration on television, which he did, in Romanian using a phonetic transcript.

Nicolae Ceaușescu was very squeamish about using the word *Jewish*, so television in Romania did its utmost to avoid the word. To its credit, Romania is one of the European countries that does not dub voices in foreign films, preferring subtitles. Consequently, when, in a foreign film, you heard a character say *Jewish*, the corresponding subtitle said *Irish*.

A Romanian Jewish friend told me an anecdote about his tribulations with red tape. An official error specifying his nationality as *Irish,* had caused his reapplication for citizenship in a Western European country to be refused, though it was his right by birth through his grandmother. 'But you're already Irish. You can't be a citizen of two countries', said the official. He objected that he wasn't Irish. 'Prove it!' they challenged him. By chance he met someone who played along with the absurdity of the situation and supplied him with an official embassy document specifying that he was not a citizen of the Republic of Ireland. He now prided himself in having an official paper enabling him to prove to Romanians that he wasn't *Jewish*!

I had made the acquaintance of a Romanian ethnic Turk. In the former Turkish region of Dobrudza whose regional capital was Constanța, they represented nearly three percent of the population. We spent a couple of evenings together, watching Romanian belly dancers in an open-air ethnic restaurant and listening to him criticising the *regime*. His mother lived in Canada and he was waiting for his visa. I started smoking once again.

Though I had paid for my hotel for a week, after a couple of days I decided to cut my losses and leave. The government had conditioned the duration of your visa on the number of coupons that you had purchased with foreign currency. I had paid for seven days, which was not enough to get me out of the country. So I spent almost a day in a paranoid rush to change money, get my visa extended by just one day, enough to get me out of the country, buy a train ticket and try unsuccessfully to reserve a seat. I never went to a country, including Albania, which gave me a comparable feeling of persecution and such an urge to get out as soon as possible. I transited through Bucharest without stopping and on to Timișoara, standing in the corridor because I hadn't succeeded in obtaining a reservation in time. I tried to buy a ticket for Belgrade, but the woman at the ticket office refused, stating that my visa would expire thirty minutes before the next train reached the border. I was desperate to leave the country. A helpful and intrepid gentleman negotiated with her, reproaching her for her bureaucratic rigidity, and she grudgingly sold me the ticket.

A young man in my compartment wore a printed white T-shirt, then uncommon in Romania. When he got up to leave I saw the letters on the front of his T-shirt, this time in Romanian script, ȚGN.

They were the three initials that I had seen in Glagolitic and Cyrillic in Bulgaria and Macedonia and – could it be a coincidence? – in Croatian Latin characters on the girl's tattoo in Bosnia.

As he got up and put on his imitation black leather jacket to go into the corridor for a smoke, I noticed two words stitched on its back,

Marea Idee

No, it was no coincidence. I recognised them immediately as Romanian for the Greek slogan of the twenties, *Megali idea*, the Great Idea.

I was reminded of what my Greek train companion had told me at the station in Piraeus about an enduring, active nostalgia for their long-lost Constantinople.

The *Great Idea* was originally that of liberating the Greeks from the Ottoman Empire and recreating a new Byzantine Empire under Greek rule, with Constantinople as its capital. Its proponents had later limited their ambitions to setting up a Hellenic state including all areas inhabited by Greeks. The new state would extend from the Ionian to the Black Sea and Asia Minor across Thrace, and from Macedonia to Crete and Cyprus, the *Greece of Two Continents and Five Seas*.

The *Megali Idea* had been one of the Greek national obsessions for more than a century, from the War of Independence in 1820 until the population exchange that followed their final defeat in the second Greco-Turkish War in 1922. A million and a quarter Greeks had forcibly emigrated from Asia Minor to the Hellenic peninsula. Even in the 1930s, after his *coup d'état*, General Metaxas had tried in vain to revive the Great Idea with his *Third Hellenic Civilisation.*

I arrived in Belgrade, relieved once again to be back in a *free* country. I crossed the city with an elderly ethnic Hungarian woman from a country village in Romania, travelling through Serbia to attend her sister's funeral in Hungary. Except that the funeral had taken place two months previously. She lived in *Erdély,* in the Hungarian-speaking part of Transylvania, less than a hundred kilometres from her late sister's home across the border in Hungary. Due to the appalling relations between Romania and Hungary she was obliged to travel through Yugoslavia, making a long detour. It had taken her the two months to obtain travel authorisation. She had her train tickets, but not enough money to cross Belgrade by bus between the two stations.

I had wasted my holiday travelling on trains and would have to wait another six years to get to appreciate Romania. A glutton for punishment, a couple of years later I decided to spend a whole week on a train, the Trans-Siberian.

10
Malbork

In exchange for a strict policy of austerity Britain obtained a loan of £3.5 Million from the International Monetary Fund, falling from its one-time fifth position in the world to the 18th in terms of GDP. In its tenth Five-Year Plan the Soviet Union reaffirmed its priority for heavy industry over consumer goods.

The announcement of a sharp increase in food prices triggered strikes in factories in the Polish People's Republic. Though Edvard Gierek, Poland's reformist First Secretary, backed down, he resorted to force to contain the demonstrations. With opposition to privileges and social inequality becoming organised, workers had become less afraid of police repression. Poland was my destination.

With four weeks' holiday, I decided to head first for the Yugoslav Adriatic for a few days by the sea. Taking my usual train as far as Trieste, I continued by bus to Koper, formerly Capodistria, in Slovenia on the Istrian peninsula. Too many tourists and impatient local hotel personnel drove me away after one night. I left the next morning early for Vienna via Ljubljana, the delightful capital of Slovenia. My travelling companion, a Croat, was satisfied to meet at last a foreigner who knew a little more about Yugoslavia than the price of its hotel rooms.

After spending a couple of days in Vienna obtaining visas for Czechoslovakia and Poland, I left for the historic town of Olomouc in Moravia, spending one night in neighbouring Přerov, where I was to join the train for Warsaw the following evening.

Back to Byzantium

Waiting for the train in the *foyer* of the hotel opposite the station I chatted in English with the hotel concierge, apparently, a student. We talked politics. The unstated rules were that each time that we saw the front door open or heard steps on the stairs our conversation stopped and we were absolutely silent until the coast was clear. The *Prague Spring* was over and Gustáv Husák, the Party Secretary, had stifled freedom of speech a good five years earlier. Out in the street of this industrial town I sensed without a trace of doubt the hostile eyes that stared into my back. As soon as I challenged them by sustaining their gaze they promptly averted them.

I joined the train for the night in a seating compartment. Opposite me sat a Polish priest returning home from a business trip to the Vatican. I had bought a bottle of *Vecchia Romagna* brandy in Trieste, and we both knew enough Italian, the language of the Vatican, to engage in a simple conversation over a swig. In the early hours of the morning in Katovice a young Polish woman entered the compartment carrying a violin case. I spoke no Polish and she spoke no other language, but I understood that she was going to Gdańsk on the Baltic on holiday and that was where I had planned to go too. After talking in a huddle with the priest in Polish, she suggested that we went there together. I learnt later what the priest had explained to her. Here was a nice young man, and her duty as a good Polish Catholic was to make sure that he left Poland with a favourable opinion. Why didn't she help me to make it favourable? A priest in the role of *Alfons*, as they say in Polish!

Her name was Elwira. Together we crossed this capital, rebuilt from scratch after the Second World War, along broad leafy avenues past identical blocks of flats, to her friend's building. Despite the ninety-five per cent destruction and too hasty reconstruction, Warsaw is a pleasant city. The historic centre was currently being rebuilt with help from old photos, *vedute* executed by Canaletto's nephew, Bernardo Bellotto, and pre-war students' drawings. Using the old bricks retrieved from the rubble, they had only just completed rebuilding the shallot-shaped dome of the red-brick royal palace from the ground up. The modern city centre was dominated by Stalin's gift to Poland, a clone of his Moscow skyscrapers, as *compensation* for Soviet occupation.

The flat was empty except for a group of bearded friends seated on the floor, who welcomed me with stewed-cherry *kompot*, offered me a bath and a bed for the night. After a night in a seating compartment I needed both. I took a bath but, in spite of my new friends' invitation to stay the night in their flat, I preferred to go through the government tourist agency, as was officially required. But this wasn't Bulgaria and the rules weren't rigorously applied in Poland.

The agency found me a room in a block of flats in the centre. I took the lift up the few flights to visit it and its obsequious occupiers. Half way up the lift stopped. Pressing all the buttons was no use. A combination of the alarm bell and my kicks against the door alerted the janitor. A conversation down a lift shaft with one party speaking Polish and the other rudimentary Bulgarian didn't immediately solve the problem. The janitor finally opened the door and I leapt a quarter storey up the lift shaft to freedom.

My violinist Elwira and her piano teacher friend Alicja were leaving for Gdańsk the next day and, following the priest's instructions, invited me to go with them, against the advice of their male colleague. However were we going to communicate, he objected. On the contrary, absence of a common language has never been an obstacle to communication. It's when you fully understand each other that you start wondering if you really have anything in common. How much Polish can you learn in one week? A fair amount, if you're with two nice girls day and night who speak no other language. We had long conversations in pidgin gestures.

So we left by train for Gdańsk, one young man and

Back to Byzantium

two young women. The pianist had a cousin who lived in the Gdańsk suburb of Oliwa. Her flat was located in what was probably the longest block of flats in Europe, built along the sand parallel to the sea, further than the eye could see. Three other cousins were already staying with them, but we all piled into the small two-room flat. The cousins slept in the living room and I slept on the bed-less bedroom floor with the two girls. Purely platonic, needless to say! Had I made a move I would surely have spoiled everything.

> Gdansk is part of the *Trójmiasto*, the municipal tri-city, composed of the towns of Gdańsk, Gdynia and Sopot. Gdańsk, the Renaissance former Hanseatic town of Danzig, had been a free city between the wars under the jurisdiction of the League of Nations. Gdynia, formerly a village named Gdingen, had been part of the Kingdom of Prussia until Poland was recreated and reunited by the Treaty of Versailles. Between the wars the Polish government turned it into its seaport and later built around it the town of Gdynia. Sopot had been the *chic* German seaside resort of Zoppot, attached to the free city of Danzig.
>
> The so-called Danzig corridor between the wars provided Poland with access to the Baltic, but it had isolated Germany from its *exclave* of East Prussia. Adolf Hitler called for an *Autobahn* and a rail link which, while connecting East Prussia to the rest of Germany, would have cut off Poland from the Baltic. It became a pretext for invading Poland.

We spent our dinners drinking Polish *wódka* and *chłodnik*, cold beetroot soup. The Poles also practised the *squirrel glance*, but with a little more serenity. In the street, I asked my friend the meaning of the expression *chervona burżuazja*. She'd tell me later, she said.

Back to Byzantium

Smoking on the balcony of the flat I asked the same question. We went inside, shut and fastened the windows. It was the *red bourgeoisie*, what the Communist bosses had become, like the pigs in the final chapter of Orwell's *Animal Farm.*

Apart from their charm, friendliness and easy-going nature, the Poles impressed you with their tidiness and cleanliness, making large detours to find a bin in the street for their waste paper. The other thing was their profound, but unobtrusive religiosity. As we walked past a new church, my friends would disappear inside for a brief prayer.

The Polish habit that I liked the most was the hand kiss. Not reserved for married women, as in Germany, but the identical routine. It was required practise for every woman that you met. Clicking your heels, taking the hand as if to shake it, turning it ninety degrees clockwise, then bending almost double to simulate a kiss a few millimetres above the hand without contact. Nothing like the southern European version that pulls the hand up to one's own mouth by the fingertips to slurp all over it, just like the senior French-snob citizens in Moscow, for whom it was no way a tradition, just ostentation. Far from being the reactionary behaviour of senior citizens, in Poland it was practised systematically by young people. After nearly thirty years of Soviet quasi-occupation, by returning to *bourgeois* or even aristocratic manners the Poles demonstrated their refusal of Soviet proletarian *tovarishch* camaraderie. As did the Hungarians verbally when they met a lady, saying *kezit csókolom, I kiss your hand*, without really acting it out.

After visiting the gilded Renaissance wonders of Gdańsk we spent a morning in Westerplatte. This was where the very first battle took place of what had just become the Second World War. Less than two hundred Poles had resisted with unbelievable valour for a full week against the vastly superior numbers and resources of the Third Reich, including *Stuka* dive-bomber attacks.

The Polish Military Transit Depot had been located on Westerplatte, a peninsula separated from the Free City of Danzig by the harbour channel. Though the League of Nations High Commissioner for Danzig had allowed Poland to keep eighty or so soldiers to guard naval ammunition stores, the Poles had unilaterally increased their numbers to two hundred. On 1st September 1939 Germany began its invasion of Poland, with the battleship *Schleswig-Holstein* opening fire without warning on the Polish garrison on the peninsula.

The Poles resisted numerous attacks, inflicting heavy losses on the Germans. Four days later Major Henryk Sucharski, the Polish commander, in a state of shell shock, urged his troops to surrender, but his second in command, Captain Franciszek Dąbrowski, opposed him and took command. Finally, a week later, on 7th September, under intense German fire, the Poles surrendered. Their defence had so impressed the German commander that he allowed Sucharski to keep his ceremonial sabre.

With Sucharski shell-shocked for the most of the battle, there has since been speculation over whether it was he or Captain Dąbrowski who effectively commanded the defence of Westerplatte. But it had remained a symbol of resistance to invasion, the Polish myth that all of the defenders had died in the battle, fighting almost to the last man.

Our last trip was to Malbork, formerly Marienburg. This was said to be the largest fortress in Europe, covering an area of more than twenty hectares, more extensive even than Carcassonne. It had been the headquarters of the Knights of the Teutonic Order. We decided to take an organised tour.

In addition to Polish, our guide, a tall thick-set Prussian with a long crew cut, spoke German, which seemed appropriate for the location, if not for the Poles, especially just after our visit to Westerplatte. He began our tour in the sunny courtyard of the Outer Castle.

'This fortress of Marienburg, as you no doubt already know, was at one time the headquarters of the Knights of the Teutonic Order. Can one of you tell us something about them?'

'Weren't they like a northern version of the Knights Templar?' I hazarded.

'They were', replied our guide 'in more ways than one. First, just before the Fourth Crusade, as a pious order, founded to set up hospitals and generally care for German-speaking pilgrims in the Holy Land, later on to become a secular colonial power on the shores of the Baltic. The Knights wore white surcoats with a black cross instead of a red one.

'Initially Pope Celestine II had ordered a contingent of the Knights Hospitallier to take over a German hospital in Jerusalem. In order to help pilgrims and crusaders who could speak neither the local language nor Latin, the friars were all to be Germans. In 1198, just six years before the Sack of Constantinople, Celestine transformed them into a military order on the model of the Knights Templar.'

'Did they take part in the Sack of Constantinople, I asked.

'In fact, they didn't. They were busy in the Holy Land at the time. The Teutonic Knights were not present during the Fourth Crusade, but they later had their own crusade in northern Europe.

'Thirteen years later, King András II of Hungary invited the Knights to move to Transylvania to help defend his borders. But after a few years they became too independent, attempting to set up a state within a state, until András expelled them from the country by force.

'Let me first say a word about the Northern Crusades. They officially began in 1195, when Pope Celestine III proclaimed a crusade against the Baltic heathens. A Papal Bull later declared that it had the same value as a crusade to the Holy Land. They were undertaken by the Christian kings of Denmark, Poland and Sweden against various non-Christian peoples around the shores of the Baltic. These included Finns, Prussians and the inhabitants of what are today the Baltic States, Estonia, Latvia and Lithuania, sandwiched between the Orthodox world to the east and the Catholic to the west. As in the Fourth Crusade, which you just mentioned, they included a campaign not only against pagans, but also against Orthodox Christians, this time Russians.

'Unlike the crusaders to the Holy Land, who left their families sometimes for years at a time, for the Northern Crusaders it was more like a jaunt. They went off to fight in spring and returned home by autumn.'

'How did the Teutonic Order come to be here

in Malbork?' Elwira's friend Alicja asked.

'When the Muslims took back the Holy Land, the Knights looked for new missions back in Europe. In 1230 they joined the Prussian Crusade, Christianising the Old Prussians by force with great brutality. They changed from being a hospice brotherhood for pilgrims into a military order, creating the independent Monastic State of the Teutonic Knights. They moved their headquarters from Venice to Marienburg to be out of reach of the big powers, gaining control of a large territory along the Baltic.'

'You mentioned the Russians', I said. 'I suppose that was *Kievian Rus'*.'

'Yes. Pope Gregory IX encouraged the Teutonic Knights to conquer the Orthodox Russian Republics of Pskov and Novgorod. All their attempts had failed when they suffered a major defeat in 1242 in the Battle of the Ice.'

'It sounds like Orthodox Christians' revenge for the Sack of Constantinople.'

'Perhaps', he replied patiently, 'but don't forget that nearly sixty years after the Sack of Constantinople, that was nearly twenty years after the Battle on the Ice, General Alexios Strategopoulos was to retake the city at the head of a small contingent of only eight hundred troops. In the absence of the Latin garrison, currently conducting a raid, he led a surprise attack, literally through the back door via a secret passage, and took back Constantinople from the Crusaders. Michael VIII Palaiologos was subsequently crowned Emperor in *Hagia Sofia*.'

'But that's another subject entirely. I am here to talk about the Knights of the Teutonic Order. Would you like me to tell you the story of the

Battle on the Ice? I wonder if you saw Sergei Eisenstein's masterpiece, *Aleksandr Nevskiï*, with a score by Sergei Prokofiev.' Most of us had.

'The Battle on the Ice', he continued ' was fought between the Republic of Novgorod, led by Prince Alexander Nevsky and the Crusader army under the Livonian branch of the Teutonic Knights. It took place in 1242, largely on the frozen Lake Peipus, situated between Estonia and Russia.

'The Knights had first attacked the neighbouring Novgorod Republic, occupying Pskov and other Russian cities. When they approached Novgorod itself, the local citizens called on Prince Alexander Nevsky for help. Alexander, who was twenty years old at the time, succeeded in retaking Pskov.

'On 5th April 1242, the day of the battle, Alexander retreated in a subterfuge to draw the over-confident Crusaders onto the frozen lake and then attack them with a pincer movement. The Russians were around five thousand, the Crusaders only half as many.

'As planned, the Teutonic Knights and Crusaders charged across the lake, but they were delayed by the Novgorod infantry. After a couple of hours of hand-to-hand fighting, the left and right wings of Alexander's army entered battle. The Crusaders, who were exhausted by fighting on the slippery surface, fled across the frozen lake in a state of panic, pursued by the Novgorod cavalry. It seems that the ice breaking under their heavy armour and the drowning of the Teutonic Knights were Eisenstein's own invention for his film *Aleksandr Nevskiï*. In any case there was mass slaughter of the Germans.

'The outcome of their defeat was that the

Crusaders never mounted another campaign eastward and the Teutonic order abandoned by treaty all territorial claims over Russian lands. It defined a permanent border dividing Western Catholicism from Eastern Orthodoxy. One hundred and thirty years later the Orthodox Church canonised Alexander Nevsky.'

'When did the Teutonic Order disappear?' asked Elwira. 'Was it at the Battle of Grünwald?'

'The answer to your question is: just before the Second World War. But it was a step-by-step process that began, as you rightly say, with the Battle of Grünwald, or of Tannenberg, as the Germans call it.

'The Teutonic Knights had failed to subdue pagan Lithuania. In 1386 its Grand Duke became baptised a Catholic and married Queen Jadwiga of Poland to become King Władysław II Jagiełło of Poland. Do you know that she was only eleven years old at the time? This personal union between Poland and Lithuania, by now both Christian, made a powerful adversary for the Teutonic Knights. Although its justification ended when Lithuania had become officially Christian, the Northern Crusade continued its attacks.

'Nearly twenty-five years later, at the Battle of Grünwald in 1410, the Lithuanians and Poles defeated the Teutonic Knights, who were forced to sign a peace treaty the following year. This was a decisive victory that broke the Order's military power, yet it managed to retain most of its territories.

'The coalition even besieged Marienburg, which it never managed to capture. During our visit you will see above the fireplace of the Summer Refectory one of Jagellon's cannon balls that missed its target.

'In the sixteenth century, the Grand Master converted to Lutheranism. The Order's territory dwindled, but it lived on throughout the centuries, until Napoleon distributed its territories among his vassals.

'Grünwald-Tannenbeg has since become a symbol for Poles and Germans alike. Hitler's attitude to the Order was ambiguous. Throughout the thirties, the Nazis used the crusades of the Teutonic Knights as propaganda, presenting them as a struggle for *Lebensraum*. Though Himmler considered his *SS* to be their reincarnation, Hitler nevertheless had the Order dismantled in 1938.

'Let us go inside.'

We finally entered the Middle Castle, led by our Teutonic guide. As he strode ahead of us I imagined him clad in a black-crossed surcoat and cylindrical face armour with crossed slits for the eyes, as in Eisenstein's film.

Entering the sumptuous Palace of the Grand Master of the Knights of the Teutonic Order, we passed through the great Knights Hall into the Summer Refectory. It had been one of the audience chambers for receiving foreign dignitaries. Beneath the palm-tree column workmen were busy scrubbing the otherwise spotless white canopy crowning the fireplace. The cannon ball dating from Jagiełło's siege had narrowly missed the central pillar to become imbedded in the wall above the fireplace. Just below, across the canopy itself, another ignoramus had scribbled his *graffiti*. Using an aerosol paint he had sprayed in black over the immaculate surface

ek vidccli cgn

Back to Byzantium

How could these morons dare to deface one of the masterpieces of European architecture? I took a closer look. At the end of the string of characters I couldn't miss the Balkan *Kilr*oy's signature once again. There were the three letters, **CGN**, that I had seen written in three distinct scripts, tattooed on a girl's arm in Bosnia, sprayed on walls and heard on the radio across Bulgaria, inscribed on an icon in Macedonia, and even printed on a T-shirt in Romania. This time it was close to the other seaboard of Central Europe, the Baltic in Poland.

Intrigued and excited, I was determined to decode it and find out what it meant, if anything.

I extracted the *CGN*, leaving EK V̄IDCCLI. Part of it looked like a date in Roman numerals. Breaking it down into groups, I found

EK V̄I DCC L I. Remembering that a Roman numeral capped with a horizontal bar was multiplied by one thousand, I converted *VI* to *6,000*. The whole number thus translated into **EK 6751** in standard Hindu-Arabic notation.

But what sort of date could it be and what did EK stand for? ***Einsatz-kommand*o**, the infamous Nazi mobile killing squads? This had to be the identification number of a Nazi *Kilroy*, encoded into Roman notation. Seeing *CGN* in Bosnia, formerly part of the Axis puppet state of Croatia, was fair enough, but why transliterate it into Cyrillic in Bulgaria and even into Romanian script? But then Bulgaria, Croatia and Romania had all three been Axis powers during the Second World War. This looked like a good lead.

No, it was more like the work of young German skinhead, glorifying what he considered to be his forefathers, the Knights of the Teutonic Order. He had sprayed over the wall the initials of the nostalgic anarcho-nazi group known as **_Chaos Gruppe Nazismus._** But then what could it have to do with the *Great Idea* in Greece, that I had seen stitched on the back of a leather jerkin on the train in Romania? Perhaps I wasn't on the right track.

We spent the final evening of my brief stay in Poland at an organ recital in the cathedral of Oliwa. Sculpted wooden angels surged from the elaborate organ waving gilded trumpets and dangling tinkling bells in sync with the music beneath the rotating golden rays of the sun and the planets. An orgy of Polish *rococo*. At the end of the concert a small army of handsome young men in cassocks surrounded us. We might have been in *Ireland.*

I was due back at work in Paris in a week. My two friends and I parted company the following morning at the station in Oliwa. They returned to Warsaw while I headed for Berlin and onwards through the Netherlands to my parents' house in the southern suburbs of London.

We were arriving in West Berlin... or was it? From a distance, it looked modern, magnificent and in fact rather Western. Immense *Alexanderplatz*, with its TV tower. And then I noticed the scattered *Trabant* cars.

The train stopped at Friedrichstraße station on platform A. *GrePo's*, East German border guards, in uniforms akin to those of the Nazis with their helmets flattened out, stood fully armed two abreast every five metres along the whole length of the platform.

> Platform A was reserved for West-bound through-trains from Poland and the Soviet Union. It was separated from platforms B and C, the terminus for West Berlin trains and the platform for East German trains respectively. A glass and metal barrier divided them hermetically into distinct railway systems. Curiously, the border crossing by train through Friedrichstraße station was not allowed for members of the Allied Forces, who had to cross by car or on foot at the nearby

Back to Byzantium

Checkpoint Charlie.

Platform A was absolutely silent, no traveller daring to say a word. For everyone on the train the presence of a small army to ensure that the train was hermetically sealed was an absolute ignominy, our first clear perception of the reality of the Cold War. Even the young Poles, who had been born with it, were quietly outraged.

Five minutes later we arrived in West Berlin at the *Ostbahnhof*, where a nonchalant immigration officer dressed like an old-time cinema commissioner hardly glanced at our passports. Then back again into *sogenannte DDR*, the so-called *German Democratic Republic*. I shared a compartment with an Iraqi and his young son. For some reason, they didn't bear the same names on their passports. Fortunately, the father had a service passport. He had no German and the East German officers had no English, so I was called upon to attempt to translate the explanation of a situation that I didn't even fully understand myself. They let us through nevertheless, probably out of exasperation, and into the *Bundesrepublik*, West Germany, and, for me, on to Rotterdam, the Hook of Holland and London.

I spent the day in Rotterdam with a young Pole, who was also travelling to London by the ferry. I took him to an Indonesian restaurant for lunch, but he wasn't hungry. The Poles never seem to be hungry at the same time as *regular* people are.

> When they wake up, Poles have *śniadanie*, a large cooked breakfast with eggs and sausages. Later, sometime during the late morning they have an optional snack with toast and sandwiches called *drugie śniadanie*, the second breakfast. Poles don't usually have lunch. *Obiad*, lunch or dinner, which is the largest and only full meal of the day, is eaten in mid to late afternoon, composed of soup, followed by a main dish of meat and vegetables. Finally, for supper, sometime during

the evening, they have a *kolacja*, a light collation. To summarise, Poles have breakfast, dinner - or should you call it high tea - and supper, hence they are never ready for lunch at 1 o'clock as you are.

This Pole was an Anglophile. His English culture came exclusively from the *BBC World Service*. What a mistake and what a disappointment when he discovered London for the first time. He reacted to Parliament Square with its pompous statues of Churchill, Disraeli, Lincoln, et al: but it was just as *naff* as in Communist Poland! And the language that the British actually spoke. Cockney he had heard of, but discovering almost the whole working population of London whining what would later be known as *Estuary English* outraged him. What had happened to the *Received Pronunciation* that he had heard on the *BBC*, he asked. The British, it seemed, like Custine's Russians, imposed on the world their very own image of their nation, significantly remote from the drearier reality.

11
Transsib

Just into the New Year a thousand persons in Czechoslovakia, including the writer Václav Havel, had signed *Charter 77*, accusing Gustáv Husák's government of serious breaches of human rights. But to no effect.

In spring, after ninety-four years, the Orient Express had made its final journey from Paris to Istanbul.

The Soviet Union had just deployed its first mobile tactical *SS-20* intermediate-range missiles, each bearing three nuclear warheads, aimed at Western European cities. I was preparing to cross the Soviet Union end to end by train.

At the close of a sunny Friday afternoon in early autumn we landed in Moscow and took a quick tour of the centre on our way from Sheremetevo airport to the mammoth Hotel *Rossia*. Past the Bolshoï Theatre we drove around Dzierżyński Square, named after the founder of the *Cheka*, ancestor of the *KGB*. His statue stood in front of the *Lubïanka*, probably the world's most notorious prison and house of interrogation. You could later find the statue prostrate in the dust of *Gorkiï Park*, the very first Soviet monument to be removed from its plinth.

The following day we boarded the *Transsibirskaïa Magistral*, the Trans-Siberian Railway, at *Ïaroslavskiï* Station on the Saturday morning. I had joined an *Inturist* group from France. Patient resigned passengers from distant Soviet republics squatted on their haunches on the floor of the station amid piles of cartons and gigantic reinforced carrier bags. Here for me was the promise of Asia. A young Russian student named Konstantin, *Kostïa* to us, accompanied us as our guide. The *Rossïa* left the station at 9:45 AM for the world's longest train journey, covering a quarter of the circumference of the Globe.

Long-distance trains in the Soviet Union, including the *Transsib*, usually have three classes.

First-class, *soft* sleeper coaches, also known as *spalniye* or *luks*, have nine two-berth compartments, with a table and a reading lamp for each berth. Under each seat there is a secure compartment for storing luggage, with enough space to hide a dead body. The sliding door can be locked from the inside by a bolt on each side. A radio can be turned on and off from within the compartment.

Second-class sleeper coaches, known as *kupe*, have nine four-berth compartments, each with a table. The upper bunk can be folded away. As in *luks*, a reading lamp lights each berth. Under each seat is a secure compartment and above the upper berths is a storage area over the corridor where their occupants can store their luggage. As in *luks* compartments, you can secure the sliding door from the inside with a bolt on each side and turn the radio on and off from inside the compartment.

The third class, known as *platskartnie*, is an open-plan sleeper coach. There are no compartments. The thirty-two, or fifty-four, bunks are laid out in bays of four berths on one side, half intersecting the aisle, and bays of two berths along the wall of the coach. This is the convivial area, with its clinging smell of *shchi*, or dill-perfumed cabbage soup. It is here, so they say, that you can really get to know the Russian people. We travelled in *kupe*.

Less than an hour after our departure we were already

passing bucolic clusters of *izbas,* blue-grey paling fences enclosing kitchen gardens. Horse-drawn *telegas* waited at level crossings. These were images out of Gogol's *Dead Souls*. Then the forest began. It would stay with us on and off for six days, until long after Lake Baïkal, beyond Chita, when it gave way to the bare hills of the Chinese border.

Ten or so passenger coaches snaked ahead of ours and as many behind, not including three other service coaches for mail, radio, restaurant and kitchen.

The *Transsib* was then the only continuous route overland from Moscow to the Pacific. Still beyond the Urals no road was suitable for motor vehicles. The *Trakt*, the so-called Siberian post road from Perm to Irkutsk, was little more than a dust or mud path, depending on the season.

We were not stopping off during our train ride. On our return journey to Moscow by air from our destination, Khabarovsk, we would be spending a night or two each in Irkutsk, Bratsk and Novosibirsk, the only towns open to foreigners.

How on earth do you spend a seven day, quasi non-stop journey on a train, you ask. Eating in the more than adequate restaurant, drinking tea and Soviet *shampanskoe*, exploring the train and watching the scenery. And, of course, reading about Russia and playing chess with Russians in the corridor. Every day our guide gave us our lesson in basic Russian. But you must get rather bored, I hear you say. On the contrary, you have the delicious lingering feeling of being in limbo, in a parenthesis from your frantic working life, outside space and time. Space, across the world's most extensive land mass, with a landscape that changes almost imperceptibly. Until the Chinese border, that is, when the taiga gives way to the bald hills of Manchuria. Time, because you change time zone every day until Khabarovsk, where you are seven hours ahead of Moscow. But the clocks on the train and in all the stations along the line continue to display

Moscow time.

We couldn't really communicate with the Russians, other than by putting their king into check. The only word they all said as they shook our hands was *kontakt*, so eager were they to meet a real foreigner as they tottered boozily down our corridor under the vigilant eye of the coach *provodnitsa*. She brought us regular glasses of sweet tea, held in ornate metal *podstakaniks,* from the enormous square metal *samovar* embedded in a recess at the end of each coach. Since then I have never drunk my tea other than black and in a glass with a metal holder, but I have never again succeeded in finding the exquisite taste of that very ordinary Russian tea.

A young self-designated *German* tried to communicate with us in the corridor. He was on his way home to Karaganda, in Northern Kazakhstan. Stalin had deported them during the War from the Volga Autonomous Republic, set up at the time of Catherine II. Ethnic *Germans* at one time came to represent up to seventy per cent of the population of Karaganda. Though he had no language other than Russian he might have been a candidate for citizenship of the German Federal Republic, following the principle of *jus sanguinis*, the right of blood.

The food and drink in the restaurant were sumptuous while they lasted. But by the time we reached Irkutsk they had started to run out and the menu began to lose its variety. They didn't sell vodka on the train, but, as soon as we reached Perm at after 9:30 on the Monday morning, we bolted across the platform for the *buffet* and brought back a bottle, hidden under our jacket.

The train was running late, so all we had time to do was to visit the station forecourt and glance at the view along the fine avenue leading to the city centre. Perm, known for some time as *Molotov* until he fell into disgrace, had 900,000 inhabitants. The enormity of these Russian cities amazed me, so far off the beaten track for

Westerners like us. Until the last quarter of the nineteenth century passengers had to leave the train here to cross the Urals on sledges.

Bring old-fashioned pyjamas, said the guide book, that's how the Russians dressed during the journey. Wrong! Strolling down the platform during stops, they all wore shiny royal blue tracksuits with a thick silver stripe down the trousers, *smart as a brand-new lorry*, as they say in France. The guide books told us to take warm clothes? Wrong again! Everyone knows that temperatures in Irkutsk can reach the minus forties in winter, when the air becomes thick with frost. Fewer know that in summer they can go well above plus thirty, when the air is thick with midges. It was now October and with temperatures in the low twenties, the pines and the azure water of Lake Baïkal were reminiscent of the *Côte d'Azur*. The taiga was a mixture of conifers in their evergreen and silver birches in their deep autumn russet. It still seemed somewhat of a heresy to see Siberia without snow.

Two and a half days after our departure, early on Monday evening, we crossed the Urals in the half-light. For an hour or so we had been climbing a gentle gradient and there at the top - don't miss it! - rose the obelisk that indicated, in the absence of any geographical evidence, that we were entering Asia. But not yet Siberia, generally considered as beginning with the Omsk *oblast'*. Now at nearly 1,800 kilometres from Moscow, this point of the Urals was only just over four hundred metres above sea level.

Half an hour later we arrived in Sverdlovsk, formerly Ekaterinburg and later to become so once again. A diesel engine took over from the electric locomotive until Omsk.

At 6:30 in the morning on Tuesday our train left Omsk, pulled once again by an electric engine. We were now in Siberia, still asleep in our berths.

On Tuesday evening, well after nine o'clock we crossed the Ob into Novosibirsk, the capital of eastern Siberia, which we were to visit on our way home. The station clock still showed 6+ PM Moscow time, though the train had already travelled 3,360 kilometres. As the train gradually lost time, the stops in stations shrunk from thirty minutes to ten.

On Wednesday morning at around 11:30, after travelling 4,120 kilometres, we stopped for a few minutes at Krasnoïarsk. Looking at a colossal poster of Lenin on the platform, I thought that if there is one thing that the Soviets share with the British, it is their common obsession with the colour red.

'The Soviets are like the British, I remarked to our guide, 'They love red.'

'You are right', said Kostïa, 'and they always have. It is not a specifically Socialist phenomenon.

'You know from our last night's lesson that in Russian the word for red, *krasnii*, used to mean beautiful, today *krasivyï*, hence *Krasnaïa ploshchad'*, Red Square, or Krasnoïarsk where we are now waiting for the train to depart. In every Russian house there used to be a *krasnyï ugol*, red or beautiful corner, where the family displayed its icon. Women's traditional costumes had prominent red components, Easter eggs were died red using onion skins.

'The Bolsheviks took the colour red,

symbolising blood, associated with socialism since the two French Revolutions, for the Red flag. The Red army opposed the White in the Civil War. If you want to give pleasure to your Russian hostess or when meeting a woman at the airport, bring her red carnations, but, remember, always an odd number.'

I mused that in Britain national symbols were also red, like St George's cross, lions *rampant* for Scotland, *couchant* for England, a red dragon for Wales, and so on. British soldiers fought traditionally in red uniforms, worn by today's Guards' regiments. In nature the two symbols of Britain are the robin red breast and the red rose. Red clad huntsmen lead the chase for red foxes

Since shortly after Rowland Hill invented the world's first postage stamps in 1840, with the *Penny Black* then the *Penny Red*, post boxes in Britain have always been red throughout the reigns of successive monarchs. Royal Mail postal vans have been red since before the adoption of motor vehicles, English phone boxes since the twenties, London underground trains, trams and double-decker buses since the thirties.

Kostïa and I agreed that the Soviet and British red was not the crimson variety found in France, but a real scarlet. We both found it paradoxical for two nations where the people never wear red, but grey for Russians and Englishmen, pastel colours for Englishwomen.

A postman from Brittany was a member of our very diverse group. As he strolled up and down the platform in Krasnoïarsk in his pyjamas the train left without him. The militia examined his passport, issued by the *Prefecture* of Brest. Perhaps that is the Brest formerly known as *Brest-Litovsk*, they first thought. No problem, this was apparently a frequent event. They contacted the train, equipped, unlike those in the West, with a radio telephone. A militia man came to our compartment to get us to inventory the contents of his suitcase. They left it for him in Irkutsk, he caught the next train at the same time on the following day and joined us a day late at our destination, Khabarovsk.

One of my three compartment companions, who worked for the *SNCF*, France's national railway company, drove a train for a living, He was surprised by the *Transsib's* state-of-the-art technology, much in advance of the ones that he drove. The radio telephone in the driver's cabin particularly impressed him. So much for Western feelings of superiority!

Krasnoïarsk was the name of the territory from which the *Samoyed* dog originated. Members of my family first introduced the breed into Western Europe.

The name comes from the *Nenets* people, whom the Russians called *Samoyed*, meaning *self-eater*. They come from the Taïmyr Peninsula, on the banks of the White Sea at the northernmost part of the mainland in what is now Krasnoïarsk territory.

They called their dog *bjelkier*, or white-breeding dog. The *bjelkier* descended from the grey wolf, and the Samoyed clan shared with wolf packs a similar social structure and talent for hunting. As animists who revered the wolf they welcomed the dog into their tent to become part of their family. The dogs took part in everyday activities, as sledge dogs, guard dogs, and for hunting and herding reindeer. The Samoyed people trusted their dogs to such a degree that they used them as nursemaids, to sleep with their children, keep them warm and mind them when the parents were outside.

The Russian royal family first brought them to

Europe as pets in the 19th century. After the October Revolution, the Bolsheviks, associating them with royalty, massacred the dogs.

For polar expeditions, both Nansen in the Arctic, and Amundsen to the South Pole, used *bjelkiers*, few of which survived. They were perfectly adapted to arctic conditions, not only for their physical characteristics, but especially for their endurance, their drive to work and will to please their master.

My great uncle and aunt were responsible for creating today's Samoyed dog. A zoologist and timber merchant, he brought back a puppy to England from an expedition to Archangel. It was brown with white spots, but through interbreeding with others from Siberia they succeeded in creating today's all-white breed.

The original dog was named *Sobaka*, meaning *dog* in Russian. It is easy to imagine my great uncle asking a *Nenets*, using sign language, what the dog was called, to receive the answer *eto sobaka, it's a dog*. To this day one of each generation of Samoyeds has borne the sacred name of *dog*. The name of the breed, and of the people, is pronounced *samma-yed* (unfortunately due to his mishearing of the correct Russian pronunciation, his descendants all insist wrongly on calling the dog a *sammid* and will invariably *correct* your appropriate pronunciation).

As we cruised through the taiga we stopped in rustic towns, where *babushka*s sold their pies, sausages, onions, boiled potatoes and red cabbage on the platform.

On Thursday morning, our sixth day, at nearly 5,200 kilometres from Moscow, we arrived in Irkutsk at 8:45 in the morning. Then for the rest of the day we followed the south bank of Lake Baïkal.

To get an idea of the distance we had covered by train

we made regular geographical comparisons. The width of the south bank of the lake was equivalent to the distance from Bordeaux to Toulouse, or London to Plymouth, its length, top to bottom, Paris to Toulouse, or Edinburgh to London. By the time we reached Irkutsk we reckoned that since Moscow we had covered by train more than the distance from Stockholm to Khartoum. Later, at the end of our journey in Khabarovsk, we would have done Paris to Cape Town, or crossed the Atlantic and back.

Until the completion of the *Transsib*, to reach Moscow from the Far East it had been quicker to cross the Pacific Ocean, North America and the Atlantic Ocean than attempt to travel east by roadless land.

To complete the *Transsib*, whose construction had begun in different sections starting from both ends, the Circum-Baïkal railway was finished in 1904. Until then the journey could be completed in various ways, depending on the season. For the five months of frost they had been able to transport goods and passengers by sledge across the frozen surface of Lake Baïkal.

During the warmer seasons rolling stock had crossed the lake on ferries. Up to twenty-four coaches were loaded onto the ferry for a four-hour long crossing. In the last decade of the nineteenth century an ice breaker named *Baïkal* had been built in Newcastle upon Tyne and transported to the lake in kit form. After its construction, they dismantled it and moved it with enormous difficulty to the shore of the lake, where they reassembled it. On the way, it got held up for a two-year-long delay in Krasnoïarsk while awaiting completion of a bridge. Though designed as an ice-breaker to penetrate ice up to one metre fifty thick, when it nevertheless became ice-bound the passengers had to complete their crossing by sledge.

It was during the Russo-Japanese war, when it was vital to supply reinforcements after the Japanese attack on the Russian Pacific fleet, that the two ice-breakers became immobilised. Tracks were laid across the frozen lake. During the test run the one-and-a-half-metre-thick ice broke over an unsuspected warm spring and the engine went under. They dismantled it and men and horses dragged it across the ice, while the army crossed on sledges.

At nearly six o'clock that Thursday afternoon we reached Ulan Ude, capital of the Buryat Autonomous Soviet Socialist Republic, where the line branches off to Ulan Bator in Outer Mongolia and on to Beijing. Travelling the whole width of Asia seeing only fair-haired blue-eyed Russians, we were eager to see some exotic faces. No luck! Three almond-eyed Buryat girls smiled at us from the platform, but all the other inhabitants had European faces.

Unbeknown to us, fast asleep, on Friday morning, our seventh day, we stopped briefly at Chita at four o'clock. We were now 6,250 kilometres and six hours ahead of Moscow. Until 1916, when the Trans-Siberian railway was completed entirely on Russian soil, the route from Chita to Vladivostok had passed through Harbin in Manchuria.

The train ran through an immense graveyard, not for elephants, but just as romantically lugubrious. For tens of minutes and as many kilometres, spooky, grey carcasses of steam locomotives and tenders from the thirties and forties closed in on our train. There were said to be many such dumps across Siberia and the Soviet Far East. With such a huge country, why bother to keep it tidy?

The *Rossiïa* was now approaching the Chinese border and from the train we saw what looked like military preparations. Here was evidence of the current antagonism between the Soviet Union and the Peoples Republic of China. For a good hour we watched through the left-hand window almost uninterrupted queues of tanks and armoured vehicles. Then the train finally emerged from the taiga to reveal a solitary horseman riding over the bald hills of Manchuria. We had now entered the seventh time zone from Moscow. The clocks in the stations and on the train still displayed Moscow time.

At nearly 2:30 on Saturday morning the train pulled into Birobidzhan for a five-minute stop. I climbed down from the train and placed my two feet on the platform, where the name was displayed in both Russian and Yiddish alphabets. The train was running even later and no time was left for tourism in the middle of the night in Stalin's would-be Israel, the administrative centre of the *Jewish Autonomous Oblast'*, where Jews by now represented only seven per cent of a population of 180,000.

Later the same morning, on Saturday at the beginning of our eighth day, we alighted in Khabarovsk at 5:15, nearly three quarters of an hour late. The clock on the station platform displayed Moscow time of 10:15 PM from the previous evening. The *Rossiïa* had covered 8,400 kilometres. We would have loved to continue the extra six hundred or so kilometres due south to Vladivostok, but, as a military zone, it was closed to foreigners and even to Russians. You could go further if you were heading for Yokohama via Nakhodka, and then only by a special train.

12
Siberia

We moved into our hotel room in Khabarovsk for our first serious wash since Moscow, albeit in a full-sized washbasin. A bearded gentleman reminiscent of Solzhenitsyn played chess on the landing outside our room, taking on all comers. Watching a game, I made the mistake of tut-tutting at his adversary's poor move. After mating him in a couple of moves he gestured to me to take his place for the ultimate humiliation, beating me three times in less than ten moves. I had been playing Russians for a week in the corridor of the *Transsib*, but none of my adversaries had been sober.

We set out on foot to discover the city. It was tempting to stare at the long queues of would-be shoppers standing patiently with their string *filets* on the off chance of finding something unusual for sale. It reminded me of holding my mother's hand in a seemingly interminable queue outside the butcher's shop in post-war Britain. The shelves of these shops, appropriately named *Gastronom* or *Delikates*, were desolately empty. With a degree of shame and embarrassment at our *voyeurism* we moved on.

As we strolled down the leafy avenues of this airy city we imagined that we could smell the air of the Pacific Ocean. Absurd, since the sea was still four hundred kilometres away, but after 8,400 kilometres on the train it didn't seem so much. But there was the vast Amur River, which, after forming the border between Russia and China, joined the Ussuri in Khabarovsk to head northwards. A huge square crowned by a gigantic war memorial overlooked the river, flanked by elegant riverside promenades.

It was only when our *Aeroflot* plane took off to take us back to Irkutsk on our return journey that we discovered the real splendour of the Amur, meandering in arabesque loops along the Manchurian border.

I had spent part of my time on the train reading Custine. Astolphe, Marquis de Custine, travelled in Russia for three months in the summer of 1839 and published his *letters* four years later.

You wonder how what was at the time Custine's nightmare caricature could become posthumously so accurate a description of the reality of Stalin's Russia a hundred years later, or even of Brezhnev's today. He foresaw a revolution in Russia that would be more terrible than the French revolution.

But Custine had already based his preconceived ideas on conversations before he even set out on his journey, or at least, as someone said, between the stage coach terminus and the inn. It reminded me somewhat of the arrogant ethnocentrism that one has come to associate with *Parisianism*. He initially despised not only the political system, the Orthodox Church, but in fact everything he saw, from the people to the architecture. He was obsessed with other countries' vulgarity as compared to the good taste of his own.

Compare Custine's chronicle of his three months stay in Russia with that of his contemporary, Matija Mažuranić, who travelled through Ottoman Bosnia for eighteen months during the same period, astride the year 1840. A young explorer from Croatia, Mažuranić described the life of Bosnjak Muslims that he encountered, at significant risk to his safety, during his unauthorised visit. I was reminded of the very old tale about the Frenchman, the Englishman, and the German, who each undertook a study of the camel.

You may remember that the Frenchman took

the metro and spent an afternoon at the Vincennes Zoo. On returning home he wrote a witty essay full of his observations. The Englishman travelled with his tent to the Sahara to spend a couple of years in the desert, returning with a rather unstructured volume containing some discoveries of real scientific interest. The German, who despised both the superficiality of the Frenchman and the Englishman's lack of metaphysical thought, shut himself up in his study to reflect on the real essence of the camel. The story says that he is still there.

Custine visited only two cities, Saint-Petersburg and Moscow, while Mažuranić travelled throughout Ottoman Bosnia. Custine wrote his letters, which he never sent, to a hypothetical reader. Mažuranić's mission was to explore Ottoman Bosnia and write a report for his brother, evaluating the readiness of its inhabitants to rebel against the Ottomans and join an *Illyrian* kingdom, a precursor of Yugoslavia, unifying all the Southern Slavs.

Custine despised Pushkin, although he had apparently never read him and by his own admission had never learnt the Russian language. Meanwhile, during his short stay, Mažuranić learnt to speak Turkish far better than most Bosnjaks.

Custine found the Russian people habitually filthy, despite their occasional outward elegance, the men drunk to oblivion and the women repulsive. He despised the borrowed architecture of Saint-Petersburg, magnificent decoration but without taste, which merely aped Western classicism. He hated its complete regularity and symmetry, opposed to Man's natural instincts. Ten years later, Haussmann would begin building modern Paris, one of the world's most uniform and rectilinear cities. He also forgot that it was Italian architects who built both Saint-Petersburg and the Moscow Kremlin.

It is easy to compare Custine's prejudice with the open mind of Mažuranić. It also compares unfavourably with that of Lady Mary Wortley Montagu during her stay in Ottoman Turkey and of Voltaire in England, both a hundred years previously. Custine's time was no longer the Enlightenment. The French Revolution and Bonaparte's conquests had come and gone, imposing French Revolutionary values on almost the whole of Europe. It was also the beginning of colonialism.

In all fairness, Custine did moderate his views somewhat during his short stay, especially the after visiting Moscow, which he considered very picturesque, a monstrous city with the *décor* of a theatre.

Custine's main obsession throughout his *letters* is despotism, which he claimed maintained the whole of society from top to bottom in a state of permanent fear of deportation. In Russia fear had paralysed thought since Ivan the Terrible, generating a discipline of silence which every man learned from birth.

For Custine, the Tsar was not only God's representative on Earth, his creative power was greater than that of God. God can determine only the future, whereas the Tsar, like Stalin, could also rewrite the past. Two nations existed, Russia as it was and the Russia they would like to show the world.

He forgot both Louis XIV and *Jacobinism* when criticising Russian centralism of Nicolas I. France only fifty years previously had its own despotic system, with arbitrary imprisonment in the Bastille through *lettres de cachet* and later the *Terreur* of the Revolution. While condemning serfdom in Russia it slipped his mind that slavery in the French colonies had by then still not been finally abolished. After a first attempt under the Revolution, re-established by Bonaparte, it would be definitively abolished nine years later. Britain had done so only the previous year.

Custine, it seems, wanted *to have his cake and eat it too*, the *Ancien Régime*, but tempered by the French Revolution.

As a result, he said, Russia was a country that you could visit only with a guide, where everyone conspired to mislead the traveller. Much vaunted Russian hospitality consisted of making one's guest happy at the expense of sincerity, with whatever you visited being politely shown, or rather hidden. They would provide answers to everything that you didn't ask to avoid you learning what you really wanted to know. He concluded that the traveller to Russia saw nothing. Escorted, he saw too much, which amounts to the same. The Russians, he claimed, were still convinced of the efficiency of the lie.

During my journey on the *Transsib*, at the time of Brezhnev, his theories still seemed to apply to some degree, particularly the hiding of reality beneath a camouflage of unasked-for statistics, while *Inturist* kept its guests constantly amused. The attitude of the Soviet people that we brushed against was that of a certain cynicism and wheeling and dealing to survive. Psychiatric hospitals were again in similar oppressive use to what Custine had described 150 years previously.

Inturist also overfed us. On each plane hop they gave us two to three full cooked breakfasts: at our hotel on departure, again at the airport and finally on arrival at our destination. At each airport the pervasive smell of dill assailed us. The Soviet people may have been struggling on buckwheat *kasha*, but we ate in style. Everything was true that I had heard about Siberian women, the bronzed statuesque blonds who served us in every restaurant.

We flew via Irkutsk into Bratsk for one night to visit *Bratskaïa GES*, then still the world's largest hydroelectric station, built across the world's deepest artificial reservoir. 'I am fed up with this lousy dam', said Kostïa, our young Russian guide. Despite its 180,000 inhabitants Bratsk felt like a frontier town dug out of the larch forest, with pinkish Soviet apartment blocks, a cellulose factory, our hotel and little else.

In the factory, paunchy balding managers in suits stood at the controls or walked about supervising, while the *popular masses* in overalls, meticulously made up for the next Saturday night ball, their hair hidden under elegant chiffon scarves, did all the heavy work. The men amongst us did their best not to ogle at the stylish beauty of the bricklayers and the street sweepers bent over their ridiculously short besom brooms in all the cities that we visited.

Piotr Mukhanov, a writer and former captain of a guards' regiment, had been deported to the Bratsk settlement after the Decembrist uprising. He described it as the most awful place he had ever seen, far worse than any of the nine prisons where he had been incarcerated. I understood how he felt.

After dinner in the only hotel, we got talking to an intense, elegant young Russian woman at a neighbouring table. She was, she said, first violin in the Novosibirsk symphony orchestra. They had just returned from a trip to Ïakutsk, in the land of *permafrost*. 'If you think Bratsk is bad, you should try Ïakutsk', she said. Her hands trembling at her temerity and fear of the consequences, she accepted our offer of *shampanskoe*, which the waiter brought to our room.

The following morning we flew back to Irkutsk.

Back to Byzantium

'My name is Natasha', she said, as the *Inturist* guides announced each time as they greeted us in the tour bus in every city. 'Irkutsk was one of the main towns where the Decembrist families settled. The Decembrist revolt took place on 26th December 1825, hence the name.'

'How did it come about', asked one of my compartment companions.

Natasha didn't seem to know very much about it, so I looked it up in my guide book.

Tsar Alexander I had died and Constantine, the first in line of his brothers, not intending to reign, had abdicated just after receiving the oath of allegiance. The revolt began when a group of officers refused to swear allegiance to his younger brother, Nicolas I, who had seized the throne.

One of the results of being around the common people in the army during the Napoleonic wars was that many aristocrats had come to reject the *regime*. They aimed to set up a constitutional monarchy and abolish serfdom. Nine years before the uprising, officers of the guard had formed a political society which, though banned, had remained secretly active in two groups, the northern in Saint-Petersburg and the southern in the Ukraine.

On 26th December 1825 in Saint-Petersburg the group of officers at the head of three thousand men refused the oath of allegiance to the new Tsar, Nicolas I. After attempts at conciliation, Nicolas ordered the cavalry to charge and then the artillery to open fire, thus ending the revolt. The southern group was defeated a year later and the leaders who were still alive were sent to trial with those from the north. Five were hanged, twice, because the ropes broke the first time. The rest were sentenced to banishment in Siberia and the

Far East, deprived of their titles, estates and children, some sentenced to hard labour, fifteen or so to exile for settlement.

Some settled in the region of Irkutsk. For members of the nobility the journey to Siberia is said to have taken place in a certain spirit of elation to be meeting with authentic Russians. It was much harder for the rank and file, who travelled fettered in chains, whipped like common criminals.

Prince Sergeï Volkonskiï, a former major general from the *Patriotic War* of 1812, was deported to a village near Irkutsk, where he worked with the peasants. The largest group, including Prince Sergeï Trubetskoï, was sent to a prison in the region of Chita, initially for hard labour, but which turned out to involve minimal work, done instead by criminal convicts.

Many wives, including Maria Volkonskaïa and Ekaterina Trubetskaïa, heroically followed their husbands into exile by sledge in appalling conditions over more than five thousand kilometres. They chose to renounce their children, their privileges and live in extreme hardship in support of their husbands. Volkonskiï and Trubestkoï, who were later allowed to live in Irkutsk, had been rich, but most exiles were poor and many didn't survive.

The people of Siberia, including the local administrators, treated the Decembrists with sympathy and respect. They considered them to be heroes, persecuted due to their loyalty to the people. The Decembrists had significant influence over life in Siberia from both economic and cultural points of view. As farmers, they implemented innovative agricultural methods and developed new crops. They set up schools, academies, libraries for themselves, for native

Siberians and even for women, triggering an intellectual awakening and becoming a permanent *intelligentsia* in Siberia, replacing the previous corrupt and despotic elites.

After thirty years of exile, when Alexander II acceded to the throne in 1856, he pardoned the Decembrists and restored their rights. Many chose to stay in Siberia, where they had built a new life, with the feeling of being free men. Those who returned contributed to the reforms concluding with the abolition of serfdom in 1861, becoming an inspiration for the revolutions of 1905 and 1917.

Irkutsk is situated by the Angara River, which has its source in Lake Baïkal. We drove south-east for an hour or so to the shores of the lake. To our immense surprise we discovered azure water overhung by vivid green conifers beneath a cloudless sky. It might have been the Mediterranean until we dabbled our toes in it. With a maximum depth in parts of 488 metres, Lake Baïkal contains alone one sixth of all the fresh water in the world.

Inturist had prepared the customary feast for lunch, with caviar, sturgeon and vodka, in a large hunting *datcha* built from logs in a clearing in the forest. Siberia represents more than seventy per cent of the territory of Russia and ten per cent of the surface of the Globe. They said that each man, woman and child in Siberia could sit down in his very own hectare of *taiga*, among the evergreen pines, spruces, larches and the deciduous silver birches, aspens and alders. We sat down in what felt like our own private hectare in the warm sunlight filtered by the trees. At the end of the day the most Soviet of vessels, a hydrofoil, sped us back to our hotel along the Angara River through the setting sun.

Enthusiastic builders had constructed wooden houses in Irkutsk with lace-carved window frames in pastel colours. The problem was that, due to subsidence and probably to superficially melted *permafrost*, the first-floor had now become the ground floor and the ground floor had disappeared into the street to become the basement.

That evening they took us to the spectacular Moscow State Circus on Ice. Two teams of brown bears on skates bearing hockey sticks played ice hockey to the applause of the paws of the reservists.

Our next hop, Novosibirsk, the third largest city in Russia, is the capital of Western Siberia. Two bridges span the river Ob, nearly a kilometre wide in the city. Our guides, probably thinking that not much in the city could interest a Westerner, took us on to a boat ride on the Ob and to a Wedding Palace to listen to the canned *Beautiful Blue Danube* waltz during the ten-minute ceremony. Brezhnev had recently implemented Khrushchëv's plan to secularise the Soviet Union by creating pseudo-religious venues and rites for events like weddings and christenings. Lenin was ubiquitous not only in statues and with his relic mausoleum, but also on stained-glass windows and as an infant on badges like a Christ-child.

Akademgorodok, the Academic City, culminated our visit. In the mid-fifties the Soviet Government had created it from scratch in the middle of the *taiga*, dug a large artificial lake within the Ob River and imported scientists and researchers from Moscow and Leningrad. The Soviet Academy of Sciences had built, ensconced in the woods, sixteen research units on a human scale, certainly atypical in Siberia, where big is beautiful. The living and working conditions there were among the best in the country. After the demise of the Soviet Union, due to lack of investment, this magnificent scientific village would fall on hard times, with some of the researchers reduced to planting kitchen gardens around the research centres to get enough to eat.

It was there that I discovered *kvas*. A small yellow tanker dispensed it from a tap at the back of the tubular tank. They said that it was brewed from fermented black rye bread and hence contained very small quantities of alcohol. This fizzy drink is in my opinion superior to Western *cola*.

We flew back to Moscow, landing at Domodedovo airport and took up our quarters again at the Hotel Rossiïa, where we had spent our first night. Our guide Kostïa asked me to accompany him on an errand. We got into a taxi together. With my naïve tourist's perception, I had begun to say something positive about Socialism when he pressed his finger to my lips. Taxi drivers were notorious informers. We arrived at the *Berïozka*, the foreign currency store, the only place where you could buy decent consumer goods. He had accumulated a thick wad of US dollars from his black-market foreign exchange transactions with members of our group, but could not spend them himself. He got me to make the purchase for him.

For the final evening he suggested a farewell dinner in one of the nine restaurants of the Hotel Rossiïa, the World's largest outside Las Vegas. We dined on caviar, sturgeon and other *zakuski*, hot and cold. I drank on my own a standard bottle of *Stolichnaya* vodka and a full-sized one of white wine. The dinner was momentous, as were the immediate and longer-term effects. Getting foreign tourists drunk was apparently a classic procedure. We left the dining room to watch the changing of the guard outside Lenin's tomb in Red Square, five minutes away on foot. My friend and I tottered the *diagonale du fou*. 'Don't fall over'; said our guide. 'As long as you remain standing the *militsia* will not bother you. Fall down and they will arrest you for drunkenness.' As I later discovered, the Hotel Rossiïa also housed a police station with its own cells, situated just behind the hairdressing *salon*. By a drunkard's miracle we managed to find our way back to the appropriate entrance to the hotel, which had at least four on each side of the rectangle, take the correct lift and succeed in sliding our key in the right door. We spent most of the night on our knees together around the same toilet bowl.

The following day they drove us to Sheremetyevo airport, where we boarded an *Aeroflot* flight to return to Paris. I spent the flight retching, which didn't seem to bother my neighbour in the least or harm his appetite. This archetypal Englishmen, totally imperturbable, continued to eat his lunch with relish while I puked. 'Next time you drink too much vodka you should chase it with tea or mineral water', he said quietly after I apologised. This is advice that I have always followed since. We landed at Orly airport in Paris, where I discovered for the first time the umbilical corridor that today connects aircraft to the terminal. Something was wrong. The whole of the rubber non-slip surface of the corridor rippled as though a herd of cats were struggling to get out from underneath. This was probably the closest I have ever got to *delirium tremens*. With three days left before going back to work I stayed in bed.

A couple of weeks later I met for dinner with my former travel companions to drink vodka, this time in moderation, and share photos. Looking closely at a shot of the splendid poster of Lenin on the station platform in Krasnoïarsk, I discovered what I had thought was part of his necktie.

No, it was the stencilled silhouette of a Byzantine cathedral. It looked familiar, but – of course – it was the tattooed *flower* on the arm of my friend Lili at the

Back to Byzantium

Turist biro in Sarajevo, this time the right way up! Beneath it were printed the same three letters, this time in Cyrillic, **ЦГН**. Perhaps it did represent the *Church of Lord Nicolas* after all, but why on a poster of Lenin?

13
Algiers

In the following autumn the papal conclave would elect 58-year-old Karol Wojtyła as pope under the name of John Paul II, the first non-Italian for more than 450 years. When I announced it to my Polish violinist friend Elwira, who was staying at my house at the time, she refused to believe me.

In the New Year, Algeria had nationalised five French petroleum companies. President Houari Boumedienne, already terminally ill, was to die at the end of the year. I was spending my summer holiday in Algiers.

An Algerian named Omar worked in our company. His sister, a German-language teacher working in Algiers, was getting married. As the eldest son and with his father no longer alive, he had inherited the role of head of the family and had to return there to organise the wedding. He invited a young French colleague and myself to come and stay with his family and keep him company during the turbulence. Omar was a Kabyle.

The Kabyle population numbered five million in Algeria and a million or so in France. While the Ottomans had left them more-or-less alone, it was the French who confiscated their land to give it to the *pied-noir* colonists. The Kabyles had been at the forefront of the fight for independence from the French.

Two years after independence, however, tensions arose with the central government, partly due to the Arabisation campaign. In their search for their national identity, Kabyles had three options to choose from. They could become a respected though specific component of the Algerian nation or, alternatively, strive for a greater Berber nation covering the whole of the Maghreb, or else finally consider Algeria itself to be a pre-Arab nation. Their language, Tamazight, would only become a national, though not yet an official, language more than a quarter century after my visit.

It is curious that in the struggle against an occupying power so many nations should have chosen a woman to lead them: Boudicca, Joan of Arc, Bouboulina in Greece and, more recently, Dolores Ibárruri, *La Passionaria*, in Franquist Spain. Kabylia was no exception.

Lalla Fadhma n'Soumer was an important figure of the Algerian resistance movement during the first years of the French colonial rule of Algeria in the mid nineteenth century. At the age of twenty-four she led an insurrection to victory against a French army that was vastly superior in numbers and equipment. Inspired by her dreams of extermination and slavery and her belief in her divine destiny, she became known as the Joan of Arc of the Djurdjura. An enormous French contingent finally defeated her and she died in captivity at the age of thirty-three.

I took the boat alone from Marseille. Charles De Gaulle had said, when Algeria was still not only a French colony but considered to be an integral part of France, 'from Dunkirk to Tamanrasset (in the south Sahara) the Mediterranean is a river'. Perhaps not a river, but it did seem like a big placid pond. Algeria had by now been independent for sixteen years. The crossing took twenty-one hours, docking in Algiers mid-afternoon. I shared a cabin with a polite, austere Arab gentleman.

Disembarking, still unstable on my sea legs, I took a

stroll while waiting for my luggage. Beneath the arcades along the seafront I got into conversation with a young clean-cut Arab, who invited me to have coffee with him in the city centre. The streets all bore new names, those of heroes of the *FLN*, the National Liberation Front, but everyone continued to use the old French names, which they pronounced *à l'algérienne*.

Algiers had a strange atmosphere. The look of the city, apart from the Casbah and some pseudo-Moorish constructions like the Central Post Office was traditionally French, with its Haussmann-style buildings and its waterfront clone of the arcades of the *rue de Rivoli*. And yet it felt mysterious and alien, with the crowds of young men idling along the pavements under the sub-tropical trees, the washing hanging down over the Second-Empire balconies and, especially, the veiled women in *haïks*, the traditional off-white sack-like robe. Young Algerians came to call them *Kinder Surprise*, because no-one knew what was underneath.

I took a taxi up the long hill to the formerly French middle-class suburb of Old Quba and located the house with its white wall surrounding a traditional courtyard.

My friend Omar's mother was a *hajji*, who had made the pilgrimage to Mecca a couple of years previously. When she went outdoors into the street she dressed traditionally in a *haïk*, her face covered by the veil. But she spoke good French and dressed as a European at home. The presence of non-Muslims in her kitchen did not bother her.

As in many developing countries, people here were polyglot, unlike those in most Western *culturally-developed* countries, where the majority are monolingual. The linguistic level may not have been high, but they managed to communicate. This family was its microcosm.

My friend Omar spoke Kabyle with his mother, French with his sister and Algerian dialectal Arabic with the younger of his two brothers, interspersed with French words, expressions and even whole sentences. The elder of his brothers, who had begun assiduously attending the Mosque, attempted to speak so-called *modern* Qur'anic Arabic, albeit without much success. No need for them to address other members of his family by their names. The language that they spoke identified their interlocutor.

We dined in the courtyard or in the kitchen, the only room that I saw. I sat at the table with Omar and his brother, while his sister served us. The salt cellar stood on the table at a short arm's length from his brother. 'Pass me the salt!' he said in French to his sister, who crossed the room, edged round the table, picked up the salt cellar and gave it to him without batting an eyelid.

My French colleague and I slept in an empty flat in a modern block, built on what looked like waste land. Not really, but the inhabitants didn't use dustbins. They just threw their rubbish out of the windows onto the ground below.

For the first week we went every evening to Omar's mother's house for dinner. That was until her second son, who had found religion, returned home on leave. He was afraid that the neighbours might learn that Christians had seen his mother without a veil, he said. So, reluctantly we gave up going to the house to eat.

I realised on the first day that, during my stay in Algiers, I would be spending it with men only. That was fine and it was fun. Almost every day we went off to the beach together, all seven of us, in a couple of beat-up cars. Each of their mothers or sisters had prepared an Algerian dish, I bought the wine, and we had a colossal picnic at the beach.

Girls in bikinis sunbathed at the beach. Later in the afternoon they got into their car and put on Western summer dresses. We happened to be driving to the same destination in the car behind. When the girls approached their village, on went the off-white *haïk* and the veil on top of the bikinis and summer dresses. From bikini to Muslim veil. It seemed again to be less a question of morality than of what the neighbours would say.

Back to Byzantium

Sitting outside on the kerbside one morning during the interminable wait for my friends, someone warned me not to get too close to the door into a courtyard. Though shut, the neighbour might think that I was trying to have a peep at his wife or daughter.

The following morning I was sitting again on the kerb, when an apparently calm young man whom I knew by sight ran into the butcher's shop and reappeared armed with a meat cleaver. The *elder brothers* managed to calm him down before he slit the throat of his rival in love.

One of my new friends invited us all to lunch at his house for a sumptuous variety of delicious exotic dishes: very spicy tripe, *bouzellouf*, sheep's head, and, strangest of all, beef stewed with pears. After he had hidden the women away, his pre-adolescent sisters served us at table.

He was getting married too, he said, showing me a small identity photo of his future bride. She looked pretty, I said, but was she fun to be with? 'I don't know', he replied. 'I haven't met her. I'll ask my mother.'

We went out to a well-known restaurant along the coast specialising in spicy king prawns. Every table was full and people were queuing outside. A very young member of our group turned out to be the youngest hero of the war of independence, having served as a messenger for the *FLN*. As a child, the French military had always overlooked him. We jumped the queue and the *restaurateur* moved the clients already seated in the window elsewhere to vacate the best table for us. Being a war hero or one of his friends earned you privileges;

FLN members and their offspring still controlled the state administration and public companies. In honour of the Pan-African Games, held in Algiers that summer, the official French-language daily, El Moudjahid, published a whole page in English, or rather a kind of English, which I understood not without difficulty. An acquaintance of mine in Paris, a gifted tri-lingual interpreter, had left Algeria to find work. Without the right politics or contacts, he had not succeeded in finding a decent job at home.

One wondered how a country with such vast potential, natural resources, a highly-educated elite and a young growing population, could fail. And yet…

My generation of Algerians spoke their local dialect. Their schooling under the colonial system had all been in French. France had published a decree in 1938 defining Arabic as a foreign language. Unable to read or write in Arabic, my friends expressed their admiration for my efforts to read my language manual.

> But what makes Arabic so difficult?
>
> First you have to decide which version of the language you want to learn. Either to learn Algerian Arabic, a dialect that is generally spoken with different variants throughout the Maghreb. It cannot be written, despite attempts made to transcribe it into Arabic characters. Not a bona-fide language, you may say. And yet I studied it both on an official course financed by the City of Paris and even purchased the *Linguaphone* method in the UK. Every time I tried to practise in Paris with someone I assumed to be an Arab, he always turned out to be a Kabyle, who was not fluent enough to help me.
>
> Or else you learn classical Arabic, or what is now known as modern Arabic, an updated version of the language of the Qur'an, which is written, but that no one actually spoke at that time in North Africa except clerics. The difficulty for foreigners learning modern Arabic resides in identifying words precisely enough to look them up in a dictionary. In modern Arabic dictionaries, words are not listed directly in alphabetical order. They are compiled in groups having the same stem. The stem is the three-or four-letter radical of a verb of which every word is composed. Learning to extract the radical took me a good year. But they say that it is only the first twenty-five years that are difficult…

Back to Byzantium

Every time the news was broadcast on television my friends' eyes glazed over. They couldn't understand it. It was only when something came on in French, usually a film, that they breathed a sigh of relief.

'Just imagine', said one of my friends. 'We can't even understand our own national television news. Our country may have become independent, but it's not easy for us to feel part of it. We no longer go down into town except when it's absolutely necessary. We feel at home up here on our hill with people like ourselves, of our generation, who speak dialect and French. We never learnt modern Arabic and we're probably too old to learn. Anyway, it's not our language.'

After deposing Ben Bella, Algeria's first president, in a blood-less coup, Colonel Boumedienne had enforced teaching of classical, so-called *modern*, Arabic progressively throughout the school system over the previous twelve years.

'Why did the government impose *modern* Qur'anic Arabic as the official language instead of the colloquial Arabic that everyone speaks?' I asked.

'For all sorts of reasons. Firstly, you know that our President received most of his education in classical Arabic in *madrasas*, Qur'anic schools, and theological universities. But in my opinion that is not the main reason. He believes that independent Algeria has two enemies. The enemy from without, France, the former coloniser, and French, the language of our nation's cultural and economic elite. But he also sees an enemy from within, our Berber population from Kabylia, and their language Tamazight.

'Classical Arabic has never been the language

of the Algerians and yet the Ministry of Education claims that our spoken language is just a degenerate version of *real* Arabic.'

'Isn't that the case?' I asked.

'Maybe so, but some modern researchers claim that its origin is Punic – remember the Punic Wars – which has been Arabized. In any case Tamazight is the original language of the Maghreb.

'Have you read anything by our national novelist and poet, Kateb Yacine? He has been an inspiration for resistance to French colonisation since the forties.'

I hadn't.

'He said, in one of his famous *bon mots*, that he had learnt French in order to inform the French that he was not French. Though he was himself a Berber, trilingual in Tamazight, *dialectal* Arabic and French, all his writing was in French, a language that he claimed to be one of Algeria's spoils of the war of independence. Faced with forced Arabisation, he had asked rhetorically if he was already an Arab, then why Arabize him, and if he was not an Arab, then why Arabize him?

'What they are teaching in schools is Oriental Arabic, quite alien to our culture. Look at our friends here in Old Quba. I'm an Arab and Omar is a Kabyle. Where's the problem? They want to turn us all into Egyptians. You know how they teach the young generation to speak *modern* Arabic? Nobody speaks it here, so they have imported teachers from Egypt, Iraq and Syria. Most of them are terrible teachers. Their method is limited to rote learning of verses from the Qur'an.

'The phenomenon is typical of many new nations after decolonisation. They behave with their own minorities in the same way as their former colonisers behaved with them. The Algerian government has reproduced French *Jacobinism*, applied here not just to the Berber minority, but to the whole population. Our President has decided to eliminate the three languages of our country, Tamazight, *dialectal* Arabic, and French, and ensure the monopoly on power of the *FLN* under the guise of pan-Africanism.'

Every year at the time of Ramadan some of my new friends came to Paris to be free to eat and drink alcohol without hindrance. A middle-aged French woman ran the only bar in this Algerian suburb, the tables filled every evening with men drinking insipid beer. Some evenings we sat with young men in a cadaver of a car, drank beer and nibbled on pure pork *saucisson*, while they repeated voluptuously 'This is a sin, this is a sin'.

I have always found Algerians fun to be with, particularly the Kabyles. So soon after independence, the Algerians gave my French colleague a hard time. He could do nothing right. I, however, could do nothing wrong. First, the British had never colonised *them*, and second, most of them had already worked as pickpockets at Victoria Station, stealing from French tourists. I was popular.

The difference between the Kabyles and the Arabs was particularly apparent on the beach. The Arabs became tanned after one afternoon in the sun. The Kabyles, with their fair skins and lapis-lazuli eyes, were an object of mockery, getting badly sunburnt partly due to their home-concocted suntan lotion, based on olive oil and crushed tomato. 'You tan, you tan, you tan, but you don't go brown', remarked a young Arab with typical Algerian wit.

I met my friend Omar's sister and her future husband, a doctor. She had taught and lived on her own for several years in Germany and, she said, she wanted to continue teaching after the wedding. 'We'll see about that later', he replied. A year later Omar would return to Algiers to set his sister free, whom her doctor husband had shut away, refusing to let her out of the house.

I had always known Omar in France as someone fully integrated into Western society. So I found it disconcerting to see him change by the day into a traditional Algerian. He realised that it was happening and we even talked about it together. Atavism, he said. With his responsibilities as head of the family and under pressure from the environment, he couldn't resist. As soon as he returned to Paris he became once again the person that I knew.

The wedding took place. The whole town was invited to the wedding breakfast, which lasted all day, but by shift. They had granted me a twenty-minute mid-afternoon shift. I arrived, gulped down my couscous and just had time to wrap my traditional honey cakes, *baklava* and *kadaif*, in a napkin to finish outside and make way for the next shift. An already-nibbled small green pepper lay on the table. Like everyone else I bit into it. My lips shrivelled, got sucked in and I could no longer open my mouth. After a glass of orangeade, the strongest liquid available, I gradually got back to normal.

I wanted to visit the Casbah. It was Sunday afternoon and I was talking with one of my new friends, whom everyone called *Mon Fils*. He wasn't their son, but he had apparently won a lot of money by backing a horse of the same name on an accumulator. 'Don't go alone', he said, 'and specially don't go there on Thursday afternoon, the beginning of the Muslim weekend. Too many people, too dangerous, pickpockets and worse. After that we'll go together to the whorehouse.' I had never been to one so I was game. We made an appointment for Monday at two o'clock in the afternoon.

I waited for him until three o'clock and thought 'Oh well, I can go tomorrow'. I met him in the street that evening, not in the least embarrassed. 'I'm sorry, I forgot, but we'll go tomorrow. But specially don't go alone and not on Thursday afternoon.' By Tuesday, after being stood up for the second time, I at last understood the nature of an Algerian date. I just meant if you are there and I am there at the same time, we will do something together.

I missed the car to the beach each time he stood me up, so I went off exploring Algiers alone on foot.

An inquisitive young man accosted me politely in the street, asking me where I came from and what I was doing in Algiers. Somewhat perturbed by his smarmy courtesy, I told him that I was an Englishmen and on holiday.

'That's interesting', he said. 'We don't see many people from England over here, only a few French, of course, those who still dare to come back, and several Belgians. The others come mainly from the Soviet bloc, especially Bulgarian medical personnel and Romanians.'

'I have heard a number of Romanian voices in the street while I've been here', I said. 'Algeria is definitely outside the British zone of influence. The English don't really share a common history with the Algerians.'

'That is not quite true', he said. 'There was a strong English presence here during the 16th century under the Ottoman Empire.'

'Really? I didn't realise that the English had colonised North Africa.'

'They didn't. They were pirates under the so-called Ottoman *Regency of Algiers*. Two brothers named Oruç and Hayreddin, privateers known collectively as *Barbarossa, Red Beard*, had moved from Tunisia to Algiers, asking protection from the Ottomans in exchange for their allegiance to the *Porte*. Attacks on shipping from Spain and slave trading with those that they had captured made up their main sources of revenue.'

'How did the English pirates fit in?' I asked.

'As Protestants, with other pirates from Holland, they had joined the Turks and Berbers to make up the *Barbary* pirates, sharing with the Turks a common enemy, the Catholic countries of Europe. At one time they numbered up to eight thousand. This was the time of the persecution of Protestants, mainly in France, Spain and Portugal. The English and Muslims collaborated with the tacit and even semi-official approval of the English crown of Elisabeth I. James I later condemned it after signing a peace treaty with Spain,'

'So this was part of British political strategy.'

'Not only. Many of the English pirates, after converting to Islam, pillaged ships of all countries, both Catholic and Protestant, selling their Christian captives as slaves across North Africa. Some of them even attacked Christian galleys to liberate their Turkish captives.'

'When did the French come on the scene?' I asked.

'In 1830 the French used a pretext to invade Algiers, after refusing to pay back what they owed for the massive quantities of food that they had purchased on credit twenty-five years previously to feed the soldiers during Bonaparte's campaigns.'

My colleague Omar was not pleased when I told him about my new acquaintance. 'I told you not to hang around with anyone that I hadn't vetted? Algiers is a dangerous place and you don't know the ropes. Better you spend time only with my friends.'

I decided to give *Mon Fils* another chance, but with the same result. Finally, on Wednesday when we did meet by chance he said, still with no embarrassment: 'I'm so sorry, I was busy. I'm afraid it will have to be tomorrow afternoon, Thursday, which is not so bad, after all. But don't go alone.'

I ended up by going alone to the Casbah on Thursday afternoon. I didn't get very far. There were just too many people. And I never did get to the brothel…

I had been walking cautiously upward through the narrow alleys of the Casbah, rubbing shoulders with the wall-to-wall Thursday afternoon population. Holding my hands tightly to my wallet in the front pocket of my jeans, I sneaked a glance left and right. I stopped in a minute square, where *graffiti* covered its grimy walls. Most of them concerned the *FLN*, the National Liberation Front. Almost hidden by the other slogans in French you could still just see faint traces of the three letters *OAS*, the initials of the defunct French terrorist Secret Army Organisation. Someone had freshly scrawled the same message several times in French.

Al Andalus – Constantinople même combat

The same struggle? Constantinople again, and this time with Andalusia, the Arab world's long-lost Iberian Caliphate, brought to an end by the Christian *Reconquista* at almost the same time as the Turks had captured Constantinople. I was perplexed. I knew that many Arabs dreamed of re-establishing their lost empire in southern Spain, but where did Turkey, their former coloniser, fit in with it?

At the end of my stay I sailed back to Marseille on the same boat.

Back to Byzantium

I had to run the gauntlet of the petty officials at passport control before embarking. Along the length of the wall sat a small army of scribes, there to help the illiterate with the red tape. I filled out the exit form. The officials didn't look easy to handle. The form required Algerians to give the number of their French resident card for them to exit Algeria. I did the same, after all I was a foreigner in France. When I passed through immigration, the official laughed, saying that was not meant for me. 'You Algerians don't have the monopoly on resident cards in France', I said. They let me through with a complicit laugh and without further hindrance.

This time they had allocated me a table in the restaurant, shared with an English couple returning from *VSO*, Voluntary Service Abroad, in Sierra Leone beyond the Sahara.

At the same table sat a young Algerian who spoke French like a Frenchman, with extreme affectation. He was obviously *gay* and very *camp*. We took the train together up to Paris. Despite his self-confident manner he was suffering from culture shock.

I saw him briefly three months later, in Pigalle, Paris's *red-light* district. I was showing the city's nightlife to my slightly strait-laced Polish violinist friend. There he stood at the end of the *rambla* near Place Pigalle. I said hello and he kissed me on both cheeks like a brother. He had been reduced for lack of funds to working as what they call *trade*, street walking as a *gay* hooker. The Polish woman looked somewhat surprised.

14
Tirana

At the end of the year, NATO countries were to decide that, unless the Soviet Union removed its *SS-20's*, they would deploy *Cruise* missiles in Western Europe, thus giving rise to the *Euromissile crisis*. It was closely followed by the Soviet invasion of Afghanistan, which thereby ended *détente*.

The previous summer, Enver Hoxha's Albania had finally broken off with Deng Xiaoping's Peoples Republic of China. Albania was now friendless and alone in the world. I was about to spend three weeks there.

Few people visited Albania under Enver Hoxha. He had turned it into one of the two hermetic countries in the world, with North Korea. Even Communist China had begun to open up to business with the West. Albania permitted Westerners to visit either with Marxist-Leninist groups or with professional organisations. A few private tour operators on the fringe had succeeded in negotiating organised trips to Albania in groups. I chose one of those.

Two weekly flights linked Tirana to the outside world, one with Budapest, the other with Belgrade. We flew with *JAT*, the Yugoslav national airline, from Orly Airport in Paris to Belgrade where we spent the night, and then on to Tirana by *JUGALB*, the Yugoslav Albanian joint-venture airline to Tirana.

We idled for four hours at Orly waiting for our delayed flight, each passenger describing his or her motivation for going to this forgotten country. Surprisingly, none was political. It was already late evening when we finally landed at Belgrade. We took the last airport bus into town, accompanied by the pilot and flight crew. To make up for the inconvenience of our delay, the *JAT* pilot with great generosity hijacked the airport bus, gave us a guided tour of Belgrade by night and transported us to our hotel, where the flight crew also stayed. We checked in and I came down for a late dinner in the restaurant, which had stayed open for us.

The pilot was sitting at the bar with a whisky. He offered me one. Like many Serbs, he was most eloquent about the path that his country had taken towards participative socialism. We talked about workers' self-management, which fascinated my generation and had made many recruits in Western Europe.

'I am a great admirer of Yugoslav self-management', I said.

'Without being chauvinistic, so am I', he said, 'but, as you no doubt know, like most democratic institutions, it is hard to get it to function efficiently. Yugoslav Socialism has always been a trial and error process between centralisation and decentralisation.

'Do you know Edvard Kardelj? He is the Slovene who devised the self-management system. Like Tito and Dimitrov, he was one of the few who survived Stalin's *Great Purge* during the thirties, working in Moscow as an economist and becoming a partisan leader during the war. His embryonic economic system was at the time one of the main reasons for the split between Stalin and Tito.

'Yugoslavia's economy today is not centrally planned. Unlike in the Soviet Union, where companies are state owned, Yugoslavia's companies are socially owned and managed by their workers through a system of delegations. Workers have the power of decision in all sorts of areas, such as production methods, division of labour, even customer relations. They also decide between paying dividends and reinvesting profits, which is probably the stumbling block of the system. They are organised in unions. Any group of workers is able to call a strike, which can frequently result in the replacement of managers. Executive decisions are taken at company level, which provides a degree of competition between different entities within the same organisation. The same system is also applied to public services, including health and education.

'You know that, except during the recession in the sixties, Yugoslavia's economy has been flourishing, with six percent growth in GDP, which you must admit is rather remarkable. Our workforce has become more educated - we have more than ninety percent literacy - health care is free and life expectancy is comparable with that of the West. And, of course, Tito's non-alignment policy has opened up commerce with the European Community.'

It was non-alignment that would later contribute to the collapse of the Yugoslav economy. Ronald Reagan soon set up trade barriers designed to overthrow Communist governments. This led to less growth, reduced *IMF* loans, debt, bankruptcy of a thousand companies and a million unemployed. It all contributed to the future collapse of the federation.

The following day we landed on the Tirana airfield in a two-prop *JUGALB* aircraft.

Albania had very strict rules concerning import of printed matter. It forbade all religious, historical and even most tourist publications. This was the world's first totally atheist state, so customs officials confiscated Bibles.

Albanian authorities considered Western fashions to

be immoral, such as long hair and bell-bottom trousers, currently in fashion for men. They not only required trousers of traditional width, but they employed a barber at the airport, one of whose tasks was to cut the hair of foreign visitors entering the country. I had taken my precautions. I wore tight trousers and I had got a Mussolini haircut on the eve of our departure.

A smart friendly woman in uniform emptied my suitcase, found nothing inappropriate and repacked it. Even my mother would not have packed it with such delicate attention, refolding each item of clothing. Her male colleague looked at my short haircut, saying 'I think you had your hair cut specially.' One of my fellow travellers from France wore a generous beard. When the barber saw him he said 'Marx'. After he had trimmed his beard the barber said 'Engels', as he let him out.

> Enver Hoxha had first allied with Stalin out of fear of Titoist revisionism, but mainly because he found Yugoslavia too close for comfort. Out of fear of Khrushchëv's revisionism and Soviet intervention he had subsequently allied with Mao Zedong. The further away the better! Since Deng Xiaoping' reforms Albania had lost its only friend.
>
> It was the Illyrians who had been the original inhabitants of Albania, with an empire far beyond present borders. Emperors Diocletian and Constantine had both been Illyrians. It had become today's *Shqipëria*, the land of eagles.
>
> In 1878 the treaties of San Stefano and Berlin had allocated areas inhabited by a very large Muslim Albanian majority to recently autonomous Bulgaria and Serbia. Albanian leaders set up their own autonomous administration, the so-called *League of Prizren*, to defend their lands while remaining loyal to the Ottoman Empire. They opposed Bulgarian and Serbian independence and did not at first seek their own. Only when, at the

Congress of Berlin, Bismarck and the Ottomans had refused the very idea of an Albanian nation, did they launch their own revolution to gain full independence in 1912.

Of all the amazing features of Albania under Enver Hoxha, what astonished foreigners the most were the national defence bunkers. They stood out in every location, in villages, towns, fields, hills facing the sea or a border and even in cemeteries. Four double pillboxes stood guard over each crossroads, gun turrets faced the sea through openings in each hill, and large concrete mushrooms emerged above the corn in every field. Enver Hoxha had deliberately created a national paranoia.

Bunkers were built of steel, iron and concrete. Some of them were linked by a system of secret tunnels. Three basic models existed, pillboxes for one or two people, command bunkers, and large ones built into mountain faces equipped with cannon. Construction had begun in the sixties and would continue into the early eighties.

The shape of the pillboxes reminded me of *Hagia Sofia* in Constantinople without the minarets, miniature Sinan mosques, Albania's secular heritage from Turkish Islam.

One third of the population were involved in defence from pre-adolescence onwards. The people's army was the continuation of the

Communist partisans, who had liberated Albania almost single-handed using guerrilla tactics.

Every foreigner asked the same question: why did Albania need the bunkers? One could only speculate. They were, first of all, a symbol of independence from potential foreign intervention, meaning Yugoslavia, the Warsaw Pact and NATO. Enver Hoxha had succeeded in creating a siege mentality with permanent mobilisation of the population. Above all he had discovered a way of intimidating and controlling the people.

It would later be revealed that, for a population of a little more than two and a half million, he had built 700,000 bunkers, or one for every three to four inhabitants. Each pillbox represented the cost of a two-room flat, without counting the number of deaths during their construction. Built at the expense of a decent road network, bunkers would have been totally ineffective without a supply system in case of attack. Needless to say, Enver Hoxha had the General who drew attention to this drawback executed as a traitor.

We felt this paranoia during the whole of our three-week stay. A professional guide-cum-security officer accompanied us at all times. There was no way of taking a step outside the hotel onto the pavement without her. When we went to the beach it was with our guide or her colleague. We found her great fun to be with on the beach, even flirting with the men in our party, but she allowed us no contact with other Albanians apart from tourist personnel.

Our beach, in front of our hotel, had been enclosed to prevent any contact. One day in the sea we took pity on a couple of boys who gazed enviously at our Hungarian inflatable mattress. When we lent it to them to play with, our guide immediately retrieved it, admonished them and sent them away.

In Albania there were no private cars, no private businesses, and there was no foreign travel. People hitched rides everywhere and our tourist bus always picked them up. If you left a tip in *café* the waiter gave it back saying that you had forgotten your money.

Enver Hoxha claimed to have created the world's first actively atheist country ten years previously. He had either destroyed churches, cathedrals and other places of worship or had had them turned in to grain silos or even a skating rink. We visited a small museum dedicated to atheism. Its gentle erudite curator had a rich collection of reactionary religious propaganda. The exhibit that gave him the most pride was a Bible. When opened, it turned out to be a box containing a handgun.

Another thing that my travel companions and I found striking was the elegance of the population, particularly the men. Their clothes, made of robust cotton, resembled those on sale in other Communist nations. And yet the Albanians managed to look elegant and stylish, unlike men in Slav countries. You could see young men walking arm in arm as in Italy and there was no reason to speculate about their sexual orientation.

I bought a cotton shirt, which I found rather elegant, and a leather watchstrap more like a wrist belt, that cost me ten times less than the price quoted at Orly airport. With what I, at least, saw as a certain *radical chic*, they lasted for years.

Their national drink was *fernet*, a bitter beverage similar to the so-called alcoholic *alka-seltzer*, *Fernet Branca*. Did the Albanians introduce this drink into Italy or was it Mussolini who introduced it into Albania?

We visited a steel works and a factory where they manufactured plastic sandals. At the end of each visit the factory manager held a question and answer session. Some of us recollected visiting factories in Russia, where you always had the impression that they were lying through their teeth, as Custine had discovered a century and a half before. 'Is there much absenteeism in your factory?' 'Oh no! Our people are conscientious in their struggle for Socialism', is something like what the Russians would say. 'Yes. It is a problem, especially on the first of January, when absenteeism may reach fifty percent' was the Albanian answer. We could have hugged the factory manager for his disarming frankness.

Later at a lecture on the condition of women in Albania one of us asked a question about contraception. 'We don't allow it', said the elegant woman. 'We consider our country to be under-populated and are trying to increase our birth rate.' It could have been Charles De Gaulle speaking.

Our hotel was located at a beach resort near the Adriatic port of Durrës. It was a historic city, formerly called Durrachium, which had been, with Thessaloniki and Constantinople, one of the three main ports of the Byzantine Empire. Each time we saw something that a tourist considers worthy of interest, our guide said 'Why don't you look at our new cultural centre?' She forbade us to take any photographs unless she had previously given her explicit permission. On leaving the country, a member of our group discovered that the authorities had secretly removed the exposed film from his camera.

They housed us in a modern holiday complex that was clean and adequate. We ate in a restaurant on the roof, where in the evenings we watched films denouncing the period of King Zog. We shared the hotel with other foreign tourist groups. Our group was more than apolitical, it included two priests travelling *icognito*. The younger one prided himself on having succeeded in smuggling a Catholic missal through customs. To my distress, he had more success on the beach than I with our flirtatious tour guide-cum-security officer. On our final evening the Albanian organisers asked each foreign group to sing a song. Each one sang the revolutionary anthem of their country. All that our group could come up with, at the instigation of the older priest, was a children's rhyme.

Back to Byzantium

The Marxist-Leninist groups were not amused.

The craggy landscapes of Albania are among the most dramatic that I have seen. The Albanians had tamed the wild hillsides to make the most of the lack of available arable land by terrace cultivation. Carved out of the hillsides signs proclaimed: *Rroft Enver*, glory to Enver…

> 'To greet Albania's chief, whose dread command
> Is lawless law; for with a bloody hand
> He sways a nation, turbulent and bold…'

Our first trip was to the Northern town of Shkodër. The Communists had destroyed the cathedral ten years previously, but, while Enver Hoxha was still their friend, the Chinese had built a modern hotel. We were staying there. The restaurant was full of Albanians carousing loudly. We wondered who they could be. 'Our people don't behave that way. They must be from Kosovo', said our guide.

Some older people still wore the local Gheg costume. Before my trip, I had learnt that two distinct cultural and linguistic groups lived in Albania. They were the *Ghegs* in the north, in Kosovo and Macedonia, and the *Tosks* in the South and in parts of Northern Greece.

Each time I asked one of my guides whether she was Gheg or a Tosk, I got the same answer: 'In Albania no Ghegs or Tosks, only Albanians'. That didn't prevent me from having a good guess, based on their morphology and general attitude.

> In fact two distinct dialects existed. Despite standardisation of the Albanian language by the Communists based on the Tosk dialect, Ghegs from remote villages still found it difficult to converse with Tosks.
>
> There were also religious differences. One Gheg in ten was Catholic, even one third of the population in Durrës, where we were staying. The

rest were Sunni Muslims. One fifth of the Tosks were Orthodox, the rest Sufi Muslims.

As for their look, the Ghegs were typically slim with a fair skin, which caused the Nazis to treat them as Aryans. The Tosks, on the other hand, were unmistakably Mediterranean, squat with a darker skin. It seemed easy to me to distinguish statuesque Ghegs from the shorter, more compact Tosks.

Gheg society was based on the clan system, with tribal assemblies for dispensing law, and blood feuds. The land belonged to the clan, and marriages were arranged for economic reasons. Characteristically they had a strong tradition of hospitality and were known for their epic poetry.

Ghegs had maintained a curious tradition. *Burrneshas*, or *he-shes*, were women who had taken a vow to remain celibate and virgin until death. They dressed and behaved as men, taking on traditional *male* responsibilities. Men consequently behaved with them as equals.

The Tosks, on the other hand, living closer to the sea, had always been open to the outside world and more progressive.

Under the Ottoman empire Tosks had been culturally closer to Istanbul, while most Ghegs were beyond the reach of the Ottoman administration, which didn't try to subdue them, but used them as mercenaries. Traditionally the Ghegs had been conservative and nationalist, the Tosks socialist. Since the creation of the Albanian state there had been constant rivalry.

Between the wars, Ahmed Zogu, self-proclaimed King Zog, a Gheg, imposed his dialect as the standard and his people dominated politics. The Tosks were poor, quasi serfs of Muslim landowners. Then, during the Second World War, the *Waffen SS* recruited many Ghegs, as Aryans, into the *Skanderbeg* division. The majority of partisans had been Tosks, making up three quarters of the Communist party. After the War, Enver Hoxha, himself a Tosk, transferred power to his people and imposed his own dialect as the national standard. The Ghegs were understandably anti-Communist. Fifteen years later, after the fall of Communism, the people would elect Sali Berisha, a Gheg, as President. He replaced the Tosks in the administration with Ghegs from the North, triggering ethnic riots.

In Shkodër we had a new guide, a statuesque young woman of character, with a morphology like that of a Serb. 'You are a Gheg, aren't you?' I asked. 'Yes, I am indeed a Gheg!' she replied.

We stopped in front of a large notice board. All sorts of hand-written posters hung on it. They looked like messages, which their author had written neatly in capital letters.

'What are these?' I asked my Gheg guide. 'They are *Fletë-rrufe'*, she replied. 'I believe the translation is *thunder papers*. They have become a pillar of the Albanian revolution.

'Our leader Enver Hoxha introduced them more than ten years ago. It was a completely new kind of communication between the masses and our officials. He wanted the people to be able to write what they thought about work, about their neighbours and colleagues, and display it publicly on special notice boards without fear of petty officials.

'You know that, until our revolution, writing in Albania was the privilege of the educated classes, the intellectuals and bureaucrats. Enver introduced reforms in two phases. The first phase was the literacy campaign immediately following the War. The people can now read the political information that the party and the government put out. The second phase was for the people to make a transition from passive reading to active participation, by expressing themselves freely. Enver wants *Fletërrufe* to be like a written protest against bureaucracy, intellectuals and the forces of conservatism.'

'They sound rather like *dazibao* from Mao Zedong's Cultural Revolution. I see that they are all neatly hand-written in capital letters.'

'You are quite right, these are our *dazibao*. They are always written in capitals, to make it easy for simple people. The aim is to improve literacy. It is like an invitation to shout out loud in writing and give it an official status.'

'This one looks interesting', I remarked. 'What is it about?'

'The one on the right is to reprimand pupils who have not worked hard enough at school. The other one criticises a teacher who has been unsuccessful in his teaching and encourages him to do better.'

In Shkodër we visited a primary school. An eight-year-old boy, very self-confident, declaimed an eloquent little speech to the glory of the great leader, which ended with the slogan that we now all recognized: '*Rroft Enver!*' Wasn't it time that Western European primary schools reintroduced courses in elocution?

Back to Byzantium

> I bought a book called *Gjuha Shqipe*, an Albanian language manual.
>
> The alphabet has unusual combinations of consonants, apparently a compromise to reconcile the different alphabets used until the country became independent. The alphabets previously in use were linked to the influence of the predominant religion of the region.
>
> Northern Albania, inhabited mainly by Ghegs, under the influence of the Catholic Church, used an alphabet composed of Latin characters. Albanian writers of the 16th and 17th century all used a Latin alphabet.
>
> Southern Albania, inhabited mainly by Tosks, under the influence of the Orthodox Church, used Greek characters. Writers busied themselves mainly with translating religious texts from Greek. The first Albanian dictionary had been compiled using Greek characters.
>
> Muslims used characters from the Arabic alphabet. Even after standardised alphabets had been developed using Latin characters, Muslim clerics still claimed that those who used a Latin alphabet had to be infidels. The followers of the Young Turk movement also tried to promote an Arabic alphabet.
>
> Until the late 19th century no Albanian-language schools had existed, all classes being held in Greek or in Turkish. Confronted by the three types of script, the League of Prizren ordered the creation of the so-called Istanbul alphabet, using Latin characters. When Albania became fully independent, the *Bashkimi* alphabet, based on accents used on Romance-language typewriters, became official.

The model farm that we visited impressed even the agronomist in our party. 'But they use the same hybridisation techniques for their maize as in the West!' he said. We visited a workshop behind the farm. Two men worked on a lathe, making brand new spare parts for their Chinese tractors, which they could no longer obtain from their former friend and ally. You had to admire the

Albanians in their heroic but absurd struggle to depend only on themselves, unfortunately with no future.

As in all Balkan countries the folk museum was one of the highlights, where we saw magnificent peasant costumes. 'When do these date from?' I asked. 'From the Middle Ages', replied our auxiliary guide, who lacked the charm of her colleagues. The Middle Ages? Of course, the *Middle Ages* was what preceded the Albanian *Renaissance*, meaning the *National Awakening* dating from the independence movement from the Ottomans. The term *Middle Ages* thus described anything dating from before 1830.

In south-east Albania we visited Pogradets on the *wrong* side of Lake Ohrid, facing Yugoslav Macedonia, stopping on our way back in Berat, the city of a thousand windows. Houses dating from the *National Awakening* covered the flank of a hill, their overlapping first floor windows reflecting the setting sun in a thousand facets onto the town below. We returned to Tirana for the last day of our stay.

Tirana is an agreeable airy city, surrounded by mountains, with an elegant central square housing the eighteenth century Et'hem Bey Mosque and its *campanile*. Skanderbeg, the enigmatic national hero, presides over the square. Raised in Constantinople after being seized from his parents following the *devşirme*, he later became the scourge of the Ottomans.

> 'Land of Albania! where Iskander rose;
> Theme of the young, and beacon of the wise,
> And he his namesake, whose oft-baffled foes,
> Shrunk from his deeds of chivalrous emprise…'

A prestigious leafy avenue leads down a slope to the columned university. We were getting rather tired of our auxiliary guide. A country girl, she obviously didn't feel at ease in a big city like Tirana. We found a way to see most of what we wanted there by first getting her lost, and

Back to Byzantium

then in finding our way without her help.

'How is it possible that you know the way?' she asked. When you had lived in a large Western capital it was easy to navigate around Tirana, but how could we explain that to a young woman raised in paranoia and who suspected us of being spies? She had obviously never felt the exhilaration of being lost in a capital city.

We flew back to Belgrade through a storm in our two-prop cuckoo. A small-town German salesman sat next to me. He was very talkative. 'What were you doing here', he asked. 'How can you spend your holiday in such an awful place?' 'I loved it', I said, "the people, the beauty of its craggy mountains, its sandy beaches, the only ones on the Adriatic. And I loved its history, but not of course the *regime*.'

'You can see that it's a Muslim country', continued the German salesman. 'Why don't the Greeks just invade Albania? For that matter, it is really about time that they took back Constantinople from the Turks once and for all. They should throw the Turks out of Asia Minor and recreate the Byzantine Empire. There are too many Turks in Germany already.'

Great minds are said to think alike. It was the same discourse that I had heard from the Greek architect in Piraeus, except that here it wasn't at all the same.

'If you don't like the Turks, it is probably because you don't know any' I replied. 'Why should I? You don't know any Pakistanis, do you?' he affirmed. I had to admit that, not living in the UK, I didn't know any. It served no purpose to tell him that I knew several Muslims from North Africa.

We remained silent until the steward served us a decent Bosnian wine. 'It's not worth a nice *Beaujolais*, served at room temperature', he said. I couldn't resist.

Back to Byzantium

'*Beaujolais* should be served slightly chilled', I said. He looked away in disgust and, when the fear of death hit him during the storm, he shut his mouth and I heard no more of him.

Back home I found traces of Albania everywhere. At a restaurant named *Les Balkans* in the Quartier Latin I became the hero of the day. The Albanian waiter sat me down at the same table as some middle-aged expatriates, who asked me questions about their lost country that I had difficulty answering.

After the others had left I stayed at the table talking with an elderly gentleman. He told me that he was a Gheg and a Catholic, originating from Shkodër.

'I am not completely clear about how the Albanians consider the Ottoman Empire and the Turks in general', I said.

'It is complex, ambivalent and not always coherent', he answered. 'We Albanians identify with our national hero, Skanderbeg, who defended us from the Turks over a period of twenty-five years, first against Murad II and then against his son, Mehmet II, the Conqueror. Uniting the Albanian tribes, he defended not only his own territory, but also the Kingdom of Naples, the Pope and even the Republic of Venice. As one of the main causes for the delay in the Ottoman invasion of Europe, he earned Albania the admiration and gratitude of the Western world.

'He also posthumously inspired the Albanian *Renaissance* in the second part of the 19th century.'

Many years later, during a stroll through Bayswater in London, at a street corner I would come unexpectedly face to face with a sculpture bust of Skanderbeg, which Westminster city council had erected in tribute to a *European hero*.

'Then the Albanians consider the Turks to be their hereditary enemy?' I asked.

'Well, no, they don't. It's more complicated than that. Don't forget that most Albanians, particularly the Tosks, became Muslims in the 17th century, for tax reasons, to avoid the *devşirme*, or simply to *join the winning team*, as the Americans say.'

'But do Albanians have collective nostalgia for a time before the Ottoman Conquest?'

'Certainly not! And at the time when Serbia and Bulgaria gained their autonomy, the Albanians preferred to remain loyal to the Ottoman Empire, already the *sick man of Europe*, rather than risk being incorporated into the newly-created Serbian principality, as they had been at the time of Stephen Dušan's empire.'

'So the Muslims acclaimed Skanderbeg as a hero for defeating the Turks and for unifying the Albanian tribes, though as a Catholic convert he was part of the Western world.'

'Precisely, in our country where Muslims were a majority, the people identified with an apostate Christian hero, allied with the Pope and the King of Naples against the Turks, at the same time as they resisted the Italian invasion by Mussolini. We are a complex nation.'

The next day I met a Greek girl whose family originated in Gjirokastër in Southern Albania. 'Its name is *Argyrokastro*', she said. 'Northern Epirus belongs to Greece anyway.'

Waiting to land from the Newhaven ferry to visit my parents I met a middle-aged English woman who had spent her holidays in Albania as a young girl during the thirties. Attempting to eliminate corruption and brigandage in the local police forces, King Zog had hired her uncle, a British former police commissioner, as his chief of police. She had few memories of the country, except for seeing her uncle put on his flashy uniform and cape, which Mussolini had graciously provided to equip the Albanian police.

A sports commentator whom I met on the same boat drove me to Godstone, in the fare-flung suburbs of London, where my parents lived. On the way we stopped at his house for a drink, where I met his daughter. Three days previously, Leka, son of late King Zog and *pretender* to the throne of Albania, had taken her out to dinner.

I never got far with the language, but I called my cat *Enver* for a little while until I changed his name to *Vlad*.

15
Transylvania

In spring a young Turkish Christian named Ali Ağca attempted to assassinate Pope John Paul II in Rome.

In France the Socialist leader François Mitterand had been elected President and had formed a government that included four ministers from the Communist Party. Meanwhile in Britain Prince Charles, the heir to the throne, was getting married to Lady Diana Spencer.

During the *Euromissile* crisis President Ronald Reagan raised the possibility of a *limited war* in Europe.

In Poland, following the demand for free elections by the congress of the independent trade union *Solidarność*, the newly-elected Prime Minister Wojciech Jaruzelski responded by decreeing a state of siege and putting its leader Lech Wałęsa in prison, probably to prevent direct Soviet intervention.

My future wife Edmonde and I set out for an advance honeymoon. We would be officially married only a year and a half later. She woke me up affectionately at a friend's house in Romans-sur-Isère, south of Lyon. Transylvania was our destination. It took a leisurely ten days to get there, even though we always seemed to be on the move, travelling through Switzerland, around Lake Geneva. We spent a night in the Vaud region, whose splendid farmhouses prefigured Saxon Transylvania. Then to Liechtenstein and down through Austrian Carinthia and into Slovenia at Maribor.

Visiting Central Europe for the first time, my wife experienced the same culture shock that had hit me in Budapest at my first visit. Aghast at the grime of this former Austrian counter-reformation town, she was unable to see the baroque glory hiding behind. It was all I could do to convince her not to turn around and go home.

We had stopped for a drink the previous afternoon in Austria in the beer garden of an inn in the middle of the Carinthian forest. As she went inside in search of the toilet, the ogling farm workers were an unnerving reminder of the film *Deliverance*. After this, the austere decadence of Maribor seemed almost too much for her, but she soon learned to look beyond and become an addict like me.

Crossing northern Croatia into Hungary, we arrived in the noon heat in Keszthely on the banks of Lake Balaton. The temperature had reached the high thirties. Everyone is not aware that Hungary is among the hottest countries in Europe and probably the driest. We stayed for three nights in what seemed to us a sumptuous hotel, set in a garden by the Lake with a private beach.

Swimming in a lake can be perilous if you are not a good swimmer, afraid of the water and used to the Mediterranean. That described my wife, but we were bathing together for the first time. She went under once and came up with her arms fluttering. She went down again and up again fluttering even more. The third time, I thought, she won't come up again. I am not a strong swimmer, but with great effort I managed to pull her to the shore. She almost drowned, and no-one except me was even aware of it.

We drove through the endless yellow fields of sunflowers to the spa town of Hévíz. They said that the mildly radioactive water had a beneficial effect on thyroid ailments. Monstrously-goitred men and women bathed in the lake that surrounded the thermal building. Concerned with the progression of both our own thyroid ailments, later operated on, we stayed no longer. The next day we left for Budapest.

I was visiting Budapest for the second time and my architectural judgement had matured. I succeeded in selling its eclectism to my wife, who had the same misgivings as I had had during my first brief visit. The walls of the buildings were totally leprous and, except for part of the castle hill in Buda, not a single one was authentic in its style. But what style! Neo-romanesque, neo-gothic, neo-baroque, neo- every style that architects had invented. Was this what they called banker's baroque and was last year's vulgarity tomorrow's good taste? It was already tomorrow! Not to mention the authentic *art nouveau* and *art deco* buildings, and the specifically Hungarian styles of Ödön Lechner and József Vágó. The topography of the city, from the hills of Buda across the fluvial boulevard of the Danube to low-lying Pest! Pest, where the *Alföld*, the Great Hungarian Plain, begins, with the *puszta*, the land of swing wells, storks and strangely-horned livestock, the anti-chamber to the Eurasian steppe! This is the only European capital that the Danube bisects. And there were the *cimbaloms* again, the hammered dulcimers, providing the bass for the syrupy but irresistible gypsy orchestras. I have loved this city like no other, as has my wife. A friend joked that I could not pronounce the name Budapest without a *tremolo* in my voice. We would soon return to live here for more than a year.

Continuing down the Danube for a while, we branched off to Szeged and then to the Romanian border at Nădlac, *Nagylak* in Hungarian.

Who on earth, with valid documents and a valid visa, has spent five hours at a European border post? The queue of cars was unending. Our turn came. The customs officer scoured every bag in the boot of our car, searched every item of clothing, felt through each pair of socks and started dismantling my wife's tampons one by one. 'What are these?' he asked. Was there any doubt that he knew? Then we had to wait and wait. He eventually let us through.

Changing money was the next ordeal. We had taken the precaution of buying travellers cheques. My wife signed the first cheque 'The signature is not the same', said the woman at the foreign exchange desk.' She pulled out and signed another. 'The corner is torn'. The woman refused six cheques, always with the same two pretexts. Edmonde was running out of travellers' cheques and she was getting angry. Realising that we were at the mercy of the bureaucrat, I tried a soft approach. I knew that there was a problem with the six previous cheques. However, if there were to be a problem with the next one, we would be out of money and would have to go home. She smiled and accepted two of our cheques with the same approximate signatures and bent corners that she had previously refused. Contrary to what I had thought, *baksheesh* was not the issue. She wanted recognition that she existed and that she had the power to refuse a rich Western tourist.

The third ordeal was finding a room. I had experience of this from Mamaia. It was question of respect and admitting that we were at their mercy. Three smart young women sat in the tourist office, which displayed a sign in French saying that no rooms were available. I tried the charm offensive. '*Buna seara, doamna. Eu sunt Engleză*' I said with a huge smile, using the only words that I knew in Romanian and, continuing in French, 'I know that rooms are scarce in Arad, but do you think that you could find us one nevertheless.' They found us an available room immediately. After five hours at Nădlac, we proceeded to Arad, in Swabian Banat, and spent the night there.

The following morning we drove on East to Hunedoara, the castle of János Hunyadi, or Corvinus, which is known in Hungarian as *Vajdahunyad*. The romantic mediaeval castle *par excellence*, heavily restored in the 19th century, stood across a wooden footbridge over a dried-up moat. An *improved* replica of the castle stands in Budapest on an island in the *Varosliget*, the city park. Contrary to Romanian tourist propaganda, eager to join the Dracula bandwagon, it was not here that János

Back to Byzantium

Hunyadi kept Vlad the Impaler prisoner, but in Visegrád, in today's Hungary, on the Danube bend. Round the castle a yellowy brown haze made the air stifling. The town contained what was then the largest steel works in Romania, hence its German name, *Eisenmarkt*. Half asphyxiated, we moved on to Sebeş for a night, then on to Sibiu. We chatted in English with an Austrian, who used only the German names for the Romanian towns. 'Why do you say *Mühlbach*, *Hermannstadt* and *Schäßburg* instead of Sebeş, Sibiu and Sighişoara? These towns are now part of Romania.' 'Why do the French say Douvres for Dover?' I am sorry, but it was not quite the same. It sounded like imperialist nostalgia.

We found a motel, not far from Sebeş. Roma children looked at our foreign car with mischievous eyes. Of course the motel was fully booked. 'I lit a cigarette and offered one to the girl at the desk. 'Keep the packet!' We had a comfortable room with hot water. Next morning we discovered that someone had removed the *F* from the boot of our car. In a state of mild paranoia, I improvised a large *F* on a piece of cardboard that I laid inside the rear window.

From Sibiu we took a loop north to Sighişoara and back for the day. We were low on petrol and, with so few filling stations, we weren't sure of making it back to Sibiu. On our way to Sighişoara we picked up a young soldier who had hitched a ride. He thanked us as he got out of the car, kissing my wife's hand. We entered the village. '*Grüss Gott*', said to my surprise a stocky russet-tanned farmer who was walking with a purpose towards the church. '*Wir sind Sachsen*', he said. '*Und ich bin Angelsachse*', I replied.

If it was true for me, it was less true for him. Though they were known as *Saxons*, most had migrated from the Western part of the then Holy Roman Empire, far distant from Saxony. *Saxons* had lived in Transylvania for eight hundred years.

Back to Byzantium

In the 12th century King Géza II of Hungary had invited the first German settlers, mainly miners, to populate the South-Eastern part of his kingdom and help defend its Carpathian borders against invaders from the steppes. They in fact came from Luxemburg and the Mosel, settling in the region of what is today Sibiu, where they founded towns and villages. He allowed them to keep their language and culture, granted them administrative and religious autonomy, while imposing on them certain obligations.

A hundred years later a second wave came from the Rhineland, the Low Countries and Bavaria, to settle in the region of what is today Sebeș. As I had learned five years before in Malbork, King András II invited the Knights of the Teutonic Order to defend the Carpathians. They helped the Saxons build the city of Kronstadt, today Brasov. When they became too powerful the King expelled them, but the Saxon settlers stayed on. The Mongols invaded and destroyed many towns and villages, which the Saxons rebuilt and protected by fortifying their churches. With its seven cities, Saxon Transylvania became known as *Siebenbürgen*.

The third wave arrived near Sibiu from Upper Austria in the 18th century to repopulate after the war against the Turks. When the Reformation came, the majority converted to Lutheran Protestantism, what they call *Evangelisch*.

'We Saxons', said the farmer, 'with Hungarians and Szeklers, had been privileged since the 15th century as members of the *Unio Trium Nationum*. But, as the Union excluded the Romanian peasantry, in the 18th century Austria tried to correct the injustice. We began to feel like a minority, opposed by both the Hungarians and the Romanians. Even so, during the Revolution of 1848 our Saxon ancestors sided with the Romanians to help them attain equal status. Hungary's objective was the annexation of Transylvania and, after the creation of Austria-Hungary, it began its policy of *Magyarisation*. We lost our seven-hundred-year-old autonomy.'

'Follow me', he said. 'It is noon and I must ring the bell.' Stepping behind our Saxon host, we clambered up a wooden staircase at the end of the church. A huge bell hung from the rafters. He didn't have a bell rope as in England, where you rang the chimes at the risk of breaking the stay and then your skull against the ceiling as the bell pulled you heavenwards. No, he clung astride it *Quasimodo* style. What better way for a minority to continue to affirm its presence in the region? That was until a few years later, when Nicolae Ceausescu sold the ethnic Germans to Helmut Kohl for hard currency and the eight hundred-year Saxon presence ceased for ever from the Carpathian forests.

'How do you get on with the Hungarians and Romanians?' I asked. 'We all work together', he said. 'And the *Zigeuner*?' We didn't yet call them *Roma*. '*Alle zusammen*', he replied, all together.

He showed us round his Evangelical church. 'The village elders are the first to enter for the service. This is where they sit and the women over here.' A well-ordered society, indeed! A long hut stood behind the church. 'This is where we hang the *Speck*', he said. 'What about the Germans in the Banat', I asked, thinking of my travelling companion from Timișoara of my last trip to Romania.

'Oh, you mean the *Swabians*. They are not at all the same as us', he said. 'They are Catholics.'

The *Swabians* no more came from Swabia than the Saxons did from Saxony. Very few of these Catholics, mostly from Alsace-Loraine, Austria and Bavaria, first originated in Swabia. In the 18th century, Maria Theresa had recruited farmers to revive the agriculture in the Banat region, offering them free land, financial support and tax relief. The Swabians settled in the desert left by Turkish attacks and ensured its defence.

The Banat covers what is now South-West Romania, North-East Yugoslavia and a very small part of South-East Hungary. The Swabian capital in the Banat was Timișoara, what the Germans called *Temeschburg*.

The Swabians, contrary to the Saxons, as Catholics, could not resist *Magyarisation*, their intelligentsia became assimilated and Hungarian bishops were nominated.

The victorious allies rewarded Romania with Transylvania for its part in the First World War. The infamous Trianon Treaty defined Romania's obligations relative to its ethnic and religious minorities, which by now represented a third of the population.

'We Saxons had given our support to the unification of Transylvania with the Kingdom of Romania in exchange for full minority rights', he continued. 'But the Romanian government recognised only two minorities, the Szeklers and the Saxons, not the Swabians, who consequently tried to form an independent Banat to resist annexation.

'The Romanian government didn't respect its treaty obligations concerning minority rights. It massively increased the taxes that both Saxons and Swabians had to pay, and added a church tax for *Evangelicals*. Then with land reform they expropriated us Saxons from our communal property. Prominent members of our community lost their jobs. The Romanians succeeded in imposing their language in all Swabian Catholic schools, despite the opposition of the German government, and they tried unsuccessfully to do the same in Saxon *Evangelical* schools.

'We Germans in Romania felt that it was particularly unjust, because we had always sided with the Romanians against *Magyarisation*. Faced with a Romanian government that wanted to eradicate our culture and reduce our political power, many of our people turned to the Third Reich, enrolling into the *Wehrmacht* and even the *SS*.

'After the Second World War a hundred thousand Germans fled from Romania to escape the Red Army, who arrested Saxons and put them in labour camps. As for the Romanians, they considered the Swabians as potential enemies, but not us Saxons. Alone among the East Bloc countries, Romania didn't expel its entire German population. Then in the early sixties, Romania granted full citizenship to its German minorities. But, of course, when Nicolae Ceauşescu came to power, he opposed all minorities.'

Many ethnic Germans would later be purchased by the German government at about five thousand dollars a head. In accordance with the law of *Jus sanguinis*, Germany considered them as *Ausland-Deutsche*, Germans abroad, who had right to settle in the Federal Republic.

With regret we left our new acquaintance and continued to Sighişoara, travelling through probably the most idyllic countryside in Europe. Peasants were busy in the fields. The Romanians, with their grey felt jerkins, high boots and conical grey felt bonnets, were certainly the most picturesque. The Hungarians and Saxons wore navy-blue aprons and wide panama hats. This was not our own nostalgia, but a vicarious version from the time when our grandparents were children, untouched villages and a landscape that hadn't changed.

Sighişoara, *Schäßburg* in German, is a small Saxon fortified city on the border region between the central Europe Latin-oriented culture and the Byzantine-Orthodox world. Saxon craftsmen and merchants had built this solid elegant German town in the 13th century. Each guild was responsible for the construction of a tower and its defence. The town itself is the model of what a small town should be, or was, when our grandparents were young. As we strolled through, my wife had an intuition. This is the sort of house where Vlad the Impaler must have lived. We turned around. A historical plaque announced that in this house *Vlad Drakul* was born. They had turned it into a café. We entered and drank a glass of the incomparable Bulgarian peach juice that they had fed me in the hospital in Plovdiv. We walked up to the Renaissance church that dominated the town. Around it, on the flank of the hill, lay a graveyard. We looked at the gravestones. All bore German names. What a tragedy, that the people who had been tilling this land and building fortified churches for eight hundred years would soon be living in council flats in Essen!

Our next stop, Brasov, was a solid elegant Saxon burgher's city, with its so-called *Black* church. We stayed two nights at an inn with a courtyard where we had our meals. Three wedding receptions were under way simultaneously when we arrived, but they found us a place. The Romanian waitress was married to a Saxon. 'How is the standard of living in Hungary?' she asked. 'Is there any milk in the shops?'

Ceauşescu had decided to reimburse the national debt. To this effect he ordered a large part of the country's production to be exported. Basic foodstuffs became unavailable in shops and the Romanian population's standard of living was steadily decreasing.

With the end of our holiday approaching, we left Transylvania, descending the bottom end of the Carpathians onto the Wallachian plain, to begin the journey home. On the way, we stopped at the spectacular but disquieting castle of Bran. Contrary to Romanian tourist propaganda, once again, Vlad the Impaler never set foot here. We continued down the mountains to Pitesti and then to Craiova, where we spent the night in an old-fashioned hotel with Central European decadent charm. The same with the inhabitants, it seemed. Elderly gentlemen kissed my wife's hand when we asked for directions.

We drove into Serbia, crossing the dam that spanned the Danube at the Iron Gates, at the end of the gorge dividing Yugoslavia from Romania. We were relieved again from the same feeling of paranoia that I had begun to feel as soon as we had left Transylvania to enter Romania proper. As Custine had written about leaving Russia, he would never forget the relief he felt when crossing the border: a bird fleeing its cage could not have been happier.

Entering Serbia with some apprehension over potholed roads, we reached a smart new motorway. Beware of the Serbs, my Macedonian friend had told me. Not long before, my niece, Janey, and her travelling companion had hitched a ride in southern Serbia. The drunken driver, after continually groping her, had stopped the car in a deserted suburb of Skopje at three o'clock in the morning and, armed with a monkey wrench, demanded payment. The passengers of a passing German car, who heroically stopped to save them, had their rear window smashed by the wrench as they drove Janey and her friend to safety.

We reached a mountain town, where we filled our tank with petrol at a filling station with friendly service. A professional waitress served us our lunch of *ćevapčići* with a smile. Does it really have to take us so long to get beyond our received ideas?

Quite exhausted, especially my wife Edmonde, who had been doing all the driving, we arrived in Belgrade, with the usual feeling of liberation to be back in the West. We found a room on the hill in the same hotel where I had stayed *en route* for Tirana. As we walked in the warm evening through *Kalemegdan* Park, overlooking the confluence of the Danube and the Sava, beneath the walls of the fortress a mighty contralto sang light opera and in another corner a group played hard rock. We slept well.

Orthodox, not Catholic or Muslim, is how Serbia has always defined itself. The Orthodox Church played a major historical role in maintaining the Serbian nation under the Ottoman yoke after the fall of the Serbian state following the defeat of Prince Lazar at Kosovo Polje. Serbia has a strong tradition of epic poetry, using the Cyrillic alphabet with a couple of its own specific characters.

Like most of today's European nations, great or small, Serbia had its hour of imperial grandeur. The Nemanja dynasty, the so-called *holy root*, descended from Stefan Nemanja, Grand Prince of Serbia in the 12th century, King Stefan I the *First Crowned*. A hundred years later, Stephen Dušan the Mighty had created the Empire of the Serbs and Greeks, his own mini Byzantium, covering Albania, Epirus, Macedonia and Greece, in addition to Serbia. As one of Europe's most powerful rulers in the 14th century, his ambition had been to conquer Byzantium. His death, followed by the battle of Kosovo Polje, signalled the end of resistance to the advancing Turks and the fall of Byzantium.

We had parked our car the previous night in front of the domed parliament building. Uncontrolled by their stone grooms, two granite horses reared from

Back to Byzantium

their pedestals at the foot of the steps. Returning in the morning, I noticed that a local punk had defaced the one of the pedestals with graffiti. I looked closely. Yes, Glagolitic again, this time not just a tag, but two whole words.

ⰂⰀⰓⰋⰃⰓⰀⰄⰟ ⰐⰀⰛ

I took out the moth-eaten page photocopied from my *Rosetta stone* Glagolitic-Cyrillic correspondence table. My hands trembled as I transliterated it onto the back of a cigarette packet.

Цариград наш

I transliterated again, this time from Cyrillic to Latin characters.

Tsarigrad nash

I believed that I had at last found the meaning of the initials that I kept seeing from country to country, from Skopje to Veliko Trnovo, from Plovdiv to Sarajevo and to Timișoara, but what did it signify?

ЦГН in Cyrillic, **Цариград наш**

CGN in Latin in Croato-Serbian,
Carigrad naš

ȚGN in Romanian, **Țarigrad nostru**

Tsarigrad was the name that the Slavs had given to the city of Constantinople, literally the city of the Caesar, today renamed Istanbul, former capital of the Eastern Roman Empire, known in the West as Byzantium.

With the Fall of Constantinople to the Turks in 1453, the embryonic Russian Empire had begun to call itself the *Third Rome*. After Ivan III had married the heiress of the last Byzantine Emperor, recapturing the city became the objective of the Tsars, encouraged by the Russian Orthodox Church. In spite of many advances throughout the centuries, the Crimean War arrested this ambition.

Though the name *Tsarigrad* had become archaic in Russian, the Bulgarians still used it occasionally when talking of the city's history. In Sofia the main thoroughfare in the direction of Istanbul still bore the name *Tsarigradsko shose*. But, apart from the Slovenians, who still called it *Carigrad*, nobody today used the name.

Once translated, it was clearly a territorial claim.

Constantinople ours

I was back once again on the station platform at Piraeus, listening to my Greek travel companion's remarks about his people's active nostalgia for their long-lost Constantinople.

Returning home, we drove the interminable road to Zagreb with an occasional stork as our only travelling companion. Stopping for lunch in a garden in Slavonsky Brod, we would never have dreamt that here in this peaceful town the war in Slavonia would break out ten years later.

The last couple of nights we spent in the mountains in Croatia, to the North of Rijeka, formerly Fiume, Hungary's last access to the sea. Edmonde bought a filigree bracelet there. The jeweller and I had a conversation, in Croatian for the jeweller, and in bad Bulgarian for myself. But we managed to communicate. I thought that it was the way it must have been at the time of the Habsburgs, Romanovs and Ottomans. In that context you had needed to speak at least the rudiments of the languages of the other peoples of the empire. That was before the USA and Britain finally succeeded in putting into effect their long-term plan to impose the English language as the world-wide *lingua franca*, thereby threatening Europe's and the World's rich cultural diversity.

We continued our return journey through Lombardy, Provence and on to our friends' house North of Avignon. Three days later we finally arrived at my parents' house in the UK just in time to have missed the Royal Wedding of Prince Charles and Princess Diana.

16
Leningrad

The *Euromissile* crisis continued throughout the year. Three European NATO member states deployed *Pershing II* and *Cruise* missiles on their territory, while the Soviet Union suspended *START* talks on strategic arms limitation and the Warsaw Pact member states withdrew from the talks on mutual and balanced force reduction. My wife and I had decided to go cross-country skiing in Leningrad.

We had just officially been married at the Town Hall of Ville d'Avray, a Western suburb of Paris. The wedding reception had already taken place six months previously. Getting married had been complicated, a question of synchronisation. When I finally succeeded in getting my foreign documents in order, the validity of Edmonde's divorce papers had expired. The French authorities required a so-called *certificate of celibacy*. The British consulate, though unable to provide one, were pleased to give me a standard photocopied document testifying that Her Majesty's Consul was unable to state whether I was, or had previously been, married or not. That was sufficient to fill the required space in my file and to check the appropriate box. The Town Hall also required the full address of my future mother-in-law. 'You forgot to put the street number', said the employee. She lived in the country and no street number existed. 'Say number 6', said my future brother-in-law. The woman checked another box.

On the day of the wedding the same employee made the announcement before the assembled guests that we

Back to Byzantium

were here to celebrate the marriage of Mr 'Gr...?' My foreign name, her dyslexia and her lack of the professionalism required to ask me previously how I pronounced it left her speechless. Fortunately a member of my family said it for her. The town councillor in his *tricolor* sash pronounced us man and wife.

I took French citizenship and Edmonde British. We went together to the British consulate in Paris, where she took the oath on the Bible and swore allegiance to 'Queen Elizabeth, her *hairs* and successors'. We celebrated it with a cross-country skiing holiday in Leningrad.

As always in the Soviet Union, it was the state organisation *Inturist* that organised our holiday with a group.

On arrival at Soviet immigration a blue-eyed Border Guards' officer in uniform examined my passport. Every traveller to the Soviet Union remembers those watery but piercing eyes. First he looked at your passport and then, without warning, shot an intense stare straight into one of your eyes, which lasted without blinking for perhaps ten seconds. Strong men flinched under that glare. Then he looked down again at the passport, and up again for another ten. They were not going to let me in, or else they were going to put me away! At the peak of your panic he stamped your passport and returned it to you. It happened every time. Pure intimidation. Going through customs with your form containing seven answers beginning with the letter 'N', 'No', 'Non', 'Nein', Nyet, Nem', etc. was pure routine and the customs officer was even pleasant. One wonders how they managed with Greeks, where they use *okhi* for *no*.

Travelling in a group is not everyone's ideal holiday. 'Hell is other people', wrote Sartre. What was this little local museum that they call the *Ermitage*? At a *CTOП* sign, why had they written *STOP* in French?'

We stayed at a hotel in Olgino, a wealthy suburb of Leningrad on the North shore of the Gulf of Finland. At dinner, just after our arrival, the hotel manager subjected us to a long welcome speech about international friendship. The subsequent visits to our rooms by members of the hotel staff, eager to purchase our jeans, shoes, in fact any item of clothing, illustrated this.

'I remember this sort of speech from my last visit to the Soviet Union five years ago. Why do the Soviets always *spontaneously* give you uninteresting information and then when you ask them a question start lying through their teeth?' I mused to a History professor in our travel group when the manager had finished speaking.

'There's nothing strictly Soviet about it', he answered. 'The Russians have apparently always done it. Have you read the *Marquis* de Custine? If you haven't, you should. He would help you to understand the permanent nature of the Russian soul.'

I replied that I had, during my last visit to Russia on the *Transsib*. As any self-respecting History teacher would, he told me about him nevertheless.

'What Custine wrote, more or less, was that since the visitor to Russia could see nothing without a guide, he had difficulty in forming a judgement on spontaneous impressions. The Russians were very good at explaining everything that you didn't really care to know, such as the number of hundredweight of corn produced this year, while giving no information on what really interested you. He talked of them tyrannising the visitor while pretending to inform him.'

Fortunately this was a winter holiday and *Inturist,* who understood to perfection the desires of foreign tourists, had prepared an entertaining program. In the mornings we went skiing and in the afternoon we took a *troïka* ride through the forest, sped across the frozen Gulf of Finland on a snow scooter, tried ice fishing through a hole in the frozen sea with little success, followed by caviar and vodka to compensate for what we didn't catch.

Back to Byzantium

Inturist took us to the *Ermitage* Museum, to the Opera for Tchaikovsky's *Queen of Spades*, taken from Pushkin's short story, to the ballet for Prokofiev's *Romeo and Juliet*. More politically, we visited on skis the haystack where Lenin had gone into hiding. Having read Gogol, *Nevskiï Prospekt* fascinated me the most, seen through the air made opaque by the extreme cold.

As we skied across country through the birch forest along the Gulf, young ski monitors followed us constantly and attentively. They must be *KGB* agents. Wrong, they were just checking that our noses hadn't turned blue, an early warning sign that they were ready to fall off from frostbite. The remedy consisted of rubbing snow onto your nose and then massaging it vigorously.

'What made the Slavs and particularly the Russians so different from us?' I asked, continuing my conversation with the History professor. 'When did the East finally separate from the West? Was it with the Sack of Constantinople by the Crusaders, or did it happen earlier with the Great Schism?'

'Both of them, and not all at once. You know that the division of the Christian world between the Eastern Orthodox and Western Catholic churches was a very gradual process, begun as early as the second century, culminating in mutual excommunication in 1054.'

'What were the main issues? Was it the

question of images?'

'You are quite right, but they eventually managed to solve that issue. It also concerned the celibacy of priests, the purpose of purgatory, the nature of original sin, the unleavened bread in the Eucharist and the famous *filioque* in the Nicene Creed, which has also been an issue for Protestants like ourselves. I assume that you are an Anglican.'

I admitted that I was, at least by birth (and also by definition, there being no separation between Church and State).

'The origins of the schism were political, linguistic and cultural, while its manifestations were doctrinal and liturgical. A major cause was language, Latin in the West, Greek in the East. As bilingual clerics became rarer and rarer, communications deteriorated, causing the rites and even the doctrines to take different directions.

'But the main issue as always was political. It was the question of universal jurisdiction and the place of Constantinople.'

'If it had been brewing for centuries, what triggered the Great Schism?' I asked.

'In the fourth century, as you know, Constantine had moved his imperial capital from Rome to Byzantium, *the New Rome*. Rome always claimed to have sole jurisdiction as the head of the congregation of the Church. Then, a hundred years later, the Council of Chalcedon had proclaimed the equality of the Bishops of Rome and Constantinople.

'In 476 the Western Roman Empire fell to Alaric. Justinian established *Caesaropapism*, whereby the *Basileus*, the Emperor of Byzantium, as God's copy on earth, had the right to control details of liturgy and doctrine. The Byzantine Empire was a theocracy, in which the Emperor held supreme authority over both church and state. This tradition is contrary to that of the Western Church, established following Jesus's commandment to 'render unto Caesar the things that are Caesar's and unto God the things that are God's', which is the basis for the separation between Church and State.

'Then came the Schism itself. In 1053 Pope Leo IX sent a letter to the Patriarch Michael I Cerularius of Constantinople, who had rejected papal primacy. He gave the legates sent by the Pope a hostile reception. After Leo IX's death, the papal legate to Constantinople placed a bill of excommunication on the high altar of *Hagia Sofia* during the liturgy, excommunicating Cerularius, who promptly returned the honour with a counter-excommunication.

'This escalation was not generally considered at the time to be really significant. Friendly relations continued between East and West until the Fourth Crusade' - here it was at last – 'cemented the schism with the Sack of Constantinople by fellow Christians from the West.'

'The Fourth Crusade fascinates me. But what happened after the Fall of Constantinople to the Turks in 1453?'

'It was very simple. *Mutis mutandis*, Mehmet the Conqueror assumed the legal function of the former *Basileus*. The Orthodox Church became the autonomous *millet*, with the Ottoman State nominating the Patriarch. Moscow became officially autocephalous, calling itself *the Third Rome*. So the entire Orthodox community became isolated from the West.'

'Yes, but didn't anyone try to reconcile the two churches?'

'Of course, there were lots of attempts to heal the rift both before and after the Great Schism, generally initiated by the church hierarchy. Each time it was the populace of the Orthodox world who rejected it.

'After he had re-conquered Constantinople from the Latins, Emperor Michael VIII Palaiologus tried to unite the two churches. Then, at the Council of Ferrara-Florence, only fourteen years before the Fall of Constantinople, John VIII Palaiologus, currently under threat from the Turks, even agreed to accept the *filioque*, the principle of purgatory and papal primacy. Though he signed the union, the people never accepted it.

'So, can you believe it, we had to wait more than five hundred years, until the Second Vatican Council less than twenty years ago, for the two Churches finally to make a joint declaration of reconciliation.'

Every evening our guide gave us a Russian lesson, though we didn't get much further than the Cyrillic alphabet and the basic rules of pronunciation, which I had learnt five years previously on the *Transsib*.

A young French woman in our group had made a deal with a Russian tenor for a *white* wedding. Imagine a regime so perverse that an opera singer would agree to leave his native country for a *Française moyenne*. On our last evening he sang for us with drunken melancholy. *Inturist* had taken us to dinner at the restaurant of the Grand Hotel Europa off *Nevskiï Prospekt*. After the end of Communism it was to become one of the finest in Europe, where I would later stay briefly for the Goodwill Games. They served us dinner to the accompaniment of sullen musicians who obviously despised the vulgarity of the heavily imbibed foreign tourists. The evening ended with

Back to Byzantium

the *chicken dance*, reason enough for the musicians to look sullen.

On the last free afternoon of our holiday I was strolling with my friend the History professor down the lower, seedier stretch of *Nevskiï Prospekt*.

'Do you know who Anna Komnene was?'

'Wasn't she the daughter of a Byzantine emperor?"

'Yes, she was the daughter of Alexios I Komnenos. As probably the world's first female historian, she has always been an inspiration for me in my profession. In her *Alexiad*, a chronicle of her father's reign, she describes how the Byzantines perceived the Crusaders.

'Alexios had called for help from the West against the Turks. You may remember that in fact he only requested mercenary forces, but Pope Urban II launched the First Crusade. Alexios was dismayed when he discovered the massive horde of Franks that was crossing his territory and even stopping in Constantinople. His daughter Anna had time to get to know the Franks. She called them *Celts*.

'Her opinion was categorical. She considered the Crusaders to be barbarians. They were an irrational people, incapable of reasoning, without self-control. They were impolite, undisciplined. They recognised no sovereign. When the crusaders finally left the Empire, the Byzantines breathed a sigh of relief.

'Anna Komnene understood that the rank and file of the Crusade were, at least in the beginning, inspired by a sincere ideal of praying in the Holy Places and by the wish to come to the aide of their Christian brothers of the Orient. She recognised that they were courageous in war and technologically superior to the Greeks. As for their leaders, their sole motivation was greed. And she was also shocked to see members of the Catholic clergy bearing arms.

'Her father, Alexios, meanwhile, did have a kind of grudging admiration for the Crusaders.'

Further down the road we stopped by a disused shop window. Someone had stuck a photo in it, just visible through the dust and grime.

ЦГН

There it lay in faded fly-bespeckled sepia, easily recognisable as the basilica of *Hagia Sofia* in Istanbul. But what had become of the minarets?

Beneath it someone had written the three same letters in Cyrillic, **ЦГН**, meaning, as I now knew, **Tsarigrad nash, Constantinople Ours**.

It looked just as it must have done before the Fall of Constantinople to the Turks in 1453. So this was the oriental temple that I had seen tattooed on the girl's arm at the *Turist Biro* in Sarajevo and stencilled onto the poster of Lenin at the station in Krasnoïarsk. The photo had of course been doctored, a tradition in this country.

'You know what these three letters mean?' I asked the historian. 'Nostalgia for Byzantium, what they call *our Constantinople*, as if the Russians had a legitimate claim to it!'

'But it did almost become *their*

Constantinople, twice. First with Catherine the Great, who devised with Joseph II of Austria a plan to calve up the Balkans. Russia was to take over Istanbul and place Catherine's grandson, appropriately name Constantine, on the throne of a recreated Byzantium (Austria was to get roughly what corresponds more or less to today's Yugoslavia). She even had a triumphal arch built bearing the inscription *The road to Byzantium*. When the major Western powers objected, she fell back on Crimea.

Then a second time a hundred and thirty years later. If Churchill had been better informed and his Gallipoli campaign in the Dardanelles had not been the disaster it was, Constantinople today might well be part of the Russian Empire.'

'How come?' I asked.

'Well, the allies in the Triple Entente, that's Britain, France and Russia, reached a secret agreement in 1915. It stipulated that, in case of victory of the allies in the war, not only Constantinople, but also the Sea of Marmara, the Dardanelles, the West bank of the Bosphorus and a large part of Thrace were to become part of the empire of the Tsar. Constantinople itself was to become a free port.'

'How on earth could Britain and France agree to this, when they had fought the Crimean War to prevent it just sixty years before?'

'With considerable reservation, of course, for what the British memorandum described as *the richest treasure of the entire war*. The purpose was to prevent the Russians making a separate peace with Germany. But it was actually a transaction. The allies were busy carving up what was left of Ottoman territory, which was still considerable. France wanted Syria and would have liked to take Palestine, while Britain wanted to extend its control over Persia.'

'Why was the agreement secret?' I asked.

'So as not to offend the Romanians and the Bulgarians, who also had territorial claims, and bring Bulgaria, unsuccessfully in fact, onto the side of the allies. But it didn't remain secret. After the Russian Revolution, Lenin revealed its existence, which France and Britain promptly denied'

'So, what prevented it from being implemented? After all, the allies did win the war.'

'Several things: first, the allied defeat in the Dardanelles, secondly, the overthrow of the government of Russia in 1917, followed by its withdrawal from the war, the allies' fear of the Bolsheviks and, lastly, the determination of Mustafa Kemal, commander of the Gallipoli campaign, to regain Constantinople for the new Turkish Republic, even at the risk of a war with Britain and France.'

Hagia Sofia had apparently become the polarisation of nostalgia that all the peoples of the Orthodox world felt for the Byzantine Empire, first destroyed by the Franks, later seized by the Turks. History only ever disappears intermittently from a people's collective memory. But was this just a manifestation of collective nostalgia or did it mean something much more sinister, covering the whole of the Orthodox world, a confirmation of my suspicions in Belgrade?

17
Istanbul

April had come and we needed a holiday. My wife, Edmonde, was three months pregnant. I wanted to return to Athens, but my fifteen-year-old stepson, Arnauld, insisted on Istanbul. Ten months previously an Armenian terrorist group had set off bomb at the Turkish Airlines check-in counter at Orly Airport and we were leaving by Turkish Airlines from Orly. My stepson had in his pocket the spark-plug spanner that he had forgotten to return to his tool box after repairing his *moped*. The security officers spotted it and after intense scrutiny of our bags, let us through, smirking at our embarrassment.

Türk Hava Yolları, the Turkish national carrier, was one of those airlines where the passengers applauded on landing. We took the airport bus to our third-class hotel in the centre. The room was adequate, but the toilet was palatial. I knew so-called Turkish toilets in Paris, simply a porcelain hole with a moon-boot printed platform for each foot. Received ideas had left me unprepared for the hygienic installation here. A short, pointed pipe equipped with a tap protruded from the back of the pan at the appropriate level. There had been no mention of it in *Fear of Flying*, but then most Americans never travelled beyond Venice or Vienna.

My stepson wanted to experience a *hammam*, so with trepidation I accompanied him to the historic *Galatasaray Hamamı* off *İstiklâl Caddesi*, the main thoroughfare of the old Greek quarter of *Beyoğlu*, or Pera. My stepson loved it. For someone who has never felt at ease in his own body, I found it a horrid experience, akin to a physical assault. We lay on a marble slab with water drip dripping above. Then an archetypally strong Turk took me into a corner and gave me a more than vigorous massage.

'*Baksheesh?*' he asked. 'OK', I answered in spite of myself. He started slapping me about aggressively, throwing copper bowls alternately of hot and cold water, while looking me in the eye with contempt. It did finally end and we got dressed again. On the way out we ran the gauntlet of fifteen men standing by the exit, all waiting for a tip. I managed to satisfy the first ten until, out of pocket, I could do nothing but shrug my shoulders and hurry to the door, with five still left waiting. Never again for me, but I had to agree with my stepson that, for the first and, hopefully, the last time in my life, I felt so clean that as I rubbed the back of my hand no trace of a roll of grime was apparent.

Edmonde became concerned about her pregnancy. We located the *Fransız Pasteur Hastanesi*, the *French* hospital, situated near *Taksim*. No-one spoke French except, as we later discovered, an Italian nun. The house surgeon received us courteously and examined my wife. He spoke only German, but his medical vocabulary was all in French. 'Das kann entweder eine *grossesse extra-uterine* oder eine *fausse couche* sein.' So it could be either a ectopic pregnancy or a miscarriage. He gave her some medicine and told her to come back the following morning, ringing us twice at our hotel to find out how it was developing.

One of my colleagues in Paris had married a Turk, who kept a *café-tabac* in Paris. He had made a quite a lot of money and was eager to show us both what he thought was authentic Istanbul and display the extent of his wealth. Accepting his invitation despite Edmonde's condition, we joined him with a couple of his friends in a traditional restaurant, where we listened to a man singing Ottoman poetry.

'Is this the music of the *Janissaries?*' I asked the more educated and communicative of his friends. 'Not at all', he said. 'The *yeniçeri* played military music, using bass drums, triangles, and cymbals. You know the origin of the name? It meant *new soldier*. It was Murad I who set up the unit in the 14th century to be his personal bodyguard. At one time they came to represent one tenth of the Turkish fighting force.'

'They were recruited through the *devşirme* process, I believe', I said, remembering my lesson in the train corridor in Yugoslavia a few years before.

'They were, at least at the beginning. At first they were recruited every five or so years across the Balkans from among Christian boys taken from their families. Janissaries may have been slaves of the *Porte*, but they had a special status, receiving salaries and retirement pensions. Severe training, almost hard labour, turned them into a well-disciplined army corps. The system was meritocratic. The most talented became members of the ruling class. Of course it broke the hearts of most Christian parents to lose their boys, but for some of them it provided social advancement.'

I remembered what Lady Mary Wortley Montagu had said about the *devşirme*. As the wife of the British Ambassador to the *Porte* she had spent a year and a half in Ottoman Turkey from 1717, keeping up a regular correspondence in which she recounted her thoughts and experiences to her friends and family. She had special appreciation for the fact that, whereas for Western Christians a man of good birth, though quite devoid of merit, could make his fortune, for the Ottomans even a man of low birth with talent could do the same. Under the *devşirme*, a page could potentially become the Grand Vizier.

'You know that they shared with Catholic priests the obligation to remain celibate', he continued. 'The corps was their *family*, the Sultan their *father*. They were forbidden to take up any non-military profession other than as engineers or sappers. They were not even allowed to grow beards either, at least at the beginning.

'Then, later on, starting from the 16th century, Janissaries gradually obtained concessions that had been refused them for nearly three hundred years and the *corps* began to degenerate. They were given permission to get married and have children. Their sons became Janissaries themselves by a shortcut, avoiding the severe training period. As you can imagine, other Turks then wanted their own children to benefit from social advancement in the Janissary corps. All this brought about a less disciplined and effective force.

'A hundred years later the *devşirme* was abolished. Protest arose in some Balkan villages. It deprived families of a vehicle for social advancement in favour of the Turks, who reserved the best positions for themselves. Janissaries took up other activities, set up businesses, joined professional guilds and neglected their military duties. The system of course ceased to be a meritocracy. The last straw was when they were eventually allowed to grow beards.

'With their numbers increasing from ten thousand to a maximum of 135,000, the Janissaries had become a reactionary force, opposed to any change to the system that might deprive them of their privileges.'

'How did it end?' I asked.

'Badly. Janissaries had gained such influence that they dominated government. They practised extortion from the Sultan by demanding wage increases and bonuses. In short, they became a law unto themselves and their abuse of power a threat to the Empire. In 1804 the Janissaries in Serbia set up a *junta*. When the Sultan threatened to oppose them with the help the local nobility, they massacred the Serbian aristocracy, triggering uprisings that led to Serbian independence. For two hundred years successive sultans had tried to reduce their power, but the Janissaries resisted all attempts at modernisation, even going as far as deposing or executing sultans. In addition, the cost in salaries for an oversized corps that had ceased to be militarily effective was reason enough to disband them.

'Finally, in 1826, Mahmud II incited them to revolt by a subterfuge. He then had their barracks set on fire, four thousand of them massacred, and those who escaped executed or exiled after confiscation of their possessions. This became known as the *Vaka-i Hayriye, the Auspicious Event.*'

My colleague's husband by this time had drunk several glasses of *raki*. 'You do not understand Turkish. You are not capable of appreciating this', he said. 'It is traditional Ottoman poetry.'

In that case, why had he brought us here? My stepson looked bored, but my colleague's husband probably wasn't sufficiently sensitive or perceptive to notice that Edmonde was in extreme discomfort on her chair due to her ill-fated pregnancy, and it wasn't his problem. 'For me it is folklore', I said. He took offence, we curtailed our dinner and went home. Edmonde was hospitalised the following day. When we really needed him he was no longer available.

The next morning we went directly to the French hospital. Edmonde was having a miscarriage, caused by toxoplasmosis. She had caught it most probably from our cat, *Vlad* (briefly called *Enver*). Friends told us to get of rid it. We kept the cat and later had children.

The hospital was rudimentary, but the house surgeon was professional. We moved into a two-bedded room, where I could stay with my wife. The bedpan had not been emptied since the previous patient. The doctor asked us to give our permission for the operation, to which my stepson and I had no choice but to agree. A surgeon arrived. He had the strange physique of some Turks, dark skinned with dark eyes but with blond hair, a result of the *devşirme* perhaps. The operating theatre consisted of a table over which hung a single naked light bulb, but the fact that Edmonde subsequently had two healthy babies may be proof of the surgeon's expertise.

The Socialist government in France had just put exchange control in place to stem the flight of capital, which increased my anxiety. How were we going to pay for the hospital? Fortunately it was only for one night.

We left the hospital the next morning. Once again, I had to give *baksheesh* to each nurse, including the chief sister. There was a risk of phlebitis, the house surgeon told us. We should force my wife to walk. My stepson and I each put an arm under her armpits and we frogmarched her up and down the hills to and from the *Souleimaniye,* discovering, in spite of the personal trauma, the charm of the different quarters in Istanbul, like little villages in Europe, each with its café and mosque.

Back to Lady Mary Wortley Montagu. She claimed to have exploded some myths brought back by commercial travellers concerning the Ottoman Empire. Not having access to Turks and especially to women, they had merely reinforced their own preconceived ideas. Her discussions with an erudite *effendi* in Constantinople had awakened in her an intellectual empathy with the Turks. The separation between men and women and the baths at the *hammam* had enabled her to have access to the intimacy of Eastern women.

Lady Mary had learnt Turkish and translated Ottoman verse, even dressing as a Turk, which gave her greater freedom of movement. She discovered that, paradoxically, within the despotism of the system, women had developed a kind of freedom and power. She believed that Ottoman women had greater freedom of movement than did the English women of her time. Her theory was that, being unrecognisable under their veil, they had nothing to fear from the indiscretion of a lover, since no one found out about their infidelity. Neither did they fear their husbands since they possessed their own money, which they took back in case of divorce. This was not the case with Western women.

She claimed that, contrary to their appalling reputation, the Turks were not a naturally cruel. Their justice was prompt, providing as little suffering as possible. She found them to be a generous people, who rarely told a lie. And they were generally tolerant of other religions of the Book, comparing favourably with the Spanish *Reconquista*, with its Inquisition and forced conversions.

On our last day we took a boat across the Bosphorus to Üsküdar, known in the West as Scutari, infamous for its hospital during the Crimean War, presided over by Florence Nightingale. We wanted to visit the Muslim cemetery with its Ottoman tombs, like the ones I had seen in Sarajevo and would see again in Budapest. We apparently witnessed a burial that we should not have seen. Still holding Edmonde up by her armpits, we were followed by a threatening bearded fundamentalist carrying a large spade. We took refuge with a middle-aged Turkish middle-class couple, who didn't understand our unease. The miscarriage and our night in the hospital had upset us considerably. I felt like the paranoid protagonist of Alain Robbe-Grillet's film *L'Immortelle*.

The next day we visited *Hagia Sofia* and the Blue Mosque. Everywhere we went, carpet-shop hustlers and unofficial tour guides would be on our heels offering their services. The only thing that seemed to discourage them was to say a couple of words in Bulgarian. We finally succumbed to a man in his forties offering his services as a guide, which we accepted at what must have been an outrageous price. He compensated for his lack of knowledge of Turkish history or of architecture by great enthusiasm for every place that we visited. 'When was this built?' I would ask. 'Very old, very beautiful', he would reply. I had to rely entirely on my guide book.

> Emperor Justinian had built *Hagia Sofia*, the Church of the Holy Wisdom, in 537. The original architects were a physicist, his son, and a mathematician. More than a thousand people worked on its construction
>
> It was here that, having ransacked it during the sack of Constantinople in 1204, the Crusaders had crowned the unfortunate Baldwyn as Emperor of the new Latin Empire.
>
> Mehmet II, after conquering Constantinople, turned it into a mosque, building a wooden minaret. His son, Beyazıd II, replaced it with two new minarets on the east side, one of brick, one of white marble. The dome was twice destroyed, once by an earthquake, once by fire. During the 16th century, Suleiman the Magnificent employed the architect Sinan to reinforce the building. He did it by constructing the two Western minarets out of white marble of different dimensions as a counterbalance to protect the building against earthquakes. Without them the building might have collapsed. It became a model for subsequent mosques that Sinan and his disciples built. I

wondered if this might not be a metaphor for the situation of the Orthodox Church after the Ottoman conquest.

In 1935 Mustafa Kemal Atatürk turned the building into a museum. Eighty years later, Prime Minister Recep Tayyip Erdoğan would attempt to turn *Hagia Sofia* into a mosque once again, but only in the afternoon and evening, leaving it as a museum during the morning.

On my return to France I bought a push-out model-cum-puzzle of *Hagia Sofia*. To my surprise I discovered that it its designer had planned it to be assembled in two distinct ways.

'We sell two different versions', the salesperson explained. Here you have the *standard* model with the four minarets, corresponding to the building as it looks today.

'Here is another version', he continued. 'The so-called **CGN** model, which has had a lot of success across the Balkans and in the Soviet Union. As you can see, without the minarets, it corresponds to the building as it looked before the Turks turned it into a mosque. This model is currently in great demand in Bulgaria.

'Which version did you have in mind, the *standard* model or the **CGN**?'

'What does **CGN** stand for?' I asked.

'***Church of the Greek Nemesis***, I believe, or something like that.'

I took the standard model.

I had been reading about the Fall of Constantinople to Mehmed II and had been surprised by the differing perceptions of the situation by the Greeks, the Russians and the Catholic West.

The Greeks considered the Fall of Constantinople as divine punishment for the Ecumenical Union at the Council of Florence between the Eastern Orthodox and Western Catholic churches. They realised on the other hand that the Ottomans had reunified the Orthodox world and provided real protection against the Catholics. The Greeks had a new hope of dominating the Orthodox Church once again. With the *millet* system the Orthodox peoples had to pay taxes, but it was no worse than before. Certain collaborationists considered the Sultan as their new *Basileus*, since the Sultan had taken for himself the title of *Kayzer-i-Rum*, Emperor of the Romans. Their persistent fear was that Eastern Christians would convert to Islam to reduce their taxes and obtain social advancement.

Russia, on the other hand, saw the Fall of Constantinople as more of a spiritual than a political loss. It was their Tsar that they considered to be the new *Basileus*, Moscow as the new Constantinople, the future capital of Orthodoxy. The Russians, like the Greeks, perceived it as a punishment for the attempted Ecumenical Union

As for the Catholic West, there was general indifference, followed by oblivion. Their only interest seemed to be in Byzantine relics, antiquities and manuscripts. Pope Pius II had prepared a new crusade, but it collapsed after his death. The Venetians and Genovese were mainly concerned with maintaining trade, protection of their ports and maritime routes and with keeping their fiscal privileges.

Later, in the 16th century, François I and Suleiman the Magnificent signed the Franco-Ottoman alliance against emperor Charles V, the so-called sacrilegious union of the *Fleur-de-Lys* and the Crescent. Even during the Crusades, the Franks had shared certain values with the Turks, such as horses, arms, courage in war, which they never shared with the Arabs. The Crusaders admired the Turks as knights, while they despised the Byzantines as intellectuals. The Franks believed that the Turks as a people were superior to the Byzantines and the Arabs. They admired them for their efficiency and cleanliness, comparing them unfavourably with the Greeks.

As for the Turks, they considered themselves to be, as knights, of the same race as the Franks. Yet they never believed in the religious motivation of the Crusaders, who had come simply as invaders with greed as their sole motivation. The Turks, like the Byzantine Greeks, considered the

Franks to be ignorant and crude.

My stepson had been dabbling in the Turkish language. He had noted that you could say *Goodbye* in two ways, depending on whether you were leaving or staying behind. *Allahaısmarladık* is what you say when you leave, to which the answer is *Güle güle*. He tried all he could to find an opportunity to say *Güle güle*, but he was always the one leaving. To his disappointment, he never found the appropriate occasion to use it.

We returned to Paris, where, to our surprise, French Social Security refunded all our hospital costs. A year and a half later my wife had a baby whom we named Chloë.

18
Budapest

The Germans had demolished the Berlin Wall a year and a half before, but Boris Eltsin had not yet succeeded in finishing off the Soviet Union.

I was standing having coffee in the offices of a huge American IT company. That was the place where you found yourself an assignment, by the coffee machine. A colleague of mine told me that he had been working in Hungary on a preliminary study for restructuring and fully computerising the Hungarian social security system. The second phase was about to begin. I got on the phone to the man in charge, an American in Brussels with whom I had previously been in phone contact. I knew his friend *X*, he said, so I must be a *good guy*. A couple of weeks later I arrived in Budapest. Nobody in our company in France except me wanted to travel abroad.

We had invited the Hungarian management team to the UK and then to France. While we dined with them on oysters in a restaurant off the *Champs Elysées*, I asked one of them what he wanted to see in Paris. 'Clémenceau's tomb!' he answered. 'Ah, why is that?' I asked. 'To spit on it!' he said.

I knew that Clémenceau, probably the politician who had contributed the most to winning the First World War by uniting the allies of the Triple Entente under a single unified command, had shown himself to be the most intransigent of all during the peace talks leading to the Treaties of Versailles. I could imagine that the Germans didn't share the French admiration for the *Le Tigre*. Didn't the Hungarians either? They had brought their interpreter with them. I asked him to explain his colleagues' remark.

'You certainly know all about the Treaty of Versailles', he said. 'Perhaps you know less about the Treaty of Trianon.

'The Treaty of Trianon was signed between the allies of the *Entente* and Hungary in Versailles in 1920. The allies dictated the treaty without any negotiation with Hungary, which had no option other than to sign under protest. It dismembered Hungary, severing it from of more than two thirds of its territory and almost two thirds of its former population. Our country lost five major cities and its only port, Fiume, now Rijeka, turning it, like Austria, into a small, landlocked country. Its new borders took into account neither ethnic, linguistic nor economic questions.

'Though a majority of non-Hungarians inhabited the regions that *Trianon* allocated to its neighbours, large Hungarian-speaking minorities remained there, representing a total of more than three million. A third of all Hungarians became *ipso facto* citizens of neighbouring countries. Though the Treaty was theoretically based on the principle of the right of peoples to self-determination, the French and British refused Hungary's proposal for referenda in disputed areas, contrary to what they permitted in East Prussia or Schleswig-Holstein. By granting former Hungarian territory to its neighbours, the *Entente* allowed them to take over whole areas where Hungarian speakers were in the majority, such as North-West Transylvania, ceded to Romania, Southern Slovakia and Northern Serbia. Hungarian speakers represented generally nearly one third of the total population of these regions. As for Transylvania, the *Entente* treated it as a monolithic entity, without taking the large Hungarian-speaking areas into account.'

'But why didn't the allies take the wishes of the Hungarian people into account? Was it Clémenceau's revenge?' I asked.

'The *Entente* aimed to contain Austria and Hungary and surround them by successor states larger than they were. In a secret pact, the *Entente* had promised Transylvania to Romania in exchange for it attacking Austria-Hungary. Clemenceau took sides with Romania, a Latin nation that spoke French, some say also due to his admiration for the beauty of British-born, half-Russian Queen Marie of Romania, who had arrived unannounced at Versailles!

'The West considered Hungary to be an oppressive colonial power, which had imposed its language on occupied nations. The small nations considered *Trianon* to be a just treaty, particularly Croatia. Hungary had tried to assimilate Croatians into the Kingdom of Hungary by denying them the right to their language and nationality.'

'But it still sounds like incredible injustice'

'So it was. The Hungarians saw *Trianon* as purely punitive, an insult to their national honour. A contemporary patriotic book even depicted the pre-*Trianon* map of greater Hungary pinned to a cross, crucified like Christ. They have never doubted that the severed regions belonged to them as part of their core national territory.'

'Then Hungary never regained any of its lost territory?'

'Well, almost. In 1938 under the infamous Munich agreement Hungary regained part of it, which it subsequently lost. Hungary's present borders are those of *Trianon*. During the Cold War, though the subject was taboo, it remained a source of tension between the Socialist sister nations of Hungary and Romania. Contemporary Hungary has a lasting feeling of historic injustice and is nostalgic for its former grandeur.'

József Antall had recently announced that he considered himself also to be the Prime Minister of fifteen million Hungarians, which included those living in Czechoslovakia, Serbia and Romania.

As I was to learn later, *Trianon* had become Hungary's national obsession. Every meeting that I attended in Hungary with a new interlocutor, without a single exception, began invariably first with coffee, then with a presentation of the injustice of *Trianon* using almost the identical words that I had heard from the interpreter in Paris.

Visiting Versailles with my nephew and his Hungarian wife a few years later, we entered the ticket office of the Grand Trianon in the grounds of the Palace. 'Where did they sign the Trianon Treaty?' I innocently asked the woman at the desk. 'You must be Hungarian', she said, unobtrusively moving her hand toward the telephone. 'You are not going to break everything?' We left quietly.

With the American project manager I made several trips to Budapest and Vienna to discuss the second phase of the project. Like many deals in my experience it dragged on for months, with moments of encouragement and others of despair. I went on holiday with my family to the French Jura region, which I spent in a state of permanent anxiety. When, towards the end, I heard the news of the *coup d'état* by the insurgents against Mikhail Gorbachëv, under house arrest in Sochi, I felt more concerned with not being able to return to Budapest than by the probable return of the Cold War.

At the end of my holiday I set off for Vienna and Budapest to get the project moving again, reporting to a manager in Vienna. Throughout the following year I travelled frequently between the two cities, three hours distant by road or by rail.

We initiated team building with the provisional Hungarian development management team. They were obsessed with including a representative member from each of the political factions in their administration. As soon as they had signed the letter of intent, I drove from Paris to Budapest. I hired ten engineers for the project internally within our company, all from the US. Due to the financing of the project by a US government agency, our team was composed only of American citizens. I was the exception.

A month later, when our team members had just arrived in Budapest, a *putsch* took place within the administration and a new management team took over the project. They decided to renegotiate the preliminary agreement. After obtaining extra financing for the project, they eventually signed the contract and we began work. Yet we worked in a climate of suspicion, based partly on anti-Western feeling and insufficient cooperation on both sides. After the end of the second phase, the administration preferred to adopt a *Bismarck-style* healthcare system, calling on an Australian company to implement it.

One of the problems that we tried to address was the time lapse required between the day when a Hungarian took retirement and the initial payment of his or her pension, currently at an average of fifteen months. Work history had been stored on paper files in cardboard binders kept vertically on metal shelves on several levels from floor to ceiling in the cellar of the main social security building. They said that it covered a linear distance approaching more than ten kilometres. The pages had become brown and brittle with age and were foxed so much at the corners as to be hardly legible. A single spark from the street through the ever-open windows could have destroyed the work history of the entire adult population of Hungary. Fortunately, the World Bank had apparently made provision for a safety net for this sort of potential disaster. A project was under way to copy the pages onto microfiches. Unfortunately, the work moved chronologically forward, starting with the oldest files, at a rhythm that could not even keep up with the creation of new paper files.

We worked with consecutive interpreters, translating in both directions. I reckoned that the duration of a conversation was multiplied by nearly three: once in the source language, once in the target language and once to iron out misunderstandings. Two situations always amused me. The first, which occurs frequently, is when the interpreter, in a state of exhaustion, repeats verbatim to the *receiver* in the source language instead of the target language what he has just heard from the *sender*. The situation that I enjoy the most is when both interlocutors get into a fit of giggles over a professional joke that they share, while the interpreter remains stony-faced, not having understood its substance, even though he has just translated it.

Back to Byzantium

I began learning Hungarian from cassettes before leaving for Budapest and continued there with a private tutor. Hungarian has the reputation for being the language that you can't learn. What makes it so difficult?

Hungarian is not an Indo-European language, but part of the so-called Finno-Ugric family. As Patrick Leigh Fermor discovered during his walk across Europe in the thirties, in fact Finnish and Hungarian are perhaps only about as closely related as, for example, English and Farsi, having parted company forty-five centuries ago on their long journey from the Urals. Hungarian has the reputation with British diplomats for being the hardest language for them to learn, closely followed by Japanese, due to its grammar and its vocabulary, bearing no resemblance to any word in European languages. It is a language that can be understood only if one has decided to learn it.

In fact, Hungarian is much easier than its reputation.

Unlike most European languages, it has no genders. Nor does it make a distinction between he and she. Anyone who has learned German knows how hard it is to guess whether a noun is masculine or neuter.

It is perfectly phonetic, with a slight stress falling on the first syllable. This means that you can spell a word that you have heard spoken once, and pronounce it correctly when you have seen it written for the first time.

Though nouns and pronouns may have more than twenty-three case endings, they are not really declensions, but just invariable suffixes that are appended to the word, having the same function as prepositions in European languages. This is called agglutination.

Hungarian is an almost perfect linguistic construction with few exceptions, like a language version of the exasperating cube that Ernő Rubik invented in 1974. The problem with Hungarian is its vocabulary, formed almost exclusively from its own store of words. For example, the word photocopy is similar in most languages, often called by the trade mark, *Xerox*. In Hungarian it is called *fénymásolás*!

Back to Byzantium

We had spent three months in our hotel rooms preparing to start a project whose existence was more and more uncertain. Finally, just before Christmas the Hungarian government signed the contract and we began working in the New Year.

Our office was located at first in the enormous dilapidated red-brick building of the Social Security Directorate, a *Kafkaesque* construction dating from before the First World War, with luxurious *salons* for management and miserable offices for the others. They housed us at first on the top floor, under the rafters of an abandoned attic. A *paternoster* lift carried employees from one floor to another.

A *paternoster* lift is a chain of open compartments, usually designed for one or two persons, which moves slowly in a loop up and down inside a building without stopping. Passengers can step on or off an ascending or a descending lift cage in motion. It looks and feels like a vertical coffin, especially when you fail to alight at the bottom floor and are afraid of being gobbled up by the mechanism. But no, there is a reassuring sign telling you not to panic and you begin your ascent on the other side. It gives you the kind of thrill that you used to feel when climbing on or off a bus in motion in London or in Paris.

Returning to visit Budapest twenty years later, I looked unsuccessfully for the lift. 'You are looking for the *Pater Noster*', said the security officer, crying on my shoulder. 'They replaced it with a modern lift.'

I moved with my family into a very large high room under the roof in the post-modern hotel complex for foreigners located near the top of one of the Buda hills, where our company housed members of the team. We looked down onto a spectacular view over the back of the Castle Hill, which hid Pest and the Danube from our view. On the other side above lay the wooded slopes of Buda. Our children attended the French school a little further up the hill. A chair lift carried you to the top, leaving your legs dangling in the air almost low enough to touch the bushes of the private gardens as you passed over them. We later moved into a sumptuous flat on two levels with two staircases and four bathrooms. In fact we lived in four hotel suites that had been merged into a single apartment.

Our company paid us generous expenses, for which government regulations required us to fill in expense reports for a fixed *per diem* amount. To justify for tax purposes the expenses that we were receiving anyway, they made us grovel by the supermarket cash desks in search of receipts to enter as plausible backup.

Edmonde and the children had arrived in Budapest on New Year's Eve in the deep snow in the most magical urban scenery we had ever seen. On New Year's Day we travelled North up the Danube to Szentendre. The town, which has since become a tourist trap similar to Montmartre in Paris, had remained untouched and empty. The roads were so icy that we could hardly remain standing. The icicle-bedecked onion spires of the churches and the high walls, pierced with rounded archways framing the streets, had turned it into the prototype for a Christmas-card. Foreign religious communities had lived here for centuries, Serbians and Dalmatians who had migrated to Hungary to escape the Ottomans. We returned to Szentendre at Easter, first to be blessed by a Croatian Catholic priest, and one week later for Orthodox Easter to give the traditional response to a Serbian *pope* that *indeed Christ is arisen*.

Anti-Western feeling was patent everywhere in Budapest. You could see the first disquieting signs of Americanisation, with fast-food chains rapidly replacing the convivial and appetising food stalls in the street. When I first arrived in Budapest, most days I would have a Hungarian lunch in the street near the office. By the time I left after a year and a half, American fast-food chains had put them all out of business.

The Hungarian attitude to the Russians was different. It was a kind of gentle sympathetic mockery, particularly when the last soldiers moved back home, taking with them all the Western consumer objects that they could scavenge. A well-known caricature showed a young Russian soldier on the rear platform of a train with five watches on each wrist. Another poster, showing the rear view of a Soviet soldier, his pimply bull-neck bulging over the collar of his uniform, bore the slogan *Tovarishchi konets*, Comrades it's all over.

The Hungarians complained that, though they had money under Communism, nothing worth buying was available in the shops and they weren't allowed to travel abroad. Today the shops were full and they were free to travel, but they could no longer afford it. The restaurants had become too expensive for Hungarians, very few of whom were to be seen there except for special occasions.

We ate out fairly frequently with other members of our team, often the only customers. The American dress culture consisted of dressing up with black-crow suits during working hours and dressing down after leaving work. Dressing down didn't mean designer jeans or what today they call *casual*. It meant looking like a tramp with a total lack of style or elegance. It embarrassed me each time we went to the restaurant to see the head waiter's hesitant disdainful look when our horde of overpaid hoboes arrived. We finally discovered the solution. We would push the only neatly-dressed member of the team in first and then, when it was too late for anyone to say that the restaurant was full, move in behind him. The waiters may have been haughty and unpleasant but, after years living in Paris, I was used to that sort of behaviour.

On returning from our Christmas holiday, a Texan in

our team decided to introduce our Hungarian *pension* staff to *Tex-mex cuisine*. He had brought back a *jalapeño* pepper, which he put on the table with a shredder. 'I should go easy on that one', he warned the hotel manager, who was eyeing the *jalapeño*. The Hungarian picked it up and nibbled it through like a bunny with a carrot.

I took a liking to one of the few elegant cafés still in existence under Communism. I enjoyed being served by buxom waitresses in pale pink dresses, their robust legs imprisoned in a kind of lace-up semi high-heeled sandal that I called the *Habsburg boot*.

As in most other countries of the former Warsaw Pact, Hungarian regulations concerning drinking and driving were of utmost severity. Any discernible trace of alcohol prohibited driving. Some said that it covered even the ferment in a jar of yogurt. The police caught me on three occasions. The first time I had had a few beers with my colleagues and we were on our way home in my car. I parked it outside the Budapest central police headquarters under a no parking sign right in front of a militia man in uniform. At his request I handed him my licence with a long outstretched arm, foolishly hoping that he would not smell my alcoholised breath. The situation was so absurd that he just told me to go home. On other occasions they were less understanding. My fear was that they would take me away for a blood test using a contaminated needle.

Budapest had an antediluvian telephone system. To communicate between the far-flung offices the most efficient method often consisted of taking a tram across town and delivering the message by hand. One of the main municipal switching systems, the *Józsefváros* phone exchange, still used the antiquated crossbar system. Our company's telecommunications specialist found a short-term solution that they never implemented, a microwave system using the tallest building in town as a hub. It sounded to me too much like science-fiction.

Finding telephoning a challenge, we purchased one of

the very first cell phones. The apparatus was the size of a table-top computer with a protruding fifty-centimetre antenna. A useful stop-gap, though it was not tram proof. A tram passing along the street below would interrupt the signal every time. When telephoning abroad, the first words that you said were always 'Don't ring off!'

Budapest never ceased to be a wonder, with its Habsburg-yellow buildings turned faecal and in an advanced state of psoriasis. In Pest the massive yet delicate houses from the *belle époque* with their multi-floor bay windows, steeples, machiculated turrets and at each street corner a tower capped with the helmet of Grand Prince Árpád. And the recent buildings. Communism had collapsed as modern architecture had gone out of style. Post-modern architects took more interest in reviving the romantic styles of Transylvania.

In the spring, deep-purple lilac and yellow laburnum sprouted from the ill-kempt hedgerows in the Buda hills. Our favourite excursion was north to Visegrád, on the Danube bend, where the river changes the direction of its flow from East to South. Storks had returned and we could hear them clattering their beaks from high up on specially constructed supports for their nests.

We knew a delightful open-air restaurant at the top of the hill dominating the Danube bend. Just above it our children could shriek their way down a roller-toboggan circuit. Below lay the remains of the *Renaissance* palace where Matthias Corvinius, otherwise known as Mátyás Hunyadi, had imprisoned Vlad the Impaler, also known as Dracula.

I had become wary since my journey through

Transylvania of the Romanian tourist authorities' unsubstantiated claims about his presence in Hunedoara, Bran and elsewhere. Here in Visegrád he was said to have lived as a semi-prisoner, some say for ten years.

'Did Dracula really live here', I asked the guide.

'Yes, he did. Do you know who he really was?'

'Perhaps not exactly, though everyone in the West knows Vlad Țepeș, the Impaler, by the name of *Dracula*, as the prototype of the vampire, thanks to Bram Stoker, the Hungarian actor Béla Lugosi and, more recently, Christopher Lee.'

'That's pure Hollywood. In fact he was the scourge of the Turks. Do you know the story of *the Night Attack*?' No, I didn't.

'At the end of the 15th century, just after the Fall of Constantinople to the Turks, Pope Pius II had called for a new Crusade. There was a general lack of enthusiasm, except for Vlad, who formed a coalition with Mátyás Hunyadi, to keep the Turks out of Wallachia.

'Aiming to control the Danube, Mehmet the Conqueror claimed Wallachia as part of the Ottoman Empire and ordered Vlad to pay the *jizya*, the tax on non-Muslims, to implement the *devșirme* by providing five hundred boys to become janissaries.

'Vlad refused to obey, so Mehmet sent him envoys. When they refused to remove their turbans in his presence, Vlad had them nailed to their heads. The Turks who crossed the Danube he had impaled. Vlad refused to go to Constantinople to negotiate and, following an attempt by the Turks to ambush him, he invaded Bulgaria and massacred more than twenty-three thousand

Turks, sparing only the Orthodox Bulgarians. Then Mehmet sent his vizier with an army of eighteen thousand men, which Vlad destroyed, leaving only eight thousand alive. You know that churches all over Europe held masses to celebrate Vlad's victory of Christianity over Islam.

'The Turks by then had become so terrified of him that, in order to conquer Wallachia, Mehmet had to raise an army of 250,000 men and lead it himself. Vlad called on Mátyás Hunyadi for help and even agreed to convert from Orthodoxy to Catholicism, but to no avail. So he used scorched-earth and guerrilla tactics, sending plague-ridden people into the enemy camp to infect them, spreading bubonic plague within the Turkish army.

'Of course, his army of only thirty thousand men, composed mainly of peasants, was too small to prevent Mehmet's professional army from crossing the Danube and advancing on Târgovişte, then capital of Wallachia. But Vlad had a diabolical plan. During the night he attacked the Turkish camp with around twenty-four thousand troops. He entered the camp himself, disguised as a Turk – don't forget that, due to his youth as an Ottoman hostage, he spoke Turkish fluently – with the aim of murdering Mehmet, but he got the wrong tent and killed the vizier instead.

'No one dared pursue Vlad, so Mehmet broke camp and fled in fear the following morning. His followers later convinced him to return and besiege Târgovişte, but he arrived to find it deserted except for twenty thousand Turks standing impaled by the roadside, which, you can imagine, quite apart from the horror, must have been a major feat of logistics. Mehmet's *unconquerable* army retreated, naturally claiming a great victory over Vlad.'

'He may have been a hero', I admitted grudgingly 'but why did Mátyás Hunyadi imprison him?'

'He was indeed a hero, despite and even thanks to his extreme cruelty. He saved Christian Europe from the Turks, at least for a while. The end justified the means. When Mehmet had finally succeeded in invading Wallachia, he placed Vlad's brother Radu on the throne. It is not clear whether it was the Saxons or Mátyás Hunyadi himself who produced a letter claiming that Vlad had offered his help to the Ottomans, but it was sufficient justification for Mátyás to have Vlad arrested and imprisoned.'

Ottoman remains in Budapest are the capital's most exotic aspect, of which Hungarians are both proud and protective. The Ottoman occupation of Buda, after the victory of Suleiman the Magnificent in 1541, lasted for more than a hundred and fifty years,

Unfortunately, after Eugene of Savoy liberated Hungary in the late 17th century, the Austrians destroyed almost all the Ottoman architecture. In a city where most of the buildings date from the late nineteenth century, the Ottoman constructions are, if you exclude the Roman remains of Aquincum in Obuda, almost the only authentic buildings in Budapest dating from before the 18th century.

I love the minute Ottoman cemetery in Buda at the bottom of Castle Hill. Tubular stone asparagus-tipped phalluses protrude at different angles from the grass of the meadow, each one crowned with a sculpted turban. The different shapes of turban indicate the quality or profession of the deceased.

Above the cemetery stand the castle fortifications, among which are Turkish structures. Two authentic Turkish baths still function in Buda, the *Rudas* and the *Király* baths, with its constellation of shallow copper domes.

It is said that nearly one word in ten in the Hungarian language is of Turkish origin. The names of two quarters of Buda are witness to the Turkish occupation. *Rozsadomb* is, with *Pasarét*, one of the wealthiest residential areas in Budapest, situated in Buda in the 2nd district. During the Ottoman occupation, *Rozsadomb*, the Hill of the Roses, was inhabited by Turks, who are said to have planted them here.

My special place in Budapest was Gül Baba's mausoleum on *Rozsadomb*, with its miraculous view over the Buda hills, the Danube and beyond to Pest and the *Alföld*, the Great Hungarian Plain. Unfortunately, the mausoleum would subsequently be over restored and a *naff* statue of Gül Baba erected beside it.

Gül Baba was a poet and a *Bektashi* dervish in the 16th century, who had taken part in numerous wars before coming to Hungary for the battle of *Budin*, as Buda was known to the Turks. *Gül* meant *rose*, a symbol of the Bektashi dervishes, which he is said to have worn in his turban. Baba meant *spiritual guide*.

The *Bektashi* were a Shia sect who were

prevalent across the Balkans. They thrived on its multi-cultural background and helped the dogmatic distinctions between Muslims and Orthodox to become blurred. Popular with new Muslims from the *devsirme*, the *Bektashi* provided chaplains to the Janissaries, who, though *Shia*, were the Sultan's personal guard.

At the time of Lady Mary Wortley Montagu, Bektashism was a joyous turbulent religion, unconcerned by the five pillars of Islam. Charity and the *Hajj* to Mecca were for the rich, prayers and *Ramadan* for the bigoted. The profession of faith was the only remaining meaningful pillar. Their enemies accused them of debauchery, as they drank wine and refused to separate the sexes in social life. In Bektashi convents gardening was a favourite activity.

Suleiman the Magnificent had called upon Gül Baba to take part in the battle, poets and dervishes being accustomed to acompany janissaries to help improve their morale. He died immediately following the victory in Buda and his funeral was held in the *Mátyás Templom*, which the Turks had converted into the *Suleiman mosque*.

They built a Bektashi monastery around his tomb, which the Habsburgs later converted into a church. It has since become a Muslim place of pilgrimage, which Hungary ceded to the Turkish government only in 1962. Gül Baba has become a well-loved subject of literature, opera and the cinema in Hungary.

Pieces began to fall off my car. The accelerator cable snapped on two occasions. We lived near the top of a high hill in Buda and, with my automatic gear box I was able to drive across the Danube and to the garage on the far side of Pest without needing an accelerator. Once the car had started, it picked up momentum running down the hill and changed gears up and down automatically. The automatic gear box went wrong on another occasion and I was unable to change up to third gear. As the garage couldn't fix it in Budapest, I had to drive it to Vienna in second.

Hungarians drove East German *Trabant* cars with a two-stroke engine. They climbed the gentle slope from Pest onto the *Erzsébet* Bridge with extreme difficulty, often conking out before reaching the middle. My Austrian boss used to claim that the *Trabant* contained no metal part. This may have been true if you excluded the engine. My wife verified it when she witnessed an accident between two of them. She stopped her car, jumped out and retrieved part of the bonnet. The body was not made of metal. In fact it was made of *Duroplast*, a hard plastic made from recycled cotton waste from the Soviet Union and phenol resin. I added it to my piece of the Berlin Wall as a relic of the Cold War.

We travelled regularly to Vienna on business or for shopping. Our final trip was in September to equip our daughters for the new school year in *Mariahilferstraße*, the main shopping street. We returned on that occasion from Vienna to Budapest by train. A young Serbian woman was struggling with a huge suitcase. I helped her put it on the luggage rack and we shared a compartment. When I asked her for her destination, she answered Belgrade. Where was she travelling from? Venice, she answered. But this was not the way, I objected, there was a direct route through Trieste, Ljubljana and Zagreb.

'There was once', she replied, 'but there is a war on and the borders have been closed between Croatia and Serbia. That is why I have to make this detour. From Budapest I shall take a bus to Belgrade.'

We left our Serbian companion at *Keleti* station in Budapest. As I helped her lift her heavy suitcase off the luggage rack, I noticed an image that had been stencilled on the side.

Цариград наш

It obviously represented *Hagia Sofia* in Istanbul, but this time the four minarets had been crossed out. This had to be more than just Orthodox collective nostalgia, the reawakening of memories buried in the collective unconscious of all the Orthodox nations, from Russia to Greece, Serbia to Bulgaria via Romania. Here was a new and aggressive polarisation, this time not just on *Hagia Sofia*, but on the minarets as the symbol of the confiscation and desecration of their collective history by what they all saw as Muslim barbarians.

The Cold War had ended, even though conflicts had broken out in former Yugoslavia and across the Caucasus. Apparently, members of the mysterious group no longer needed to express themselves with a three-character code in Glagolitic or even in Cyrillic. The Serbian woman had unashamedly stencilled *Tsarigrad nash* underneath. It had begun to look like a sign of something menacing. At the time of Slobodan Milošević's struggle for a Greater Serbia and on the eve of the massacres of Bosnjak Muslims, it was a sinister political slogan. *TseGeeN* was certainly the code name of the action group and *Tsarigrad nash*, *Constantinople Ours*, its rallying cry.

Back to Byzantium

After the end of the project I stayed on for a few months until our country's short-lived manager for Europe decided, after a lightning visit, to repatriate all foreigners. I would have sold one of my close ancestors to stay here. Budapest was and has remained my paradise lost. Before leaving I worked on several price quotations for public tenders within the framework of the privatisation of public companies. On one particular deal for a bank, for which we had received the request for tender almost at the last moment, I had worked all night to provide a costing for three proposals at different cost levels. Hardware would be provided from Germany, Slovakia and Bulgaria, and I had to do the costing in five different currencies. At four o'clock in the morning, tired but satisfied, I completed the proposal that had to be submitted by nine o'clock. Our company had deposited a warranty of a million dollars for the right to submit. But I had made an error of one zero in the low-cost proposal, potentially the most attractive. Of course it was, the price was ten times lower than it should have been. Fortunately we didn't get the contract, but my days in Budapest were numbered.

To complete our proposal I had needed the cost of human resources. 'How much does a clerk cost?' I asked my Hungarian colleague. 'Two hundred and fifty dollars' was the answer. 'And how much does a manager cost?' 'Two hundred dollars.' 'A clerk can't earn more than a manager.' 'Oh, yes!' he replied, 'the clerk has only one job, while the manager has several.' I added in a whole lot of computers. 'Too expensive', said my colleague. 'Put in clerks instead, they work out cheaper.'

Early on the fifth day of the New Year, after more than a year in Budapest, with the heaviest of hearts, we set out in the snow and ice for Paris in two cars loaded to the roof. The black ice was so bad when we arrived that evening in Munich that we had no choice but to stay a couple of nights. We found a hotel in a suburb with the disquieting name of Dachau and I visited Munich for the first time for twenty years. It was Epiphany and choirs in every church celebrated the arrival of the Three Kings. A lunch with two litres of beer each in the *Hofbraühaus* almost annihilated us. '*Ein halbes Mass Bier, bitte!*' '*Kein halbes Mass, nur Mass*', *No halves, only full measures*, meaning a litre, replied the waitress. We left the bar and managed to stagger up the three hundred steps to the top of the steeple of the *Alter Peter* church.

We succeeded in returning to Paris over the ice and through the mist, despite the breakdown of Edmonde's old *BMW*, without communication between the two cars. I re-joined my company in search of a new project. Leaving to go abroad was always easy. It's was coming back home that was so difficult.

A week after our return, we drove to Normandy with our two daughters for our nephew's twenty-first birthday party. My elder daughter had just learnt to read in Budapest and you could see the exhilaration in her eyes as she discovered for the first time, displayed on the shop fronts, the words that she had learned to read at school. She had learnt *pharmacie*, *restaurant* and *patisserie*, but had never seen them written before except as *gyógyszertár*, *étterem* and *cukrázda*.

19
Moscow

In the New Year, Presidents George Bush and Boris Eltsin had signed the *START2* agreement on strategic arms reduction. The USA, the United Kingdom and the Soviet Union had suspended nuclear tests.

The Maastricht Treaty defining the Single European Market would come into force at the end of the year.

'They are looking for someone to go to Russia.' I was at the coffee machine again. They wanted a manager to work with the Russian IT company that was developing software applications for the Goodwill Games. Once again I was the only candidate, so, with my experience in a former Communist country, they gave me the job.

Never having heard of the *Goodwill Games,* I rang the International Olympic Committee in Lausanne. A helpful female voice answered.

Nothing much is happening this year in the sporting world', she said. The Goodwill Games will fill the gap. It is organised by Ted Turner. You know, the founder of *CNN.*'

'I know *CNN*, of course, but I had never heard of the Games before. Have they been going for a long time?'

'Since 1986, in fact. You remember the double boycott of the Olympics. To protest against the Soviet invasion of Afghanistan, the Western countries, goaded by the USA, boycotted the 1980 Moscow Summer Olympics. The Soviet Union and its satellites retaliated four years later by boycotting the Los Angeles Olympics. We all thought here at the *IOC* that the future of the Olympic movement had been seriously compromised.

'Then Mikhaïl Gorbachëv came to power. Ted Turner, founder and owner of *TBS* and *CNN*, with Gorbachëv's encouragement, created his own games to ease cold-war tensions and build a bridge between East and West. The first Goodwill Games were held in Moscow in 1986, the second in Seattle four years later, and the third are to be held in 1994 in Saint-Petersburg.'

'It sounds a bit like a crackpot event.'

'Not at all! Major world athletes have taken part in the previous Games, setting close to ten world records. For the Saint-Petersburg Games next year they are expecting two thousand athletes from nearly sixty countries to take part in twenty-four different sports. It's like a smaller combination of both Summer and Winter Olympics.

'Anatoly Sobchak is the president of the organising committee. He's the mayor of Saint-Petersburg. Both President Eltsin and Juan Antonio Samaranch, our *IOC* President, will be attending the opening ceremony. It is certainly not a crackpot event but, due to low TV ratings for the previous Games, Ted Turner loses money every time, which he says he is willing to do to have his own Olympics.'

We were to work in Moscow for more than a year with a Russian company to prepare the Games, and then move to Saint-Petersburg three months before the event itself. My management in Dallas sent me to Moscow and Saint-Petersburg to do a *due diligence* reconnaissance trip. It was the most difficult time in Russia, a couple of years after the collapse of the Soviet Union. In addition to high inflation in food prices there was a climate of insecurity. Dual economies functioned in parallel, with Russian shops, on the one hand, where goods were payable in roubles, and Finnish, Irish and Swiss stores, on the other, stocked with Western goods, payable in US dollars.

I visited the Moscow offices of the Russian service company providing the computer applications for the Games. My future colleague drove me round the sights in his *Zhiguli*, known in the West as a *Lada*. To the top of the Lenin Hills, in front of the *Lomonosov* Moscow State University, the last of Stalin's seven skyscrapers in the wedding-cake style, for a spectacular view of the city.

They put me up in a disquieting place called the Hotel Sport. Heavies in camouflage fatigues armed with *AK47*s blocked the access to the upper floors to intruders. Rather than reassuring me, it only increased the feeling of insecurity that I felt as soon as I entered the foyer. White tiles covered the walls of the bedroom and the shower areas which were not even separate rooms.

My Russian opposite number seconded a young woman to accompany me to the food stores in a classy black *Volga*, driven by the company chauffeur. I compiled a weighted consumer price index, based on prices in the dollar stores. Inflation was high in the Rouble economy, but prices were stable in US dollars. My management in Dallas agreed for me not to justify my expenses as in Budapest, all of it being cash payments in this bank-less society, a non-negligeable part of which were just *bakhchich* or extortion payments. So I kept a ledger, calling them *gratuities*.

The next day I flew from Moscow to Saint-Petersburg to meet the team from *Turner Broadcasting*. The chauffeur drove me to the airport, scaring me rigid as he skidded through the icy streets. The air in Saint-Petersburg was so thick with damp, cold and fog that you could only guess at the phantom outlines of the cars.

I flew back home via Frankfort. It was illegal to take roubles out of the country. I spent all that I had on vodka, but I still had some small change remaining. I had to spend it or forfeit it, said the customs officer. When I protested that it was so little, he replied to my embarrassment: 'It's a lot of money for me!' This was the country where I was to live for a year and a half.

Arriving in in Moscow in May to initiate our project, I booked into the Hotel Rossiya where I had stayed during my previous visit sixteen years previously. What had once been a decent hotel, the world's largest outside Las Vegas, had become very seedy. The friendly booking clerk recommended that I stay in the North wing, where, she said, I would be safer from the Caucasian *mafia*. What had become of this despotic but well-ordered country that I had visited in 1977? Most nights a knock on the door woke me up. A prostitute offered her services. My tiny room had a TV where I could watch Spanish and Turkish channels.

In a couple of weeks my colleagues would arrive and I had to find housing for us in Moscow. A French woman had set up an estate agency for Western expats. A regiment of *Matriochki* of all sizes and shades of scarlet filled her office, encircling every variant of Lenin's bust. She apparently still needed to reassure her patrons of her loyalty to her defunct host country. A young officer reminiscent of William Hurt in *Gorky Park*, shod with black officer's riding boots, accompanied us on our rounds of the flats. A washing machine was one of our prerequisites. Where was the machine, I asked. 'Here it is', said the flat owner, pointing to a *babushka* smiling meekly in the corner of the kitchen. We would employ an elderly woman a few months later to baby sit our two young daughters. We had a bed made up for her to spend the night, but just as Custine had discovered hundred and fifty years previously, she would not agree to sleep elsewhere than on the bare boards of the corridor.

Back to Byzantium

I finally identified three flats in buildings that atypically did not overpower you from your very first step into the communal corridor permeated with a reek of encrusted urine.

We moved into a tall yellow-brick block of flats, constructed during the Khrushchëv period to house medium level *nomenclatura*. It was located in a garden near the *Oktïabrskaïa* Square. Just down the road stood the *Donskoï* monastery. We chose it because it was close to the French *lycée* and the French Embassy.

The building was secure on all levels. You opened the main entrance door first with a key. Then you passed through a kind of air lock under the scrutiny of the *dezhurnaïa*, a *Cerberus* who supervised entries and exits, and you unlocked the second door key by typing a code. Arriving by lift at your floor, you opened a first door with a key, revealing a second door that you opened with another key. The padded inner door to the flat provided sound proofing to ensure inaudible conversation.

Our landlord, a writer, had moved to his *datcha* to let out his flat and benefit from the high rents that foreigners were obliged to pay. He had succeeded in maintaining a decent standard of living by writing dull books about Soviet institutions, which he found somewhat embarrassing. His masterpiece, of which at the time he was far from proud, was a bread-and-butter book about a factory and the people who worked there.

What he was proud of was to have revived the *All Moscow Directory*, edited for the first time since the October Revolution. He gave us a dedicated copy, numbered eight, proudly showing us a manuscript letter of thanks from President George Bush Senior, who owned number six. It contained among other useful items a VIP phone directory. Unfortunately, he had sorted the names in hierarchical, instead of alphabetical order, starting with the President of the Russian Federation and descending ministry by ministry and department by department. Not the best way to find a name and number.

Back to Byzantium

Elegant rows of never-to-be-opened books lined the shelves that covered every centimetre of the walls of the corridor, probably purchased by the metre. Although perhaps not, as the landlord was a writer of sorts, and as such had probably been given them.

The flat, like my grandfather's, had been decorated in different shades of brown. Unlike my grandfather, who was colour blind, our landlord had just bought what had been available under the twelfth five-year plan. Until going to Russia I never understood that designing an armchair in which you could sit comfortably or a toaster that actually made toast was in fact a fairly complex business. I had never before seen a sofa in a kitchen. It was the room where we spent most of our time, listening to CDs to the backdrop of the unending eerie cawing of the hooded crows in the tree tops on the level of our fourth-floor flat.

It was now the end of May, Edmonde had arrived with the children, as had my colleagues, and we had begun work. We had hired a driver, the son of my Russian opposite number. He had two words of English and two of French and Edmonde had no Russian. Nevertheless, they managed to communicate with French expressions such as *j'ai acheté*, which could mean *I have bought, I am buying* or *I shall buy*.

As he drove us to work the Moscow streets were covered with snow. Except that it wasn't, but what was it?

'It's just *pukh*', our driver Evgeny managed to explain. 'We get it every year in June. It's the pollen from the poplar trees.

'In the thirties Stalin planted balsam poplars and later on, at the time of Khrushchëv, they did the same. They are now several hundred thousand of them, which is more than a quarter of all the trees in Moscow. As Stalin's gardeners planted practically only the female variety, there is never any cross-pollination. The trees need pruning every two years or so. They did it in Soviet times, but there's no money these days and anyway it doesn't have high enough priority. So we just have to put up with it. At least the pollen doesn't melt and turn into slush.

'I remember when older people called it Stalin's revenge or Lenin's snow. *Pukh* is highly inflammable, you know, and it's also an irritant. So much so that they say that an American ambassador had to leave Russia briefly after he got asphyxiated by swallowing *pukh*!'

In the suburb of Toulouse where I live today, the mayor made the same mistake as Stalin, but naturally on a smaller scale and the city council can afford to prune the poplars every three years.

We all remember the border control ordeal when entering the Soviet Union, the bleached blue eyes that looked up from your passport to glare into yours for ten seconds without flinching. They were the famous Border Guards and today was their own special day.

Drunken *heavies* in horizontal blue and white striped *marinière* T-shirts and dangerously tilted peak caps staggered arm in arm like lovers across eight lane highways, stopping the traffic and unnerving the Muscovites. Water from the fountains where they had been bathing dripped from their clothes and vodka from the empty bottles that they still clutched in their huge pink fists.

'What's is this circus, Evgenyï?' I asked.

'It's just Border Guards' Day? It takes place every year and the Moscow becomes a *bardak*, a bloody mess.'

'So these are the people who used to intimidate us when we entered the Soviet Union?'

'I am too young to remember that period, but

yes they must be the same ones. They don't look so impressive today, just irritating.'

Border guards were first formed in the 14th century to defend the Principality of Muscovy from invaders. Catherine the Great officially established them by decree in the 18th century to provide border security and customs control.

Just after the Revolution the General Directorate of Border Guards was set up, reporting first to the *Cheka* and its successors and after the Second World War to the *KGB*. They currently report to its successor, the *FSB*. There are 200,000 of them, controlling borders with fourteen countries over a distance of more than 20,000 kilometres. In addition to border protection, they are in charge of the fight against organised crime, contraband, illegal immigration and traffic in arms and drugs.

Border Guards' Day is an official holiday, held every year on 28th May, the anniversary of their establishment in 1918.

'How do they celebrate Border Guards' Day, Evgenyï? What are the events?'

'There are parades and fireworks, of course. But mainly it is just the guards enjoying themselves by getting drunk in city parks, wallowing in the fountains, blocking traffic on eight lane roads, bottle in hand, hardly managing to walk straight or even remain standing. It's a very Russian event!'

The old Soviet system was defunct, but as yet nothing existed to replace it. It was a particularly difficult time in the young Russian Federation. As foreigners, we lived with a constant feeling of insecurity. One of the first things that I did after the initial rush was over, was to compile a contingency plan, covering physical security, health questions and the ever-imminent *coup d'état*. Moscow at this time was a perilous place.

Firstly it was physically dangerous. Westerners told horror stories that chilled your bones. My children went to school in the French *lycée*, ten minutes down the road on foot. One morning, the manager of a large western IT company found protruding from beneath his door pictures of his children playing in the school yard, accompanied by an extortion demand for several million dollars. Our children played in the same school yard. Without hesitating, he left his apartment with all his belongings, picked up his wife, a teacher at the school, and his children and drove straight to the airport. The co-director of a large joint-venture hotel had been murdered a week before we arrived. The manager of a Saint-Petersburg hotel also left after receiving threats, to be replaced by his assistant, who subsequently got beaten up inside the diplomatic compound where he lived. Closer to home, a Croatian friend of ours was also terrorised by *mafia* racketeers. He just abandoned everything and returned to Zagreb.

Each time we left our building small-time hoods with woollen ski bonnets pulled down over their ears watched us from the entrance hall of a crummy hotel. So when we left our house on foot with our children we tried to vary our itinerary. Otherwise our driver took them to school by car. We tried to keep ourselves as anonymous as possible, not publishing the fact that we worked for a subsidiary of the world's largest company.

There were also health issues. Diphtheria was said to be resurgent in Moscow, so we got the French school medical officer to vaccinate us. As an expert in tropical medicine, typically it was to Moscow that he had been sent to do his military service. Tap water contained heavy metals and bacteria. Like all westerners we filtered all our water and then boiled it. They told us not to buy mushrooms, which had been radioactive since Chernobyl, but nobody told us to avoid apples. We made amazing apple pies with those that we bought on the market by *Bielorusskiï* Station, until we discovered that they too came from a contaminated region.

At the office in the Olympic Committee building I had lunch at the canteen every day. None of my western colleagues would touch the food there and the American visitors didn't even dare to approach the food service line quite literally closer than a couple of metres. It seemed alright to me, though the food didn't taste spectacular. I got to know that *kotlet* meant *hamburger*. One day I asked for meat balls, saying *kotlet*. That was not *kotlet*, said the cook indignantly, it was *bifshteks*.

The offices of the Olympic Committee were located close to the *Luzhniki,* previously Lenin, Stadium. This historic venue now housed in its access corridors a free market for clothes, shoes and other consumer goods. Central Asians with long exotic faces and incredibly high cheekbones carried enormous pale blue-, yellow- and pink-striped carry-all bags to take home cheap items. The once elegant park leading to the stadium now housed their tents and campfires.

Why did they make the corridors in Russian office and apartment building proportionately so wide, compared to the tiny rooms themselves? For storing bicycles, infrequently used equipment and just family junk, of course. In the corridor of our offices the remains of political announcements and Soviet propaganda still adorned the notice board covering one wall. Two years after, nobody had bothered to take them down.

The Russians love plants. But why do they always plant them in sawn-off plastic bottles?

The time came for us to get official status at the Ministry of Sports. They called us one morning to get a mug shot for a *Propusk*, the ID card used in all government offices, including the *KGB*. I at last understood why Soviet officials all have that double-chinned pompous look in official photos. It was the *Polaroid* cameras they used. Though I am a regular-looking Western European, my Russian ID photo was that of a *Homo Sovieticus,* or *homocus,* as Aleksandr Zinoviev would later call them. The father of one of my children's school friends was a Belgian of Russian extraction. On seeing my card he became suspicious, almost panicking. But that was a *KGB* card. Of course it wasn't, but it turned out to be useful for things like reductions at museums, reservations, though it didn't help me when a racketeer extorted an outrageous surcharge from me on a train.

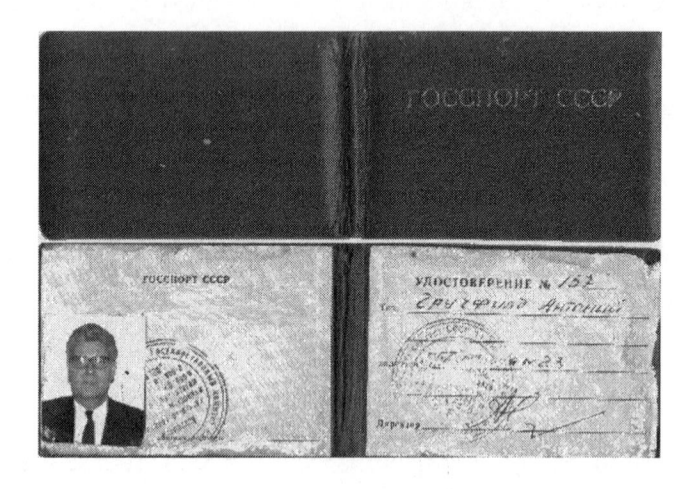

Telephoning was even more laborious than it had been in Hungary. Dialling a number outside Russia took an average of fifty attempts, passing through the special exchange that allowed them to monitor your call. If and when it got through, the person that you were ringing first heard a beeping sound resembling that of a fax. Naturally they rang off. Our first words, as in Hungary, were always 'Don't hang up!' At the end of the month you received a thick wad of telephone invoices, one slip per call. It is easy to imagine how thick ours was. If one slip was missing when you went to pay, they cut your phone off.

Without a banking system, Russia remained a cash society. Each month Evgeny, our driver, drove me to the

Back to Byzantium

Radisson-Slavïanskaïa Hotel near the *Kievskiï* Station to withdraw dollars in cash. On the ground floor at end of the corridor stood a cash desk, the only place in Moscow where you could withdraw foreign currency transferred from abroad. I would put the cash for the month in my case, get in the car looking right and left, and return home each time by a new itinerary. The cash found its place on my landlord's bookshelves behind a discreet portrait of Lenin, the only one in the house.

When it came time to move to Saint-Petersburg, I needed to pay three months' rent in advance for our future flats. It was payable up front in cash, but no way existed of transferring it to Saint-Petersburg or of withdrawing cash there. I had no option other than, with the authorisation of my management in Dallas, to carry the fifteen thousand dollars in my bag on the overnight train. Holdups on the *Krasnaïa Strela* train were not uncommon. I knew the routine, taking a less prestigious train and trying to travel *incognito*, always in second class. I liked to think that in a compartment with a non-commissioned officer, a school teacher and a *babushka*, I was less at risk than with foreigners. The routine for securing baggage consisted in taking the lower bunk and placing your case in the hideaway container underneath that you could access only by lifting the bunk that you were lying on. You could lock the door, once with the bolt by the door handle and a second time with a small protruding metal finger that blocked on the other side. That day the train was late and Edmonde went nearly berserk with panic, not having heard from me. Communications were hazardous before mobile phones.

I really took a great liking to the Russians. I exclude the so-called *new Russians*, who threw their weight around, both literally and metaphorically, as they flashed their bulky wads of US Dollars and flung them down in front of the cashier at the till of a Western store. The other Russians seemed to me more educated, more sensitive than Westerners, with that streak of fantasy and enthusiasm that is so appealing. The only thing that really exasperated me was their queuing behaviour at the canteen. One of them would come down and stand in line as an advance guard. All the members of the office would then join him, jumping the queue. Did they learn this from the Germans on holiday beaches?

I had become acquainted with Soviet toilets sixteen years previously during my journey on the *Transsib*. You get the surprise of your life when you turn round from the urinal to discover a *babushka* and an army officer squatting over individual Turkish toilets without a door, facing you full frontal without the least embarrassment.

In the new-born Russian Federation they had not improved much. At our Moscow office the programmers had got into the habit of going out to smoke by the urinals under the *No-smoking* sign. In August, when the cleaner took her month's holiday with no backup, they continued to congregate for their social smoke each mid-morning under the same sign, impervious to the month-old unflushed stench from the adjacent stalls.

Twice a month I took the night train from Moscow to Saint-Petersburg. I thrived on getting off the metro at *Komsomolskaïa* at midnight to board the train at *Leningradskiï* Station. Losing one's autonomy, carried forward by several thousand others all moving through the corridor wall to wall in the same direction, gave me a feeling of elation of being in communion with the popular masses, straight out of out of *Eisenstein*. The proximity of a couple of thousand people in a station at a given moment had something almost erotic.

My Russian colleagues usually made my travel arrangements to Saint-Petersburg, but I had to purchase my own return ticket. It reminded me of the difficulty a foreigner has making any kind of transaction in a Paris shop, when he learns that there is no such thing in France: *Mais enfin, Mossieu, ça n'existe pas en France!* But this was far worse. Buying a ticket at the station was not possible, and purchasing it through the special desk at the transport office required both perseverance and negotiating skills.

Edmonde found shopping trying, especially with our driver breathing down her neck, telling her that the item she wanted to purchase was too expensive. She got exasperated by the bad service. One day in a shop, unable to get the attention of a shop assistant busy meticulously sorting documents into several tall piles, she knocked the piles over, saying *Seïchas rabotite, Now do some work.* Our driver was aghast at her audacity.

One of our joys was going to the ballet. Not to the *Bolshoï* Theatre, with its *new Russians* in flashy suits and a professional applause-cue leader. No, we preferred the Congress Hall in the Kremlin. The ultimate excitement was getting off the metro at *Aleksandrovskiï Sad* station, hurrying through a foot tunnel and then up the drawbridge over the wall into the Kremlin.

We never tired of the other ballet in Moscow, that of the changing of the guard at Lenin's mausoleum. Even watching a film of it frame by frame I still couldn't understand how the permutation took place. There was the excitement of hearing the carillon from the Kremlin announcing the three-man guard exiting the gate in the *Spasskaïa* Tower with palm-held erect rifles and fixed bayonets at a slow goose step echoing across Red Square.

A place that fascinated me, with its *kitch* Social Realist decadence, was *VDNKh*, the Exhibition of Achievements of the People's Economy. Since the end of Soviet Union, car show rooms had replaced many of the exhibitions, but it had not lost its degenerate charm. I loved the gilded life-size peasant girls from the different Republics, encircling fountains spurting out of enormous gilded ears of corn.

Though I had been initiated to the Russian language on my two previous trips to Russia, I hadn't really progressed beyond the Cyrillic alphabet, which I already knew from my stay in Bulgaria. Through an acquaintance we found a woman who came to teach us every Sunday afternoon. She came by train from Tula, where they manufacture the *samovars*, more than 170 kilometres South of Moscow, just to give us our lesson, an indication of how needy the Russians were at that time. I was so busy with the project and exhausted at weekends, that I made little progress with her. And then the Russian language is so difficult.

Since returning home, I have made amends by seriously studying the language. In another twenty-five years, I may even be fluent. I travelled to Kiev for a two-week Russian course. Unlike the Russian Federation, Ukraine no longer required a visa for Westerners. Thanks to my excellent teacher and to the Russian-speaking Ukrainian family with whom I was staying, I improved my spoken Russian no end. The classes and educational supports in the language school targeted US Army personnel, who represented fifty per cent of all the pupils. They were more interested in decoding Russian news bulletins than in Russian language and culture. Almost all the vocabulary in the language manual was army-oriented, with detailed army procedures and etiquette. 'How are you going to keep up your Russian when you go home?' I asked a young non-commissioned officer in my class. 'I will do so only as long as it's useful', he answered, 'and when it is no longer useful I will forget it.'

Back to Byzantium

Edmond Wilson described in the forties the different phases and obstacles in learning Russian. Though students begin learning with enthusiasm, when they encounter difficulties they gradually drop out of class.

First the easy part. Russian is an Indo-European language, which has adopted many words from French and German, keeping more or less the same meaning. Although it has a different alphabet, three quarters of Cyrillic characters are taken from Greek, making it fairly easy to learn. It is almost perfectly phonetic, once you know the rules and the two or three exceptions. Learning the alphabet corresponds to the initial phase of enthusiasm. Though there are three genders, unlike German, it is usually possible to guess the gender of a noun from its appearance.

Then what is so difficult? Even though it is phonetic, Russian is hard to pronounce. As in English and contrary to French, it's not always possible to predict, for a word that one has never heard before, on which syllable the stress is going to fall. The stress can also move about from one syllable to another depending on its case in the declension system, with the vowel *o* pronounced as an *a* when it is not stressed. Pronunciation is difficult also because the consonants are not *clean*, like in Bulgarian or Serbian, but can be *softened* by the succeeding vowel. But this still does not discourage the determined pupil. It is when he gets a little farther and meets the difficulties of the grammar, that Wilson's student becomes appalled. Nouns and adjectives are declined in six cases and three genders. Adjectives are also declined, but quite differently from nouns. For a string of adjectives preceding a noun, each one is declined.

There are two ways of expressing plurals in Russian, one from two to four and another from five to twenty. Then when you get to twenty-one you start all over again. Not only are numbers declined, like nouns and adjectives, but each separate digit of a number is declined individually. This is what Edmond Wilson calls the *true horrors* of Russian.

For verbs, there are fewer tenses than in Romance and Germanic languages, but for each verb in those languages there are at least two aspects in Russian, to express a continuous or else a completed action, which is not always obvious. There is neither a verb *to be* nor do they really use the verb *to have*.

Russian is an ancient language, descending from the Slavonic spoken in *Kievian Rus'* and it has consequently had time to generate numerous exceptions and irregularities.

Back to Byzantium

November was approaching and we began to be apprehensive of the Russian winter. We had brought thermal underwear with us from France and had purchased one-piece ski equipment for our children in Vienna the previous year. They said that the most important heat loss was through the scalp, so I bought a silver-fox *shapka* at one of the stalls in the *GUM,* the *Gosudarstvennyï Universal'nyï Magazin,* the state department store on Red Square. The *shapka* looked like a huge Christmas cake.

We stuck insulating tape around the windows. This was not necessary since the triple-glazed windows let in no air and, as in all Moscow flats, we were over-heated by the municipal central heating system.

On the first day of November it really began to snow and it some of it would remain on the ground until the last day of March. We strolled down the street in the twilight as far as the *Donskoï* monastery, pulling our girls along on a sledge. This is what we had come to Moscow for and what my Muscovite colleague had been impatiently awaiting. The virgin snow, so firm and luminous, turned grimy after a day. The bulldozers banked it at the sides of the road, its accumulation eventually reducing their width by a third.

It got so cold that the air became almost opaque. The hairs in my nose froze, but we kept warm in our thermal underwear. The Muscovites said that you only really felt it below fifteen degrees Celsius. No need to say *minus*, or *degrees of frost* to a Russian in winter. It felt much colder in Saint-Petersburg at the same temperature with the wind factor and sea air. They had built ice sculpture in Gorky Park and ice slides, to our children's delight. When do Muscovites eat ice creams? In winter, of course, when it's cold outside. We were perplexed when my younger daughter giggled as her ice lolly turned pink, until we saw a baby tooth protruding from it.

We tried to spend a Sunday afternoon skating on the pond in Gorky Park. Anyone who saw the film of the

Back to Byzantium

same name remembers the ominous theme music and the *Beautiful Blue Danube* playing while the three friends skate on the very same pond before being murdered and their faces skinned with a hunting knife. The loudspeakers played the same music as we attempted to skate. Edmonde and the children had never tried before. I learned there and then that skating is not like riding a bike. As you grow older and put on weight your centre of gravity changes. I could hardly stay upright on the ice and Edmonde fell over, hurting her coccyx. We needed expert help, but the risk of going in a Russian ambulance to a local hospital was daunting. A local first-aid centre gave her some folk medicine which enabled her to drag herself the kilometre up the road to our house.

On 9th November I went with my driver to pick up my Croatian colleague at his flat just down the road. He was watching *Euronews*. 'Look what my people have done!' he said. The *Stari Most* in Mostar in Hercegovina, the bridge commissioned by Suleiman the Magnificent more than four hundred years before, was collapsing on the screen under shells from the Bosnian Croat artillery. We drove to work. Why didn't the West intervene? Britain was in favour of maintaining the arms embargo. We are not concerned with this war, said a senior government spokesman. 'In that case how can Britain justify its permanent seat on the Security Council?' asked my colleague. It did seem reminiscent of Chamberlain's *quarrel in a faraway country between people of whom we know nothing*.

In early spring the following year I exceptionally took the *Krasnaya Strela,* the *Red Arrow* train to Saint-Petersburg, usually travelling for security reasons on a less prestigious train. It had been the first important line built within the limits of Russia, Thousands had died out of the fifty thousand serfs who had spent eight years constructing it. As we pulled into the station I was surprised to see a horde of screaming schoolgirls on the platform. No, it wasn't for me, but for the perennial Russian pop star, Alla Pugachëva, who was descending from the next-door coach with her most recent husband.

>Alla Pugachëva is a Russian singer and performer born in 1949, who sings popular songs and has played in occasional films. She has won numerous Soviet, Russian and international awards and become an international star, especially in Japan and Sweden. She is the closest thing to a megastar in Russia, excluding sportsmen and women.
>
>She sang with the Bulgarian pop star, Emil Dimitrov, whose hit song had been ubiquitous during my stay in Bulgaria. She is particularly well-known for having recorded the songs mimed by the Polish actress Barbara Brilska in the Soviet Union's most popular film, *Ironija sudby, ili s lëgkim parom!, The Irony of Fate or Sweet Vapours!* Millions of Russians watch it on television every New Year's Eve. It was one of the few cassettes that we found in the apartment. I watched it a countless number of times.
>
>After three previous marriages, she had recently wed Filipp Kirkorov, a pop singer eighteen years younger than she. He climbed down from our train in her wake like a prince consort.

We had tried to have our children baptised since birth and they were already little girls. Not that we felt religious, Christianity being more of a cultural thing for us. We had first tried the Catholics in France. *Chloë* was not a saint's name, they told us, but the priest could baptise her as *Clovis* or *Clotilde*. We tried the Anglicans. 'God is like the motor under the bonnet of my car', said the vicar. 'I don't know how it works, but when I press the accelerator He moves forward.' Not for us!

In Moscow we sometimes attended the French

Catholic church, *Saint-Louis-des-Français*, situated just behind the former torture chambers of the notorious *Lubïanka* prison. Not only the French, but the Irish community also frequented it. We discovered there a priest whom Edmonde had known when we both worked for *Bayard Presse*, the French Catholic publisher owned by the order of the Assumptionists. We invited him to dinner. Yes, he would baptise our daughters as Catholics. We would kill three birds with one stone, so to speak, two baptisms and one first communion. We knew a Belgian woman who could be godmother to our elder daughter, but who else did we know that was Catholic? ... Of course, the Croats are Catholic!

We entered the church with our daughters, both wearing *albs*, the traditional off-white cassocks used in France by boys and girls for first communion. The French expatriate community occupied the first row. They say that expatriation reinforces national characteristics. This seemed to be the case in Moscow. The small community practised *high-society* rites forgotten even in the snottiest circles in France. You could see their scraggy wives in short tight skirts, stork legs on high heels perambulating in front of the French *lycée*. They had succeeded in creating a caricature of *Parisianism*, with extreme mannerism, elitism, snobbery, aloofness to newcomers and rejection of strangers. Western civilisation had left them behind. I was tempted to react with a slap in the face to the men's maladroit attempts at a hand-kiss, quite unnatural for the French, each time they saw my wife. But people like them had a special talent for intimidating those accustomed to a degree of courtesy.

By the time that the Croatian godfather and godmother arrived, the church was already full, with the French *notables* seated in the front row. My gigantic colleague and his huge friend with his *chetnik* beard arrived in navy-blue alpaca suits. The *mafia* had arrived and, to my satisfaction, you could sense apprehension in the eyes of the French community in the front.

Back to Byzantium

A young Bulgarian girl was being baptised with our daughters. No problem with pagan first names. What was her name, asked the priest. *Rumïana,* whispered the deacon. 'Saint Rumïana pray for her!' Next *Chloë,* 'Saint Chloë pray for her!' The ceremony was nearly finished when our younger daughter leaned too far forward and her candle on a rod set fire to the *alb* in front.

We celebrated in a Russo-American restaurant. We were the only guests. The previous day the *mafia* had shot its American owner dead.

Above the television set in our Moscow apartment ten or so video cassettes lay on a shelf. A voice over, Russian style, reciting in a monotone, prevented you from hearing distinctly either the original voices or the translation. The same reader dubbed all the voices, both male and female. *Pokrovskie Vorota* was one of the cassettes, a nostalgic comedy made in the eighties, idealising life in the fifties in a Moscow *komunalka,* a communal apartment. We must have watched it twenty times and I still didn't fully understand the ending.

It was spring and we discovered the charm of Moscow, walking between *Ploshad' Nogina* and the *Taganka* in search of the location where they had shot the film. Behind one of Stalin's sky scrapers, along a leafy street ran a short, rickety tram. Among the charms of the city were the courtyards filled with gangly trees, the neo-classical buildings disposed at different angles. I loved the magical views from the walled-in balconies over the city to Stalin's seven skyscrapers.

Despite our exploratory walks, apart from the centre, we never really got a general view of this largest of European cities, only pieces of a puzzle that I never quite fitted together.

On the same shelf above the television as the video cassettes I discovered a board game that I didn't know. It was in English and was called **RECONQUEST**.

The aim of the game was to recreate former empires of the Middle-Ages by retaking lost territories. Up to four persons could play it, each one taking the role of one of four former/would-be empires.

The groups and their objectives were as follows:

1. The Arabs: retake Andalusia and recreate the Umayyad Califate.
2. The Turks: retake the Balkans, Arabia, Crimea, the Holy Land and recreate the Ottoman Empire.
3. The Orthodox Christians: retake Constantinople and recreate the Byzantine Empire.
4. The Crusaders: retake the Holy Places and recreate the Empire of the Franks.

The different national groups could make or break alliances with each other. They used primary and secondary itineraries across Southern Europe, North Africa and the Mediterranean.

The box displayed a present-day map of the Mediterranean, with pictures of the Alhambra, the church of the Holy Sepulchre, *Hagia Sofia* before the addition of minarets and the Cathedral of *Aleksandr Nevskiï* in Sofia.

The armies were represented symbolically by a Byzantine Varangian Guard, a Saracen, a Janissary and a Crusader, but in fact a picture of modern-day soldier reminded the player that the game took place today.

Back to Byzantium

This looked eerily familiar, reminiscent of *Al Andalus-Constantinople - même combat*, the slogan that I had seen scribbled on the wall of the Casbah in Algiers. Shared nostalgia, certainly, but could it correspond to a shared political struggle?

Most surprisingly, in the board game they had cast the Americans in the role of the modern-day Franks.

Who published this game, I wondered. At the rear of the box I found out. The company, located in Hackney, London, was named ***TseGeEn Publications PLC***. Hackney was said to be the area of London with the largest Balkan population in the United Kingdom.

20
Coup

Churchill described Russia as *a riddle wrapped in a mystery inside an enigma*. With my colleagues we compared discovering Russian complexity to opening a *Matrïoshka* doll, except that inside each nested doll what you found was not a smaller, but a larger one. Two years had gone by since Eltsin stood defiantly on a tank confronting the *putschists* and we watched a new disaster approaching with foreboding.

The constitutional crisis of autumn 1993 resulted from a fight between the President of the Russian Federation in one corner, and the Congress of People's Deputies, the supreme government institution, and its emanation, the Supreme Soviet, in the other. Increasing its own power at the expense of those of the President had come to dominate Parliament's agenda.

In January 1992 President Boris Eltsin had put in place his economic reforms, reducing government spending and introducing new taxes. Prices had shot up and a credit squeeze had brought the country into depression. Aleksandr Rutskoï, the Vice-President of the Russian Federation, and Ruslan Khazbulatov, the Speaker of the Supreme Soviet, denounced the reforms as an *economic genocide*.

Eltsin was then governing by decree, a privilege that was about to expire. The Congress of People's Deputies refused the constitutional amendment that he required to implement his privatisation plan. When Khazbulatov tried to reduce the President's control over the government, Eltsin called for a referendum, which the Congress voted to cancel. Despite the majority vote of confidence in Eltsin when the referendum took place, the Supreme Soviet passed a resolution against him.

On 1st September Eltsin suspended his Vice President, Rutskoï, accusing him of corruption. Three weeks later he dissolved the Supreme Soviet by decree in breach of the constitution, which he then proceeded to abolish, granting himself extraordinary powers in order to transition the Russian Federation to a market economy. The USA backed this move, which made it all the more unpopular with the Russians.

By this time we were receiving frequent alarmed phone calls from both London and Dallas, but unsurprisingly not from my home office in Paris. Looking after its employees was a company tradition in *EDS*. Fifteen years previously its founder Ross Perrot had set up a private army to get two of its executives out of prison in Iran. Before we had left for Moscow, the person in charge of *expats* for Europe had warned us that, though Americans were very good with their own people, they were less diligent about helping other nationals. When the *coup d'état* became imminent she tried unsuccessfully to encourage Edmonde to return to France with our children. Then, thanks to her moving mountains in Dallas, they put the corporate jet on standby for us, giving me a direct number to ring in case of necessity. Would they have been able to land on *Leninskiï Prospect*, as Mathias Rust had done on Red Square, which the Muscovites had since then jokingly called *Sheremetyevo III*, the airport's third terminal? It seems doubtful, but the need never arose.

Though we were all dual citizens in my family, Edmonde and our children, travelling on a French passport, had registered with the French consulate in Moscow, while I had registered with the British. As soon as the crisis became serious, the French Embassy set up a support network for its nationals. In case of emergency my wife would be contacted and she in turn would contact three other families.

No word for my British colleague or myself from our Embassy. When I did ring them to ask what support system they had set up, I sensed an embarrassed or more like a baffled hesitation on the line. The person answered that, though the Embassy had recently discouraged their nationals from travelling to the Russian Federation, that recommendation now seemed to have been lifted.

> Rutskoï called it a coup d'état. The Supreme Soviet, chaired by Khazbulatov, declared Eltsin's decree null and void and proclaimed Rutskoï president, who, after taking the oath, dismissed Eltsin and Pavel Grachev, the Minister of Defence. Russia now had two Presidents and two Ministers of Defence.

My brother-in-law had come with his friend to stay with us. It gave me no little satisfaction to wake him up from the couch where he slept, with the announcement that there had been a *coup d'état* and that consequently there were now two presidents. It was the calm before the storm.

On that cloudy Sunday afternoon of 26th September Mstislav Rostropovich directed the National Symphony Orchestra of Washington in Red Square in the presence of an ostensibly jovial Eltsin. My children sat in a tree in front of the *GUM*, while we listened with the same trepidation as the tens of thousands of others in the square to the ominous booming cannon fire and the bells from the Kremlin for the *finale* of Tchaikovsky's *1812 Overture*.

The bells! Their romantically monotonous clanking in the monasteries, rung using a *cat's cradle* of cables and levers, is, with the cawing of the rooks, something that still triggers my nostalgia for Moscow. The bells from the coronation of Boris Godunov.

Six hundred armed men with large quantities of ammunition had already occupied the *White House*, the Parliament building. Eltsin cut off their electricity, telephones and hot water. Patriarch Alexiï II made a fruitless last-ditch attempt at arbitration between Eltsin and the Parliament.

On the following Saturday, supporters of the Parliament set up barricades and broke through police cordons and into the *White House*. Rutskoï harangued the crowd from the balcony, calling on them to seize the Mayor's office and the Ostankino TV centre, while Khazbulatov called on them to storm the Kremlin. Eltsin decreed a state of emergency.

The Saturday's weather was fine enough for us to go for an afternoon walk in Gorky Park, just a kilometre down the road from our house. Not only Communists, but also neo-fascists were marching along *Leninskiï Prospect*. Frightened by a not so distant roar of confrontation, we left the park and hurried back up the hill. The demonstration had now become violent with the *OMON*, the Interior Ministry's special forces, attacking the demonstrators. We each grabbed a small hand and sprinted with our girls through the underpass beneath the demonstration and up to our flat. Our teacher arrived from Tula and I began my Russian lesson with little enthusiasm. Half way through it I heard blasts of gunshot, very close. They came from the garden. We looked out to see a *babushka* vigorously beating her carpet.

That evening the nationalist general, Albert Makashov, elegant in his overlarge black beret, eerily reminiscent of Pétain's militia, led a group of gunmen to invade the Mayor's Office in the former *Comecon* building known as the *Open Book*. Later in the day, using an armoured vehicle, they rammed the glass front of the Ostankino TV centre. Sixty people were killed and the ten or so

TV channels all immediately went off the air.

Imagine suddenly losing all the TV stations. For us it was the ultimate in anxiety. Soon they would be sealing the borders and we would be stuck in an updated version of the Soviet Union. We were frightened. I remembered that Russian expats had told Custine that to enter Russia the gates were wide, to leave they were narrow.

Later that evening broadcasting resumed on a single channel with a very flustered young journalist reading from a flurry of loose papers. We were somewhat reassured. That night we heard the tanks rolling down *Krymskiï Val*, past the Ministry of the Interior, two hundred metres from our house. We felt a certain relief.

Yegor Gaidar and many other personalities appealed on TV for support for the President. The army sided with Eltsin, as Rutskoï, neglecting to consult lower-ranking officers, had also failed to convince the top brass. Pavel Grachev, the official Minister of Defence, grudgingly saved Eltsin by ordering special troops to encircle the White House at dawn on Monday 4th October. They began to shell the building. By noon the White House had caught fire and troops had broken in.

We heard my younger daughter talking on the phone with her school friend, who lived in a building almost adjacent to the *White House* and in the line of fire. The mother and daughter lay on the floor, trying to remain below the crossfire. 'What colour are your tanks?' I heard my daughter ask.

Rutskoï surrendered during a lull in the fighting. Both he and Khazbulatov were charged with organising mass disorders and imprisoned. Four months later and they were released under an amnesty. All criminal charges were dropped against them.

Each week a young Muscovite student came to teach our daughters painting. She had been enthusiastic. 'Russian children paint everything in grey and brown. Your children use vivid colours'. After the *coup* the sole subject of my children's painting was tanks, and in different shades of brown.

The next day we stayed at home. Following our contingency plan, we had laid in a stock of staple foods. Snipers were still shooting sporadically from the roofs. The second day we went back to work. 'Welcome back, Antonin!' said my Russian colleague, 'You are not yet accustomed to this situation. When you have lived longer in Moscow it will not impress you anymore.' Nevertheless, my Russian colleagues spent the afternoon super-glued to *CNN*, the only channel providing news. The broadcaster had had the foresight to rent the top floor of the Hotel *Ukraïna*, with a plunging view over the *White House* in flames.

Two weeks later we returned to France for two weeks' holiday. We spent a night in Trouville on the Normandy coast recovering from the stress. Each time before returning to Moscow we felt the same apprehension, yet an hour after regaining our Moscow flat we always felt elated to be back.

> This *second* October revolution turned out to be the deadliest event in civil conflict in Russia since the revolution of 1917. Estimations of the number of dead varied between four hundred and two thousand.
>
> More than half of the Russian population approved Eltsin's use of force, blaming Rutskoï and Khazbulatov, though nearly a third blamed the legacy of Gorbachëv. Ten years later, public opinion would lay the blame for the crisis on Eltsin's privatisation programme, which had handed out public property to individuals who were to become the *oligarchs*.

Eltsin consolidated his power and Russia remained a presidential system. The president became unimpeachable, gaining sweeping new powers. Eltsin decreed parliamentary elections for December, in which the extremist right-wing, so-called *Liberal Democratic Party* of Vladimir Zhirinovskiï, won nearly a quarter of the vote.

My Russian opposite number, Andreï, invited me and my family to make an excursion in his car to Sergiev Posad, the Trinity Monastery of Saint Sergeï, sometime known as *Zagorsk*, a marvel of ecclesiastical architecture in what is one of the largest monasteries in Russia. Rastrelli, the Italian architect who built the Winter Palace, designed much of it. The monastery had survived both the plague and the Bolsheviks. I made the discovery that apparently rational Russians, like this cybernetician, a specialist in brain functions, can also be true believers. He followed all the rituals of the liturgy, elaborately crossing himself, lighting votive candles, kissing icons and buying their miniatures.

On the return journey we stopped in a village by a convent. Young nuns in black scurried about amongst the chickens, dressed like Boïarina Morozova in the painting by Vasily Ivanovich Surikov. A young monk hurried by. We stopped the car and strolled through the village.

'Who are these?' I asked my colleague;

'These are *Starovery*, Old Believers.'

'What makes them different from other Orthodox monks, Andreï?'

'Oh, nothing really important, in my opinion, not questions of doctrine, only liturgy and rituals. Being raised in the Soviet Union, we never learned about religious questions. We can ask the *pope*.'

A young priest in a black cassock with a

hirsute russet beard walked by. He looked approachable. Andreï spoke to him and helped with his answers.

'We *Starovery* separated from the Russian Orthodox Church in 1666, after the patriarch Nikon introduced reforms to the liturgy.

'The reformers had noticed differences in texts and rites with those of the Greek Orthodox Church. They considered them to be Russian innovations or errors in translation from the Greek. Nikon consequently modified the liturgy without consulting the clergy. He changed the spelling of *Jesus*, added *begotten not made* to the Creed, imposed the sign of the cross with three fingers, representing the Trinity, instead of two, and enforced the direction of processions to be made anti-clockwise instead of clockwise, with three Alleluias instead of two. Changes to the texts seemed to be quite arbitrary, each occurrence of *сынъ, the son*, being replaced by *Христос, Christ*, and vice versa.

'The Old Believers maintained the existing texts and rejected the reforms, considering them to be the work of the Antichrist. We were known as *raskol'niki,* or schismatics.'

'It all sounds somewhat futile to me', I said.

'That may seem so to you, but the motivation behind the reforms was as much political as religious. Russia's ambition was for Moscow to become the *Third Rome* and the liberator of all Orthodox Christians currently under the Ottomans. An anathema was put on us *Starovery* and for 250 years our forefathers were either double-taxed or tortured, depending on the sovereign, until in 1905 Nicolas II authorised religious freedom. Our forebears often chose to be burned alive rather than deny their beliefs.

'Then, in the 19th century, researchers discovered that the liturgy condemned by the Russian church was in fact genuine and unchanged, whereas it had been altered by the Greeks in the 15th and 16th centuries. The former Russian liturgy had in fact been closer to Byzantine practises than that of the Greeks.'

As we returned to the car, I noticed a black and white image stencilled a wall of the village. It resembled the one I had noticed on the Serbian woman's suitcase on the train from Vienna a year earlier.

Beneath it read the caption

Цариград наш

Tsarigrad nash, Constantinople Ours, the same slogan that I had seen across the Balkans, now apparently covered the whole of the Orthodox world. But here, instead of crossing out the minarets, they had replaced the two of them on the left-hand side with twin blunt pencil-like towers.

Inspired by our visit to the two monasteries, Andreï gave me a short history lesson.

'You remember that Russian Orthodoxy began

Back to Byzantium

with the conversion of the Grand Prince of Kiev in the 10th century. Prince Vladimir had married Emperor Basil II's younger sister, Anna. As a result he got baptised and converted the people of *Kievian Rus'* to Orthodoxy, when necessary even by force. He provided his Scandinavian troops for the Byzantine Emperor to create the Varangian guard as his personal bodyguard. This process led to Moscow becoming the *Third Rome* after the fall of Constantinople.

'Anecdotally, they say that Vladimir had sent envoys to study the religions of his neighbours. After investigating Islam, they reported that it was a sad and a *smelly* religion that banned consumption of pork and especially of alcohol, which, as you know, has always been one of the joys of the Russian people. As for Judaism, they considered that the loss of Jerusalem by the Jews was proof that God had abandoned them. Byzantium, however, with its desire to create heaven on earth by its liturgy and its *mise-en-scène*, was of such beauty compared to Catholicism that he converted to Orthodoxy.

'In 1510 the monk Filofeï wrote a letter to Vassily III, the Grand Prince of Muscovy in which he made the following declaration. Ancient Rome had fallen to the Goths, due to its heresies. Constantinople had fallen to the Turks because its people had ceased to be true Christians. All other Orthodox states had merged into the Ottoman Empire. Moscow had become the *Third Rome*. It must stand firm, because there would not be a fourth.'

Five hundred years later, at the beginning of the 21st century, the Archimandrite Tikhon would make a documentary for the state-controlled channel *Rossia* called *Gibel' imperii: vizanskiï urok, the Fall of the Empire: the lesson from Byzantium*. Tikhon makes an interesting parallel between Russia since the fall of Soviet Communism and the fall of Byzantium to the Turks.

He equates Russia with Byzantium. His premise is that Russia has preserved its continuous messianic destiny across the centuries, beginning with Byzantium, continuing through Tsarism, enduring and even becoming reinforced during the time of the atheistic Soviet Union, right up to the Russian Federation. Tikhon explains the fall of Byzantium and draws lessons from it.

He claims that the collapse could have been avoided had Byzantium been sufficiently autocratic and nationalistic against the West and against the local lords. In the case of both Byzantium and present-day Russia, the rise of corrupt local lord-oligarchs weakened the central bureaucratic state, and the separatist movements in the borderlands put imperial unity in peril. While the Byzantine state abandoned a centralised financial system, replaced by Venetian and Genovese merchants, the current Russian Federation has given way to the free international market and to the oligarchs.

Just before the fall of Constantinople to the Turks, Byzantium had reached an agreement at the Council of Florence for ecumenical union with Catholic Rome and for the adoption of Western values. Tikhon parallels the creation by the West of an image of Byzantium as heretical with Ronald Reagan's characterisation of Russia as *the Evil Empire*.

He doesn't consider the invasion by the Turks as an event of major importance. The Franks, however, like the USA today, both with their so-called Western values, he sees as the eternal villain. His conclusion is that to maintain the spiritual tradition of Vladimir I, the Prince of Kiev, Vladimir Putin should become an autocrat and refuse Western values.

Reaching home we turned on the TV and started watching the evening news on *NTV*. They were screening a report on a visit by a congregation of Orthodox dignitaries to Istanbul for a meeting with their counterparts at the Patriarchy of Constantinople. The *popes*, all dressed in cassocks, came from different countries and regions, each with a local variant in headgear, the Bulgarians in trilbies, the others in *skufias,* stove-pipes for the Greeks, pointed for the Russians, and with raised edges for the Romanians. The reporter interviewed a Bulgarian cleric.

'We are finally returning to our imperial capital', he said 'which we lost, but which we have always known that we would regain one day.'

A Romanian cleric added: 'Țarigrad belongs to us and we will not rest until it becomes ours again, if necessary by force.'

So **ЦГН** was no longer just a fringe group of nostalgic freaks. It was an active and probably violent political movement, which had now received a kind of legitimacy from maverick *popes* of the Orthodox churches. Most disturbing!

21
Games

At our first joint meeting with the Goodwill Games Organising Committee the previous year in Saint-Petersburg we had watched an elderly veteran organiser of sports-events present a project for an outrageously luxurious but totally *naff* opening ceremony. Outsize corks were to pop out of gigantic champagne bottles from a platform supported on the backs of a horde of motor-cycle riders. 'And who is going to pay for this?' the Americans asked affirmatively.

The contrast between the silhouettes of members of the two groups struck me: overweight former American football players gone to seed, lean underfed Russians. They too contrasted with the Russian executives in the now decrepit, once-elegant Olympic Committee building of the sixties in Moscow, also erstwhile sportsmen now with prominent spare tires.

As the woman at the IOC had told me, the Goodwill Games turned out to be by no means an unimportant sports event. Two thousand world-renowned athletes from nearly sixty countries took part in twenty-four different sports. Marina Pluzhnikova broke a world record in the 2,000 metres steeplechase. But the real medal should have gone to the engineers of the Russian IT company in charge of the results system, with whom we worked.

They were veterans of the Moscow Olympics, which had taken place fourteen years previously. Their computer applications were also veterans of 1980. They had ambitions of developing a brand-new system, but the time was too short. At the Barcelona olympics the results system had already undergone live testing a full year before the event. The Russians had less than a year left to develop the complete system.

Software developers worldwide are used to missing deadlines while still retaining the scope of the project. With event management, however, the deadline is set in stone. You can throw resources at it or reduce the scope, but the due date cannot be moved.

They had assembled specifically for the Goodwill Games a team of engineers and technicians from different professional groups, all with experience in sports events. The system from the Moscow Olympics was most rudimentary, allowing only one output for each input. This meant that for multiple outputs, such as scoreboards and printed results, data had to be captured twice, with all the risk of error that it entailed.

I had travelled overnight from Moscow to Saint-Petersburg with the Russian IT management team a few months before the Games. We arrived in the early morning as usual at the *Moskovskiï* Station. I was hungry and suggested that we had breakfast at our company's expense. We went to a Western hotel. They looked ill at ease with the prices and uncomfortable with the atmosphere that Westerners took for granted. Eight years later one of them would laughingly admit how impressed he had been and how normal it now all seemed to him now.

We stayed in a third-class hotel on *Krestovskiï* Island. Sitting together in one of our rooms, we drank beer and nibbled on whatever we could together lay our hands on, a tin of ham, dried up *piroshky* and some biscuits. Here at last was the atmosphere that I had been looking for in Russia. Each time I meet with Russians today, whatever there is to eat and wherever we get together, home or restaurant, modest or *chic*, even the simplest meal always turns into a feast, more often with music and song. Quite recently, dining one Friday evening with Russian friends at our kitchen table, we decided to contact a mutual friend in Russia from a mobile phone via Skype. He was in Moscow, where it was already midnight, but he got out his *bayan* chromatic accordion, poured himself glass of Caucasian wine and joined in our party from beyond the computer screen. With whom else but Russians could you have a spontaneous convivial celebration with wine, music and song across cyberspace?

There is never any formality like in France, where dishes must be eaten in a predetermined order, each accompanied by the appropriate wine. A few years later in a restaurant on the Normandy coast, I lunched with some other friends from Moscow. They were Russians, I announced sheepishly. '*J'ai l'habitude*', answered the waiter. They ordered oysters, *foie gras* and *bouillabaisse* which they ate all at the same time, accompanied with red wine. Had we been Westerners he would have turned up his nose up at us. As it was, he served us with radiant benevolence. In contrast, Russian meals are spontaneous, convivial, and festive and above all there is that lavish generosity unknown to Westerners. Each person brings what they happen to have and you put it all together pell-mell on the table. Russians eat and enjoy almost everything and afterwards not a crumb of food nor a drop of drink remain. That is the sort of party that I would miss so much after returning to France.

The Goodwill Games were less than three months away and it was time for us to move house from Moscow to Saint-Petersburg. In early June, spring had finally arrived in Northern Russia. Lilacs and laburnums had just begun to flower in the Field of Mars in Saint-Petersburg. I had crossed it in almost broad daylight in mid-June the previous year at 11 o'clock in the evening to get the night train to Moscow. That was during the *White Nights*. Awakening in my couchette early the following morning to watch suburbanites ambling to work in the early light along overgrown railway paths, crossing the tracks to await their train on bucolic station platforms, as ours dawdled past small elegant *izbas* with not so well-tended kitchen gardens. Sunrise from the night train always cheered me up.

If Moscow, with its skyscrapers, is a vertical city, Saint-Petersburg, with its Italianate palaces and perspectives, is horizontal. In winter, to our children's dismay, we had crossed over the partly-frozen Neva on foot from the Peter and Paul fortress to the tip of Vasilevskiï Island, a distance of three-or-so hundred metres. Six months later, it was under the water that we would travel for the first time through the recently opened Channel tunnel.

We had found a couple of flats just off Nevskiï Prospect, the grandiose main thoroughfare acclaimed by Gogol. In fact the whole city was reminiscent of Russian literature. Walking through the former corn market you expected to encounter *Raskolnikov* creeping home after murdering his awful landlady. We lived in a former *komunalka*, a three room flat previously occupied by three separate families. It was located on the second floor above a butcher's shop. Twice a week we watched them delivering the meat, dumping whole sides of beef onto the ground of the muddy courtyard, the hangout of cats and birds.

The triple apartment was comfortable, except that each time we used the washing machine we had to rush downstairs to warn our colleague in the *kommunalka* below to prepare empty buckets. It was an improvement on Moscow, where, during the summer period when they turned off the municipal hot water, the only way to have a bath was to run the washing machine to heat the water and feed the bathtub through the drain hose.

While our Russian colleagues transported our goods and chattels by van, we took the night train with our children and our cat. We had plugged him with a triple dose of tranquilisers for the journey to keep him quiet, knowing that they didn't allow domestic animals on the train. Our seven-year-old daughter insisted on sleeping on the upper bunk. Unlike Western couchettes, Russian berths have no strap to prevent you falling out. During the night she did fall a couple of metres down onto the bag in which the cat was sleeping. It softened her fall, but the caterwauling lasted for the rest of the night. It took twenty-four hours for the cat to recover in our new apartment.

The unmovable deadline was nearly upon us. In Saint-Petersburg, due to critical delays in delivery of equipment, unavailability of venues, absence of timely specifications, large-scale testing of the results system was just not possible.

Nevertheless, the Russians completed on-schedule a simple results and inquiry system for twenty-four sports against almost insurmountable difficulties. I often heard it said that Soviet systems always worked once, usually on-time, though they looked awful and were neither maintainable nor duplicable. By contrast, the Americans, despite constant chasing up, did not provide all the specifications in time. They might have taken a lesson from the Russians.

Hardware was delivered at the last minute. Cable for the local area network, the servers and TV interface machines were delivered not more than a week before. Printers were installed only on the first day of the Games, those that were available that is, since a whole consignment of printers got lost or stolen. One of the consequences was that, due to lack of time to run live tests at full capacity, the local area networks functioned with only eight workstations per server. Twenty-five per cent of the workstations in the Main Press Centre had to be switched off.

CoCom restrictions dating from the recent Cold War had until very recently prevented hardware from the West being available in Russia. The Russian team had been obliged to develop their own somewhat primitive, but functioning local area network. The Russians had that remarkable talent for making do with situations which in the West would be unbearable.

Despite favourable presidential decrees, customs regulations kept changing, thus delaying delivery. You got the feeling of an arbitrary system, sometimes even designed to frustrate legitimate activity. After difficulties trying to obtain a vital spare part the size of your finger through regular Russian channels, we purchased it directly from Croatia and, thanks to *DHL*, had it delivered at record speed.

The systems software provider was able to supply the basic systems software in time, but still only in test status. The communications link with a major press agency in London was obtained only at the end of the first week. The link to Paris never materialised.

Most venues became available less than a week before the beginning of the Games and some never became available, causing several events to be cancelled.

Due to lack of ice in the *Iubileinyï Palace* for Figure Skating, the resourceful Russian team had managed to put in place a last-minute contingency solution on another ice rink, which belonged to the Russian Army, setting up connectivity on a duplicate local area network within a few hours. When the ice finally solidified in *Iubileinyï* on the day preceding the event, they had to move all the equipment back again. It was then that a French champion at first refused to skate on it.

The *SKA* swimming pool was totally empty of water a week before the Swimming and Diving events. A gentle trickle eventually managed to fill it, but the water had the colour of rotting seaweed. One Northern European team refused to swim in it. It took a dive on local TV by Anatoly Sobchak, the Mayor of Saint-Petersburg and co-Chairman of the Games with his American opposite number to convince them.

A month before the Games, Atlanta had still not supplied specifications for TV captions for several events. They never supplied them at all for some sports and modified many of them on the day preceding the event. We communicated with the US first via *DHL*. When later, following Russian regulations, they no longer accepted diskettes, even when we had camouflaged them between several layers of paper, we had no option than to have them transmitted via a diplomatic pouch.

My Croatian colleague needed to spend five days in Atlanta to try to obtain on site the specifications that the Americans had still not supplied to enable him to complete the development of his TV interface. For this he required a visa. He had already spent four mornings waiting in a long queue outside the US Embassy, first arriving too late to enter before the offices closed, then, when he did manage to penetrate the building, getting a rebuttal due to a missing document, although he had presented an official invitation from Atlanta. He was due to leave in a couple of days, so I decided to go with him on the fifth day to share his burden and help give him credibility.

The queue was long but, with a palm-to-palm contribution to the official in charge of filtering the entries, we might have moved more quickly up the line. But our company didn't bribe US citizens. When we finally did get inside, a young woman with a strong first-generation accent in English called us to a desk, where she conducted the whole conversation over a microphone. Everything she said, or rather bellowed, was audible to every person in the hall. You could hear women at the other desks shouting to their own visa applicants. I showed her our contract. 'What proves that you didn't type out this contract yourself?' she yelled.

Back to Byzantium

I recalled what the Croatian writer, Slavenka Drakulić, had said about the yellow line that only recently ensured privacy during a transaction in a Croatian post office. It wasn't as if my colleague were an asylum seeker or had even asked to enter US territory on his own behalf. He had no real wish to go there. It was a requirement for an international sports event, sponsored by the President of the Russian Federation, with an invitation from *TBS*.

After more violent language she finally granted him the visa. The five days that it had finally taken to obtain it was the duration of his stay in the USA.

I had a meeting with a charming but inefficient *KGB* officer to find a solution for the protection of the pool of computers in the Main Press Centre. He put a muscular contingent of guards at each access to protect them. When the guards wouldn't let me out with my own laptop, I started negotiating with them. 'Look! Antonin is having a fight with the *KGB*', exclaimed my Russian colleagues, surprised by my naïve audacity. The following morning we discovered that, while under the security guard which had refused to permit access to accredited technicians to the Main Press Centre, someone had tampered with key computers and had broken one of them. When a *KGB* officer got bored, what did he do? He played computer games, of course, and with brutality.

A couple of veterans of the Barcelona Olympics arrived in Saint-Petersburg to help operate the results system and TV captions. I recruited help from my wife to pick one of them up at the airport. While waiting at the arrivals gate with a large cardboard sign bearing his name written in bold capitals, a Russian goon accosted her. 'Which company you work for? Who you come to meet?' he asked menacingly. 'I am waiting for my husband' answered Edmonde, brandishing her cardboard sign with aplomb.

The *Lenexpo* Main Press Centre had filled up with technicians from Atlanta. I had spent most of my working life with well-travelled American expats. But these were the real thing, straight from the backwoods. My colleagues had always told me to leave the door ajar if ever I found myself alone in an office with an American woman. I worked with one such young woman. One day when she looked particularly glamorous, I said 'You look great!' She never spoke to me again.

On the run-up to the Games I got so stressed that a chronic abscess, caught while sitting for a week in the *Transsib*, erupted, as it had every six months for fifteen years. I had to get it cut out without an anaesthetic at the American clinic the day before the opening ceremony. I was also suffering from warts on my right foot. Their origin is viral, said the chiropodist, but their cure is incantatory: 'You have to demonstrate that you are stronger than your warts.' What could he mean by that? I had been in disagreement with one of my colleagues for months until I decided to terminate his contract. The same day my warts fell off like sores from the Galilean leper.

My Belgian colleague had brought his wife and accident-prone son over for the event. The son succeeding in cutting his head open. Another colleague had left his girlfriend in his flat while he was away on holiday. She had an attack of paranoia and started throwing saucepans three floors down into the street onto the police cars that the neighbours had summoned. The restraint of the Saint-Petersburg militia amazed us.

A couple of colleagues from Barcelona, staying in a hotel on the North Bank of the Neva, got stuck most of the night on the wrong side of the river. Each night the bridges in Saint-Petersburg are raised to allow ships to pass. They returned to their hotel only after walking the streets on the opposite bank until the early hours of the morning.

Despite all our efforts to put in place a change management system, procedures were never implemented or, in the rare cases where they were followed, were overridden by management. Programming methods were purely individual. The lack of project tracking and release control caused a small disaster in Figure Skating.

The basic source programs for Figure Skating were either lost, undocumented or of such bad quality that any change to the application was impossible. Even the engineer who had programmed it was unwilling to touch it. Returning from a liquid lunch, he made last-minute changes to a program interfacing with TV, which he recompiled using the wrong set of libraries to calamitous effect. Applications in Russia generally worked, but they could often be modified by no-one other than the person who developed them. Development legacy was unprotected and Quality control inexistent.

The Russians took risks that would have been unacceptable in the West, but did they have other options? The central applications ran on a midrange computer, which had to be transported from Moscow to Saint-Petersburg. No padded removal vans were available in Russia, so they just removed the disk unit, laid the central processing unit down on its side on some blankets and drove it in a camper van over seven hundred kilometres of among the bumpiest road surfaces in Europe. The server was up and running the following day.

Poor levels of service were generally accepted in post-Soviet Russia. Russians felt that, given time, problems would just sort themselves out.

As the deadline for the event approached, the Organising Committee, with the Americans' approval, had hired a former Soviet political commissar, one of those unproductive people who had for decades been poisoning the lives of regular workers. It made the members of the Russian team who knew him ill at ease. He summoned me to an office in the Committee building. Do you know the *Lobnoë Mesto*?' he asked. *The Place of Skulls* is a round stone platform situated in Red Square in front of the Cathedral of Saint-Basil. 'That is where the pillory used to be and that is where I am going to put you personally if the results system doesn't work as it should.

I felt too ill at ease to reply. I turned my chair around and sat astride it in defiance with my elbows on the upright back.

On the first day of the Games a Canadian from the *TBS* team, known for his *short fuse*, came into the computer room and subjected me to a violent verbal attack in front of the Russians, who, despite their difficult history, were aghast at such barbaric behaviour. No thanks to me, ninety-five per cent of the results had been made available in a timely manner by the second day. Another visit on the third day of the Games gave me pleasant surprise. This time it came from the political commissar. With a broad smile he patted me on the back and congratulated me on a job well done.

The sun shone, albeit sometimes pallidly, for the duration of the Games. The first drop of rain fell just a minute after the closing ceremony. The Soviets had gained expertise in cloud busting since Stalin initiated research during the thirties. Chernobyl had given them hands-on experience protecting the Pripïat River. Specially equipped aeroplanes using ecologically clean chemicals prevented a single drop of rain from falling for the two weeks of the Games. The whole of the city centre had a face lift. A regiment of painters daubed the stucco of the historic buildings with a single coat of paint without any prior washing, what they call *lipstick on the bulldog*?

The Russian IT company found itself in a difficult financial situation. High inflation and unethical procedures by banks to delay payment had eaten up their meagre financial resources, leading to major cash flow problems and irregular payment of personnel. By the time the Games began, the organising committee was six months in arrears of payment for even the basic services. This had already happened a few months previously. The Russian company was unable to honour the salaries of its employees, pay its rent or its electricity bills. Its office landlord, the Olympic Committee, consequently switched off the electricity for two weeks. What did an IT company do without power? They switched off the computers and halted development and testing for the same period. Six engineers left the company due to non-payment of their salaries

On the last Friday of the Games the Russian employees, again unpaid, posted a notice on the computer room door in the Main Press Centre in the *Lenexpo* exhibition hall saying in English **ON STRIKE**. I warned the American director of the Games, who tried to avert the strike by bringing the Russian managers to talk with the Organising Committee.

We all marched off to see Anatoly Sobchak. Inconspicuous in a back corner of the same room stood a creepy new Russian, full in the face, his chin and hairline both receding, dressed in an ill-fitting loud maroon double-breasted blazer. 'Put your complaint in writing', he said. I had noticed him more than once during presentations, sitting with a spooky scowl away from the official dais, always dressed the same way. How could Sobchak work with such a man? This ex-*KGB* officer was soon to become one of the most powerful men on earth.

Twenty minutes later, the three managers of the Russian development team were still busy composing the letter, stuck at the first line, quibbling over the appropriate form of address. Sobchak's receding blond double-breasted sidekick lost patience and stormed out. A heavyweight American woman, blocking the door with arms and legs akimbo, tried to discourage him from leaving the room. Large as she was, she was no match for an 8th *dan* black-belt *karateka*. He forced his way through. The strike had been averted, but was payment ever made?

A Slovene woman won a gold medal in the 100 metres hurdles. The Russian judges mistook the country and displayed Slovakia instead of Slovenia. After all, the Slovenes call themselves *Slovenski* and the Slovaks *Slovenský*. The Russians consulted with the Americans.

Back to Byzantium

They didn't know the difference, they explained. Nobody in the US knew the difference either, they answered, let's just leave it that way. So that's just how they left it, at least for the moment.

A couple of weeks after the closing ceremony, with the heaviest of hearts we flew back to Paris. Our children returned to school in September to discover that their friends had moved on. No-one took any interest in their *unique* experience. I found a job working for a major international sports event that was to take place across France. I had never liked Paris, or at least not recently, and I found the job and our customer hard to bear.

Not long after, I took early retirement. At last I had the time to start learning Russian seriously. To give myself the illusion of progressing in this arduous language, I would occasionally buy *Russkaïa Mysl'*, the weekly newspaper published in Paris since 1947 for the diaspora in France, which I could find in a Russian bookshop near the Place Maubert.

Epilogue
A. Malakoff

In *Russkaïa Mysl'* I discovered a small ad in the Associations column, in both Russian and in French.

> ПАРИЖ
>
> Ц-Г-Н
>
> Информационная встреча
>
> Вторник 13 апреля 2004 г
> в 20 часов
>
> Ассоциация Франция-
> Византия
>
> 13 rue de Constantinople
> **MALAKOFF**
>
> ЭК 6713
> 800 лет
>
> Помните!

Back to Byzantium

Translated into English, the small ad said:

> **PARIS**
>
> **Tse-Ge-eN**
>
> **Information meeting**
>
> **Tuesday 13 April 2004**
>
> **8 PM**
>
> **Association France-Byzantium**
>
> **13 rue de Constantinople MALAKOFF**
>
> **EK 6713**
> **800 years**
>
> **Remember!**

There was the number again, 6713, preceded by EK, like the one scrawled, using Roman numerals, across the chimney canopy in the Grand Master's Palace in the fortress of Malbork. Except that there was a gap of 38 between the two numbers. It was now clearly a date, and I seriously doubted whether EK stood for *EinsatzKommando*. No, this had nothing to do with the Nazis.

13th April 1204 was the date of the Sack of Constantinople by the Franks and Venetians. This was an anniversary commemoration that I did not intend to miss. Today was only the 1st of April and I had a good twelve days before the meeting and time to do some research using the new tool that I had recently discovered, the internet. I started to browse the web about the re-conquest of Constantinople. What I found surprised me.

I came across the site of a well-known French writer, who had launched in 1965 the *Association française pour la delivrance de Constantinople*. He considered it to be just as relevant today, Turkey being, in his words, a lackey of the USA since the war. I also identified a *Community for Ethnic Westerners*, which asked whether the West should conquer-reconquer Constantinople, Alexandria, and Jerusalem. An article bore the title *Do Greeks have a legitimate claim on Istanbul?* Others were *Tsarigrad ou le rêve brisé*, *Will Greece retake Constantinople from the Turks*? The list was considerable and the subject apparently still newsworthy.

While I was about it, why not look for *TseGeeN*? Another surprise was the site at the address **www.tse-ge-en.com**, with the confirmation of all the symbols that I had been seeing over the years, but not really much more. I would have to wait for the meeting for a full explanation.

At 7:45 PM on 13th April I arrived at the meeting hall in Malakoff. Named after a defensive tower near Sebastopol captured by the French during the Crimean War, once a working-class suburb of Paris with small factories and workshops, the suburban town was undergoing gentrification.

The meeting room was a non-descript space on the ground floor of a former factory. A large trestle table at the far end of the room dominated the auditorium from a low stage improvised on wooden blocks. Sixty-or-so folding chairs were lined up in rows, two thirds of them already occupied by whispering groups of two or three men. Long-haired bearded *Chetniks* sat next to ear-pierced, shaven-headed youths in parka jackets. In one corner distinguished elderly Mediterranean gentlemen glanced benevolently at newcomers from behind their flamboyant moustaches. I wrote down my name and email address on an exercise book lying on a small table beside the door and sat down in one corner.

Portrait photos and posters lined three of the walls with little apparent attempt at symmetry or elegance. I recognised a number of writers and politicians from across Europe and the Balkans.

At precisely 8 o'clock a door opened at the end of the room and a grey man in his early fifties entered and sat down at the table. Short pepper and salt unkempt hair stood spikily over bifocals as thick as beer bottles. His ill-cut jacket as grey as his hair covered a shirt of a doubtful shade of white, half untucked over his ill-matching grey trousers. A scrawny tie held his collar together askew, not quite covering a stubbly protuberant Adam's apple.

He welcomed us. 'I believe that you all know why I have summoned you to this meeting', he said quietly in a melodious voice, rolling his *Rs*, tongue to teeth, with a strong foreign accent. 'This is about fund raising.

'But first let us stand for a minute's silence in remembrance of events that took place eight hundred years ago today. I refer of course to the Sack of Constantinople by the Franks during the Fourth Crusade, which led two hundred years later to its fall to the Heathen.'

Back to Byzantium

Chetniks, skinheads and Balkan gentlemen all arose to attention and stood with remarkable discipline until our host told us to be seated.

'Let me remind you of the aims of our movement, which our members and sympathisers know across Europe by its code name *Tse-Ge-eN*. Our purpose is to recreate our long-lost Byzantine Empire, which our enemies the Turks and the Franks stole from us.'

Our host had confirmed my suspicions. I began to feel most uncomfortable and thought that it was time that I left, but some ominous looking bearded Balkan types stood by the door looking suspiciously over the assembly. I would just have to sit it out.

Our grey chairman continued. 'But how can we achieve this?' He paused ponderously.

'Our strategy is based on a struggle against the USA to bring about the isolationism that a large part of its population has always yearned for. The USA will soon withdraw from Europe, Turkey and the Middle East and cease to support its ally, Israel.' He paused again. 'Turkey, once definitively excluded from the European Union will turn towards its cousins, the Turkic lands of Asia.

'Under increasing military threat from Russia, Turkey will accept a transaction, an exchange of territory between Europe and Asia. It will reluctantly agree to surrender Istanbul-Constantinople, Edirne-Adrianople and its European provinces. Realising that its renewed greatness lies in a new hegemony over Central Asia, Turkey will accept compensation by major territorial concessions from Russia: Azerbaijan, Russian Tartary, Kazakhstan, Kirghizstan, Turkmenistan and Uzbekistan.

'Due to demography and immigration, Catholics will come to dominate the USA, reducing Protestant and Jewish influence, and create widespread anti-Semitism. Again through demography, Palestinians will take over

Israel without military reaction from the USA.

'New Byzantium will share domination of Europe with the Arabs, after their re-conquest of *Al Andalus* and the creation of a new Caliphate.'

Help, where on earth have I set foot, I thought, in a panic that the chairman could not help noticing in my eyes despite all my efforts to hide it.

'You, Sir, you seem a little sceptical. Did you have a question?'

The *Chetniks* at the door looked menacingly in my direction. I had no choice. 'You mentioned the Franks. Are you referring to the French and Germans?' I asked, desperately trying to say something that sounded relevant while hiding my apprehension.

'Not at all', he replied. 'Let me reassure you. The Franks were Western barbarians. Though historically the Normans and the *Toulousains* were major participants in the Crusades with the Flemish and Germans, modern French influence and that of the Europeans in general today is based on soft power. France has always been the country of predilection for Orthodox peoples since Catherine the Great and the voyage of Lamartine. The French have a traditional love for the Russians and for the Serbs. Bulgaria and Romania are part of *Francophonie*, the French-speaking world. France and Germany have always resisted Turkey entering the European Union. No, on the contrary, the French and Germans are our friends and potential allies.'

'Who then are your enemies exactly? Who do you refer to as the Franks?' Getting involved in the discussion I forgot my anxiety to some extent.

'There has been a displacement. When I talk of the Franks I refer of course to the North Americans. They have a strong Catholic and Protestant heritage, contrary to most European nations, which with a few exceptions have become mainly secular. American Protestants identify with the Crusaders.

'The USA has camouflaged its motives of mercantilism and domination beneath religious and ideological clothing. Its aim since the Second World War and especially since the fall of Communism has been hegemony and neo-colonialism. The Americans have allied themselves with our principal enemy, the Turks, providing them with aid and arms against the Slavs. They intervened to help the *Bosnjak* Muslims against the Serbs and even bombed Belgrade to set up an independent Muslim Kosovo. The Orthodox Serbs were subsequently expelled from what used to be the cradle of their culture and the British set up their Embassy near the historical site of the battle of Kosovo Polje, the founding myth of Serbian cultural identity.

'Despite the fall of the Soviet Union, the Americans have maintained their hostility to Russia with a policy of encirclement, setting up bases in the neighbouring Turkic nations which were formerly part of the USSR. You may not remember the Cuban missile crisis, which the Americans claim to have won. On the contrary, it was the Soviets who forced them to withdraw their missiles from Turkey. But today US bases are now in almost every Turkic nation in Asia.

'They also use their own version of soft power. For decades, in fact since Marshall Aid, the USA has deliberately been diligently destroying all cultural diversity in the world through its cinema, music and fast food industries, designed for children and adolescents, a culture that requires no intellectual effort from consumers. It has imposed its language on the world, following a plan devised with the British after the Second World War. This means that a monolingual nation has forced a multilingual world to abandon all languages except the only one that it understands. Imagine a poor man requiring the rich man to become as poor as he wishes to remain himself. Gradual insidious Americanisation of the world is reminiscent and comparable to the Ottomanisation of Montenegro denounced by Bishop Danilo in the *Golden Wreath*.

'The USA has become today's symbol of the barbaric West, as the Franks were previously. Just consider American behaviour in Middle-East. Aren't *Abu Graib* and water-boarding at Guantanamo comparable to the atrocities of the Crusaders? Who is the *Evil Empire* now?'

Here at last was the full confirmation of my suspicions and fears. I had got too involved, but I had to learn more. 'How long has your movement existed?' I asked.

'The answer to your question is obvious', the grey man replied. 'It has lain in the collective unconscious of the Orthodox peoples since the fall of Constantinople in 1453. I would say that the movement itself has existed in an embryonic state since 1878.

'It really came alive during the fall of the Ottoman Empire, with the Balkan Federalist movement and later briefly with the *Megali Idea* in Greece. Then it fell back into slumber during most of the life of the Soviet Union to reawaken under Khrushchëv after the Cuban missile crisis. We became really active only after the fall of the Soviet Union.

'Even before our resurrection after the end of the Cold War, people with our ideas in masonic lodges and secret societies have always been active, financing individual actions, influencing political decisions.

'We inspired and financed Gavrilo Princip through *Crna ruka*, the Black Hand, in the assassination of Franz Ferdinand. We instigated the *Megali idea* in Greece. We failed in our project for Balkan federation with Tito and Dimitrov, when Stalin murdered him. It was we who armed the Turkish Christian, Ali Ağca, against the anti-Orthodox Catholic Pope, thereby compromising Turkey. Our followers financed Milošević and the ethnic Serbs in

Krajina, Bosnia, Slavonia and later in Kosovo. This was one of our great failures. We inspired the movement for *Enosis* in Cyprus and *Eoka* terrorism. We are allied with the *PKK* for Kurdish independence and with *ASALA* in Armenia. Our lodges in France and Germany have lobbied successfully against Turkey's entry into the European Union. We subsidize European cultural organisms and associations, such as Russian choirs in France. Here is the logo of one of them. He pointed to a poster on the wall.

'Our movement is omnipresent.

'If you have no other questions I will pass a hat around. I must insist on your generosity. It is mainly thanks to your contributions that we can keep our movement alive. Please give generously, but remember that any contribution, however small, is better than nothing. Remember too that the most important thing is your continued mobilisation.'

I put in the hat the smallest bank note that I thought the scrutinous *Chetnik* holding it would accept and got up to look at the pictures on the walls. I had been quite intrepid so far and wanted to have my money's worth.

'I recognise some of these figures. Can you identify the others for me?' I asked the chairman.

We started on the right-hand wall. 'These are our heroes', he said.

'First Bulgaria, with its Tsars, Boris and Simeon, and Cyril, Methodius and Clement of Ohrid;

'Then Serbia, with Stefan Dušan, Prince Lazar, Miloš Obilić, the poet-prince Petar Petrovic Njegos and the meek looking peasant with his adolescent moustache, Gavrilo Princip;

'Russia, with Alexander Nevsky, the hero of the Battle on the Ice against the Teutonic Knights, Ivan Groznyï, the Terrible, scourge of the Tatars, and Catherine the Great, who, after a failed attempt to restore Byzantium, crushed the Khanate of Crimea, liberating it from the Turks.' Beside them hung a reproduction of Ilya Repin's famous painting of *The Cossacks of Saporog defying Sultan Mehmed IV*.

'Then Wallachia, with a reproduction of the portrait of Vlad Țepeș, the Impaler, the terror of the Ottomans.

Further along hung a portrait of Gotthold Ephraim Lessing, whose *Nathan der Weise*, written as early as the 18th century Enlightenment in Germany, was a condemnation of the Templars and of religious intolerance.

'And here is our hero and your compatriot, Lord Byron. You remember these lines?

> 'If Greece one true-born patriot can boast:
> Not such as prate of war but skulk in peace,
> The bondsman's peace, who sighs for all he lost,
> Yet with smooth smile his tyrant can accost,
> And wield the slavish sickle, not the sword…'

Other portraits hung on the facing wall, including Ali Ağca, who had shot Pope John-Paul II. We identified them all to the last figure, a portrait of Winston Churchill. 'What does he have to do with your movement?' I asked. 'He launched the attack, albeit abortive, on the Turks in the Dardanelles', he replied.

'If these are your heroes, who are your enemies', I asked.

Back to Byzantium

'Our enemies are the Habsburgs, with their century-old persecution of Orthodox populations; Lenin and Stalin with their multi-national, multi-cultural, multi-religious Soviet Union; Tito and Yugoslavia, with its federation of Catholic, Orthodox and Muslim nations; the Nazis and the Croatian Ustaša, for their persecution of Orthodox Slavs; of course John Paul II, the Catholic supremacist, and Ronald Reagan, with his *Evil Empire* rhetoric; and Vladimir Putin for his plan for a Eurasian Empire.

'Everything that you have been saying seems to be in line with Samuel Huntington's description', I said. 'He claimed that dialogue which, despite ideological differences, had been possible between East and West since Lenin, ceased to be possible between the Catholic-Protestant West and Orthodox Russia, due to irreconcilable cultural and religious differences and a refusal of Westernisation. He also described the common enmity of Orthodox nations for Turkey.'

'Huntington had an erroneous belief in a Western entity', he objected, 'he was unaware of the degree of anti-Americanism in Europe. He was a mono-lingual, whose only concrete experience was of the USA, and whose knowledge of the rest of the world came from books. He didn't understand Western European cultural diversity and didn't realise that its peoples are condemned to coexist on a microcosmic level.

'Huntington located the fault line in his *clash of civilisations* in Bosnia. What he didn't realise was that, historically, the different religious communities lived there side by side. Muslims, Christians and Jews were often blood brothers since childhood, joined as adults in the same labour unions. In case of illness a Muslim might call for help from a Christian priest or even from a Jewish rabbi. The differences, at least in urban areas, were blurred. And he didn't see that the conflict between Bosnian Serbs and Bosnjak Muslims was at least partially a class struggle.

'He also didn't understand that with globalisation today there is a thirst for other cultures, foreign cooking, music, dance, martial arts and, especially, mixed marriages. Nor did he foresee the continued antagonism between the two Koreas. Particularly, he seemed to be unaware of the century-old Franco-Russian friendship. And, of course, he didn't envisage the successful entry of Bulgaria, Romania and Croatia into the European Union, or the candidacy of Serbia, Turkey, the Ukraine and other Balkan nations.

'You are very well-informed and extremely curious', he said, giving me a sinking feeling in my stomach. 'You ask a lot of questions.'

I said goodbye and left the meeting room as fast and as discreetly as possible, leaving his followers chatting in the same groups as before. I took a bus to the metro terminus and went back to my flat.

The first thing that I did as usual was to turn on my computer. Instead of my usual wallpaper a not unfamiliar image invaded the screen.

e k 7510

Someone had just hacked my computer.

Epilogue
B. Ramstein

After rebooting my computer I found that everything was working correctly again.

Unable to make a screen print of the image that had been displayed, I had taken a snapshot on my mobile phone. There were the twin towers that I had seen before, replacing two of the minarets of *Hagia Sofia*. But what were the numbers below and what could *EK* stand for?

I felt in my pocket and withdrew the small ad that I had cut out of *Russkaïa Mysl'*. It said:

EK 6713

800 years

Remember!

The previous evening had confirmed that it referred to the Sack of Constantinople in 1204 during the Fourth Crusade, exactly eight hundred years ago. So the number was probably a date in another chronological system, like the Islamic calendar, *AH* or *anno Hegirae,* the year of the *Hijra*. No, of course not, the number would be much smaller. This was something else. Subtracting 1204 from 6713, I found 5509. I made the same operation on the number on the screen image: 7510 minus 5509 came to 2001.

Of course, they were the towers of the World Trade Center. I almost fell off my chair. So *Tse-Ge-eN* had been involved in that atrocity, or were at least sympathisers.

But that was not the date that I had seen in Malbork; it was 6751. By the same operation I arrived at 1242, thirty-eight years after the Sack of Constantinople. What had happened of note that year? Fortunately I was something of a *cinephile*. Of course, I remembered Eisenstein's film *Aleksandr Nevskiï*, with Prokofiev's score. It was the year of the Battle of the Ice, marking the Catholic Crusaders' defeat and humiliation at the hands of Orthodox Russians, a symbolic revenge for Orthodoxy. Like Dunkirk, Kosovo Polje or Vercingetorix's submission to Caesar at Alesia, defeats often make more inspiring national symbols than do victories.

But what was *EK*?

I found the answer the following morning by the coffee machine at the office in *La Défense*. I was working on a project with a Cretan and we had stopped for a break. I explained my enigma to him.

'It stands for *'Etos Kosmou*, he said, '*Annus Mundi* in Latin, or the era of the creation of the world. Byzantium used it as its official calendar from the 6th century until its fall in 1453 and Russia continued to use it until the new-born Soviet Union adopted the Gregorian calendar in 1918.

'The Julian calendar started from the date of the creation of the world, 1st September in the year 5509 BC. That means that Jesus Christ was born in EK 5509. To convert from *'etos kosmou* to the Gregorian calendar, you add 5509 years, taking into account that 1st January has replaced 1st September. So, as you correctly deduced, EK 7510 is the year 2001 in antique Orthodox notation.'

I left my office early and waited for the bus in the street in front, perturbed by what I had discovered. A car stopped. 'Which way to Paris?' asked the driver, opening the front-passenger door. I was leaning over to tell him, when I felt an irresistible pressure from behind and found myself sitting in the passenger's seat with something metallic pressing on the nape of my neck. 'Stay calm, no move and everything OK', said a voice in *Globish* from behind. I am no hero and I just did as they told me.

When we were out of the suburban area they blindfolded me. We drove for more than four hours along what sounded like a motorway. The car stopped, they removed the blindfold and, as far as I could see through the night air under the full moon, I found myself surrounded by low, rough-cast utility huts amid a scrubby forest of conifers. We entered one of them, they gave me a glass of water, took me by the toilet and then locked me into an empty windowless room.

After hours of anxiety, but mainly of boredom, the door opened and a large, clean-shaven, middle-aged man in army fatigues came in with a cup of coffee. 'Do you wish to complain?' he asked. 'We mean you no harm, but you have become too inquisitive. We had no other option than to keep you locked up until we have finished preparing our new operation.'

'Who are you' I asked with trepidation, 'and what are you preparing?'

'We are preparing an attack on a US air base', he answered with surprising frankness. 'I am busy now, but I shall return later and we can talk. It will be a pleasure to have a conversation with someone a little more cultured than the brutes that surround me.' He left and I discovered what he meant through the crack of the door.

The adjacent room was fifty metres square with windows looking out into the woods. Trestle tables had been set up in rows and on most of them stood a microcomputer. A disparate group of large men in army fatigues sat drinking tea. Half of them were dark-haired with fair skins. The other half were very dark-skinned. They had one thing in common. They all had long unkempt beards.

I spent a couple of days in captivity more of boredom than anxiety, much reassured by my jailor's apparently benevolent attitude to me. Through intermittent observation each time the door opened, it had become clear to me that there were two distinct groups working here, Balkan *Chetniks* and Russian Cossacks, on the one hand, and Arab *Salafists*, on the other. Communication between the two groups, mostly in *Globish*, was reduced to a minimum. Two functional groups existed also. Regardless of their ethnicity, most of them were apparently programmers, bowed all day in front of their computers. The minority were fighters, who seemed to spend their whole time cleaning their automatic rifles.

They fed me with palatable Turkish food. It seemed paradoxical that it was the Turks who had taught most of the Orthodox and Arab worlds how to cook.

My charming captor returned after a few hours with a cup of sweet tea and some *baklava* to put me as much at ease as was possible in the circumstances.

'As you may already have understood', he said, 'we are engaged in cyber-warfare.'

Hacking was beginning to have a long history, with cyber-attacks in the USA, at the Pentagon, against aviation security, against embassies. A couple of years later, a massive attack would put Estonia offline for three weeks by disabling its infrastructure, including everything from online banking and mobile phone networks to government services and access to health care information.

'The *jihadis* need people from the Balkans, mainly Bulgarians, but also Russians, who have expertise in hacking and virus attacks. We need petro-dollars. We decided to join forces, at least until our mid-range objectives have been met.'

'You are not telling me that your movement has allied with *al Qaeda*?' I said.

'Precisely. He who sups with the devil needs a long spoon, as they say, and I only hope ours is long enough.'

'But you have nothing in common', said I, 'neither religious, cultural, ethnic, nor even alimentary. It can only be a short term tactical alliance.'

'On the contrary, we have much more in common than you think.

'First of all, there is our common enmity for the USA and shared traditional hostility to the Turks, that

> '... those who loath alike the Frank and Turk
> Might once again renew their ancient butcher work.'

'Then there is the desire to restore former grandeur and the great hegemonies of history. We share the aim of re-establishing the geopolitical situation of the past, meaning Byzantium and *Al Andalus*. The fall of Constantinople in 1453 and the end of the *Reconquista* with the fall of *Al Andalus* in 1492, were almost simultaneous.

'You know there has never been a war between Slavs and Arabs and we have no traditional anti-Arab feeling. During the Cold War there was an entente between the Soviet Union and most Arab nations.

'Most important, we share the vision of a new division of the world.

'To be frivolous, we even have the same style: beards, common to all fanatics, puritanism, extreme asceticism, victimisation, the cult of death in combat, the ideal of martyrdom and exultation of violence.'

'So we are co-financing this project and sharing tools and methods.'

This didn't surprise me. Bulgaria had long been a hub of international crime and terrorism. During the Cold War, *DS*, *Darzhavna Sigournost*, the so-called hand of Moscow, had been involved in arms and drug trafficking to finance revolutionary movements and destabilise the West. It was the Bulgarians who had hired Ali Ağca to assassinate the anti-Soviet Pope. And, of course, there was the Bulgarian umbrella, used to kill the dissident Georgi Markov on Waterloo Bridge.

Ayman Al-Zawahiri, Osama Bin Laden's right-hand man, who would later replace him as head of *al-Qaeda*, stayed in the Rhodope Mountains on two occasions during the nineties. The agent Aleksandr Litvinenko, later to be assassinated, alleged that the *FSB* had been training Al-Zawahiri there. The first attacks against the USA had been organised from Bulgaria.

'But who actually finances your activities?' I asked.

'Individuals, fanatics, but also oligarchs, the *mafia* and, of course, some Arab nations. The Russian state and the *FSB*, at least to destabilise the West, and the Moscow Patriarchate, for ideological reasons. Milošević has given us foot-soldiers and moral support. A large part came from the Serbian and Bulgarian *mafia*, who wanted to regain their financial domination in Constantinople. We use the same methods for financing as the *mafia* do for money laundering.'

'It is clear that you want to create a new world order', I said. 'Can you explain the advantages and disadvantages are for the different protagonists?'

'Let us start with Russia. It will reunify and gain hegemony over the whole of the Orthodox world. It will fulfil its century-old ambition of gaining access to the warm seas. It will once again be able to oppose US hegemony.

'The only disadvantage that I can see for Russia is that Moscow will cease to be the *Third Rome*. Constantinople will supplant the religious Patriarchates of Moscow and Kiev as the political capitals of Orthodoxy. I must admit that Moscow currently has no real will to accomplish any of this, just stir up discord.

'Turkey will have lost Istanbul and will be geographically and politically excluded from Europe, but it will have created a new empire with hegemony over all the Turkic nations of Central Asia.

'As for the US, there are only disadvantages. It will lose its hegemony in a multi-polar world. It will be pushed out of Europe and Central Asia. NATO will collapse. The state of Israel will disappear. The American people, however, will at last have the isolationism that they always dreamed of.'

'Who are your friends and allies?' I asked.

'Our friends? Naturally, they are the Orthodox nations, the Bulgars, Greeks, Macedonians, Montenegrins, Russians, Romanians, Serbs and non-Uniate Ukrainians. Our allies, those who hate the Turks, the Kurds, the Armenians and, as you can see, some Arabs.'

He hadn't the imagination to foresee that, in the near future, *al-Qaeda's* descendant *Daech*, otherwise known as *ISIS*, would make his Arab allies look like choir boys.

Something was going on in the main room. I could hear shouts of joy. 'What is happening?' I asked my jailer. 'We have just seen on TV that there has been an important terrorist attack against a US cultural installation in Ankara. We have reason for jubilation. It is time to celebrate.'

In his excitement he had forgotten to lock my door. I heard a clatter of plates and the plop of champagne corks being pulled, followed almost immediately by shouts and recriminations in English and then in Arabic. They were soon screaming, brandishing chairs and throwing computer keyboards and at each other. Guns went off.

Blood-stained laptops lay on the floor and groaning bodies obstructed my path as I crept out through the mayhem. I ran out into the woods under the full moon and down the road as fast as I could for what seemed like half an hour. I reached a checkpoint, where two very spotty young men in US Air Force uniforms pointed their automatic rifles into my neck. After three days in captivity I must have looked like a freak. They took me into the guard room for interrogation. 'Where on earth am I', I asked. 'Welcome to Ramstein!' said the officer without a trace of conviviality.

I had arrived at Ramstein-Miesenbach, in Rhineland-Palatinate, the headquarters of the United States Air Force in Europe

I recounted my experience with the terrorists.

Two hours later the US troops had arrested all those who had survived. They told me how it had ended. Apparently the *Chetniks* had started to celebrate by opening a bottle of Russian *shampanskoe*. They started cooking *ražniči*, marinated pork and veal grilled on a skewer, which they offered to the *Salafists*. 'You give us pig to eat. You celebrate by drinking wine. Today is Thursday and the full moon. It is a day of fasting. You uncircumcised miscreants.' Both groups had produced knives and automatic weapons. By the time the troops arrived several of them were dead or wounded and the others came along without a fuss.

Their aim had been to sabotage the complete IT system of the base, including security, then send in a *kamikaze* commando to blow up the NATO command centre.

But their spoon had not been quite long enough.

Back to Byzantium

Postscript

A few years after taking early retirement in Paris, I had moved to Toulouse in South-West France, where the meteorological and human climate were both more clement.

The President of The Executive Committee of UEFA, the Union of European Football Associations, had just announced on television its choice of Turkey as the site for the Euro 2024, the UEFA European Football Championship. Istanbul had failed in its candidacy for the 2020 Summer Olympics, but Turkey had received its consolation prize.

I saw it an hour later, posted on my Facebook page:

TSARIGRAD
etos kosmou **7533**

This looked like a practical joke. After all, *Tse-Ge-eN* had been dismantled once and for all after the Ramstein fiasco. I thought no more about it and made the most of my retirement in Toulouse.

Toulouse is a wonderful place to live. It is a very young city. On the one hand, 110,000 students are registered in its different universities and schools of higher education. On the other, it is the capital of the

Back to Byzantium

European aerospace industry. The town is quiet until late morning, when the students arise, hungover from their rowdy late-night libations. At the weekend the streets fill with the families of engineers and technicians from different European nations who work for *Airbus* or its sub-contractors in the vast northern aeronautical suburb.

It is a cosmopolitan city, with many cultural associations. One of the most exciting events is the annual *Forom des Langues*. One or more stands in the central *Place du Capitole* represents each, or almost, of the languages spoken in the city. Here you can be initiated to the Amharic language from Ethiopia, taught by a bald-headed *Rastafarian*. You can get acquainted with Tamazight from a dark-skinned Kabyle teacher with flashing lapis-lazuli eyes. You can learn about agglutination with a Hungarian, discover the Armenian alphabet, and of course meet with Russian, Italian and German speakers. Even the English language is represented on a stand, though one wonders why, for a language that has for long successfully busied itself with destroying cultural diversity throughout the World.

The years passed and it was time for the European Cup. I have never been a fan of soccer, always preferring rugby. It started in primary school when the captain always chose me last of all for his team and then sent me off out of sight to the end of the pitch. They made me the goalkeeper. I never understood why you would entrust the most strategic position on the field to the weakest player and then shout at him when the opposing team scored a goal. I later got my revenge by working for the World Cup in France. Even though I was never a sports fan, I enjoyed the atmosphere of a sports event, particularly the opening ceremony.

The UEFA 2024 Opening Ceremony was about to begin at Atatürk Olympic Stadium in Istanbul, built for the would-be Olympics. I turned on the television.

The President of UEFA had just declared the

Back to Byzantium

tournament open, when I heard a colossal detonation and the screen filled with smoke and flames. Insipid Turkish folk *muzak* interrupted the programme. A French newscaster came on the air, very flustered.

'A terrorist attack has destroyed the Atatürk Olympic Stadium. With its capacity of more than 75 thousand, major loss of life is to be expected.' He was interrupted, apparently by a word in his earphone. 'We have just received news, as yet unconfirmed, that a second attack has taken place in another part of Istanbul. The four minarets on *Hagia Sofia* have all been blown up.'

I remained stuck to my TV set, as they showed the same images over and over of *Hagia Sofia* amid a pile of rubble, once again as it must originally have looked. Half an hour later, on all French channels, the President of the Republic appeared on screen behind a lectern.

'My dear compatriots, following the tragic events in Istanbul today, I have just learned that the NATO IT system in Europe has been hacked. A significant part of NATO military defence infrastructure in Central and Eastern Europe and in Central Asia has been destroyed by drones. This is a situation of the greatest concern not only for the security of our ally, Turkey, but it is a threat to all our democracies. We are not yet aware if they are coordinated terrorist attacks or whether other powers are involved. In cooperation with our NATO allies we are in the process of evaluating the situation in detail to prepare the appropriate collective response. I will inform you of the situation as it evolves and of the measures that we have taken. I can assure you that this attack will not go unanswered and that it will be punished with the utmost severity. *Vive la République! Vive la France!*'

The newscaster reappeared on the screen, even more flustered. 'NATO surveillance satellites have observed that the Russian Black Sea fleet has weighed anchor in its naval headquarters in Sebastopol. More than thirty warships are heading in a southerly direction across the Black Sea towards the Bosphorus.'

My mobile phone beeped to inform me that I had received an *SMS*. I opened it. It contained just two words:

CGN NIKA

A Latin transliteration of the inscription on the cross of the icon from Skopje:

ЦГН НИКА,

Цариград наш: *Tsarigrad nash:* *Constantinople ours*

CGN NIKA

TseGeeN **vanquishes**

The End

Appendix 1
Timetable Trans-Siberian 1977

City	kms.	Day		lag	local	Moscow
Moscow	0	1	Saturday	0	09:45	09:45
Kirov	958	2	Sunday	0	01:28	01:28
Perm (Molotov)	1,464	3	Monday	2	09:30	07:30
Ural border Europe-Asia	1,777	3	Monday	2	17:15	15:15
Sverdlovsk/Ekaterinburg	1,79	3	Monday	2	17:49	15:49
Omsk	2,694	4	Tuesday	3	06:31	03:31
Novosibirsk	3,36	4	Tuesday	3	21:06	18:06
Taïga	3,702	5	Wednesday	4	01:40	21:40
Krasnoïarsk	4,127	5	Wednesday	4	11:01	07:01
Irkutsk	5,18	6	Thursday	5	08:19	03:19
Ulan-Ude	5,612	6	Thursday	5	17:14	12:14
Chita	6,252	7	Friday	6	03:30	21:30
Birobidzhan	8,184	8	Saturday	7	01:47	18:47
Khabarovsk	8,363	8	Saturday	7	04:35	21:35

Appendix 2
Chronology of Author's Travels

1-2	**1971**	June	Greece	Piraeus
				Poros
			Yugoslavia	Skopje
3-4	**1972**	September	Bulgaria	Sofia
				Plovdiv
				Veliko Trnovo
5-6	**1973**	February --->	Austria	Vienna
		---> March	Bulgaria	Plovdiv
				Sofia
			Hungary	Budapest
7	**1974**	June	Yugoslavia	Sarajevo
				Dalmatia
				Montenegro
8	**1975**	June	Romania	Bucharest
9	**1976**	June	Poland	Warsaw
				Gdansk
			Germany	Berlin

Back to Byzantium

10-11	**1977**	September	USSR	Moscow
				Transsib
				Khabarovsk
				Irkutsk
				Novosibirsk
12	**1978**	July	Algeria	Algiers
13	**1979**	June	Yugoslavia	Belgrade
			Albania	Tirana
				Durrës
14	**1981**	July	Yugoslavia	Maribor
			Hungary	Balaton
				Budapest
			Romania	Transylvania
			Yugoslavia	Belgrade
15	**1983**	February	USSR	Leningrad
16	**1984**	April	Turkey	Istanbul
17	**1991**	October --->	Hungary	Budapest &
	1992	---> December	Austria	Vienna
18-20	**1993**	May --->	Russia	Moscow &
	1994	---> August		St-Petersburg

Appendix 3
Chronology of Current Events

1971 Switzerland — Introduction of women's suffrage
Britain — Decimalisation of currency
Decision by Parliament to join EEC
Yugoslavia — Leonid Brezhnev visit to Marshal Tito

1972 Soviet Union — Richard Nixon visit to prepare SALT 1

1973 Britain — Joins European Economic Community
United States — Devaluation of the dollar
Greece — Proclamation of a republic by the junta
USA & USSR — Signature of SALT 1, start of *détente*

1974 Soviet Union — Publication of the Gulag Archipelago
Sweden — Solzhenitsin awarded Nobel Prize
Cyprus — Coup d'état, triggering Turkish invasion
Greece — Junta overthrown, democracy restored

1975 Helsinki — Agreement on Security & cooperation

1976 Britain — IMF £3.5M loan for strict austerity
Soviet Union — 5-year plan: heavy industry priority
Poland — Strikes over food prices

Back to Byzantium

1977	Czechoslovakia	Signature of *Charter 77*
	Paris-Istanbul	Final journey of the Orient Express
	Soviet Union	SS-20 missiles deployed
1978	Rome	Karol Wojtyła elected Pope
	Algiers	Petroleum companies nationalized
1979	Europe	NATO *Cruise* missiles threaten USSR
	Soviet Union	Invasion of Afghanistan
	Albania	Relations broken off with China
1980	Moscow	US boycott of Olympic Games
1981	Rome	Assassination attempt on the Pope
	France	Communists in Socialist government
	Britain	Prince Charles weds Diana Spencer
	Europe	*Euromissile* Crisis
	Poland	Declaration of a state of emergency Lech Wałęsa imprisoned
1983	Europe	*Cruise* & *Pershing* missiles deployed
	Soviet Union	Arms reduction talks withdrawal
1984	Paris-Orly	Armenian terrorist bomb explosion
	Los Angeles	Soviet boycott of Olympic Games

Back to Byzantium

1985	Soviet Union	Gorbachëv introduces *perestroïka*
1986	Soviet Union	First Goodwill Games held in Moscow
1989	Germany	Demolition of the Berlin Wall
1990	United States	Goodwill Games held in Seattle
1991	Soviet Union	*Coup d'état* fails Communism collapses
	Russia	Russian Federation created
1993	Russian Fed.	Failed *coup d'état* by parliament
1994	Russian Fed.	Goodwill Games held in St-Petersburg

Appendix 4
Chronology of Relevant Historical Events

Year	Place	Person	Event
324	Bosphorus	Constantine the Great	Constantinople founded
476	Rome	Alaric	Fall of Roman Empire
537	Constantinople	Justinian I	Construction of *Hagia Sofia*
700s	Byzantium	Constantine V	1st period of iconoclasm
800s		Michael II	2nd period of iconoclasm
843		Regent Theodora	Triumph of Orthodoxy
863	Great Moravia	Cyril & Methodius	Creation Glagolitic alphabet
890s	Bulgaria	Clement of Ohrid	Creation Cyrillic alphabet
988	Kiev	Grand Prince Vladimir	Christianisation Kievian Rus'
1054	Rome-Byzantium	Pope Leo IX	Great Schism consummated
1071	Manzikert	Seljuq Turks	Defeat of the Byzantines
1081-1118	Byzantium	Alexios I Komnenos	Reign as Emperor
1095	Clermont	Pope Urban II	First Crusade initiated
1099	Holy Land	Crusaders	Capture of Jerusalem
1100s	Transylvania	Germans	Arrival of first settlers
	Balkans	Roma	First migrations from India
1118–1180	Byzantium	Manuel I Komnenos	Reign as Emperor
1148	Byzantium	Anna Komnene	*The Alexiad* completed
1187	Holy Land	Saladin	Capture of Jerusalem
1198	Holy Land - Acre	Pope Celestine II	Teutonic Order established
1202	Zara, Constantinople	Pope Innocent III	Fourth Crusade initiated

Back to Byzantium

1204	Byzantium	Franks and Venetians	Sack of Constantinople
	Constantinople	Baldwyn of Flanders	Crowned Emperor of Outremer
1205	Veliko Tarnovo	Ivan II Kaloyan	Baldwyn of Flanders slain
1209	Languedoc	Pope Innocent III	Albigensian Crusade initiated
1261	Byzantium	Alexis Stragopoulos	Greeks retake Constantinople
1242	Novgorod Republic	Alexander Nevski	Teutonic Order defeated
1346–1355	Balkan Peninsula	Stefan Dušan	Empire of Serbs & Greeks
1365	Ottoman Empire	Murad I	Janissary corps established
1389	Kosovo Polje	Ottomans	Mythical defeat of the Serbs
1410	Grünwald	Władysław Jagiełło	Teutonic Order annihilated
1439	Florence	Rome, Byzantium	Ecumenical Council
1443-1468	Balkans, Italy	Skanderbeg	Wars against Ottomans
1453	Byzantine Empire	Mehmet the Conqueror	Fall of Constantinople
1462	Wallachia	Vlad the Impaler	Night Attack on the Turks
1652-1658	Moscow	Patriarch Nikon	Reform Orthodox texts/rites
1666	Moscow	Old Believers	Schism in Russian Orthodoxy
1682–1725	Russia	Peter the Great	Tsar and Emperor
1784	Crimea	Catherine the Great	Annexation of Taurida
1788	London	Lord Byron	Birth
1812	Russia	Napoleon	Patriotic War
1824	Missolonghi	Lord Byron	Death
1825	Saint-Petersburg	Russian officers	Decembrist revolt

Back to Byzantium

1826	Ottoman Empire	Mahmud II	Janissaries disbanded
1830	London	Britain, France & Russia	Kingdom of Greece created
	Algeria	French	Conquest of Algiers
1839	Petersburg	Marquis de Custine	Voyage to Russia
	Serbia & Bosnia	Matija Mažuranić	Travels in Ottoman Bosnia
1847	Vienna	Petar II Petrović-Njegoš	*Mountain Wreath*
1868	Congress of Berlin	Serbia	Formal independence
	San Stefano	Bulgaria	Independence from Turkey
1878	Cyprus	Britain	Protectorate over Cyprus
1904	Far East	Russia	Completion Transsiberian
1905	Far East	Japan	Defeat of Russian army
1912	Vlorë	Albanian Assembly	Declaration independence
1914	Sarajevo	Gavrilo Princip	Franz Ferdinand murdered
1917	Petrograd	Bolcheviks	October revolution
1918	Petrograd	Peoples Commissars	Gregorian calendar adopted
	Compiègne	Triple Entente & USA	Armistice First World War
1919	Paris	Triple Entente & USA	Treaty of Versailles
1920	Trianon	Triple Entente & USA	Hungary dismembered
1923	Turkey	Mustafa Kemal	Declaration of the Republic
	Asia Minor, Thrace	Greece, Turkey	Population exchange
	Italy	Benito Mussolini	March on Rome
1933	Berlin	Van der Lubbe	Burning of the Reichstag
		Adolf Hitler	Granted plenary powers
1934	Leibzig	Imperial High Court	Dimitrov tried & acquitted
1939	Westerplatte	Nazi Germany	Start of Second World War
1945	Berlin	Allies	Victory in Europe
1948	Yugoslavia	Stalin-Tito	Expulsion from *Cominform*

Back to Byzantium

1949	Moscow	Georgi Dimitrov	Suspicious death
1953	Moscow	Josef Stalin	Death
1956	Moscow	Nikita Khrushchëv	20th Congress: destalinisation
1962	Algeria	F.L.N.	Independance from France
1964	Moscow	Leonid Breznev	Khrushchëv deposed

Glossary of Proper Names

- *24 Chasa - 24 часа:* Bulgarian tabloid
- *Aeroflot - Аэрофлот:* Soviet national airline
- *Air France:* French national airline
- *Airbus:* European civil aircraft manufacturer
- *AK47 - Kalashnikov – Калашников:* Soviet assault rifle
- **Al-Zawahiri, Ayman:** leader of al-Qaeda (1951-)
- **Alaric I:** King of the Visigoths (370/375-410)
- *Albigensian heresy:* 12th-century French Catharist movement
- **Alexander I Pavlovich - Александр Павлович:** Tsar of All the Russias (1777-1825)
- **Alexander II Nikolaevich - Александр II Николаевич:** Tsar of All the Russias (1818-1881)
- **Alexiï II - Патриарх Алексий II:** Patriarch of Moscow and all Rus' (1929-2008)
- *Alexiad:* biographical text by princess Anna Comnene (1148)
- **Alexios I Komnenos - Ἀλέξιος Α′ Κομνηνός:** Byzantine Emperor (1048/56-1118)
- **Alexios III Angelos - Ἀλέξιος Γ' Ἄγγελος:** Byzantine Emperor (1153–1211)
- **Alexios IV Angelos - Ἀλέξιος Δ' Ἄγγελος:** (young) Byzantine Emperor (1182-1204)
- **Alexios V Doukas, Muzurfulos - Ἀλέξιος Ε′ Δούκας Μούρτζουφλος:** Byzantine Emperor (1140-1204)
- **Ali Ağca, Mehmet:** political militant and assassin (1958-)
- **Ali Pasha of Ioannina:** Ottoman Albanian ruler (1740-1822)
- **Amin Dada, Idi:** president dictator of Uganda (1923/1928-2003)
- **Amundsen, Roald:** Norwegian explorer (1872-1928)
- *Ancien Régime:* political system of the Kingdom of France before the French Revolution
- **András II:** King of Hungary and Croatia (1188/90-1208/10)
- **Andrić, Ivo:** Yugoslav Nobel Prize winning writer (1892-1975)
- *Animal Farm:* allegorical novel by George Orwell (1945)

- **Antall, József:** Hungarian Prime Minister (1932–1993)
- *Arabs:* ethnic group from Western Asia and North Africa
- **Árpád:** Grand Prince of the Hungarians (845-907)
- *Aryan:* adopted by Gobineau as a racial category
- *ASALA:* Armenian Secret Army for the Liberation of Armenia
- *Assumptionists:* congregation of Catholic friars in France
- *Auspicious Event - Vaka-i Hayriye:* forced disbandment of the Janissary corps
- *Austroslavism*: political movement of Slav people in the Austro-Hungarian Empire

- *Baj Ganjo - Бай Ганьо*: comic Balkan stereotype created by Aleko Konstantinov
- **Baldwyn I:** King of Constantinople (1172-1205)
- **Balkans, Les**: Paris Latin-Quarter restaurant
- *Balkan wars:* two conflicts in the Balkan Peninsular (1912, 1913)
- *Balkanturist:* Bulgarian tourist agency
- **Barbarossa:** Bey of Algiers, Hayreddin Pasha (1478-1546) and Oruç, (1474-1518)
- *Barbary pirates:* Berber Muslim privateers
- *Bashkimi alphabet:* used today in Albania
- **Basil II - Βασίλειος Β΄:** Byzantine Emperor (958-1025)
- *Basileus - βασιλεύς:* title used by Byzantine Emperors
- *Battle of the Ice - Ледовое побоище:* defeat of the Teutonic Knights by the Republic of Novgorod (1242)
- *Bayard Presse:* French Catholic press group
- **Bayezid I, the Thunderbolt - Beyazıt Yıldırım:** Sultan of the Ottoman Empire (1360 -1403)
- *BBC World Service:* British news broadcaster
- *BCMS:* language of Bosnia, Croatia, Montenegro, Serbia
- **Bellotto, Bernardo:** urban landscape painter, nephew of Canaletto, aka (1721- 1780)
- **Ben Bella, Ahmed:** President of Algeria (1916-2012)
- *Berbers - Amazighs:* ethnic group indigenous to North Africa

Back to Byzantium

- **Beria, Lavrenti Pavlovich:** Soviet politician, head of NKVD (1899-1953)
- *Berïozka - Берёзка:* Soviet Russian hard-currency retail store
- **Berisha, Sali:** Albanian Prime Minister (1944-)
- *Berlin Wall:* barrier dividing Berlin rueing the Cold War (1961-1989)
- **Beyazıd II - II. Bayezid:** Sultan of the Ottoman Empire (1447-1512)
- *Bible, The:* collection of sacred scriptures for Jews and Christians
- **Bin Laden, Osama:** founder of al-Qaeda (1957-2011)
- **Bismarck, Otto von:** Prussian statesman and Chancellor of Germany (1815-1898)
- *Black Lamb and Grey Falcon:* travel book on Yugoslavia by Rebecca West (1941)
- *Blue Danube, The Beautiful - An der schönen blauen Donau:* waltz by Johann Strauss II (1866)
- *BMW - Bayerische Motorische Werk:* West German automobile manufacturer
- *Bogomil - Богомил:* member of a religio-political sect founded in the First Bulgarian Empire
- *Bolsheviks - Большевики:* political party taking power in Russia during the October Revolution (1917)
- **Bonaparte, Napoleon:** Emperor of the French (1769-1821)
- **Boniface of Montserrat:** leader of the Fourth Crusade (1150-1207)
- *Border Guards, Soviet - Пограничные войска СССР:* militarized guard, part of state security
- **Boris I - Борис I:** Tsar of Bulgaria (bapt. 864-907)
- **Bouboulina, Laskarina - Λασκαρίνα Μπουμπουλίνα:** heroine of the Greek War of Independence (1771-1825)
- **Boudicca - Boadicea:** British Celtic warrior queen (-60/61)
- **Boumedienne, Houari:** President of Algeria (1932-1978)
- **Branković, Vuk - Вук Бранковић:** Serbian general, son-in-law of Prince Lazar, mythical traitor of the Battle of Kosovo Polje (1345-1397)

Back to Byzantium

- **Brezhnev, Leonid Ilyich - Леонид Ильич Брежнев:** President of the Soviet Union and General Secretary of the Communist Party (1906-1982)
- *Bridge on the Drina - Na Drini ćuprija - На Дрини ћуприја:* historical novel by Ivo Andrić (1945)
- **Brilska, Barbara:** Polish actress (1941-)
- *Burrnesha:* Albanian virgins who have taken a vow of chastity, dressed as men
- **Bush, George H.W.:** President of the USA (1924-)
- **Byron, Lord George Gordon:** poet and politician (1788-1824)
- *Byzantium - Βυζάντιον:* capital of the Eastern Roman Empire

- *Caesar:* title given to Roman emperors
- *Caliphate:* area governed by a caliph, a religious successor to the prophet Muhammad
- **Cambronne, Vicomte Pierre:** General of the French Empire (1770-1842)
- **Canaletto, Giovanni Antonio Canal aka:** painter of urban landscapes - *vedute* (1697-1768)
- **Carter, James Earl Jr.:** President of the USA (1924-)
- **Catherine II the Great - Екатерина II Великая:** Empress of all the Russias (1729-1796)
- *Catholic:* Western, self-styled universal and apostolic church
- *Cathars:* members of a mediaeval Christian dualist movement in South-West France
- **Ceaușescu, Nicolae:** President of Romania and General Secretary of the Communist Party (1918-1989)
- **Celestine II:** Pope of Rome (?-1144)
- **Celestine III:** Pope of Rome (1106-1198)
- **Cervi, Gino:** Italian actor (1901-1974)
- *Chalcedon*, **Council of:** the fourth ecumenical council (451)
- **Charles Windsor:** Prince of Wales (1948-)
- **Charles V:** Holy Roman Emperor (1519-1556)
- *Charter 77:* document criticizing the Czechoslovak government on human rights (1977)
- *Cheka - ЧК:* Soviet state security organisation (1917)

Back to Byzantium

- ***Chetniks - Четници:*** Yugoslav liberation movement in Serbia during 2nd World War
- ***Childe Harold's Pilrimage:*** narrative poem by Lord Byron
- **Christ:** Jesus of Nazareth (0-30/33)
- **Christie, Agatha née Miller:** English detective writer (1890-1976)
- **Churchill, Winston:** British statesman and Prime Minister (1874-1965)
- ***CIA: Central Intelligence Agency:*** foreign intelligence service of the federal government of the USA
- **Clemenceau, Georges - *Le Tigre:*** French statesman and Prime Minister (1841-1929)
- **Clement of Ohrid, Saint - Свети Климент Охридски:** a creator of the Cyrillic alphabet (830/40-916)
- ***CNN: Cable News Network:*** American cable and satellite television news channel
- ***CoCom - Coordinating Committee for Multilateral Export Controls:*** for implementing arms embargo on *COMECON* countries
- ***Cold War:*** state of political and military tension between nations of the Warsaw Pact and thoe of NATO
- ***Columbo:*** American TV detective series starring Peter Falk
- ***Comecon - Council for Mutual Economic Assistance - Совет Экономической Взаимопомощи:*** Eastern Bloc economic organization
- ***Comintern:*** Communist (Third) International (1919-1943)
- **Conan Doyle, Arthur:** British writer (1859-1930)
- ***Congress of Berlin:*** meeting of the Great Powers and Balkan states following the Russo-Turkish War (1878)
- **Constantine Pavlovich - Константин Павлович:** Tsar of All the Russias (1779-1831)
- **Constantine II - Κωνσταντῖνος Β':** King of Greece (1940-)
- **Constantine V- Κωνσταντῖνος Ε':** Byzantine Emperor (718-775)
- ***Crimean War:*** defeat of the Russian Empire by France, Britain and the Ottomans (1853-1856)
- ***Cruise:*** guided missile used against terrestrial targets

Back to Byzantium

- *Crusade, Fourth:* leading to the sack of Constantinople (1201-1204)
- *Culloden, Battle of:* Scotland, final defeat of the Jacobite rising of Charles Edward Stuart (1746)
- **Custine, Astolphe marquis de:** French diplomat and travel writer (1790-1857)
- **Cyril & Methodius, Saints - Кирилл и Мефодий:** Apostles to the Slavs, creators of the Glagolitic alphabet (826-869 & 815-885)
- *Cyrillic alphabet:* developed in the First Bulgarian Empire (9th century), used in east and south Slav countries

- **Dąbrowski, Captain Franciszek:** Polish officer, hero of Westerplatte (1904-1962)
- **Dandolo, Enrico:** Doge of Venice (1107-1205)
- **Danilo Šćepčević - Данило Шћепчевић:** Metropolitan of Cetinje (1670- 1735)
- **Dassin, Julius aka Jules:** American film director (1911-2008)
- *Dazibao - big-character reports:* handwritten posters used in Communist China for popular communication
- *DDR - Deutsche Demokratische Republik:* East Germany during the Cold War
- **De Gaulle, Charles:** French general, President of France (1890-1970)
- *Dead Souls - Мёртвые души:* novel by Nikolaï Gogol (1842)
- *Decembrist uprising - Vosstanie dekabristov - Восстание декабристов:* protest by Russian army officers at Nicolas I's assumption of the throne (December1825)
- *Deliverance:* American film by John Boorman (1970)
- **Deng Xiaoping:** Chinese Communist statesman (1904-1997)
- *Détente:* easing of the geopolitical tensions between the Soviet Union and the United States in the middle of the Cold War
- *DHL - Deutsche Post:* international express mail service
- **Diana Spencer:** Princess of Wales (1961-1997)
- **Dimitrov, Emil - Емил Димитров:** Bulgarian pop singer (1940-2005)
- **Dimitrov, Georgi Mikhailov - Георги Михайлов Димитров:** Bulgarian Communist statesman (1882-1949)

Back to Byzantium

- **Diocletian:** Roman Emperor (244-312)
- **Disraeli, Benjamin:** British statesman and writer (1804-1881)
- **Djilas, Milovan - Милован Ђилас:** Yugoslav officer and statesman (1911-1995)
- *Doge:* elected head of state in Italian crowned republics
- **Dracula:** *see Vlad Țepeș*
- **Drakulić, Slavenka:** Croatian writer and journalist (1946-)
- *Duroplast:* a resin plastic reinforced with fibres, used in the Trabant car
- **Durrell, Lawrence:** British writer (1912-1990)
- **Dürrenmatt, Friedrich:** German Swiss writer (1921-1990)
- **Dzierżyński, Feliks - Феликс Эдмундович Дзержинский:** creator of the Soviet secret police system (1877-1926)

- *EDS - Electronic Data Systems*: American international information services company headquartered in Plano, Texas
- *EinsatzKommando:* mobile killing squads whose mission was to exterminate Jews in captured territories
- **Eisenstein, Sergei Mikhailovich - Сергей Михайлович Эйзенштейн:** Soviet film director (1898- 1948)
- *El Moudjahid:* Algerian French-language newspaper, formerly organ of the *FLN*
- **Elisabeth I:** Queen of England and Ireland (1533-1603)
- **Elizabeth II:** Queen of the United Kingdom, Canada, Australia, New Zealand and twelve other former British colonies (1926-)
- **Eltsin, Boris Nikolayevich - Борис Николаевич Ельцин:** statesman and president of the Russian Federation (1931-2007)
- **Engels, Friedrich Engels:** German political philosopher (1820-1895)
- *Enlightenment:* intellectual movement which dominated the world of ideas in Europe during the 18th century
- **Erdoğan, Recep Tayyip:** Turkish statesman (1954-)
- *Esperanto:* constructed international language, developed by L.L.Zamenhof
- **Eugene of Savoy, Prince:** Hapsburg Imperial army general (1663-1736)

Back to Byzantium

- *Euromissiles:* project for installation of Pershing II ballistic missiles in Europe
- *Euronews:* multilingual European news media service
- **EEC - *European Economic Community:*** later *European Union*

- **Falk, Peter:** American actor (1927-2011)
- **Fernandel, Fernand Contandin aka:** French comic actor (1903-1971)
- *Fernet Branca:* bitter Italian herbal liqueur
- **Filofeï - Филофей:** Russian monk (1465-1542)
- *Fletërrufe - thunder papers:* handwritten posters used in Communist Albanian for popular communication *(see Dazibao)*
- **FLN - *Front de Libération Nationale:*** nationalist movement of the Algerian War and sole ruling political party in Algeria
- *Forom des Langues:* annual multi-language event in Toulouse (since 1993)
- *Franks:* originally Germanic tribes settled in Gaul; a generic term used by Byzantine Greeks for western crusaders
- **Franz Ferdinand:** Archduke of Austria, assassinated in Sarajevo (1863-1914)
- *French revolution - Révolution française:* period of violent social and political upheaval in France (1789-1799)

- **Gaidar, Egor Timurovich - Егор Тимурович Гайдар:** Russian economist and politician (1956-2009)
- **Gavras, Konstantinos aka Costa-Gavras - Κωνσταντίνος Γαβράς:** Greek film director (1933-)
- **Géza II:** King of Hungary and Croatia (1130-1162)
- *Ghegs:* ethnic group of Albania
- **Gierek, Edvard:** First Secretary of the Polish United Workers' Party (1913-2001)
- **Giotto di Bondone:** Florentine painter (1266/7-1337)
- *Gjuha Shqipe:* Albanian language manual
- *Glagolitic alphabet:* first Slavic alphabet, developed by brothers Saints Cyril (9th century)
- **Godunov, Boris Fïodorovich - Борис Фёдорович Годунов:** Tsar of all the Russias (1551-1605)

Back to Byzantium

- **Goebbels, Joseph**: propaganda minister of Nazi Germany (1897-1945)
- **Goering, Hermann**: aviation minister of Nazi Germany (1893-1946)
- **Gogol, Nikolai Vasilievich - Николай Васильевич Гоголь:** Russian/Ukrainian writer (1809-1852)
- *Goodwill Games:* international combined summer and winter sports event created by Ted Turner
- **Gorbachëv, Mikhail Sergeyevich - Михаил Сергеевич Горбачёв:** Soviet statesman (1931-)
- **Gorki, Maxim - Alexei Maximovich Peshkov aka - Алексей Максимович Пешков:** Soviet Russian writer (1868-1936)
- **Grachev, Pavel Sergeevich - Павел Сергеевич Грачёв:** Russian general and politician (1948-2012)
- *Great Purge - Большой террор:* intense political repression in the Soviet Union (1936-1938)
- *Great Schism:* break between Eastern Orthodox and Western Catholic churches (1054)
- *Gregorian calendar:* universally civil calendar. Introduced by Pope Gregory XIII (1582).
- **Gregory IX:** Pope of Rome (1145-1241)
- **Grivas, Georgios - Γεώργιος Γρίβας:** Greek general, leader of EOKA (1897-1974)
- *Grünwald – Tannenberg, Battle of:* defeat of the Teutonic Knights by the Polish-Lithuanian alliance (1410)
- **Gül Baba:** Ottoman Bektashi dervish poet, warrior and gardner (?-1541)
- *Gulag Archipelago - Архипелаг ГУЛАГ:* book by Aleksandr Solzhenitsyn about the Soviet labour camp system (published 1973)
- *GUM - Glavnyï Universal'nyï Magazin - Гла́вный универса́льный магази́н:* main Moscow department store

- *Habsburg:* family reigning over the Holy Roman Empire and later the Austro-Hungarian Empire
- *Hastings, Battle of:* defeat of the English by the Norman-French (1066)
- **Haussmann, Baron Georges Eugène:** French prefect, renovator of Paris (1809-1891)

Back to Byzantium

- **Havel, Václav:** Czech writer, dissident and president (1936-2011)
- **Heath, Edward:** British Prime Minister (1916-2005)
- **Hill, Rowland:** British reformer of the postal system (1795-1879)
- **Himmler, Heinrich:** interior minister, head of police of Nazi Germany (1900-1945)
- **Hitler, Adolf:** Führer of Nazi Germany (1889-1945)
- *Hospitalliers:* Knights of the Hospital of Saint John of Jerusalem, medieval Catholic military order
- **Hoxha, Enver:** Albanian Communist leader (1908-1985)
- *Humanité, L':* French newspaper, official organ of the French Communist Party
- **Huntington, Samuel:** American political scientist (1927-2008)
- **Hunyadi, John - Hunyadi János - Ioan de Hunedoara:** Hungarian military and political leader (1406-1456)
- **Hunyadi, Mátyás - Matthias I Corvin:** King of Hungary and Croatia (1443-1490)
- **Hurt, William:** American actor (1950-)
- **Husák, Gustáv:** President of Communist Czechoslovakia (1913-1991)

- **Ibárruri Gómez, Dolores aka La Pasionaria:** Spanish Republican heroine of the Spanish Civil War and Communist politician (1895-1989)
- *IMF - International Monetary Fund:* international organisation working to foster global monetary cooperation
- **Innocent III:** Pope of Rome (1160/61-1216)
- *International Criminal Court:* tribunal to prosecute individuals for crimes of war, against humanity, and genocide
- *Inturist - Интурист:* official state travel agency of the Soviet Union
- **Ioannidis, Dimitrios - Δημήτριος Ιωαννίδης:** Greek officer, leader of the military junta (1923-2010)
- *IOC - International Olympic Committee - CIO - Comité international Olympique:* supreme authority of the worldwide Olympic movement

Back to Byzantium

- *Iron Curtain:* nick name for the boundary dividing Europe during the Cold War
- **Isaac II Angelos - Ἰσαάκιος Β' Ἄγγελος:** Byzantine Emperor (1156-1204)
- **Isaac I Komnenos - Ισαάκιος Α' Κομνηνός:** Byzantine Emperor (1007-1060/61)
- *Islam:* revealed religion professing that there is no other god than God and that Muhammad is his prophet
- **Ivan IV Groznyï, the Terrible - Иван Грозный:** Tsar of All the Russias (1530-1584)
- **Ivan III the Great - Иван III Васильевич:** Grand Prince of all Rus'(1440-1505)

- **Jadwiga:** Queen of Poland (1373/4-1399)
- *Jacobinisme:* political doctrine defending the sovereignty and indivisibility of the French Republic
- **James I:** King of Great Britain and Ireland (1566-1625)
- *Janissaries – Yeñiçeri:* elite infantry units of the Ottoman Sultan's household guards
- **Januarius, Saint - San Gennaro:** saint of the Roman Catholic and Eastern Orthodox Churches (?-305)
- **Jaruzelski, Wojciech:** Polish officer and First Secretary of the Polish United Workers' Party (1923-2014)
- *JAT - Jugoslovenski aerotransport:* national airline of Yugoslavia
- Jesus: *see Christ*
- **Joan of Arc - Jeanne d'Arc:** heroine of the France struggle against the English in the Hundred Years' War, later canonized (1412- 1431)
- **John II Komnenos - Ἰωάννης Β' Κομνηνός:** Byzantine Emperor (1087-1143)
- **John VIII Palaeologus - Ἰωάννης Η' Παλαιολόγος:** Byzantine Emperor (1392-1448)
- **John Paul II - Karol Józef Wojtyła:** Pope of Rome (May 1920-2005)
- *JUGALB:* joint Yugoslav-Albanian airline

Back to Byzantium

- *Julian calendar:* reform of the Roman calendar proposed by Julius Caesar (46 BC), gradually replaced by the Gregorian calendar
- **Justinian the Great - Ἰουστινιανός:** Byzantine (East-Roman) Emperor (482-565)
- **Kaloïan, Ivan II - the Greek Slayer - Иван II Калоян Ромеоубиец:** Tsar of Bulgaria (1169-1207)
- **Karamanlís, Konstantinos - Κωνσταντίνος Καραμανλής:** President of Greece (1907-1998)
- **Kardelj, Edvard:** Yugoslav Slovene partisan and politician, creator of workers' self-management system (1910-1979)
- *KDC - Komitet za dăržavna sigurnost - Комитет за държавна сигурност:* Communist Bulgarian secret service
- **Kemal, Mustafa aka Attatürk:** officer, revolutionary, founder and President of the Republic of Turkey (1881-1938)
- *KGB - Komitet gosudarstvennoy bezopasnosti – КГБ - Комитет государственной безопасности:* Committee for State Security of the Soviet Union
- **Khazbulatov, Ruslan Imranovich - Руслан Имранович Хасбулатов:** Russian Chechen politician (1942-)
- **Khristo, Khristo Vladimiroff Javacheff aka:** Bulgarian artist specialising in wrapping monuments (1935-)
- **Khrushchëv, Nikita Sergueïevitch - Никита Сергеевич Хрущёв:** First Secretary of the Communist Party and Chairman of the Council of Ministers of the Soviet Union (1894-1971)
- *Kievian Rus' - Киевская Русь:* Principality of Kiev, federation of Slavic tribes under the Rurik dynasty
- *Kinder Surprise:* chocolate egg containing a small toy, manufactured by Ferrero
- **Kirkorov, Filipp Bedrosovich - Филипп Бедросович Киркоров:** Russian-Bulgarian pop singer (1967)
- *Knights Hospitallier: see Hospitalliers*
- *Knights of the Teutonic Order: see Teutonic Knights*
- *Knights Templar: see Templars*
- **Kohl, Helmut:** Chancellor of the German Federal Republic (1930-2017)
- **Komnene, Anna - Ἄννα Κομνηνή:** Byzantine princess, historian and biographer (1083- 1153)

- *Kommunalka - коммуналка:* communal apartment in the Soviet Union
- **Konstantinov, Aleko - Алеко Константинов:** Bulgarian writer, creator of the character *Baj Ganjo* (1863-1897)
- **Kusturica, Emir - Емир Кустурица:** Bosnian Serb film director (1954-)

- **Lalla Fadhma n'Soumer:** leader of resistance against French colonial conquest of Algeria (1830-1863)
- **Lamartine, Alphonse de:** French poet and politician (1790-1869)
- **Lazar, Prince - Лазар Хребељановић:** ruler of the Serbian Empire (1329-1389)
- **Lawrence of Arabia, Thomas Edward aka:** British officer, diplomat and writer (1888-1935)
- *League of Nations - Société des Nations:* international intergovernmental organisation, established after the First World War to maintain world peace (1920)
- **Lechner, Ödön:** Hungarian architect (1845-1914)
- **Lee, Christopher:** British actor (1922-2015)
- **Leigh Fermor, Patrick:** British travel writer (1915-2011)
- **Leka:** Crown Prince of Albania (1939-2011)
- **Lenin, Vladimir Illich Ul'ianov aka - Владимир Ильич Ульянов:** Russian Bolshevik politician, head of government of the Soviet Union (1870-1924)
- **Leo IX:** Pope of Rome (1002-1054)
- **Lessing, Gotthold Ephraim:** German dramatist and philosopher (1729-1781)
- **Lincoln, Abraham:** President of the USA (1809-1865)
- *Linguaphone:* self-study language audio teaching provider
- **Litvinenko, Aleksandr Valterovich - Александр Вальтерович Литвиненко:** assassinated defector from Russian FSB (1962-2006)
- **Louis XIV:** King of France and Navarre (1638-1715)
- **Lugosi, Béla:** Hungarian-American actor (1882-1956)
- *Lutherans:* followers of the branch of Protestant Christianity which identifies with the theology of Martin Luther

Back to Byzantium

- *Maastricht Treaty:* Treaty on European Union, leading to creation of the single currency (1992)
- *Madonna of the Sleeping Cars:* novel by Maurice Dekobra
- **Mahmud II:** Sultan of the Ottoman Empire (1785-1839)
- **Makarios III, Archbishop, Michail Christodoulou Mouskos - Μακάριος Γ΄, Μιχαήλ Χριστοδούλου Μούσκος:** President of Cyprus (1913-1977)
- **Makashov, Albert Mikhailovich - Альберт Михайлович Макашóв:** Russian officer and nationalist-communist (1938-)
- **Manuel I Komnenos - Α' Κομνηνός:** Byzantine Emperor (1118-1180)
- **Mao Zedong:** Chairman of the Communist Party of China (1893-1976)
- **Maria Theresa:** Empress of Austria (1717-1780)
- **Marie of Romania:** Queen Consort (1875- 1938)
- **Markov, Georgi Ivanov - Георги Иванов Марков:** dissident writer, defector from Bulgaria, assassinated by the *Bulgarian umbrella* (1929-1978)
- **Marshall, George Catlett Jr.:** US Secretary of State and Secretary of Defense (1880-1959)
- *Martenitsa - мартеница:* coloured tassels worn in Bulgaria to celebrate spring
- **Marx, Karl:** German philosopher, economist, writer and revolutionary socialist (1818-1883)
- *Matrïoshka - матрёшка:* Russian traditional set of wooden dolls of decreasing size placed one inside another
- **Mažuranić, Matija:** Croatian travel writer (1817-1881)
- *Megali idea - Μεγάλη Ιδέα - Great Idea:* Greek nationalist goal of restoring a Greek state comprising all Greek-inhabited areas still under the Ottoman Empire
- **Mehmet II, the Conqueror - Meḥmed-i s̱ānī el-Fātiḥ:** Sultan of the Ottoman Empire, conqueror of Constantinople (1432-1481)
- **Mehmed IV:** Sultan of the Ottoman Empire (1642-1693)
- *Mercedes Benz:* **West German automobile manufacturer**
- **Mercouri, Melina - Μελίνα Μερκούρη:** Greek actress and Minister for Culture (1920-1994)

- **Metaxas, Ioannis - Ιωάννης Μεταξάς:** Prime Minister of Greece (1871-1941)
- **Methodius:** *see Cyril*
- **Metternich, Klemens Wenzel von:** Foreign Minister and Chancellor of the Austrian Empire (1773-1859)
- **Michael I Cerularius - Μιχαὴλ Α΄ Κηρουλάριος:** Patriarch of Constantinople (1000-1059)
- **Michael VIII Palaiologus - Μιχαὴλ Η΄ Παλαιολόγος:** Byzantine Emperor (122- 1282)
- *Middle Ages:* in Western Europe, period between the fall of the Western Roman Empire and the Renaissance; in the Balkans, the period before the *National Revival*
- **Milošević, Slobodan - Слободан Милошевић:** President of Serbia and of Yugoslavia (1941-2006)
- **Mitterand, François:** President of France (1916-1996)
- **Mladić, Ratko - Ратко Младић:** Bosnia Serb military leader (1943-)
- **Molotov, Vyacheslav Mikhailovich - Вячеслав Михайлович Молотов:** Foreign Minister of the Soviet Union (1890-1986)
- *Mongols:* ethnic group native to east-central Asia, today Mongolia, Buriats in Russia
- **Morozova, Boïarina Feodosia Prokopievna - Феодосия Прокопьевна Морозова:** Old Believer (1632-1675)
- *Moscow State Circus:* run by the Soviet centralized circus administration
- *Mountain Wreath:* dramatic poem by Petar II Petrović-Njegoš
- **Mukhanov, Piotr Aleksandrovich - Пётр Александрович Муханов:** officer and *Decembrist* (1799-1854)
- **Murad I:** Sultan of the Ottoman Empire (1326-1389)
- **Murad II:** Sultan of the Ottoman Empire (1404- 1451)
- *Muslim:* person practicing Islam
- **Mussolini, Benito:** Italian politician, journalist, leader of the Fascist Party (1883-1945)

- **Nansen, Fridtjof:** Norwegian explorer and scientist (1861-1930)
- *National Awakening/Revival:* period in the late 19th century, when the Balkan peoples began to shake off the *Ottoman yoke*
- *NATO:* North Atlantic Treaty Organization

Back to Byzantium

- *Nazi:* pertaining to the German National Socialist Party
- *Never on Sunday:* film by Jules Dassin
- **Nevskiï, Aleksander Iaroslavich - Александр Ярославич Невский:** Grand Prince of Kievan Rus' (1221-1263)
- **Nicolas Thaumaturgos, Saint - Ἅγιος Νικόλαος ὁ Θαυματουργός:** the Wonder worker (270- 343)
- **Nicolas I Pavlovich - Николай I Павлович:** Tsar of all the Russias (1796-1855)
- **Nicolas II Aleksandrovich - Николай II Александрович:** Tsar of all the Russias (1868-1918)
- **Nightingale, Florence:** English social reformer, founder of modern nursing (1820-1910)
- **Nikon - Никон:** Patriarch of Moscow (1605-1681)
- **Nixon, Richard Milhous:** President of the USA (1913-1994)
- *Nobel Prize:* international award bestowed by Swedish and Norwegian academies
- *Nők Lapja:* Hungarian women's periodical
- *Normans:* people descended from Norse Vikings who settled in Normandy in France
- *NTV - НТВ:* independent Russian TV channel

- *OAS - Organisation armée secrète - Secret Army Organisation:* extremist pro-French paramilitary organization during the Algerian War
- **O'Toole, Peter Seamus:** British Irish actor (1932-2013)
- **Obilić, Miloš - Милош Обилић:** Serbian general, son-in-law of Prince Lazar, mythical hero of the Battle of Kosovo Polje, assassin of Sultan Murad I (?-1389)
- *Ochi Chërnije - Очи чёрные - Dark Eyes:* world-famous Russian romance song
- *October Revolution:* overthrow of the Provisional Government in Petrograd by the Bolsheviks led by Lenin (1917)
- *Olympic Committee: see IOC*
- *Olympic Games - Jeux olympiques:* leading international sports held every four years, with the Summer and Winter Games
- *OMON - Отряд мобильный особого назначения - Otryad Mobilny Osobogo Naznacheniya:* special purpose mobility unit of Soviet, Russian police

Back to Byzantium

- ***Orient Express - Direct Simplon:*** long-distance passenger train service linking Paris to Istanbul
- ***Orthodox:*** Eastern Christian Church, communion of autocephalous churches, prominently in the Byzantine Empire
- **Oruç:** *see Barbarossa*
- **Orwell, George - Eric Arthur Blair aka:** British writer (1903-1950)
- ***Ottoman Empire - Osmanlı İmparatorluğu:*** Turkish Empire, ending the Byzantine Empire by the conquest of Constantinople (1453)

- ***Pan-African Games:*** a continental multi-sport event held every four years
- ***Pan-Slavism:*** movement aiming for the political unity for Slavic peoples
- **Papadopoulos, Georgios - Γεώργιος Παπαδόπουλος:** officer leading the military junta in Greece (1919-1999)
- **Papandreou, Georgios - Γεώργιος Παπανδρέου:** Prime Minister of Greece (1888- 1968)
- ***Paternoster:*** passenger lift consisting of open compartments that move up and down in a loop without stopping
- **Pattakos, Stylianos – Στυλιανός Παττακός:** officer member of the military junta in Greece (1912-2016)
- ***Paulicians:*** Christian sect originating in in Armenia and the eastern Byzantine Empire
- **Pavelić, Ante:** Croatian fascist, leader of the Ustaše movement (1889-1959)
- ***Pavlov, Ivan P. Infektsiozna Klinika:*** clinic for infectious diseases in Plovdiv, Bulgaria
- ***Pershing II:*** nuclear-capable theatre-level ballistic missile
- **Pericles - Περικλῆς:** Greek statesman of Athens during the Golden Age (495-429 BC)
- **Perrot, Ross:** American entrepreneur, founder of Electronic Data Systems (1930-)
- **Pétain, Marshal Philippe:** hero of the Battle of Verdun, Head of State of Vichy France (1856-1951)
- **Petar II Petrović-Njegoš - Петар II Петровић-Његош:** Prince-Bishop of Montenegro (1813-1851)

Back to Byzantium

- **Philip of Swabia:** King of Germany (1177-1208)
- **Pius II:** Pope of Rome (1405-1464)
- *PKK - Partiya Karkerên Kurdistanê - Kurdistan Workers' Party:* organization in armed struggle against Turkey for Kurdish self-determination
- **Plato - Πλάτων:** philosopher in Classical Greece (428/23-348/47 BC)
- **Pluzhnikova, Marina - Марина Плужникова:** Russian athlete, steeplechase champion (1963-)
- *Pokrovskie Vorota - Покровские ворота - Pokrovsky Gate:* Soviet nostalgic comedy film by Mikhaïl Kozakov about life in a *kommunalka*
- *Porte, The Sublime - Bāb-ı Ālī:* metonym for the government of the Ottoman Empire
- **Powell, Enoch:** British politician (1912-1998)
- *Prague Spring - Pražské jaro:* period of political liberalisation in Czechoslovakia, crushed by invasion by forces of the Warsaw Pact (1968)
- **Princip, Gavrilo - Гаврило Принци:** Bosnian Serb nationalist who assassinated Archduke Franz Ferdinand in Sarajevo (1894-1918)
- *Prizren, League of - Besëlidhja e Prizrenit:* political organization to protect Albanians in states recently independent from the Ottoman Empire (1878)
- *Programme Commun:* reform programme, signed in France by the Socialist, Communist and Left Radical Parties (1972)
- **Prokofiev, Sergeï Sergeevich - Сергей Сергеевич Прокофьев:** Russian composer and pianist (1891-1953)
- *Propusk - пропуск:* Russian entry permit
- *Protestants:* members of Christian churches originating with the Reformation, against perceived errors in the Roman Catholic Church
- **Pugachëva, Alla Borisovna - Алла Борисовна Пугачёва:** Russian pop idol (1949-)
- *Pukh - пух:* white pollen from female balsam poplars covering the ground in Moscow with 'snow' in June
- *Punic Wars:* three wars fought between Rome and Carthage
- **Pushkin, Aleksandr Sergeyevich - Александр Сергеевич Пушкин:** Russian poet (1799-1837)

Back to Byzantium

- **Putin, Vladimir Vladimirovich - Владимир Владимирович Путин:** President of the Russian Federation (1952-)

- *Quasimodo:* hunchback in Victor Hugo's novel *Notre-Dame de Paris*
- *Qur'an:* central text of Islam, revealed by God to Muhammad

- **Radu III, the Handsome - Radu cel Frumos:** Voïvode of Wallachia (1437/39-1475)
- *Ramadan:* ninth month of the Islamic calendar, observed by Muslims as a month of fasting
- *Raskolnikov:* central character of Crime and Punihment by Crime and Punishment Fëdor Dostoevskiï
- **Rastislav:** ruler of Moravia, host of Cyril and Methodius (?-870)
- **Rastrelli, Francesco Bartolomeo:** Franco-Italo-Russian baroque architect (1700-1771)
- **Reagan, Ronald:** actor, President of the USA (1911-2004)
- *Reconquista*: period of the Christian reconquest of the Iberian Peninsular from the Moors
- *Red Army - Красная армия:* army and air force of the Soviet Union
- *Reformation:* schism from the Roman Catholic Church initiated by Martin Luther and continued by Jean Calvin
- *Regency of Algiers:* Ottoman territory centred on Algiers and the coast of modern Algeria
- *Renaissance:* period in European history of discovery and rediscovery, marking the beginning of the Modern Age
- **Repin, Ilya Yefimovich - Илья Ефимович Репин:** Russian painter (1844-1930)
- **Robbe-Grillet, Alain:** French writer (1922-2008)
- *Roma: gypsy* poplations in central and eastern Europe since 14th century, who originated in the Indian subcontinent
- *Roman Empire - Imperium Romanum:* ancient Roman civilisation with government headed by emperors over territories around the Mediterranean Sea (100 BC-400 AD)
- **Romanovs - Романовы:** second dynasty to rule over Russia (1613-1917)

- ***Rome Treaty:*** international agreement leading to the creation of the European Economic Community, to become the European Union (1957)
- ***Rosetta stone:*** inscribed with three versions of a decree of King Ptolemy V in hieroglyphic and Demotic scripts, and in Greek, the key to the deciphering Egyptian hieroglyphs
- **Rostropovich, Mstislav Leopoldovich - Мстислав Леопольдович Ростропович:** Russian cellist and conductor (1927-2007)
- **Rubik, Ernő:** Hungarian architect, inventor of the Rubik's cube (1944-)
- ***Russian Revolution:*** two revolutions in Russia, which deposed the Tsar and led to rise of the Soviet Union (1917)
- ***Russkaïa Mysl'- Русская мысль - Russkaya Mysl:*** Russian language monthly published in Paris for expatriates
- ***Russki Club:*** elite Russian restaurant in Sofia, Bulgaria
- ***Russo-Japanese war:*** defeat of the Russian Empire by Japan (1904–1905)
- **Rust, Mathias:** amateur pilot who landed illegally near Red Square in Moscow (1968-)
- **Rutskoï, Aleksandr Vladimirovich - Александр Владимирович Руцкой:** Russian politician (1947-)

- *Sack of Constantinople:* Fourth Crusade (1204)
- **Saladin - Ṣalāḥ ad-Dīn Yūsuf ibn Ayyūb:** Sultan of Egypt and Syria (1137-1193)
- **Samaranch y Torelló, Juan Antonio:** Spanish Minister of Sports and President of the International Olympic Committee (1920-2010)
- *Samoyed – Самоед:* Russian name for indigenous peoples of Siberia, also given to their *Bjelkier* dog
- **Sampson, Nikos - Νίκος Σαμψών:** journalist and briefly President of Cyprus after the coup d'état (1935-2001)
- *San Gennaro: see Januarius*
- *San Stefano:* treaty signed between Russia and the Ottoman Empire (1878)
- *Saracen:* a term that became synonymous with *Muslim* in the Middle Ages

Back to Byzantium

- **Sartre, Jean-Paul:** French philosopher, playwright, novelist and political activist (1905-1980)
- *Saxons, Transylvanian - Siebenbürger Sachsen:* ethnic Germans who settled in Transylvania (12th century)
- **Scott, Ernest Kilburn:** British engineer and dog breeder (1868-1941)
- *Shadok:* French satirical TV cartoon series
- **Shakespeare, William:** English poet and dramatist (1564-1616)
- **Simenon, Georges:** Franco-Belgian writer (1903-1989)
- **Simeon I the Great - Симеон I Велики:** Tsar of the Bulgarians (864/5-927)
- **Simon IV de Montfort:** Count of Toulouse (1164/75-1218)
- **Sinan Agha, Koca Mi'mâr Sinân Ağâ - the Grand Architect:** chief Ottoman architect and civil engineer (1489/90-1588)
- **Skanderbeg, George Castriot - Gjergj Kastrioti:** Lord of Albania, military commander and rebel against Ottoman expansion (1405/17-1468)
- *Skype:* computer application providing free video and voice call services
- *SNCF - Société nationale des chemins de fer français:* French national railway corporation
- **Sobchak, Anatoly Aleksandrovich - Анатолий Александрович Собчак:** Russian politician, Mayor of Saint-Petersburg (1937-2000)
- *Solidarność - Solidarity:* independent trade union using civil resistance to advance social and political change in Poland
- **Solzhenitsyn, Aleksandr Isayevich - Александр Исаевич Солженицын:** Nobel Prize winning Russian writer who revealed the Soviet Gulag labor camp system (1918-2008)
- *SS - Schutzstaffel - Protection Squadron:* responsible for security, surveillance and terror in Nazi Germany and occupied territories
- *SS-20 - RSD-10 Pioneer:* intermediate-range ballistic missile with a nuclear warhead deployed by the Soviet Union
- **Stalin, Iossif Vissarionovitch Dzhugachvili aka – Сталин, Иосиф Виссарионович Джугашвили:** General Secretary of the Communist Party of the Soviet Union (1878-1953)
- *Starovery - Староверы - Old believers:* persecuted schismatics from the Russian Orthodox Church in protest to church reforms

Back to Byzantium

- *START - Strategic Arms Reduction Treaties:* between the USA and USSR (1991, 1993)
- **Stefan IV Dušan, the Mighty - Стефан Урош IV Душан:** Emperor of the Serbs and Greeks (1308-1355)
- **Stefan Nemanja - Стефан Немања:** Grand Prince of Serbia (1113/14-1199)
- **Stendhal, Marie-Henri Beyle aka:** French author (1783- 1842)
- **Stoker, Bram:** Irish author (1847-1912)
- *Stolichnaya – Столичная:* Russian vodka distilled from wheat and rye grain
- **Strategopoulos, Alexios Komnenos - Ἀλέξιος Κομνηνός Στρατηγόπουλος:** Byzantine general (?-1270)
- **Štrosmajer, Josip Juraj:** Croatian Roman Catholic bishop and politician (1815-1905)
- *Stuka - Sturzkampfflugzeug:* German dive bomber used by the Luftwaffe
- **Sucharski, Henryk:** Polish officer, commander of Westerplatte (1898-1946)
- *Sufi:* a branch of Islamic mysticism
- **Suleiman I the Magnificent, the Lawgiver - Kanunî Sultan Süleyman:** Sultan of the Ottoman Empire (1494- 1566)
- **Surikov, Vasiliĭ Ivanovich - Василий Иванович Суриков:** Russian painter (1848-1916)
- *Swabians, Danube - Donauschwaben:* ethnic Germans who settled in southeastern Europe, mainly in the Banat (18th century)
- *Szekler – Székelyek:* subgroup of the Hungarian people living mostly in Romania

- *Tamazight:* Berber language indigenous to North Africa
- **Tamerlane - Timūr Leng:** Turco-Mongolian warrior, conqueror of Central and Western Asia (132?-1405)
- *Tannenberg, Battle of:* see Grünwald
- **Tchaikovsky, Pëtr Il'ich - Пётр Ильич Чайковский:** Russian composer (1840-893)
- **Theodorakis, Michael aka Mikis - Μιχαήλ Θεοδωράκης:** Greek composer (1925-)

Back to Byzantium

- *Third Reich - Dritte Reich:* Germany under the Nazi regime (1933-1945)
- *Third Rome:* Moscow, claimed by Russia to have replaced the *Second Rome*, Constantinople, as head Christendom since the fall of Byzantium
- *Templars - Order of Solomon's Temple:* religious and military order founded initially to aid pilgrims in the Holy Land (1129-1312)
- *Terreur, La:* period of the French Revolution characterised by arbitrary rule and mass executions
- *Teutonic Knights, Order of:* German and Catholic religious and military order founded in Acre to aid German-speaking pilgrims (1190)
- **Tikhon, Archimandrite - Архимандрита Тихон:** Russian Orthodox cleric and popular writer (1958-)
- *Time of Anika - Aska i vuk:* historical novel by Ivo Andrić (1968)
- **Tito, Josip Broz aka - Јосип Броз Тито:** Yugoslav Partisan, revolutionary and statesman, President of Yugoslavia (1892-1980)
- *Tosk:* ethnic group of Albania
- **Toynbee, Arnold:** British historian and philosopher (1889-1975)
- *Trabant:* East German automobile
- *Trianon, Treaty of:* peace agreement signed in 1920 between the Allied Powers and Hungary, amputating it of two thirds of its territory
- *Triple Entente:* agreement linking the Russia, France and the United Kingdom, as a counterweight between the Triple Alliance of Germany, Austria-Hungary and Italy
- **Trubetskaïa, Ekaterina Ivanovna née Laval - Екатерина Ивановна Трубецкая:** wife of the *Decembrist* (1800-1854)
- **Trubetskoï, Sergeï Petrovich - Сергей Петрович Трубецкой:** officer and exiled *Decembrist* (1790-1860)
- *Tsarigrad - Царьград:* Slavic name for the city of Constantinople
- *TSUM - Tsentralen universalen magazin - ЦУМ - Централен универсален магазин:* Central Department Store, Sofia, Bulgaria

Back to Byzantium

- **Turks:** people originating from the steppes of central Asia, settled in Anatolia from 11th century
- **Turkish Airlines - Türk Hava Yolları:** Turkish national airline
- **Turner, Ted:** American media mogul, founder of CNN and the Goodwill Games (1938-)
- **Turner Broadcasting System:** American media conglomerate founded by Ted Turner

- **UEFA:** Union of European Football Associations
- **Umayyad Califate:** based in Damascus covering lands from the Caucusus across northern Africa to the Iberian Peninsula
- **Unità, L':** Italian newspaper, official organ of the Italian Communist Party
- **United Nations:** international intergovernmental organisation, established after the Second World War to promote international co-operation and prevent another conflict (1945)
- **Urban II:** Pope of Rome (1042-1099)

- **Vágó, József:** Hungarian architect (1877-1947)
- **Varangian Guard - Τάγμα τῶν Βαράγγων:** elite unit of the Byzantine Army, bodyguard to the Byzantine Emperors, composed of mainly of Norsemen
- **Vartan, Sylvie Vartanian aka:** Franco-Bulgaro-Armenian pop singer (1944-)
- **Vassili III - Василий III Иванович:** Grand Prince of Muscovy (1479-1533)
- **Vatican Council, Second - Vatican II:** convened by Pope John XXIII to address relations between the Catholic Church and the modern world
- **Vecchia Romagna:** Italian brandy
- **Versailles, Treaty of:** peace agreement signed in 1920 between the Allied Powers and Germany, officially ending the First World War
- **Vercingetorix:** chieftain of the Gauls in revolt against the Roman Empire (86-46 BC)
- **Vikings:** Nordic seafarers, who raided and traded across wide areas of Europe

Back to Byzantium

- *Vitus' Day - Видовдан - Vidovdan:* Serbian feast day commemorating the Battle of Kosovo; the day chosen by Gavrilo Princip to assassinate Archduke Franz Ferdinand
- *Vlachs:* term used by their Balkans neigbours for Romance-speaking peoples of Romania and Moldova, by extension a pejorative name for shepherd
- **Vlad III, the Impaler - Vlad Țepeș - Vlad Dracul:** Voïvode of Wallachia (1428/31-1476/77)
- **Vladimir Sviatoslavich - Владимир Святославич:** Grand Prince of Kiev (958-1015)
- **Volkonskaïa, Maria Nikolaevna née Raevskaya - Мария Николаевна Волконская:** wife of the *Decembrist* (1805-1863)
- **Volkonskiï, Sergeï Grigorievitch - Сергей Григорьевич Волконский:** officer and exiled *Decembrist* (1788-1865
- **Voltaire, François-Marie Arouet aka:** French Enlightenment writer and philosopher (1694-1778)
- *VSO - Voluntary Service Overseas:* international development charity for a world without poverty

- *Waffen SS:* the armed wing of the *SS* organisation in Nazi Germany
- **Wałęsa, Lech:** dissident trade-unionist and President of Poland (1943-)
- *War, First World, the Great War:* between countries of the Triple Entente and those of the Triple Alliance (1914-1918)
- *War, Second World:* a state of total war involving the majority of the world's countries, opposing the Allies and Axis Powers, with the Holocaust, the deadliest conflict in history (1939-1945)
- *Warsaw Pact:* collective defence treaty between the Soviet Union and satellite states in Central and Eastern Europe during the Cold War
- *Wehrmacht:* army of the Third Reich in Germany
- **West, Rebecca:** British journalist and travel writer (1892-1983)
- *White Nights - Белые ночи - Belye nochi:* summer solstice in Saint-Petersburg with the midnight sun, an open-air music festival
- **Wilson, Edmond:** American writer and critic (1895-1972)
- **Wilson, Harold:** British Prime Minister (1916-1995)

- **Władysław II Jagiełło:** Grand Duke of Lithuania and King of Poland (1352/62-1434)
- *Women's Day, International:* celebrated on 8th March every year for women's rights and equality
- *World Cup, FIFA:* international association football competition which takes place every four years
- **Wortley Montagu, Lady Mary:** English traveller and letter writer (1689-1762)

- **Yacine, Kateb:** Algerian Berber writer (1929-1989)
- *Young Turk - Jeunes Turcs - Jön Türkler:* political reform movement for the replacement of the Ottoman absolute monarchy by constitutional government

- *Z:* film by Costa-Gavras
- *Zhiguli - Жигули - Lada - VAZ-2101:* compact passenger car, produced by the Soviet manufacturer AvtoVAZ
- **Zhirinovskiĭ, Vladimir Volfovich Edelstein aka - Владимир Вольфович Жириновский Эйдельштейн:** Russian nationalist politician (1946-)
- **Zhivkov, Todor Khristov - Тодор Христов Живков:** First Chairman of the State Council of Bulgaria and General Secretary of the Communist Party (1911-1998)
- **Zinoviev, Aleksandr Aleksandrovich - Александр Александрович Зиновьев:** Soviet philosopher, writer and humorist (1922- 2006)
- **Zog I - Ahmet Zogu:** King of the Albanians (1895-1961)

Glossary of Place Names

- **Adriatic Sea:** part of the Mediterranean Sea situated between the Italian and Balkan peninsulars
- **Aegean Sea:** part of the Mediterranean Sea situated between the mainlands of Greece and Turkey
- **Akademgorodok - Академгородок:** Siberian scientific centre, Novosibirsk, Western Siberia, Russia
- **Al-Andalus:** Muslim Spain covering today's Spain and Portugal *(see Andalusia)*
- **Aleksandr Nevskiï Cathedral - Храм-паметник „Свети Александър Невски":** Sofia, Bulgaria
- **Aleksandrovskiï Sad - Александровский сад:** park and metro station adjacent to the Kremlin, Moscow, Russia
- **Alesia:** location of the defeat of the Gauls by Julius Caesar, France
- **Alexanderplatz:** central square, formerly east Berlin, Germany
- **Alföld:** The Great Hungarian Plain, Hungary
- **Algiers - Dzayer:** capital city of Algeria
- **Alsace-Loraine:** region in France bordering on Germany
- **Alter Peter:** historic Saint Peter's church in Munich, Germany
- **Amersham:** north-western suburb of London, United-Kingdom
- **Amur - река Амуур:** river bordering Russian Far East and Chinese Manchuria
- **Andalusia - Andalucía:** autonomous Community in southern Spain
- **Angara - река Ангара:** tributary of the Yenesei River, flowing from Lake Baïkal, eastern Siberia, Russia
- **Aquincum:** ruins of ancient Roman city, Budapest, Hungary
- **Arad:** capital of Romanian Banat, Romania
- **Athens - Αθήνα:** capital city of Greece
- **Atlanta:** capital of the state of Georgia, USA
- **Attica - Αττική:** region of Greece
- **Avignon:** town in south-eastern France

Back to Byzantium

- **Baïkal, Lake - озеро Байкал:** world's largest freshwater lake, southern Siberia, Russia
- **Balaton, Lake:** Central Europe's largest freshwater lake, Hungary
- **Balkans:** peninsula in south-eastern Europe situated between the Adriatic, the Danube, the Black Sea and the Aegean
- **Baltic Sea:** part of the Atlantic Ocean enclosed by Scandinavia, Finland, the Baltic countries, parts of western Russia, Poland and eastern Germany
- **Banat:** border region in Romania and Serbia
- **Banja Luka - Бања Лука:** city in Bosnia-Herzegovina (Republika Srpska), former Yugoslavia
- **Barcelona:** capital city of Spanish Catalonia, Spain
- **Bastille:** square and metro station in Paris, France, location of the infamous prison linked to the French Revolution
- **Bavaria - Bayern:** federal *land* of Germany
- **Beijing:** capital city of the Peoples Republic of China
- **Belgrade - Београд:** Serbia, former Yugoslavia
- **Belvedere:** baroque palace, Vienna, Austria
- **Berat:** town in Albania
- **Berïozka - Берёзка:** Soviet state-run hard-currency retail stores
- **Berlin Wall - Berliner Mauer:** concrete barrier dividing Berlin from 1961 to 1989
- **Bielorusskiï vokzal - Белорусский вокзал:** main-line station, Moscow, Russia
- **Birobidzhan - Биробиджан:** Jewish Autonomous Oblast, Russian Far East
- **Black Sea:** body of water between eastern Europe and western Asia
- **Blue Mosque – Sultan Ahmet Mosque, Sultan Ahmet Camii:** Istanbul, Turkey
- **Bolshoï Theatre - Большой театр:** home of the Russian opera and ballet, Moscow, Russia
- **Bordeaux:** city in south-western France
- **Borromeo Islands:** Lake Maggiore, Italy
- **Bosphorus:** straits dividing Europe and Asia at Istanbul, Turkey
- **Brasov - Brassó - Kronstadt:** city in Transylvania, Romania

Back to Byzantium

- **Bratsk - Братск:** city on the Angara River, Eastern Siberia, Russia
- **Bratskaïa GES - Братская ГЭС:** hydroelectric dam in Bratsk
- **Brest:** town in the region of Brittany, France
- **Brest - Брест:** city of Belarus at the border with Poland, formerly Brest-Litovsk, Soviet Union
- **Brittany:** region of western France
- **Bruck an der Leitha:** town in Austrian Burgenland, border with Hungary
- **Brussels - Bruxelles - Brussel:** capital city of Belgium and the European Union
- **Bucharest - București:** capital city of Romania
- **Buda:** part of Budapest, Hungary, situated on the right (west) bank of the Danube
- **Budapest:** capital city of Hungary
- **Budva - Будва:** town on the Mediterranean coast, Montenegro, former Yugoslavia
- **Burgas - Бургас:** town on the Black Sea coast, Bulgaria
- **Calais:** port on the Channel coast in north-eastern France, facing Dover
- **Cape Town - Kaapstad:** southernmost coastal city in South Africa
- **Capitole, place du:** prestigious central square, Toulouse, France
- **Carinthia - Kärnten:** federal *land* in southern Austria
- **Carpathians:** mountain range across central and eastern Europe
- **Casbah:** walled traditional Arab quarter, Algiers, Algeria
- **Caucasus - Кавказ:** border region between Europe and Asia, the Black Sea and the Caspian
- **Champs Elysées:** prestigious avenue in Paris, France
- **Channel tunnel:** undersea rail link between Folkestone, United Kingdom, and Coquelles, France
- **Checkpoint Charlie:** crossing point between East and West Berlin during the Cold War
- **Chernobyl - Чернобыль - Чорнобиль:** town in Ukraine, site of a nuclear catastrophe
- **Chita - Чита:** city in eastern Siberia, Russia

Back to Byzantium

- **Constanța:** town on the Black Sea coast, Romania
- **Constantinople - Κωνσταντινούπολις - Цариград:** today Istanbul, Turkey *(see Istanbul)*
- **Costa Brava:** northern Mediterranean coast in Catalonia, Spain
- **Côte d'Azur:** French Riviera on the southeast Mediterranean coast of France
- **Crete - Κρήτη:** largest Greek island in the Mediterranean Sea, Greece
- **Crimea - Крим:** disputed peninsular on the northern coast of the Black Sea, formerly Soviet Union

- **Dallas:** city in the state of Texas, USA
- **Dalmatia - Dalmacija:** region of Croatia along the Adriatic Sea, former Yugoslavia
- **Danube:** longest river in the European Union, flowing through central and eastern Europe to the Black Sea
- **Dardanelles:** historically Hellespont, strait in Turkey dividing Europe from Asia, connecting the Sea of Marmara with the Aegean
- **La Défense:** business district close to Paris, France
- **Derbyshire:** county in the Midlands of England, United Kingdom
- **Dijon:** city in the region of Bourgogne, France
- **Djurdjura:** mountains of the Atlas range in Kabylia, Algeria
- **Dobrudzha - Dobrogea - Добруджа:** region between the Danube River and the Black Sea, shared by Bulgaria and Romania
- **Domodossola:** town in the region of Piedmont, Italy
- **Donskoï monastery - Донской монастыр:** Moscow, Russia
- **Dover:** port on the Channel coast in southeastern England, facing Calais
- **Dubrovnik:** historically Ragusa, city on Adriatic Sea coast, Croatia, former Yugoslavia
- **Dunkirk - Dunkerque:** port on the Channel coast in north-eastern France
- **Durrës:** historically Durrachium, port city on the Adriatic Sea, Albania

Back to Byzantium

- **Edinburgh:** capital city of Scotland, United Kingdom
- **Ekaterinburg - Екатеринбург:** briefly Sverdlovsk, administrative centre of Sverdlosk oblast, Russia
- **Epirus:** area in southeast Europe, split between Albania and Greece
- **Erdély:** *see Transylvania*
- **Ermitage - Государственный Эрмитаж:** prestigious museum in Saint-Petersburg, Russia *(see Winter palace)*
- **Erzsébet híd:** road bridge over the Danube in Budapest, Hungary
- **Et'hem Bey:** historic mosque in Tirana, Albania

- **Falkland Islands - Islas Malvinas:** British Overseas Territory in the South Atlantic, claimed by Argentina
- **Far East:** *part of Russia situated in northeast Asia*
- **Field of Mars - Марсово поле:** park in Saint-Petersburg, Russia
- **Florence - Firenze:** regional capital of Tuscany, Italy
- **Fontainebleau:** town in the region Île-de-France, France
- **Frankfurt:** financial capital of Germany
- **Fransız Pasteur Hastanesi:** French hospital Pasteur, Istanbul, Turkey
- **Frasne:** rail junction on the Jurassian plateau in eastern France
- **Frauenkirche:** Cathedral of Our Dear Lady, Munich, Germany
- **Friedrichstraße:** railway station, border between East and West Germany during the Cold War

- **Galatasaray Hamami:** historic hamam in Istanbul, Turkey
- **Gallipoli - Gelibolu Yarımadası:** peninsular between the Aegean Sea and the Dardanelles, Turkey
- **Gare de l'Est:** eastern mainline station, Paris, France
- **Gare de Lyon:** southeastern mainline station, Paris, France
- **Gare du Nord:** northern mainline station, Paris, France
- **Gdańsk - Danzig:** port on the Baltic coast, capital of the Voivode of Pomerania, Poland
- **Gdynia - Gdingen:** Baltic seaport in Pomerania, Poland

Back to Byzantium

- **Geneva, Lake - lac Léman:** straddling Suisse Romande, Switzerland and Haute-Savoie, France
- **Genoa - Genova:** capital of the region of Liguria, Italy
- **Gevgelija - Гевгелија:** border town with Greece, Macedonia, former Yugoslavia
- **Gjirokastër - Αργυρόκαστρο:** historic town in northern Epirus, Albania
- **Giurgiu:** city on the Danube in southern Romania, facing Ruse in Bulgaria
- **Godstone:** distant southern suburb of London, United Kingdom
- **Gorkiï Park - Центральный парк культуры и отдыха имени Горького:** park in Moscow, Russia
- **Great Plain - Alföld:** eastern Hungary
- **Gulf of Finland - Финский залив:** easternmost arm of the Baltic Sea, bordering Estonia, Finland and Russia

- *Hagia Sofia - Άγία Σοφία*: formerly Greek Orthodox church of the Holy Wisdom, later an Ottoman imperial mosque, today a museum, Constantinople-Istanbul, Turkey
- **Hague, The - Den Haag - 's-Gravenhage:** seat of the government and parliament of the Netherlands
- **Hackney:** borough of London, United Kingdom
- **Harbin:** city in Manchuria, People's Republic of China
- **Helsinki:** capital city of Finland
- **Hercegovina:** region of Bosnia and Herzegovina, former Yugoslavia
- **Hévíz:** spa town in southwestern Hungary
- **Hofbraühaus am Platzl:** historic beer-hall and brewery in Munich, Germany
- **Holy Sepulchre:** traditionally the site of the crucifixion and tomb of Jesus, Jerusalem, Israel
- **Hook of Holland - Hoek van Holland:** North Sea port, The Netherlands
- **Hotel Rossia - Гостиница «Россия»:** formerly the largest hotel in Europe, since demolished
- **Hotel Ukraina - Гостиница «Украина»:** hotel in Stalinist skyscraper, Moscow, Russia

Back to Byzantium

- **House of Commons:** lower house of the Parliament of the United Kingdom, Westminster, London
- **Hunedoara - Vajdahunyad - Eisenmarkt:** historic castle and city in western Transylvania, Romania
- **Hydra - Ύδρα:** Aegean island, Greece

- **Ïakutsk - Якутск:** capital city of the Sakha Republic, Russia
- **Ïaroslavskiï vokzal - Ярославский вокзал:** main-line station, Moscow, Russia
- **Irkutsk - Иркутск:** administrative centre of Irkutsk oblast, eastern Siberia, Russia
- **Istanbul:** capital city of Turkey, formerly Constantinople
- **İstiklâl Caddesi:** (Independence) avenue of the district of Pera, Istanbul, Turkey
- **Ïubileynyï Sports Palace - Спортивный комплекс "Юбилейный":** indoor sports arena, Saint-Petersburg, Russia

- **Jean Jaurès:** central metro station, Toulouse, France
- **Jesenice - Assling:** border town with Austria, Slovenia, former Yugoslavia
- **Jerusalem - Yerushalayim, al-Qods:** administrative centre of Israel, holy city for Judaism, Christianity and Islam

- **Kabylia:** historical Berber region in northern Algeria
- **Kalemegdan Park - Калемегдански парк:** cliff-top park at the confluence of rivers Sava and Danube in Belgrade, Serbia, former Yugoslavia
- **Karaganda - Караганда:** city in northern Kazakhstan, formerly Soviet Union, once home to a majority of ethnic Germans
- **Katovice:** capital of the Voivode of Silesia, Poland
- **Keleti pályaudvar:** 'Eastern' mainline station, serving western destinations, located in southern Budapest, Hungary
- **Keszthely:** town on the western shore of Lake Balaton, Hungary
- **Khabarovsk - Хабаровск:** city in the Far East of Russia
- **Khartoum:** capital city of Sudan
- **Kiev - Київ - Киев:** capital city of Ukraine, formerly Soviet Union

Back to Byzantium

- **Kievskiï vokzal - Киевский вокзал вокзал:** main-line station, Moscow, Russia
- **Király fürdő:** thermal bath in Budapest, Hungary, dating from the Ottoman period
- **Komsomolskaïa - Комсомольская:** metro station serving Leningradskiï, Ïaroslavskiï and Kazanskiï railway terminals in Moscow, Russia
- **Koper - Capodistria:** Mediterranean resort in Slovenia
- **Koprivshtitsa - Копривщица:** historic town in central Bulgaria
- **Kosovo - Kosova - Косово:** disputed territory, formerly Autonomous Province of Kosovo and Metohija, Yugoslavia
- **Kosovo Polje - Косово Поље – Field of Blackbirds:** location of the historical and mythical Battle of Kosovo between the Serbs of Prince Lazar and the Ottomans of Sultan Murad (1448)
- **Kotor - Котор:** coastal town on the Gulf of Kotor, Montenegro, former Yugoslavia
- **Krasnaïa Strela - Красная стрела:** Red Arrow, overnight sleeper-train connecting Moscow and Saint-Petersburg, Russia
- **Krasnoïarsk - Красноярск:** city in central Siberia, Russia
- **Kremlin - Московский Кремль:** fortified complex, seat of the government of Russia, formerly of the Soviet Union
- **Krestovskiï Island - Крестовский остров:** island in Saint-Petersburg, Russia
- **Krymskiï val - Крымский вал:** thoroughfare of Moscow, Russia
- **Kumanovo - Куманово:** town in northern Macedonia, former Yugoslavia

- **Latin Quarter - Quartier latin:** traditionally students' quarter on the left bank of Paris, France
- **Lausanne:** city on Lake Geneva, capital of the canton of Vaud, Switzerland
- **Lenexpo:** exhibition centre in Saint-Petersburg, Russia
- **Leningrad - Ленинград:** *see Saint-Petersburg*
- **Leningradskiï vokzal - Ленинтралский вокзал:** main-line station, Moscow, Russia
- **Leninskiï Prospect - Ленинский проспект:** prestigious main thoroughfare and metro station in Moscow, Russia

Back to Byzantium

- **Lobnoë Mesto - Лобное место:** stone platform in Red Square, Moscow, Russia
- **Lombardy - Lombardia:** region of northwestern Italy
- **Lomonosov Moscow State University - Московский государственный университет имени М. В. Ломоносова:** МГУ – MGU, Moscow, Russia
- **London:** capital city of the United Kingdom
- **Los Angeles:** city megalopolis on the Pacific coast of California, USA
- **Lubïanka - Лубянка:** headquarters of the FSB, formerly KGB, and affiliated prison
- **Luxemburg:** Grand Duchy
- **Lyon:** capital of the region of Auvergne-Rhone-Alpes, France

- **Maggiore, Lake - Lago Maggiore:** straddling Ticino, Switzerland and Piedmont and Lombardy, Italy
- **Maghreb:** region of North Africa including Algeria, Marocco, Tunisia
- **Malakoff:** close suburb of Paris, France
- **Malbork - Marienburg:** town in Pomerania, Poland, former seat of the Knights of the Teutonic Order
- **Mamaia:** Black Sea resort of Constanţa, Romania
- **Manchuria:** northern region of the People's Republic of China
- **Manzikert - Malazgirt:** town in eastern Turkey, site of the historic defeat of the Byzantines by the Seljuk Turks
- **Maribor:** city in Slovenia, former Yugoslavia
- **Maritsa - Марица:** Balkan river, flowing from the Rhodopes through Bulgaria, Greece, Turkey to the Aegean Sea
- **Mátyás Templom:** Matthias Church of Our Lady, Budapest, Hungary
- **MariahilferStraße:** main shopping street in Vienna, Austria
- **Marseille:** Mediterranean seaport, capital of the region of Provence-Alpes-Côte d'Azur, France
- **Mea She'arim:** old, mainly Hassidic quarter of Jerusalem, Israel
- **Mestre:** mainland area of Venice, Italy
- **Milan - Milano:** capital of the Lombardy region, business capital of Italy

Back to Byzantium

- **Milano Centrale:** main-line station of Milan, Italy
- **Moldavia - Moldova:** region in northern Romania, also republic of Moldova, former Soviet Union
- **Mosel - Moselle:** wine-growing region and tributary of the Rhine, flowing through France, Luxembourg and Germany
- **Montmartre:** historic hilltop district of Paris, France
- **Montreux:** town on Lake Geneva in the canton of Vaud, Switzerland
- **Morava, Great - Велика Морава: Serbia, former Yugoslavia**
- **Moravia - Morava:** historical country in the eastern Czech Republic, former Czechoslovakia
- **Moscow - Москва:** capital city of Russia, formerly of the Soviet Union
- **Moskovskiï vokzal - Московский вокзал:** main-line station, Saint-Petersburg, Russia
- **Mostar:** city of Herzegovina region in Bosnia Herzegovina, former Yugoslavia
- **Munich - München:** capital of the federal *land* of Bavaria, Germany

- **Nairobi:** capital city of Kenya
- **Nakhodka - Находка:** port city on the Sea of Japan, close to Vladivostok, Russia
- **Naples - Napoli:** capital of the region of Campania, Italy
- **Neva - река Нева:** river flowing from Lake Ladoga through Saint-Petersbur to the Gulf of Finland, Russia
- **Nevsky Prospekt - Невский проспект:** prestigious avenue in Saint-Petersburg, Russia
- **New York:** financial capital of the USA
- **Newhaven:** port on the Channel coast in south-eastern England, United Kingdom
- **Niš - Ниш:** city in southern Serbia, former Yugoslavia
- **Nogina, Ploshad - Площадь Ногина:** square and metro station adjacent to the Lubïanka, Moscow, Russia
- **Normandy:** region of western France
- **Novgorod - Великий Новгород:** historic administrative centre of the Novgorod oblast, western Russia

Back to Byzantium

- **Novosibirsk - Новосибирск:** administrative centre of Novosibirsk oblast, western Siberia, Russia

- **Ob, River - река Обь:** river flowing from the Altaï mountains through Novosibirsk to the Arctic Ocean
- **Obuda:** district of Budapest, Hungary
- **Ohrid, Lake - Охридско Езеро - Liqeni i Ohrit:** straddling Macedonia, former Yugoslavia, and Albania
- **Oktïabrskaïa - Октяябрьская:** square and metro station in Moscow, Russia
- **Old Quba:** eastern residential suburb of Algiers, Algeria
- **Olgino - Ольгино:** northern residential suburb of Saint-Petersburg, on the banks of Gulf of Finland, Russia
- **Oliwa:** district of Gdańsk, Poland
- **Olomouc:** city in Moravia, Czech Republic, former Czechoslovakia
- **Omsk - Омск:** administrative centre of Omsk oblast, western Siberia, Russia
- **Orly:** second international airport of Paris, France
- **Ostankino - Останкино:** district of Moscow, Russia, location of the TV and Radio tower and VDNKh park
- **Ostbahnhof:** Eastern mainline station, formerly East Berlin, Germany

- **Pamporovo - Пампорово:** ski resort in the Rhodope Mountains in southern Bulgaria
- **Paris:** capital city of France
- **Parliament Square:** historic area adjacent to the Parliament in Westminster, London, United Kingdom
- **Pasarét:** residential district in Budapest, Hungary
- **Peipus, Lake - Псковско-Чудское озеро:** lake on the border between Estonia and Russia, former Soviet Union
- **Peloponnese - Πελοπόννησος:** peninsular region in southern Greece
- **Pera - Beyoğlu:** district by the by the Golden Horn, formerly Genovese, Venetian and Greek quarter, Istanbul, Turkey
- **Perm - Пермь:** city in the European part of the Urals, Russia

Back to Byzantium

- **Pest:** forms with Buda and Óbuda the capital city Budapest, Hungary
- **Peter and Paul fortress - Petropavlovskaya Krepost:** citadel of Saint-Petersburg, Russia
- **Petrograd - Петроград:** *see Saint-Petersburg*
- **Pigalle:** red-light district in Paris, France
- **Piraeus - Πειραιάς:** port city of Athens, Greece
- **Ploče:** town on the Adriatic coast of Dalmatia in Croatia, former Yugoslavia
- **Plovdiv – Пловдив:** second-largest city in Bulgaria
- **Plymouth:** city in southwestern England, United Kingdom
- **Pogradets:** town on Lake Ohrid, Albania
- **Poros - Πόρος:** small island off the Peloponnese, Greece
- **Přerov:** town in Moravia, Czech Republic, former Czechoslovakia
- **Provence - Provença:** region of southeastern France
- **Prussia, East - Ostpreußen:** former province of Prussia, today the enclave of Kaliningrad, Russia
- **Pskov - Псков:** administrative centre of Pskov oblast, western Russia
- **Puszta:** Pannonian Steppe in eastern Hungary

- **Radisson-Slavïanskaïa Hotel - Гостиница Рэдиссон Славянская:** prestigious hotel, Moscow, Russia
- **Ragusa:** *see Dubrovnik*
- **Ramstein-Miesenbach:** town in Rhinelan-Palatinate, Germany, location of the headquarters for the United States Air Forces in Europe
- **Red Square - Красная площадь - Krasnaïa ploshchad':** prestigious square adjacent to the Kremlin, Moscow, Russia
- **Reichstag:** former and present seat of the German Parliament, Berlin, Germany
- **Rennweg:** street in the Landstraße district of Vienna, Austria
- **Rhineland-Palatinate - Rheinland-Pfalz:** federal *land* of Germany
- **Rhodope - Родопи - Ροδόπη:** mountain range in southern Bulgaria and northern Greece

Back to Byzantium

- **Rijeka - Fiume:** seaport in Croatia, former Yugoslavia
- **Rivoli, rue de:** prestigious street adjacent to the Louvre and Tuileries, Paris, France
- **Romans-sur-Isère:** town in southeastern France
- **Rome - Roma:** capital city of Italy, location of the Vatican City
- **Rotterdam:** North Sea port in the Netherlands, Europe's largest
- **Rozsadomb:** residential district in Budapest, Hungary
- **Rudas fürdő:** thermal bath in Budapest, Hungary, dating from the Ottoman period
- **Rumelia - Ρωμυλία:** Turkey in Europe, the Balkans under Ottoman administration
- **Ruse - Русе:** city on the Danube in northern Bulgaria, facing Giurgiu in Romania

- **Sahara:** desert covering much of northern Africa
- **Saint-Basil's Cathedral - Собор Василия Блаженного:** historic church in Red Square, Moscow, Russia
- **Saint-Louis-des-Français - Храм Святого Людовика Французского:** traditionally a French Roman Catholic church, located behind the Lubyanka, Moscow, Russia
- **Saint Mark's - Basilica di San Marco:** historic cathedral in Venice, Italy
- **Saint-Petersburg - Санкт-Петербург:** Baltic Sea port, second-largest city in Russia
- **Salzburg:** capital of the federal *land* of Salzburg, Austria
- **Sarajevo:** capital of Bosnia and Herzegovina, former Yugoslavia
- **Sava - Сава:** river flowing through Slovenia, Croatia, along the border of Bosnia and Herzegovina, through Serbia into the Danube in Belgrade
- **Scutari - Üsküdar:** district of Istanbul, Turkey, on the Anatolian shore of the Bosphorus
- **Schleswig-Holstein:** federal land of Germany, adjacent to Denmark
- **Schwarzenbergplatz:** historic square in Vienna, Austria, briefly renames Stalinplatz
- **Sea of Marmara - Marmara Denizi:** inland sea in Turkey, connecting the Black Sea to the Aegean

Back to Byzantium

- **Sebastopol - Севастополь:** Black Sea port in the Crimea, formerly Soviet Union, home of the Russian Black Sea fleet
- **Sebeş - Szászsebes - Mühlbach:** city in Transylvania, Romania
- **Sergiev Posad - Сергиев Посад:** seat of one of the largest monasteries in Russia, briefly renamed Zagorsk
- **Sežana - Sesana:** border town with Italy, Slovenia, former Yugoslavia
- **Sheremetevo - Международный Аэропорт Шереме́тьево:** main international airport in Moscow, Russia
- **Shkodër:** city in northwestern Albania
- **Shqipëria:** *see Albania*
- **Sibiu - Nagyszeben - Hermannstadt:** city in Transylvania, Romania
- **Siberia - Сибирь:** vast region covering northern Asia, Russia
- **Siebenbürgen:** *see Transylvania*
- **Sighişoara - Schäßburg - Segesvár:** town in Transylvania, Romania
- **Simplon tunnel:** railway link between Switzerland and Italy
- **SKA pool - бассейн СКА:** indoor olympic pool, Saint-Petersburg, Russia
- **Skopje - Скопје:** capital city of Macedonia, former Yugoslavia
- **Slavonia - Slavonija:** region of eastern Croatia, former Yugoslavia
- **Slavonsky Brod:** city in the region of Slavonia, Croatia, former Yugoslavia
- **Sofia - София:** capital city of Bulgaria
- **Sopot - Zoppot:** resort town on the Baltic coast in Pomerania, Poland
- **Spasskaïa Tower - Спасская башня:** Saviour Tower in the Kremlin, overlooking Red Square, Moscow, Russia
- **Split - Spalato:** city on the Adriatic coast of Dalmatia, Croatia, former Yugoslavia, location of Diocletian's Palace
- **Srebrenica, Republika Srpska:** former Yugoslavia
- **Stalinplatz:** *see Schwarzenbergplatz*
- **Stara Zagora - Стара Загора:** city in south-central Bulgaria
- **Stockholm:** capital city of Sweden

Back to Byzantium

- **Südbahnhof:** southern mainline station, Vienna, Austria
- **Sverdlovsk - Свердловск:** *see Ekaterinburg*
- **Szentendre:** historic town on the Danube bend, north of Budapest, Hungary

- **Taganka - Таганский район:** district of Moscow, Russia, location of the Taganka art theatre
- **Taksim - Taksim Meydanı:** central square in Istanbul, Turkey
- **Tamanrasset:** Touareg oasis city in southern Algeria
- **Târgoviște:** city, former capital of Wallachia, Romania
- **Thessaloniki - Θεσσαλονίκη:** regional capital of Macedonia, Greece
- **Thrace – Θράκη – Тракия - Trakiya:** area in southeast Europe, split between Bulgaria, Greece and Turkey, between the Balkan Mountains, the Aegean and Black Seas
- **Timișoara - Temesvár - Temeschburg:** regional capital of Banat, Romania
- **Tirana:** capital city of Albania
- **Toulouse:** regional capital of Occitanie, France
- *Trakt, Sibirsky - Сибирский тракт:* historic route connecting European Russia to Siberia
- *Trans-Siberian - Транссибирская магистраль - Transsibirskaïa Magistral - Transsib – Транссиб:* rail route between Moscow and Vladivostok
- **Transylvania - Ardeal - Erdély - Siebenbürgen:** region of Romania, formerly part of Austria-Hungary
- **Trieste:** Adiatic sea port on the border with Slovenia, Italy

- **Ulan Bator - Улаанбаатар:** capital city of Mongolia
- **Ulan Ude - Улан-Удэ:** railway junction of the Trans-Siberian and Trans-Mongolian lines, capital of the Republic of Buryatia, Russia
- **Urals - Уральские горы:** mountain range running north-south through Russia, separating Europe from Asia
- **Üsküdar:** *see Scutari*
- **Ussuri - река Уссури:** tributary of the Amur River, bordering Russia and China

Back to Byzantium

- **Vajdahunyad:** castle in Budapest, Hungary, copy of the castle of Hunedoara in Romania *(see Hunedoara)*
- **Vallorbe:** town in the canton of Vaud, Switzerland
- **Varna - Варна:** resort city on the Black Sea coast, Bulgaria
- **Varosliget:** city park, Budapest, Hungary
- **Vasilevskiï Island:** Saint-Petersburg, Russia
- **Vaud:** canton in Suisse romande, Switzerland
- **VDNKh - ВДНХ - Выставка достижений народного хозяйства - Vystavka Dostizheniy Narodnogo Khozyaystva:** Exhibition of Achievements of the People's Economy, Moscow, Russia
- **Veliko Trnovo - Велико Търново:** city in north central Bulgaria
- **Venice – Venezia:** regional capital of Veneto, Italy
- **Verona:** city in the region of Veneto, Italy
- **Vienna - Wien:** capital city of Austria
- **Villa Opicina:** border town with Slovenia, Italy
- **Villach:** city in the federal *land* of Carinthia, Austria
- **Ville d'Avray:** suburb of Paris, France
- **Vincennes Zoo:** Paris, France
- **Visegrád:** town on the Danube Bend, Hungary
- **Višegrad:** town in Hercegovina on the Drina River
- **Vodno - Водно:** mountain in Macedonia, former Yugoslavia
- **Volga - Волга:** longest river in Europe, flowing through Russia to the Caspian Sea

- **Wallachia - Muntenia:** region of Romania
- **Warsaw - Warszawa:** capital city of Poland
- **Westerplatte:** peninsular in Gdańsk, Poland, site of the first battle of the Second World War
- **White House - Белый дом:** seat of the Government of the Russian Federation, formerly of the Supreme Soviet, Moscow, Russia
- **Winter Palace - Зиимний дворец:** home of the Ermitage Museum, Saint-Petersburg, Russia

Back to Byzantium

- **Yalta - Ялта:** resort city on the Black Sea coast in Crimea, formerly Soviet Union
- **Yantra - Янтра:** tributary of the Danube River, Bulgaria
- **Yokohama:** port city situated in Tokyo Bay, Japan

- **Zagorsk:** *see Serguiev Possad*
- **Zagreb:** capital city of Croatia, former Yugoslavia
- **Zadar:** historically Zara, city on Adriatic Sea coast, Croatia, former Yugoslavia

Bibliography

- **ANDREEVA, E.** *Georges Dimitrov.* Sofia: Sofia-Presse, 1977.
- **ANDRIC, Ivo.** *Anika's Times (Anikina vremena).* Belgrade: 1931.
- **ANDRIC, Ivo.** *Bife Titanic.* Belgrade: 1950.
- **ANDRIC, Ivo.** *The Bridge on the Drina (Na Drini ćuprija – На Дрини ћуприја).* Belgrade: 1945.
- **ANDRIC, Ivo.** *The Damned Yard (Prokleta Avlija).* Belgrade: 1954.
- **ANDRIC, Ivo.** *The Vizir's Elephant (Priča o vezirovom slonu).* Belgrade: 1948.
- **ANDRIC, Ivo.** *Omer Paša Latas.* Belgrade: 1975.
- **ANGOLD, Michael.** *The Fall of Constantinople to the Ottomans.* London: Pearson Education, 2012.
- **ASCHERSON, Neal.** *Black Sea.* London: Jonathan Cape, 1995.
- **AUTY, Phyllis.** *Tito.* London: Longman Group, 1970.
- **BÁNFFY, Miklós.** *The Phoenix Land.* London: Arcadia Books, 2003.
- **BARBERO, Alessandro.** *Benedette Guerre: Crociate e Jihad.* Roma: Laterza, 2009.
- **BARRET, Pierre & GURGAND, Jean-Noël.** *La Part des Pauvres.* Paris: Editions Robert Laffont, 1978.
- **BARTLETT, W.B.** *An Ungodly War.* Stroud: Sutton Publishing, 2000.
- **BARTLETT, W.B.** *God Wills It!* Stroud: Sutton Publishing, 1999.
- **BECK, MAST & TAPPER.** *Eastern Europe for Beginners.* New York: Writers and Readers Publishing, 1978.
- **BEESON, Trevor.** *Discretion and Valour.* British Council of Churches, 1974.
- **BRACEWELL & DRACE-FRANCIS.** *Balkan departures.* New York, Berghahn Books, 2011.
- **BROOK, Stephen.** *The Double Eagle.* London: Hamish Hamilton, 1988.
- **BUMÇI, Zef.** *Maska te Çjerra.* Tirana: 8 Nentori, 1976.

- **BYRON, Lord George Gordon.** *Childe Harold's Pilgrimage.* London: John Murray, 1812-1818.
- **CASTELLAN, Georges.** *Histoire des Balkans.* Editions Arthème Fayard, 1991.
- **CAZACU, Matei.** *Dracula.* Paris: Tallandier Editions, 2004.
- **CONTE, Arthur.** *Yalta.* Paris: Robert Laffont, 1964.
- **COOPER, Artemis.** *Patrick Leigh Fermor.* London: John Murray, 2013.
- **CUSTINE, Marquis de.** *Lettres de Russie (préface de Pierre Nora).* Paris: Editions Gallimard, 1975.
- **DARUVAR, Yves de.** *Le Destin dramatique de la Hongrie.* Paris: Editions Albatros, 1970.
- **DELORME, Olivier.** *La Grèce et les Balkans.* Paris: Gallimard, 2013
- **DIMITROVA, Alexenia.** *The Iron Fist.* London: Artnik, 2005.
- **DJILAS, Milovan.** *Wartime.* New York: Harper, Brace, Jovanovich, 1977.
- **DRAKULIC, Slavenka.** *Café Europa.* New York: W.W.Norton, 1997.
- **DRAKULIC, Slavenka.** *How we Survived Communism and even Laughed.* London: Hutchinson, 1987.
- **DUCELLIER, Alain.** *Les Byzantins.* Paris: Seuil, 1988.
- **DUMAS, Alexandre.** *Ali Pacha.* Paris: 1819.
- **DURHAM, Edith.** *High Albania.* London: Edward Arnold, 1909.
- **DURREL, Lawrence.** *White Eagles over Serbia.* London: Faber & Faber, 1963.
- **FEJTÖ, François.** *La Fin des Démocraties populaires.* Paris: Seuil, 1997.
- **FERMOR, Patrick Leigh.** *A Time of Gifts.* London: John Murray, 1977.
- **FERMOR, Patrick Leigh.** *Between the Woods and the Water.* London: John Murray, 1986.
- **FERMOR, Patrick Leigh.** *Roumeli.* London: John Murray, 1966.
- **FERMOR, Patrick Leigh.** *The Broken Road.* London: John Murray, 2013.

- **FLORI, Jean.** *Guerre sainte, Jihad, Croisade.* Paris: Seuil, 2002.
- **FONSECA, Isabel.** *Bury me Standing.* London: Chatto and Windus, 1995.

- **GALLAND, Nicole.** *Crossed, a Tale of the Fourth Crusade.* New York: Harper, 2008.
- **GARDE, Paul.** *Fin de Siècle dans les Balkans.* Paris: Editions Odile Jacob, 2001.
- **GARDE, Paul.** *Les Balkans: Héritages et Evolutions.* Paris: Flammarion, 2010.
- **GARTON-ASH, Timothy.** *The Uses of Adversity.* London: Granta Books, 1989.
- **GARTON-ASH, Timothy.** *We the People.* London: Granta Books, 1990.
- **GIBBON, Edward.** *The Fall of Constantinople* from *The Decline and Fall of the Roman Empire.* London, 1776.
- **GLENNY, Misha.** *The Fall of Yugoslavia.* London: Penguin Books, 1992.
- **GOLDSWORTHY, Vesna.** *Inventing Ruritania.* London: Yale University Press, 2013.
- **GOODWIN, Jason.** *Lords of the Horizons.* London: Chatto & Windu, 1998.
- **GOODWIN, Jason.** *On Foot to the Golden Horn.* London: Vintage, 1996.
- **GOODWIN, Jason.** *The Janissary Tree.* London: Faber & Faber, 1988.
- **GREENE, Graham.** *Stamboul Train.* London: Heinemann, 1932.

- **HALL, Brian.** *Stealing from a Deep Place.* London: Heinemann, 1988.
- **HARDING, Georgina.** *In Another Europe.* London: Hodder and Stoughton, 1990.
- **HARPER, Tom.** *The Mosaic of Shadows.* New York: Random House, 2003.
- **HAŠEK, Jaroslav.** *Les Formes du Secret (Velitelem města Bugulmy).* Praha: Tribuna, 1921.
- **HAŠEK, Jaroslav.** *The Good Soldier Švejk (Osudy dobrého vojáka Švejka).* Praha: Adolf Synek, 1921.
- **HERGÉ.** *L'Affaire Tournesol.* Brussels: Casterman, 1956.

- HERGÉ. *Le Sceptre d'Ottokar.* Brussels: Casterman, 1942.
- HITZEL, Frédéric. *L'Empire Ottoman.* Paris: Les Belles Lettres, 2001.
- HOXHA, Enver. *Albania Challenges Krushchev Revisionism.* New York: Gamma Publishing, 1976.
- HUNT, Nick. *Walking the Woods and Water.* London: Nicholas Brealey Publishing, 2014.
- HUNTINGTON, Samuel P. *The Clash of Civilizations and the Remaking of World Order.* New York: Simon & Schuster, 1996.
- JUDAH, Tim. *The Serbs.* New Haven: Yale Nota Bene, 2000.
- KAPLAN, Robert B. *Balkan Ghosts.* New York: St. Marton's Press, 1993.
- KARDELJ, Edvard. *Les Contradictions de la Propriété sociale dans le Système socialiste.* Paris: Editions Anthropos, 1976.
- KINDERSLEY, Anne. *The Mountains of Serbia.* London: John Murray, 1976.
- KISS, Csaba G. *Understanding Central Europe: Nations and Stereotypes.* Budapest: Nap Kiado "Sun"Publishing, 2013.
- KONSTANTINOV, Aleko. *Baj Ganju (Бай Ганю).* Sofia, 1895.
- KRISTEVA, Julia. *Meurtre à Byzance.* Paris: Librairie Arthème Fayard, 2004.
- KUKRYNIKCY. *По Врагам Мира (Po Vragam Mira).* Moscow: Plakat, 1982.
- LÉGRÁDY, Ottó. *Justice pour la Hongrie.* Budapest. Pesti Hirlap, 1930.
- LEMERLE, Paul. *Histoire de Byzance.* Paris. Presses Universitaires de France, 1943.
- LEWIS, Bernard. *What Went Wrong.* London. Weidenfeld and Nicholson,2002.
- MACLEAN, Fitzroy. *Eastern Approaches.* London: Jonathan Cape, 1949.
- MAGRIS, Claudio. *Danubio.* Milan: Garzanti, 1986.

- **MASPERO, François.** *Balkans - Transit.* Paris: Editions du Seuil, 1997.
- **MAZOWER, Mark.** *The Balkans.* London: Weidenfeld a Nicholson, 2000.
- **MAZURANIC, Matija.** *A Glance into Ottoman Bosnia (Pogled u Bosnu, ili, kratak put u onu krajinu, učinjen 1839-40).* Zagreb, 1842.
- **MICHISON, Naomi.** *Anna Comnena.* London: Gerald Howe, 1928.
- **MONTAGU, Lady Mary Wortley.** *Letters from Turkey.* London, 1725.

- **NEWBY, Eric.** *The Big Red Train Ride.* London: Weidenfeld a Nicholson, 1978.
- **NJEGOS, Petar II Petrovic.** T*he Mountain Wreath (Горски вијенац – Gorski vijenac).* Cetinje, 1847.

- **PECHOU & SIVIGNON.** *Les Balkans.* Paris. Presses Universitaires de France, 1971.
- **PLOMER, William.** *The Diamond of Jannina.* New York. Taplinger Publishing 1970.

- **SAID, Edward.** *Orientalism.* London: Routledge & Kegan Paul, 1978.
- **SCHREIBER, Thomas.** *Enver Hoxha.* Paris: Editions Jean-Claude Lattes, 1994.

- **THIERIOT, Jean-Louis.** *François-Ferdinand d'Autriche.* Paris: Editions de Fallois, 2005.
- **THIESSE, Anne-Marie.** *La Création des Identités nationales.* Paris: Editions du Seuil, 1999.
- **TODOROVA, Maria.** *Imagining the Balkans.* Oxford: Oxford Unversity Press, 1997.
- **TURTLEDOVE, Harry.** *Agent of Byzantium.* New York: Congdon & Weed, 1987.

- **VAISSIÉ, Cécile.** *La Fabrique de l'Homme nouveau après Staline.* Rennes: Presses Universitaires de Rennes, 2016.
- **VASOV, Ivan.** *Under the Yoke (Под игото).* Sofia, 1890.

- **WARE, Timothy.** *The Orthodox Church.* London: Penguin Books, 1963.
- **WEST, Rebecca.** *Black Lamb and Grey Falcon.* London, Macmillan, 1942.
- **WILSON, Edmund.** *A Window on Russia.* New York: Macmillan, 1972.
- **WINDER, Simon.** *Danubia.* London: Picador, 2013.

- **YACINE, Kateb.** *Nedjma.* Paris: Seuil, 1956.

- **ZECEVIC, Miodrag.** *Le Système de Délégations.* Belgrade: Jugoslovenski Pregled, 1977.
- **ZINOVIEV, Aleksandr.** *Homo Sovieticus (Гомо Советикус).* Paris: Editions l'Age d'Homme, 1983.

Index

24 Chasa, 37
Adriatic Sea, 52, 120, 182, 189
Aegean Sea, 44, 52, 71
Aeroflot, 148, 159
Air France, 108
Airbus, 321
AK47, 254
Akademgorodok, 157
Alaric I, 212
Albigensian heresy, 101
Aleksandr Nevskiĭ, 129, 273, 313
Aleksandrovskiĭ Sad, 265
Alesia, 313
Alexander I, 154
Alexander II, 156
Alexanderplatz, 133
Alexiad, 215
Alexiĭ II, 278
Alexios I Komnenos, 57, 60, 215
Alexios III Angelos, 65
Alföld, 195, 246
Algiers, 161, 162, 163, 164, 165, 170, 171, 172, 274
Ali Ağca, Mehmet, 193, 307, 309, 316
Ali Pasha of Ioannina, 11
Alsace-Loraine, 200
Alter Peter, 251
Al-Zawahiri, Ayman, 317
Amersham, 75
Amin Dada, Idi, 76
Amundsen, Roald, 144
Amur River, 148, 149
Ancien Régime, 152
Andalusia, 173, 273

András II, 127, 198
Andrić, Ivo, 52, 100, 338, 357
Angara River, 156
Animal Farm, 124
Antall, József, 234
Aquincum, 245
Arabs, 60, 169, 173, 229, 273, 305, 316, 318
Arad, 111
Árpád, 242
Aryan, 40
ASALA, 308
Assumptionists, 271
Athens, 4, 22, 219
Atlanta, 293, 294
Attica, 15
Auspicious Event, 223
Austroslavism, 95
Avignon, 207
Baĭkal, Lake, 138, 140, 144, 145, 156
Baj Ganjo, 55
Balaton, Lake, 194
Baldwyn I, 47, 71
Balkan wars, 51, 93
Balkans, 6, 9, 11, 19, 23, 24, 40, 42, 50, 52, 53, 54, 71, 82, 86, 92, 94, 95, 111, 113, 114, 190, 217, 221, 227, 247, 273, 283, 303, 315
Balkanturist, 35, 41, 51
Baltic Sea, 51, 121, 123, 126, 127, 128, 132
Banat, 196, 199, 200
Banja Luka, 99
Barbarossa, 171
Barbary pirates, 172
Barcelona, 288, 294, 295

Bashkimi alphabet, 187
Basil II, 284
Basileus, 60, 64, 69, 90, 212, 213, 228, 229
Bastille, 152
Battle of the Ice, 128, 313
Bavaria, 74, 198, 200
Bayard Presse, 271
Bayazid, 25
BBC, 135
BCMS, 105
Beijing, 146
Belgrade, 3, 4, 6, 32, 34, 73, 74, 76, 77, 92, 93, 94, 96, 109, 111, 117, 119, 175, 189, 204, 218, 248, 306
Bellotto, Bernardo, 121
Belvedere, 75
Ben Bella, Ahmed, 167
Berat, 188
Berber, 162, 167, 168, 169
Beria, Lavrenti Pavlovich, 37, 94
Berïozka, 158
Berisha, Sali, 185
Berlin Wall, 231, 248
Bible, 181, 209
Bielorusskiï Station, 261
Bin Laden, Osama, 317
Birobidzhan, 87, 147
Bismarck, Otto von, 179, 235
Black Lamb and Grey Falcon, 103
Black Sea, 45, 46, 50, 52, 112, 118, 322
Blue Danube, 157, 269
BMW, 251
Bogomils, 100, 101, 102
Bolsheviks, 83, 141, 144, 218, 281

Bolshoï Theatre, 136
Bonaparte, Napoleon, 151, 152, 172
Boniface of Montserrat, 64
Bordeaux, 145
Border Guards, 209, 258, 259
Borromeo Islands, 5
Bosphorus, 69, 217, 225, 323
Bouboulina, Laskarina, 162
Boudicca, 23, 162
Boumedienne, Houari, 161, 167
Branković, Vuk, 25, 26, 29
Brasov, 198, 202
Bratsk, 138, 153
Brest, Belarus, 142
Brest, France, 142
Brezhnev, Leonid Ilyich, 3, 7, 149, 152, 157
Bridge on the Drina, 52, 100
Brilska, Barbara, 270
Brittany, 142
Bruck an der Leitha, 54
Brussels, 231
Bucharest, 111
Buda, 195, 238, 242, 245, 246, 247
Budapest, 2, 54, 92, 96, 175, 193, 194, 196, 225, 231, 234, 235, 237, 238, 239, 241, 242, 245, 246, 248, 250, 251, 254
Budva, 103, 106, 109
Burgas, 45, 46
Burrneshas, 184
Bush, George H.W., 252, 256
Byron, Lord George Gordon, 309
Byzantium, 15, 53, 57, 58, 59, 60, 61, 62, 67, 85, 204, 206,

212, 216, 217, 284, 285, 301, 305, 309, 313, 316
Caesar, 205, 213, 313
Calais, 54
Caliphate, 173, 305
Cambronne, Vicomte Pierre, 70
Canaletto, Giovanni Antonio Canal aka, 121
Cape Town, 145
Capitole, 321
Carinthia, 74, 193
Carpathians, 52, 114, 198, 203
Carter, James Earl Jr, 79
Casbah, 163, 170, 173, 274
Cathars, 68, 71, 101
Catherine II the Great, 139
Catholic, 30, 31, 66, 68, 69, 90, 95, 102, 106, 121, 127, 130, 172, 182, 183, 187, 190, 191, 201, 204, 211, 216, 221, 228, 229, 239, 271, 285, 305, 307, 310, 313
Caucasus, 249
Ceaușescu, Nicolae, 50, 99, 112, 116, 201, 202
Celestine II, 126
Celestine III, 127
Cervi, Gino, 37
Chalcedon, 212
Champs Elysées, 231
Channel tunnel, 290
Charles V, 36, 229
Charter 77, 136
Checkpoint Charlie, 134
Cheka, 136, 259
Chernobyl, 260, 297
Chetniks, 71, 303, 304, 305, 315, 319
Chita, 138, 146, 155

Christ, 14, 25, 30, 31, 42, 43, 44, 97, 157, 233, 239, 282, 313
Christie, Agatha, 44
Churchill, Winston, 88, 135, 217, 275, 309
CIA, 13, 14
Clemenceau, Georges, 233
Clement of Ohrid,, 91
CNN, 252, 253, 280
CoCom, 292
Cold War, 13, 46, 108, 134, 234, 235, 248, 249, 292, 307, 316
Columbo, 116
Comecon, 278
Comintern, 36, 37, 93
Conan Doyle, Arthur, 44
Congress of Berlin, 179
Constanța, 112, 115, 117
Constantine II, 13
Constantine V, 44
Constantinople, 1, 9, 10, 15, 47, 56, 59, 61, 64, 67, 68, 69, 70, 71, 118, 128, 173, 179, 182, 188, 189, 205, 206, 212, 213, 214, 215, 216, 217, 218, 224, 226, 228, 229, 243, 249, 273, 274, 283, 284, 285, 286, 300, 301, 302, 304, 307, 316, 317, 323
Costa Brava, 8, 50
Costa-Gavras, Konstantinos, 14
Crete, 118
Crimea, 217, 273, 309
Crimean War, 206, 217, 225, 302
Cruise missiles, 175, 208

Crusade, 47, 48, 49, 55, 56, 57, 59, 60, 61, 64, 65, 66, 67, 68, 69, 71, 101, 126, 127, 128, 130, 213, 215, 243, 303, 312
Culloden, Battle of, 23
Custine, Astolphe marquis de, 18, 135, 149, 150, 151, 152, 181, 203, 210, 255, 279
Cyril and Methodius, 37, 90, 308
Cyrillic, 40, 48, 84, 90, 91, 92, 97, 98, 105, 109, 118, 132, 160, 204, 205, 214, 216, 249, 265, 267
Dąbrowski, Captain Franciszek, 125
Dallas, 253, 254, 263, 276
Dalmatia, 102, 106
Dandolo, Enrico, 65, 66, 67, 68, 70, 71
Danilo Šćepčević, 107, 307
Danube River, 2, 49, 54, 114, 195, 197, 203, 204, 239, 242, 243, 244, 246, 247
Dardanelles, 217, 218, 309
Dassin, Julius aka Jules, 53
Dazibao, 186
DDR, 134
De Gaulle, Charles, 162, 182
Dead Souls, 138
Decembrist, 153, 154
Deliverance, 194
Deng Xiaoping, 175, 178
Derbyshire, 73
Détente, 33, 78, 175
DHL, 292, 293
Diana Spencer, 193, 207
Dijon, 4
Dimitrov, Emil, 80
Dimitrov, Georgi Mikhailov, 7, 36, 37, 38, 71, 92, 93, 94, 176, 270, 307
Diocletian, 108, 178
Disraeli, Benjamin, 135
Djilas, Milovan, 25
Djurdjura, 162
Dobrudzha, 117
Doge of Venice, 65, 66, 67
Domodossola, 4, 5
Dover, 197
Dracula
  see Vlad Țepeș, 10, 196, 242, 243
Drakulić, Slavenka, 294
Dubrovnik, 103, 104, 106, 108
Dunkirk, 23, 162, 313
Duroplast, 248
Durrell, Lawrence, 6
Dürrenmatt, Friedrich, 44
Durrës, 182, 183
Dzierżyński, Feliks, 136
Edinburgh, 145
EDS, 276
EEC, 73
EinsatzKommando, 302
Eisenstein, Sergei Mikhailovich, 129, 131, 264, 313
Ekaterinburg, 140
El Moudjahid, 165
Elisabeth I, 172
Eltsin, Boris Nikolayevich, 231, 252, 253, 275, 276, 277, 278, 279, 280, 281
Engels, Friedrich, 178
Enlightenment, 53, 151, 309
Epirus, 192, 204
Erdély
  see Transylvania, 119

Erdoğan, Recep Tayyip, 227
Ermitage Museum, 209, 211
Erzsébet Bridge, 248
Esperanto, 50, 96
Et'hem Bey Mosque, 188
Eugene of Savoy, 245
Euronews, 269
Falk, Peter, 116
Falkland Islands, 76
Far East, 145, 146, 155
Fernandel, Fernand Contandin aka, 37
Fernet Branca, 181
Field of Mars, 289
Filofeï, 284
Fletërrufe, 186
FLN, 163, 165, 169, 173
Florence, 8, 228, 285
Fontainebleau, 33
Forom des Langues, 321
Frankfurt, 46
Franks, 56, 58, 59, 60, 61, 62, 65, 67, 69, 70, 114, 215, 218, 229, 273, 274, 285, 302, 303, 304, 305, 307
Fransız Pasteur Hastanesi, 220
Franz Ferdinand, 27, 102, 103, 307
Frasne, 5
Frauenkirche, 73
French Revolution, 142, 151, 152
Friedrichstraße, 133
Gaidar, Egor Timurovich, 279
Galatasaray Hamamı, 219
Gallipoli, 217, 218
Gare de l'Est, 73
Gare de Lyon, 99, 111
Gare du Nord, 3, 4, 34
Gdańsk, 121, 122, 123, 124

Gdynia, 123
Geneva, 5, 193
Genoa, 59, 61
Gevgelija, 4
Géza II, 198
Ghegs, 183, 184, 187
Gierek, Edvard, 120
Giotto di Bondone, 31
Giurgiu, 49
Gjirokastër, 192
Gjuha Shqipe, 187
Glagolitic, 90, 91, 92, 98, 109, 118, 205, 249
Godstone, 192
Godunov, Boris Fïodorovich, 277
Goebbels, Joseph, 36
Goering, Hermann, 36
Gogol, Nikolai Vasilievich, 138, 211, 290
Goodwill Games, 214, 252, 253, 287, 288, 289
Gorbachëv, Mikhail Sergeyevich, 234, 253, 280
Gorkiï Park, 136
Grachev, Pavel Sergeevich, 277, 279
Great Purge, 37, 176
Great Schism, 57, 58, 211, 212, 214
Gregorian calendar, 23, 83, 313
Gregory IX, 128
Grivas, Georgios, 20, 21
Grünwald - Tannenberg, Battle of, 130, 131
Gül Baba, 246, 247
Gulag Archipelago, 99
Gulf of Finland, 210
GUM, 268, 277
Habsburg, 51, 95, 241, 242

Hackney, 274
Hagia Sofia, 47, 70, 71, 128, 179, 213, 216, 218, 226, 227, 249, 273, 312, 322
Hague, The, 29
Harbin, 146
Hastings, Battle of, 23
Haussmann, Baron Georges Eugène, 150, 163
Havel, Václav, 136
Heath, Edward, 76
Helsinki, 78, 111
Hercegovina, 269
Hévíz, 194
Hill, Rowland, 142
Himmler, Heinrich, 131
Hitler, Adolf, 39, 123, 131
Hofbraühaus, 251
Holy Sepulchre, 43, 68, 273
Hook of Holland, 134
Hospitallier, 126
Hotel *Ukraïna*, 280
House of Commons, 3
Hoxha, Enver, 175, 178, 179, 180, 181, 183, 185
Humanité, L' newspaper, 12
Hunedoara, 196, 243
Huntington, Samuel, 310
Hunyadi, János, 196, 197
Hunyadi, Mátyás - Matthias I Corvin, 242, 243, 244, 245
Hurt, William, 255
Husák, Gustáv, 121, 136
Hydra, 17
Ïakutsk, 153
Ïaroslavskiï Station, 136
Ibárruri Gómez, Dolores aka La Pasionaria, 162
IMF, 177
Innocent III, 64, 71

International Criminal Court, 28, 29
Inturist, 136, 152, 154, 156, 209, 210, 211, 214
Ioannidis, Dimitrios, 19, 21
IOC, 253, 287
Irkutsk, 138, 139, 140, 143, 144, 145, 148, 153, 154, 155, 156
Iron Curtain, 34, 35
Isaac II Angelos, 64
Islam, 8, 11, 28, 42, 43, 52, 53, 60, 100, 102, 107, 172, 179, 228, 244, 247, 284
Istanbul, 10, 15, 32, 35, 78, 103, 136, 184, 187, 205, 206, 216, 217, 219, 220, 224, 249, 286, 302, 304, 317, 320, 321, 322
İstiklâl Caddesi, 219
Ïubileinyï Sports Palace, 292
Ivan Groznyï, the Terrible, 309
Ivan III, 206
Jacobinism, 151, 169
Jadwiga, 130
James I, 172
Janissaries, 220, 221, 222, 247
Januarius, Saint, 88
Jaruzelski, Wojciech, 193
JAT, 175, 176
Jean Jaurès metro station, 2
Jerusalem, 32, 58, 61, 68, 126, 284, 302
Jesenice, 74, 76
Jesus
   see Christ, 44, 97, 213, 282, 313
Joan of Arc, 162
John II Komnenos, 61

Back to Byzantium

John Paul II, 193
John VIII Palaiologus, 214
JUGALB, 175, 177
Julian calendar, 83, 313
Justinian the Great, 70, 212, 226
Kabylia, 162, 167
Kalemegdan Park, 96, 204
Kaloïan, Ivan II, 48, 71
Karaganda, 139
Karamanlís, Konstantinos, 99
Kardelj, Edvard, 176
Katovice, 121
KDC, 81
Keleti Station, 248
Kemal, Mustafa aka Attatürk, 218, 227
Keszthely, 194
KGB, 136, 211, 259, 261, 294, 298
Khabarovsk, 138, 143, 145, 147, 148
Khartoum, 145
Khazbulatov, Ruslan Imranovich, 275, 277, 278, 279, 280
Khristo, Khristo Vladimiroff Javacheff aka, 39
Khrushchëv, Nikita Sergueïevitch, 7, 42, 45, 157, 178, 256, 257, 307
Kiev, 266, 284, 286, 317
Kievian Rus', 128, 267, 284
Kievskiï Station, 263
Kinder Surprise, 163
Király baths, 246
Kirkorov, Filipp Bedrosovich, 270
Kohl, Helmut, 199
Kommunalka, 290
Komnene, Anna, 215

Komsomolskaïa Station, 264
Konstantinov, Aleko, 55
Koper, 120
Koprivshtitsa, 88
Kosovo, 23, 24, 25, 26, 27, 28, 29, 103, 107, 183, 204, 306, 308, 313
Kotor, Gulf of, 106
Krasnaïa Strela, 263
Krasnoïarsk, 141, 142, 143, 145, 159, 216
Kremlin, 151, 265, 277, 278
Krestovskiï Island, 288
Krymskiï Val, 279
Kumanovo, 7
Kusturica, Emir, 54
La Défense, 313
Lalla Fadhma n'Soumer, 162
Lamartine, Alphonse de, 69, 305
Lausanne, 4, 5, 252
Lawrence of Arabia, Thomas Edward aka, 81
Lazar, 24, 25, 26, 28, 29, 204, 309
League of Nations, 125
Lechner, Ödön, 195
Lee, Christopher, 243
Lee, Ken, 62, 63
Leigh Fermor, Patrick, 237
Leka, 192
Lenexpo Centre, 294, 298
Lenin, Vladimir Illich Ulïanov aka, 17, 35, 37, 38, 46, 141, 157, 158, 159, 160, 211, 216, 218, 254, 255, 258, 263, 265, 310
Leningrad, 116, 157, 208, 209
Leningradskiï Station, 264
Leninskiï Prospect, 276, 278

Lessing, Gotthold Ephraim, 309
Lincoln, Abraham, 135
Linguaphone, 166
Litvinenko, Aleksandr Valterovich, 317
Lobnoë Mesto, 296
Lombardy, 6, 207
Lomonosov Moscow State University, 254
London, 17, 20, 33, 44, 72, 97, 133, 134, 135, 142, 145, 192, 238, 274, 276, 292
Los Angeles, 253
Louis XIV, 151
Lubïanka prison, 136, 271
Lugosi, Béla, 243
Lutheran, 198
Luxemburg, 198
Lyon, 193
Maastricht Treaty, 252
Madonna of the sleeping cars, 4
Maggiore, Lake, 5
Maghreb, 162, 166, 168
Mahmud II, 223
Makarios III, Archbishop Michail Christodoulou Mouskos, 19, 20, 21, 99
Makashov, Albert Mikhailovich, 278
Malakoff, 300, 302
Malbork, 120, 125, 128, 198, 302, 312
Mamaia, 111, 115, 116, 196
Manchuria, 138, 146, 147
Manuel I Komnenos, 61
Manzikert, Battle of, 57
Mao Zedong, 178, 186
Maria Theresa, 200
MariahilferStraße, 248

Maribor, 193, 194
Marie of Romania, 233
Maritsa River, 55, 62, 68
Markov, Georgi Ivanov, 317
Marmara Sea, 217
Marseille, 162, 173
Marshall, George Catlett Jr., 306
Martenitsa, 82
Marx, Karl, 42, 178
Matrïoshka, 275
Mátyás Templom, 247
Mažuranić, Matija, 103, 149, 150, 151
Megali Idea, 118, 307
Mehmed IV, 309
Mehmet II, 190, 226
Mercedes Benz, 46
Mercouri, Melina, 14
Mestre, 32
Metaxas, Ioannis, 119
Metternich, Klemens Wenzel von, 54
Michael I Cerularius, 213
Michael VIII Palaiologus, 214
Middle Ages, 25, 53, 91, 188
Milan, 4
Milano Centrale Station, 6
Milošević, Slobodan, 28, 29, 249, 307, 317
Mitterand, François, 193
Mladić, Ratko, 29
Moldavia, 113
Molotov, Vyacheslav Mikhailovich, 94, 139
Mongols, 26, 198
Montmartre, 239
Montreux, 5
Morava River, 6
Moravia, 90

Morozova, Boïarina Feodosia Prokopievna, 281
Moscow, 36, 37, 79, 83, 94, 116, 122, 124, 136, 138, 140, 141, 144, 145, 146, 147, 148, 150, 151, 157, 158, 176, 213, 229, 252, 253, 254, 255, 256, 257, 258, 260, 263, 264, 265, 266, 268, 270, 271, 272, 276, 277, 280, 282, 284, 287, 288, 289, 290, 296, 316, 317
Moscow State Circus, 157
Mosel, 198
Moskovskiï Station, 288
Mostar, 269
Mountain Wreath, 24, 27, 106, 107, 108
Mukhanov, Piotr Aleksandrovich, 153
Munich, 8, 73, 233, 250
Murad I, 25, 103, 221
Murad II, 190
Muslims, 108
Mussolini, Benito, 6, 17, 178, 181, 192
Nairobi, 112
Nakhodka, 147
Nansen, Fridtjof, 144
Naples, 88, 190, 191
National Awakening, 27, 188
NATO, 13, 19, 175, 180, 208, 318, 319, 322
Nazi, 36, 51, 86, 132
Neva River, 290, 295
Never on Sunday, 53
Nevskiï Prospekt, 211
Nevsky, Aleksandr Iaroslavich Nevskiï, 129, 130, 309
New York, 32, 92
Newhaven, 192

Nicolas I, 151, 154
Nicolas II, 282
Nicolas *Thaumaturgos*, 31
Nightingale, Florence, 225
Nikon, 282
Niš, 4, 32, 33
Nixon, Richard Milhous, 33, 73, 78, 82
Nobel Prize, 99
Nogina Square, 272
Nők Lapja, 2
Normandy, 251, 280, 289
Normans, 57, 61, 305
Novgorod, 128, 129
Novosibirsk, 138, 140, 153, 157
NTV, 286
O'Toole, Peter Seamus, 81
OAS, 173
Ob River, 140, 157
Obilić, Miloš, 25, 27, 103, 108, 309
Obuda, 245
Ochi Chërnije, 80
October Revolution, 144, 256
Ohrid, 91, 188, 308
Oktïabrskaïa Square, 256
Old Quba, 163, 168
Olgino, 209
Oliwa, 123, 133
Olomouc, 120
Olympic Committee, 252, 261, 287, 297
Olympics, 79, 252, 253, 288, 294, 320, 321
OMON, 278
Omsk, 140
Orient Express, 3, 4, 73, 136
Orly, 159, 175, 181, 219

Orthodox, 9, 11, 19, 23, 25, 28, 29, 41, 51, 54, 55, 56, 57, 85, 87, 95, 101, 102, 106, 113, 127, 128, 130, 149, 184, 187, 202, 204, 206, 211, 213, 214, 218, 227, 228, 239, 244, 247, 249, 273, 281, 282, 283, 284, 286, 305, 306, 307, 310, 313, 315, 317, 318
Orwell, George, Eric Arthur Blair aka, 124
Ostankino, 278
Ostbahnhof, 134
Ottoman Empire, 9, 20, 51, 53, 54, 85, 93, 100, 109, 118, 171, 178, 190, 191, 224, 243, 273, 284, 307
Pamporovo, 77, 88
Pan-African Games, 165
Pan-Slavism, 93, 95
Papadopoulos, Georgios, 13, 14, 19, 73
Papandreou, Georgios, 13
Paris, 2, 3, 8, 14, 33, 41, 45, 72, 73, 74, 75, 82, 92, 97, 108, 109, 112, 133, 136, 145, 150, 159, 165, 166, 169, 170, 174, 175, 208, 209, 219, 220, 230, 231, 234, 235, 238, 239, 240, 250, 251, 264, 276, 292, 299, 302, 313, 320
Parliament Square, 135
Pasarét, 246
Paternoster lift, 238
Pattakos, Stylianos, 13, 17
Paulicians, 101
Pavelić, Ante, 105
Pavlov, 77
Peipus, Lake, 129
Peloponnese, 3
Pera, 219

Pericles, 15
Perm, 138, 139
Perrot, Ross, 276
Pershing II missiles, 208
Pest, 96, 195, 239, 242, 246, 247, 248
Pétain, Marshal Philippe, 278
Petar II Petrović-Njegoš, 24, 106, 107
Peter and Paul fortress, 290
Petrograd, 83
Philip of Swabia, 64, 67
Pigalle, 174
Piraeus, 2, 3, 4, 15, 16, 18, 32, 52, 118, 189, 206
Pius II, 229, 243
PKK, 308
Plato, 19
Ploče, 104, 106
Plovdiv, 2, 33, 36, 41, 45, 48, 55, 56, 62, 71, 72, 73, 74, 77, 84, 88, 89, 92, 95, 98, 202, 205
Pluzhnikova, Marina, 287
Plymouth, 145
Pogradets, 188
Pokrovskie Vorota, 272
Poros, 3, 16
Porte, The Sublime, 171, 221
Powell, Enoch, 76
Prague Spring, 108, 121
Přerov, 120
Princip, Gavrilo, 27, 102, 103, 307, 309
Prizren, League of, 178, 187
Programme Commun, 79
Prokofiev, Sergeï Sergeevich, 129, 211, 313
Propusk, 261

Protestant, 42, 172, 304, 305, 310
Provence, 207
Prussia, 123, 232
Pskov, 128, 129
Pugachëva, Alla Borisovna, 270
Pukh, 257, 258
Punic Wars, 168
Pushkin, Aleksandr Sergeyevich, 150, 211
Puszta, 195
Putin, Vladimir Vladimirovich, 286, 310
Quartier Latin, 190
Quasimodo, 199
Qur'an, 166, 168
Radisson-Slavïanskaïa, 263
Radu III, the Handsome, 245
Ragusa, 106
Ramadan, 169
Ramstein-Miesenbach, 319
Raskolnikov, 290
Rastislav, 90
Rastrelli, Francesco Bartolomeo, 281
Reagan, Ronald, 79, 177, 193, 285, 310
Reconquista, 173, 225, 316
Red Army, 201
Red Square, 141, 158, 265, 268, 276, 277, 296
Reformation, 31, 194, 198
Regency of Algiers, 171
Reichstag, 36
Renaissance, 123, 124, 190, 202, 242
Rennweg, 54
Repin, Ilya Yefimovich, 309
Rhineland-Palatinate, 319

Rhodope, 45, 72, 77, 87, 88, 317
Rijeka, 206, 232
Rivoli, rue de, 163
Robbe-Grillet, Alain, 226
Roma, 11, 12, 22, 55, 69, 113, 114, 197, 199
Roman Empire, 212
Romanov, 51
Romans-sur-Isère, 193
Rome, 3, 35, 67, 108, 193, 212, 284, 285
Rome Treaty, 3
Rosetta stone, 89, 205
Rossia Hotel, 136
Rossia TV channel, 284
Rostropovich, Mstislav Leopoldovich, 277
Rotterdam, 134
Rozsadomb, 246
Rubik, Ernő, 237
Rudas baths, 246
Rumelia, 9, 54, 113
Ruse, 49
Russian Revolution, 218
Russkaïa Mysl', 299, 312
Russki Club, 72
Russo-Japanese war, 146
Rust, Mathias, 276
Rutskoï, Aleksandr Vladimirovich, 275, 276, 277, 278, 279, 280
Sack of Constantinople, 47, 49, 56, 62, 126, 127, 128, 211, 213, 302, 303, 312
Sahara Desert, 150, 162, 174
Saint Mark's Basilica, 70
Saint-Basil's Cathedral, 296
Saint-Louis-des-Français Church, 271

Saint-Petersburg, 150, 154, 253, 254, 260, 263, 264, 268, 269, 287, 288, 289, 290, 291, 293, 294, 295, 296
Saladin, Ṣalāḥ ad-Dīn Yūsuf ibn Ayyūb, 61
Salzburg, 74
Samaranch y Torelló, Juan Antonio, 253
Samoyed, 143, 144
Sampson, Nikos, 19
San Gennaro
   see Januarius, 88
San Stefano treaty, 178
Saracen, 273
Sarajevo, 27, 99, 100, 102, 103, 105, 109, 160, 205, 216, 225
Sartre, Jean-Paul, 209
Sava River, 204
Saxon, 193, 198, 199, 201, 202
Schleswig-Holstein, 125, 232
Schwarzenbergplatz, 74
Scutari, 69, 225
Sebastopol, 302, 322
Sebeș, 197
Sergiev Posad, 281
Sežana, 4, 34
Shadok, 34
Shakespeare, William, 25, 89, 106
Sheremetevo, 136
Shkodër, 183, 185, 186, 190
Shqipëria, 178
Siberia, 140, 144, 146, 148, 154, 155, 156, 157
Sibiu, 197, 198
Siebenbürgen
   see Transylvania, 198
Sighișoara, 197, 201, 202

Simenon, Georges, 44
Simeon I the Great, 308
Simon IV de Montfort, 68
Simplon, 3, 4, 5
Sinan Agha, Koca Mi'mâr Sinân Âǧâ, 10, 179, 226
SKA pool, 292
Skanderbeg, George Castriot, 10, 185, 188, 190, 191
Skopje, 3, 4, 7, 12, 16, 22, 29, 31, 32, 35, 97, 113, 203, 205, 323
Skype, 289
Slavonia, 206, 308
Slavonsky Brod, 206
SNCF, 143
Sobchak, Anatoly Aleksandrovich, 253, 293, 298
Sofia, 2, 35, 39, 41, 47, 50, 72, 81, 88, 89, 92, 94, 206, 249, 273
Solidarność, 193
Solzhenitsyn, Aleksandr Isayevich, 99, 148
Sopot, 123
Spasskaïa Tower, 265
Split, 108, 109
Srebrenica, 29
SS-20 missiles, 136, 175
Stalin, Iossif Vissarionovitch Dzhugachvili aka, 6, 7, 27, 36, 37, 45, 74, 87, 94, 95, 122, 139, 147, 149, 151, 176, 178, 254, 257, 258, 272, 297, 307, 310
Stalinplatz, 74
Stara Zagora, 45
Starovery, 281, 282
START, 208, 252
Stefan IV Dušan, 94, 309

Stefan Nemanja, 204
Stendhal, Marie-Henri Beyle aka, 6
Stockholm, 145
Stoker, Bram, 243
Stolichnaya, 158
Strategopoulos, Alexios Komnenos, 128
Štrosmajer, Josip Juraj, 105
Stuka, 125
Sucharski, Henryk, 125
Südbahnhof, 74
Suleiman the Magnificent, 226, 229, 245, 247, 269
Surikov, Vasiliĭ Ivanovich, 281
Sverdlovsk, 140
Swabian, 196, 200, 201
Szekler, 198, 200
Szentendre, 239
Taganka, 272
Taksim, 20
Tamanrasset, 162
Tamazight, 162, 167, 168, 169, 321
Tamerlane, Timūr Leng, 26
Tannenberg
  see Grünwald, 130
Târgovişte, 244
Tchaikovsky, Pëtr Ilïich, 211, 277
Templars, 58, 309
Terreur, 152
Teutonic Knights, 127, 128, 129, 130, 131, 309
Theodorakis, Michael aka Mikis, 14
Thessaloniki, 4, 12, 15, 182
Third Reich, 125, 201
Third Rome, 206, 213, 282, 284, 317

Thrace, 47, 118, 217
Tikhon, Archimandrite, 284, 285
Time of Anika, 100
Timişoara, 117, 199, 200, 205
Tirana, 175, 177, 188, 189, 204
Tito, Josip Broz aka, 3, 6, 7, 12, 27, 37, 92, 94, 95, 105, 176, 177, 307, 310
Tosks, 183, 184, 187, 191
Toulouse, 2, 145, 258, 320
Toynbee, Arnold, 54
Trabant, 46, 133, 248
Trakt, Siberian, 138
Trans-Siberian Railway, 119, 136, 146
Transylvania, 113, 114, 119, 127, 193, 197, 198, 199, 200, 203, 232, 233, 242, 243
Trianon, 200, 232, 233, 234
Trieste, 4, 5, 6, 109, 120, 121, 248
Triple Entente, 217, 231
Trubetskaïa, Ekaterina Ivanovna née Laval, 155
Trubetskoï, Sergeï Petrovich, 155
Tsarigrad, 205, 206, 216, 249, 283, 302, 323
TSUM, 81
Turkish Airlines, 219
Turks, 8, 9, 11, 20, 21, 23, 24, 25, 26, 29, 41, 51, 53, 54, 56, 57, 60, 71, 88, 93, 100, 103, 107, 172, 173, 189, 190, 191, 198, 204, 206, 213, 214, 215, 216, 218, 222, 224, 225, 227, 229, 243, 244, 245, 246, 247, 273, 284, 285, 302, 304, 306, 309, 315, 316, 318

Turner, Ted, 252, 253, 254
UEFA, 320, 321
Ulan Bator, 146
Ulan Ude, 146
Umayyad Califate, 273
Unità, L' newspaper, 12
United Nations, 83
Urals, 138, 140, 237
Urban II, 57, 215
Üsküdar
  see Skutari, 225
Ussuri River, 148
Vágó, József, 195
Vajdahunyad, 196
Vallorbe, 4
Varangian guard, 284
Varna, 50
Varosliget, 196
Vartan, Sylvie Vartanian aka, 62
Vasilevskiï Island, 290
Vatican Council, 214
Vaud, 193
VDNKh, 265
Vecchia Romagna, 121
Veliko Trnovo, 46, 47, 48, 49, 56, 64, 72, 98, 205
Venice, 4, 6, 31, 32, 59, 61, 65, 66, 128, 190, 219, 248
Vercingetorix, 313
Verona, 4
Versailles, 123, 231, 232, 233, 234
Vienna, 54, 74, 97, 120, 219, 234, 235, 248, 268, 283
Viking, 59
Villa Opicina, 4
Villach, 77
Ville d'Avray, 208
Vincennes Zoo, 150
Visegrád, 197, 242, 243

Višegrad, 52
Vitus' Day, 24
Vlach, 114
Vlad III, the Impaler, 10, 192, 197, 202, 203, 223, 242, 243, 244, 245, 309
Vladimir, 284, 286
Vodno, 29
Volga, 87, 139, 254
Volkonskaïa, Maria Nikolaevna née Raevskaya, 155
Volkonskiï, Sergeï Grigorievitch, 155
Voltaire, François-Marie Arouet aka, 151
VSO, 174
Waffen SS, 184
Wałęsa, Lech, 193
Wallachia, 113, 114, 243, 244, 245, 309
Warsaw, 120, 121, 133, 180, 208, 241
Warsaw Pact, 180, 208, 241
Wehrmacht, 201
West, Rebecca, 103
Westerplatte, 124, 125, 126
White House, 278, 279, 280
White Nights, 290
Wilson, Edmond, 267
Wilson, Harold, 76
Winter Palace, 281
Władysław II Jagiełło, 130
Women's Day, 83
World Cup, 321
Wortley Montagu, Lady Mary, 39, 103, 151, 221, 224, 247
Yacine, Kateb, 168
Yalta, 50, 79
Yantra River, 47

Yokohama, 147
Young Turk, 187
Z, 14
Zadar, 66
Zagorsk
   see Sergiev Posad, 281
Zagreb, 4, 6, 34, 99, 109, 206, 248, 260
Zhiguli automobile, 254
Zhirinovskiĭ, Vladimir Volfovich Edelstein aka, 281
Zhivkov, Todor Khristov, 42, 50
Zinoviev, Aleksandr Aleksandrovich, 262
Zog I, Ahmet Zogu, 182, 184, 192

Antonin Grook is an Englishman who has spent his adult life in France. He travelled extensively during the Cold War in countries of the East Bloc, including totalitarian Albania, and was laid up in a Bulgarian hospital. He lived and worked in Hungary and in Russia in the challenging conditions that followed the dissolution of the Soviet Union, where he witnessed an attempted *coup d'état*. He has a good understanding of the Orthodox world and what makes it different and antagonistic to the West.

He is married, with two daughters and a grand-daughter, retired and living in Toulouse.

Made in the USA
Columbia, SC
09 August 2017